The Illustrator 10
WOW! Book

Sharon Steuer

The Illustrator 10 Wow! Book

Sharon Steuer

Peachpit Press

1249 Eighth Street

Berkeley, CA 94710

510/524-2178

510/524-2221 (fax)

Find us on the World Wide Web at: http://www.peachpit.com

To report errors, please send a note to errata@peachpit.com

Peachpit Press is a division of Pearson Education

Contributing writers: Steven H. Gordon, Victor von Salza, Dave Awl, Lisa Jackmore, Sandee Cohen
Tech editors: Pierre Louveaux, Mordy Golding
Book design: Barbara Sudick
Cover design: Andrew Faulkner, afstudio
Cover Illustration: Javier Romero Design Group

ISBN 0-201-78481-5

9 8 7 6 5 4 3 2

Printed and bound in the United States of America.

The Illustrator 10 Wow! Book Writers and Editors

Sharon Steuer is the originator of *The Illustrator Wow! Books*. In addition to being author of this book, she is a painter and illustrator, and author of *Creative Thinking in Photoshop: A New Approach to Digital Art*. Sharon lives in Connecticut with her cats, Puma and Bear, and soon-to-be radio star husband Jeff Jacoby. She is extremely grateful to her co-authors, editors, and *Wow!* team members (past and present) for making this revision of the book possible.

Steven H. Gordon is a returning co-author for Step-by-Steps and Galleries. He has too many boys to stay sane. If only they wouldn't fall off cliffs in Bryce—the National Park, not the software. Steven runs Cartagram, a custom mapmaking company located in Madison, Alabama. He thanks Monette and his mom for their encouragement, and the boys for their cessation of hostilities.

Victor von Salza, new to the *Wow!* team, worked on chapter Introductions, Step-by-Steps, Galleries, the CD, testing, and anything else we threw his way. Working on the book has been an exciting challenge, too fun to call a job. He and Mary Anne live in Portland, Oregon with their bouncy bearded collie Spencer; besides their work, they enjoy gardening, day hikes, and movies.

Pierre Louveaux is the chief technical editor for major portions of this edition. A resident of the San Francisco Bay Area since 1990, he holds degrees in Computer Science from U.C. Berkeley and Stanford University. As an engineer for Adobe, Pierre has worked on Illustrator 8, 9, and 10. He is the primary inventor of the advanced transparency model used in Illustrator and PDF.

Dave Awl is a Chicago-based writer, editor, and webmaster. As the newest member of the *Wow!* team, he helped revise and edit the chapter Introductions, and wrote the OS X section. Dave is also a poet, playwright, and performer known for his ten-year stint in the fringe theater hit *Too Much Light Makes the Baby Go Blind*. You can visit some of the web sites and online communities he's created via his web site Ocelot Factory (www.ocelotfactory.com).

Additional contributing writers and editors: **Mordy Golding** (Technical editor for a number of chapter Introductions, Mordy is an Adobe Illustrator Product Manager), **Mindi Englart** (Copy editor and designer for the second time, Mindi is an author of children's books and other projects), **Lisa Jackmore** (Contributing writer for Galleries and the Course Outline, Lisa is an artist on and off the computer), **Sandee Cohen**, a.k.a. vectorbabe.com (our emergency technical consultant; she provided help on the OS X section for this edition). Please see the Acknowledgments for a more thorough listing of the *Wow!* team contributors.

Acknowledgments

As always, my most heartfelt gratitude goes to the more than 100 artists and Illustrator experts who generously allowed us to include their work and divulge their techniques.

Thank you Adobe for letting us include the *Adobe Illustrator 10* demo on the *Wow! CD*. And thanks to all at Adobe who answered our zillions of questions, and came through with our special requests. Special thanks to: Mordy Golding, Ted Alspach, Marcus Chang, and Pierre Louveaux.

This revision required a major team effort, and would not have happened without an amazing group of people. Thankfully, Steven Gordon agreed to return to the team to tackle a batch of new Step-by-Steps and Galleries—Steven adds a dose of humor to his incredible resourcefulness, for which we're all exceedingly grateful. Victor von Salza did a great job of getting up to speed in record time; Victor wore every hat we threw his way, from Step-by-Steps and Galleries, to introductions and organizing the *Wow! CD*, which included co-developing the comprehensive Illustrator-to-Photoshop 7 technical document (AI&PS.pdf.) under the direction of Pierre Louveaux. Thank you Victor! Thanks to Mordy Golding for rescuing us and providing a technical edit of Chapter 1 and many of the introductions. Pierre Louveaux deserves a standing ovation for being the most thorough technical editor ever born on this planet. As he metamorphosed from tester to technical editor, he proved that he was also a better grammarian than most of us who call English our first language. His expertise in transparency and the Illustrator-to-Photoshop work flow, throughout the book and in the AI&PS.pdf, is an invaluable addition to this book. Dave Awl wins an award for joining a team at the goal line; thank you Dave for making it possible to get this book out—your writing and editing are great! Thank you Lisa Jackmore for your help with Galleries and the *Illustrator 10 Wow! Course Outline* on the *Wow! CD*. Thanks to talented Laurie Grace for the screenshot help. Thank you Mindi Englart for the wonderful job copyediting the book, and managing production of the Quark documents. Thank you Janet Reed for the meticulous proofread. Thank you to Peg Maskell Korn for being involved since the beginning, and thanks to Diane Hinze Kanzler for your work on the book. As always, thanks also go to our stellar team of testers and consultants, especially Pierre Louveaux, Adam Z Lein, Jean-Claude Tremblay, Bob Geib, and Rich Marchesseault. Thank you to Sandee Cohen who continues as our official kibbitzer; she helped us immensely with the OS X section. And thanks to the industry's most concientious indexer, Rosemary Michelle Simpson. Thank you Javier Romero and Andrew Faulkner for the cool new cover.

Thank you to the folks at Commercial Document Services for the fabulous printing job. And thanks also to Aridi, Dynamic Graphics, Image Club Graphics, Photosphere, and Ultimate Symbol for allowing us to include them in the *Wow! CD*. Last but not least, thanks to Linnea Dayton for being the *Wow!* series editor (and sometimes our copyeditor), and to everyone at Peachpit Press (especially Connie Jeung-Mills, Nancy Davis, Victor Gavenda, Kim Lombardi, Gary-Paul Prince, Paula Baker, and Nancy Ruenzel) for making this book happen.

WOW! BOOK PRODUCTION NOTES:

Interior Book Design

Barbara Sudick is the artist behind the *Illustrator Wow!* design and typography. Using Jill Davis's layout of *The Photoshop Wow! Book* as a jumping-off point, she designed the pages in QuarkXPress, using Adobe fonts Frutiger and Minion.

Hardware and Software

With the exception of some of the testers, all of the *Wow!* staff use Macintosh computers. We use QuarkXPress 4, ALAP's XPert Tools II, Photoshop 6 or 7 (depending on the user), and SnapzPro2 for the screenshots. We used Adobe Acrobat 5 for distribution of the book pages to testers, the indexer and the proofreaders.

How to contact the author...

If you've created artwork using the newer features of Illustrator that you'd like to submit for consideration in future *Wow!* Books, please send printed samples to: Sharon Steuer, c/o Peachpit Press, 1249 Eighth Street, Berkeley, CA 94710. Or email us a web address that contains samples of your work (no files please!): **wowartist@ssteuer.com**

Contents

3

Brushes, Symbols & Hatches

10

11

Web & Animation

12

Illustrator & Other Programs

Important: Read me first!

Critical print resolution issues

Illustrator's new features require that you manually set the proper resolution for output of images that include transparency or live effects! For details, see the *Transparency* chapter introduction.

Lots of artwork on the CD!

We're putting more and more of our Illustrator *Wow!* artists' artwork on our *Wow! CD*. Now you will find more than sixty examples of artwork from the book so you can follow along, or simply pick the art apart to see how it was constructed.

Additional Illustrator training

You'll find additional lessons in the "Ch02 The Zen of Illustrator" folder on the *Wow! CD*, including the *Zen Lessons* (which supplement the *Zen* chapter). These lessons walk you through some basics of working with the Pen tool, Bézier curves, layers, and stacking order. (If you're looking for more help with the Pen tool, look at the demo for zenofthpen.org on the *Wow! CD*). If you're new to Illustrator, you may even want to begin with a class. If you're teaching a class in Illustrator, don't miss the *Illustrator Wow! Course Outline* on the *Wow! CD*.

This book has been fully updated, reworked, and expanded for Illustrator users of all levels to master the exciting (and sometimes perplexing) features of Adobe Illustrator. You'll find hundreds of essential production techniques, timesaving tips, and beautiful art generously shared by *Illustrator Wow!* artists worldwide. All lessons are deliberately kept short to allow you to squeeze in a lesson or two between clients, and to encourage the use of this book within the confines of a supervised classroom.

In order to keep the content in this book tantalizing to everyone—from novice to expert—I've assumed a reasonable level of competence with basic Mac and Windows concepts, such as opening and saving files, launching applications, copying objects to the clipboard, and doing mouse operations. I've also assumed that you've read through "An Overview of Adobe Illustrator" in the beginning of the *Adobe Illustrator 10 User Guide*, and understand the basic functionality of the tools.

I'd love to tell you that you can learn Adobe Illustrator just by flipping through the pages of this book, but the reality is that there is no substitute for practice. The good news is, the more you work with Illustrator, the more techniques you'll be able to integrate into your creative process.

Use this book as a reference, a guide for specific techniques, or just as a source of inspiration. After you've read this book, read it again, and you'll undoubtedly learn something you missed the first time. As I hope you'll discover, the more experienced you become with Adobe Illustrator, the easier it will be to assimilate all the new information and inspiration you'll find in this book. Happy Illustrating!

Sharon Steuer

How to use this book...

Before you do anything else, read the *Wow! Glossary* on the pull-out quick reference card at the back of the book. The *Glossary* provides definitions for the terms used throughout *The Illustrator 10 Wow! Book* (for example, ⌘ is the Command key for Mac).

WELCOME TO *WOW!* FOR WINDOWS AND MAC

If you already use Adobe Photoshop or InDesign you'll see many interface similarities to Illustrator 10. The similarities should make the time you spend learning each program much shorter (especially if you're a new-comer to all three products). Your productivity should also increase across the board once you adjust to the new shortcuts and methodologies (see "Shortcuts and keystrokes" following, and the *Illustrator Basics* chapter). If you're using OS X (or are considering using it), don't miss our *Illustrator & OS X* following this section.

Shortcuts and keystrokes

Because you can now customize keyboard shortcuts, we're eliminating most of the keystrokes references in the book. We will keep keystroke references when it's so stan-dard that we assume you'll keep the default, or when there is no other way to achieve that function (such as Lock All Unselected objects). We'll always give you Macin-tosh shortcuts first, then the Windows equivalent (⌘-Z/Ctrl-Z). For help with customizing keyboard shortcuts, and tool and menu navigation (such as single key tool access and Tab to hide palettes), see the *Basics* chapter.

With the All Swatches icon selected, hold the Option or Alt key and choose "Sort by Name" and "List View" from the pop-up menu

Choose Select All Unused from the Swatches pop-up; then immediately click the Trash icon to safely remove unused swatches

Setting up your palettes

In terms of following along with the lessons in this book, you'll probably want to disable the "Type Area Select" option (see Tip "One option you may not want" in the *Type* chapter). Next, if you want your palettes to look like our palettes, you'll need to set swatches to be sorted by

Phantom Swatches

In order to delete ALL your unused swatches, you'll need to first delete unused Brushes and Styles.

1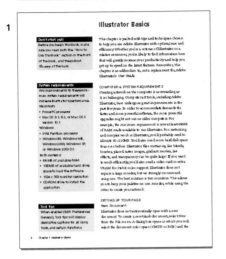

2 The CD icon indicates that related artwork can be found on the Wow! CD

Tip boxes

Look for these gray boxes to find Tips about Adobe Illustrator.

Red Tip boxes

The red Tip boxes contain warnings or other essential information.

3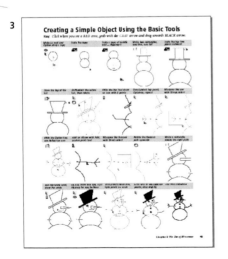

name: hold down Option (Mac) or Alt (Win) and choose "Sort by Name" and "List View" from the Swatches pop-up menu (see figures on previous page).

By default, Illustrator sometimes has the habit of filling palettes with excess styles; in order to customize the default settings loaded into new documents, see the Tip "Using Startup documents" in the *Basics* chapter. To clear out an existing Swatches palette of unwanted, unused swatches, first click on the All Swatches icon, then choose "Select All Unused" from the Swatches pop-up, and immediately click the Trash icon to remove these unwanted extras (see Tip "Phantom Swatches" at left).

HOW THIS BOOK IS ORGANIZED...

You'll find six kinds of information woven throughout this book—all of it up-to-date for Illustrator 10: **Basics, Tips, Exercises, Techniques, Galleries,** and **References.**

1 Basics. *Illustrator Basics* and *The Zen of Illustrator* qualify as full-blown chapters on basics and are packed with information that distills and supplements your Adobe Illustrator manual and disk. Every chapter starts with a general overview of the basics. Although these sections have been designed so advanced users of Illustrator can move quickly through them, I strongly suggest that the rest of you read them very carefully. Please keep in mind that this book serves as a supplement to, not a substitute for, your Adobe Illustrator *User Guide.*

2 Tips. When you see this icon, you'll find related artwork in the Artists folder on the *Wow! CD.* Look to the information in the gray and red boxes for hands-on Tips that can help you work more efficiently. Usually you can find tips alongside related textual information, but if you're in an impatient mood, you might just want to flip through, looking for interesting or relevant tips. The red arrows⟶, red outlines and red text found in tips (and sometimes with artwork) have been added to emphasize or further explain a concept or technique.

3 Exercises. (Not for the faint of heart.) we have included step-by-step exercises to help you make the transition to Illustrator technician extraordinaire. *The Zen of Illustrator* chapter and the *Zen Lessons* on the *Wow! CD* are dedicated to helping you master the mechanics (and the soul) of Illustrator. Take these lessons in small doses, in order, and at a relaxed pace. All of the Finger Dances are customized for Mac and Windows.

4 Techniques. In these sections, you'll find step-by-step techniques gathered from almost a hundred *Illustrator Wow!* artists. Most *Wow!* techniques focus on one aspect of how an image was created, though I'll often refer you to different *Wow!* chapters (or to a specific step-by-step technique, Tip, or Gallery where a technique is introduced) to give you the opportunity to explore a briefly-covered feature more thoroughly. Feel free to start with almost any chapter, but, since each technique builds on those previously explained, try to follow the techniques within each chapter sequentially. Some chapters conclude with **Advanced Technique** lessons, which assume that you have assimilated all of the techniques found throughout the chapter. *Advanced Techniques* is an entire chapter dedicated to advanced tips, tricks, and techniques.

5 Galleries. The Gallery pages consist of images related to techniques demonstrated nearby. Each Gallery piece is accompanied by a description of how the artist created that image, and may include steps showing the progression of a technique detailed elsewhere. *Illustrator & Other Programs* consists almost entirely of Gallery pages to give you a sense of Illustrator's flexibility.

6 References. *Technical Notes, Resources, Publications* and *Artists* appendixes, *Glossaries*, and *General Index* can be found in the back of this book. In addition, we'll occasionally direct you to the *User Guide* when referring to specific information already well-documented in the *Adobe Illustrator User Guide*.

4

5
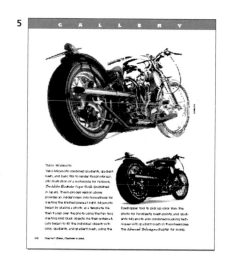

6
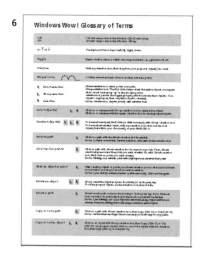

Illustrator & OS X

by Dave Awl

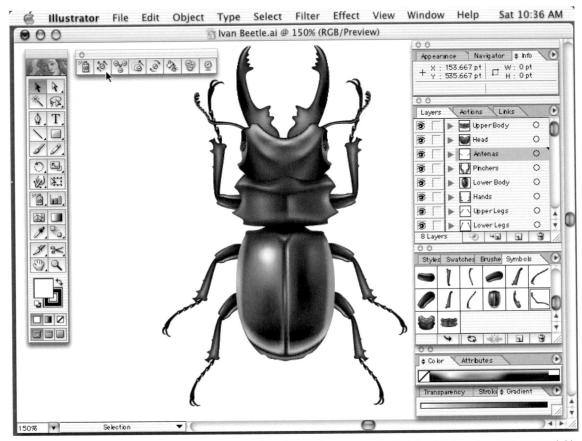

We're using Ivan Torres's beetle artwork to give you a look at Illustrator's workspace in OS X. For details on how Torres created this image using Illustrator 10's symbols feature, see his Gallery in the Web & Animation chapter.

NOTE: *We gratefully acknowledge the wisdom and generosity of our friend Sandee Cohen, the Vectorbabe herself, who supplied us with much of the information about OS X in this section. Thanks also to OS X guru Maria Langer for screen shot assistance!*

Apple's new operating system, Mac OS X, is a big step forward for the Macintosh platform, and it involves some major changes, not only to the look and feel of the OS but also to the way that basic tasks are accomplished. The good news is that using Illustrator in OS X isn't a whole lot different from using Illustrator in Mac OS 9 or Windows. Adobe has been very careful to preserve as much consistency as possible. There are some added conveniences and improvements that come with using OS X, but nothing that's going to make your life any more difficult. (Go ahead and breathe a sigh of relief.)

Just what are these added conveniences and improvements? Two notable features are a handy new Illustrator application menu on the title bar and increased support for making and using PDF files. We'll cover both, but first let's take a look at the basic improvements in OS X's interface that affect the look and function of windows and dialogs.

OS X's candy coating

Apple's creative guru, Steve Jobs, must have a serious sweet tooth. First, he gave us the famous "fruit-flavored" iMacs in bright candy colors; when it came time to design the "Aqua" look for OS X, he decided to create an interface that would make people want to lick it. The results are enough to make Willy Wonka green with envy: OS X's windows are decorated with translucent, candy-colored buttons, tabs, scroll-bars, and drop-down menus that appear to glisten like drops of water.

Improved windows and dialogs

In addition to the new aesthetic touches, there are a few basic functional differences in the way OS X's windows and dialogs are set up compared to OS 9 and earlier. First, instead of the close and minimize boxes we're used to, each window in OS X has three colored, drop-like buttons in the upper left corner: red, yellow, and green (visible in the beetle screen shot on the facing page). The red button closes, the yellow button minimizes, and the green button zooms. Similarly, Illustrator for OS X's palettes have a close button and a minimize button in the upper left corner, but note that the palette buttons are colored red and yellow (respectively) only when you

Everyone's a critic

It should be noted that not everyone is a fan of the new look: OS X's candy colors send some artists and designers into sugar shock. Sharon Steuer, for instance, complains: "OS X's design and shadows interfere with my austere space...which in turn competes with my work! I had an art teacher who wouldn't even let us use colored thumbtacks to put things up on the wall because they added a color element. With OS X you have those red, green, and yellow buttons everywhere."

Thanks for the memory

One of the best advantages of working in OS X: by all accounts, it's a virtually crash-free experience, thanks to OS X's protected memory. OS X uses *pre-emptive multitasking* (as opposed to OS 8 and 9's *cooperative multitasking*), which means that if one application crashes, it won't bring the whole operating system down with it. And you no longer have to worry about memory management—OS X handles all that for you! (Note that you can still allocate memory for Classic applications when you need to, using the Show Info window.)

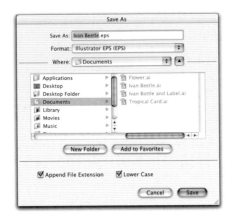

OS X's Save As dialog offers a file browser with column view for more direct navigation

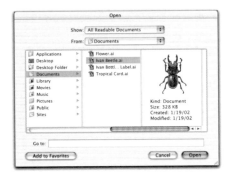

The Open dialog in OS X offers a bigger, better preview of the files you're browsing, including key file data

The Illustrator application menu lives right next to the Apple menu on the menu bar. You'll find Illustrator's preferences there, as well as About Illustrator and Quit Illustrator

move your mouse over them—the rest of the time they're gray. (The grayed-out close and minimize buttons can be seen in the beetle screen shot at the beginning of this section, on the various palettes shown.)

OS X's dialogs are set up a little differently, too. Take the Save As dialog (shown at left), for example. In the OS 9 version, the Name field and Format menu are in the middle of the box; in OS X, the Save As field (which is the Name field renamed) and the Format menu are at the top of the dialog. A more significant (and very helpful) improvement is the double browsing area you'll notice in the center of the dialog—the right side shows you the contents of items you select on the left side.

Similarly, OS X's Open dialog (shown at left) helps you find the file you're looking for by supplying a bigger, better, and more robust preview of the files you're browsing. (In the screen shot of the Open dialog, you'll see the preview area at the right side of it.) In addition to the larger preview image, you also get information about the file: kind, size, date created, and date modified.

The handy Illustrator Application menu

In OS X, every application has its own Application menu, which appears right next to the Apple menu on the Menu bar. The Application menu is named for the application you're in. So in Illustrator for OS X, you'll find a convenient new menu called Illustrator (shown at left). It brings together a number of menu items previously found in other places, including About Illustrator (formerly under the Apple menu), Preferences (formerly under the Edit menu), and Quit Illustrator (formerly under the File menu).

PDF: Here, there, and everywhere

The PDF (Portable Document Format) is becoming an

increasingly popular method for sharing documents electronically. With OS X, you'll find that it's easier than ever to make, share, and use PDF documents, because OS X has PDF functionality woven into it. (In fact, OS X's display engine, called Quartz, was built using the PDF format.) The upshot is that it's possible to make PDF files using OS X itself.

You can easily generate PDFs in any application that uses OS X's Print dialog (File: Print). You'll find a Save as PDF File option when you choose Output Options from the third pop-up menu in the dialog (shown above right). When you select that option, your file gets saved as a PDF instead of printed out. Yes, it's really that easy. You don't even need to have a printer hooked up to take advantage of this functionality, since you aren't actually printing anything. The Print Preview in many OS X applications can also be saved as a PDF. Click the Preview button to generate a preview (see an example of this button in the Print dialog screen shot at right). In some applications, you'll find a Save as PDF option right under the File menu. How's that for convenience?

This widespread ability to save files in the PDF format is especially useful for Illustrator users, because it means that charts, graphics, and text documents from other applications can be easily converted into Illustrator documents. All you have to do is save them as PDFs, and then open the PDF files in Illustrator.

The bottom line

Change can be intimidating, and making the switch to OS X is a big step for some users. But once you get there (assuming you haven't made the move already), you're likely to find that the advantages of using Illustrator in OS X are more than enough to reward you for your bold leap forward.

OS X lets you save files in the PDF format right from the Print dialog (File: Print). Just choose Output Options from the third pop-up menu, check Save as File, choose Format: PDF, and then click Save

The Print dialog's Preview function offers another way to create a PDF of your document; just click Preview and you'll have the option to save the preview as a PDF (File: Save as PDF)

Once you've saved your file from another application as a PDF, it can be easily opened in Illustrator

Illustrator Basics

1

Illustrator Basics

Don't start yet!

Before you begin this book, make sure you read both the "How to Use This Book" section in the front of the book, and the pullout *Glossary* at the back.

System requirements

Any improvements to these minimum system requirements will increase Illustrator's performance.

Macintosh:
- PowerPC processor
- Mac OS 9.1, 9.2, or Mac OS X version 10.1

Windows:
- Intel Pentium processor
- Windows 98, Windows ME, Windows 2000, Windows XP, or Windows 2000 OS

Both systems:
- 64 MB of available RAM
- 105 MB of available hard drive space to load the software
- 1024 x 768 monitor resolution
- CD-ROM drive to install the application

Tool tips

When enabled (Edit: Preferences: General), tool tips will display descriptive captions for all icons, tools, and certain functions.

This chapter is packed with tips and techniques chosen to help you use Adobe Illustrator with optimal ease and efficiency. Whether you're a veteran of Illustrator or a relative newcomer, you're likely to find information here that will greatly increase your productivity and help you get up to speed on the latest features. Remember, this chapter is an addendum to, not a replacement for, Adobe Illustrator's *User Guide*.

COMPUTER & SYSTEM REQUIREMENTS

Creating artwork on the computer is as rewarding as it is challenging. Computer art tools, including Adobe Illustrator, have undergone great improvements in the past few years. In order to accommodate demands for faster and more powerful software, the more powerful upgrades might not run on older computers. For example, the minimum requirement is now at least 64MB of RAM made available to run Illustrator. For rasterizing and complex work in Illustrator, you'll probably need to allocate 90–120MB. You'll also need more hard disk space than ever before: Illustrator files containing live blends, brushes, placed raster images, gradient meshes, live effects, and transparency can be quite large! If you want to work efficiently, you'll also need a video card or extra VRAM for 24-bit color support. Illustrator does not require a large monitor, but we strongly recommend using one. The best solution is two monitors. This allows you to keep your palettes on one monitor, while using the other to create your artwork.

SETTING UP YOUR PAGE
New Document

Illustrator does not automatically open with a new document. To create a new blank document, select New from the File menu. A dialog box opens in which you will select the document color space (CMYK or RGB) and the

Artboard Size (the document dimensions). The default page size is 612 pts x 792 pts, which is equivalent to 8.5" x 11". Illustrator does not allow you to create new art that uses both CMYK and RGB colors in the same document. You can choose from the pop-up list of different page sizes (for print or web purposes) and page orientation, and you can also choose your preferred measurement system. Pages can be as small as 1 pixel x 1 pixel, or as large as 227" x 227".

The Artboard

A box with a solid black outline defines the Artboard dimensions and the final document size. The dotted line indicates the printable area of the current selected printer. Double-click the Hand tool to fit your image to the current window. Use View: Hide Page Tiling to hide the dotted lines. Use the Page tool to click-drag the dotted-line page parameters around the Artboard; only objects within the dotted line will print to your printer.

Page Setup

Use Page Setup if you want to change the paper size and page orientation for the currently selected printer. Select your desired page size from the Paper Size pop-up menu, and choose portrait or landscape orientation. Only the paper sizes your target printer can support will display in the Paper Size pop-up menu.

There are times when you want to change the size of your Artboard. You might create a large image that you'll eventually print to an imagesetter, but will first need to proof on your local laser printer. For Mac only, you have the option to scale your image in relation to the Page Setup by reducing the image size to fit your current printer's paper size. Alternatively, you can enlarge your Page Setup to tile your image onto smaller pages. Then you can paste the sheets together to simulate the larger page size. This is a terrific way to scale something quickly to see how it looks when printed smaller or larger. A 4" line of a 4-pt weight, printed at 25% reduction (the

A zoomed-out view of the Artboard

Using startup documents

In your Plug-ins folder (in the Adobe Illustrator folder) are two files called "Adobe Illustrator Startup_CMYK" and "Adobe Illustrator Startup_RGB"; these files automatically load information into the application—such as colors, patterns, brushes, and gradients—when you open a new document. To create a *custom* Startup file, make a duplicate of the original and move the original to a safe place (out of the Plug-ins folder). Open the copy from within Illustrator, add or subtract styles from your document, then save. The next time you launch Illustrator, this Startup file will determine the set of styles available to new files. (For more details see the *Adobe Illustrator User Guide*.) **Note:** *You can make different Startup files for each project!*

Resizing and stroke weight

If you double-click the Scale tool, you can resize your selection with or without altering line weights:

- To scale a selection, while also scaling line weights, make sure to enable the Scale Strokes & Effects checkbox.
- To scale a selection while maintaining your line weights, disable Scale Strokes & Effects.
- To decrease line weights (50%) without scaling objects, first scale the selection (200%) with Scale Strokes & Effects disabled. Then scale (50%) with it enabled. Reverse to increase line weights.

STEUER

Changing keyboard shortcuts

To assign a shortcut to a menu item or tool, select Edit: Keyboard Shortcuts. Making any changes will rename the set "Custom." If you choose a shortcut already in use, you will get a warning that it is currently being used and that reassigning it will remove it from the item it is currently assigned to. When you exit the dialog you will be asked to save your *custom* set. You can't overwrite a *preset*.

maximum you can reduce), will print as a 1", 1-pt line. In addition, Page Setup only scales your image in relation to the current printing setup. It won't affect the size of the image when placed into another program or document. **Note:** *The Document Setup can be different from the Page Setup. If you change one, you should update the other.*

MAKING YOUR MOVES EASIER

Look over this section to make sure you're aware of the many ways to select tools and access features. Learning these simple techniques will free you from mousing to the toolbox or using the pull-down menus.

Single key tool-selection and navigation

Need to access a tool? Press a key. Press "T" to choose the Type tool, "P" for the Pen tool, and so on. Choose any tool in the toolbox by pressing its single-key equivalent. To learn the default single-key equivalents for your tools, with Show Tool Tips enabled (by default this is on), hold the cursor over any tool in the toolbox, and its single-key shortcut will appear in parentheses next to the tool name (toggle the Tool Tip option in Edit: Preferences: General). **Note:** *Single-key navigation won't work inside a text block.*

Keyboard shortcuts

To change a shortcut for a tool or menu item, open the Keyboard Shortcut dialog (Edit: Keyboard Shortcuts). Making a change to a shortcut will change the *Set* name to "Custom." When you're finished making changes and want to exit the dialog box, you will be asked to save your shortcuts to a new file. This file will be saved in the Illustrator application folder and will end in ".kys". As long as these file types are located in the application folder, they will be available as choices in the *Set* pop-up menu. In addition, every time you make any changes to a saved set (not a default preset), you'll be asked if you want to overwrite that set. You can also use the Save button to create a new keyboard shortcut file. Click the Export Text button if you need a text file as a reference

for a specific set of shortcuts or need to print them.
Note: *You cannot customize any palette items, such as the
Pathfinder filters or palette pop-up menu items.*

Context-sensitive menus

If you're not already familiar with context-sensitive
menus, you might find them a great timesaver. Windows
users merely click the right mouse button. If you're on a
Mac, press the Control key while you click and hold the
mouse button. In both cases a menu pops up (specific to
the tool or item you are working with) providing you
with an alternative to the regular pull-down menus.

Tear-off palettes

The Illustrator Toolbox lets you *tear off* subsets of tools so
you can move the entire set to another location. Click on
a tool with a pop-up menu, drag the cursor to the arrow
end of the pop-up, and release the mouse.

WORKING WITH OBJECTS

Anchor points, lines, and Bézier* curves

Instead of using pixels to draw shapes, Illustrator creates
objects made up of points, called "anchor points." They
are connected by curved or straight outlines called
"paths" and are visible if you work in Outline (formerly
Artwork) mode (View: Outline). Illustrator describes
information about the location and size of each path, as
well as its dozen or so attributes, such as its fill color and
its stroke weight and color. Because you are creating
objects, you'll be able to change the order in which they
stack. You'll also be able to group objects together so you
can select them as if they were one object. You can even
ungroup them later, if you wish.

If you took geometry, you probably remember that
the shortest distance between two points is a straight line.
In Illustrator, this rule translates into each line being
defined by two anchor points that you create by clicking
with the Pen tool, or drawing with the Line tool.

In mathematically describing rectangles and ellipses,

* Named after the software engineer who pioneered its use, Pierre Bézier

How to allocate RAM (OS 9 only)

Just because your computer has a
lot of RAM doesn't mean Illustrator has enough memory to run
effectively (Adobe only presets
a minimum amount of RAM).
To improve the speed and performance, increase the memory allo-
cation. *Single*-click the Illustrator
application icon to select it when
the program isn't running, and
choose File: Get Info: Memory and
adjust the Minimum and Preferred sizes. Reserve enough RAM
to run the operating system and
any other applications you'll want
open simultaneously.

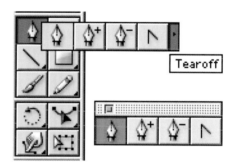

Tear-off tool palettes

Changing measurement units

To set units of measurement for
rulers, palettes, and some dialog
boxes or filters, choose File:
Document Setup. To set units for
new documents, change units in
General Preferences.
Note: *Control-click (Mac) or
right mouse-click (Win) the rulers
to select alternate units.*

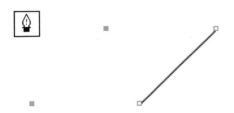

Clicking with the Pen tool to create anchor points for straight lines

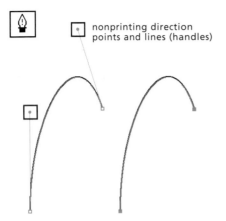

nonprinting direction points and lines (handles)

Click-dragging with the Pen tool to create anchor points and pulling out direction lines for curves

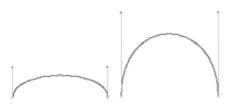

When direction handles are short, curves are shallow; when handles are long, curves are deep

The length and angle of the handles determine the gesture of the curves

Illustrator computes the center, the length of the sides, or the radius, based on the total width and height you specify. For more complex shapes involving free-form curves, Adobe Illustrator allows you to use the Pen tool to create Bézier curves, defined by nonprinting anchor points (which literally anchor the path at those points), and direction points (which define the angle and depth of the curve). To make these direction points easier to see and manipulate, each direction point is connected to its anchor point with a nonprinting direction line, also called a "handle." The direction points and handles are visible when you're creating a path with the Pen tool or editing the path with the Direct-selection tool. While all of this might sound complicated, manipulating Bézier curves can become intuitive. Mastering these curves, though initially awkward, is the heart and soul of using Illustrator.

More about Bézier curves

If you're new to using Bézier curves, take some time to go through the Adobe training materials. The *Wow! CD* includes several "Zen" practice lessons that will help you fine-tune your Bézier capabilities (found in the Training folder).

Many graphics programs include Béziers, so mastering the Pen tool, though challenging at first, is very important. Friskets in Corel Painter, paths in Photoshop, and the outline and extrusion curves of many 3D programs all use the Bézier curve.

The key to learning Béziers is to take your initial lessons in short doses and stop if you get frustrated. Designer Kathleen Tinkel describes Bézier direction lines as "following the gesture of the curve." This artistic view should help you to create fluid Bézier curves.

Some final rules about Bézier curves

• The length and angle of the handles "anticipate" the curves that will follow.
• The length of the handles is equal to approximately one-third the length of the curve, if it were straightened.

- To ensure that the curve is smooth, place anchor points on either side of an arc, not in between.
- The fewer the anchor points, the smoother the curve will look and the faster it will print.
- Adjust a curve's height and angle by dragging the direction points, or grab the curve itself to adjust its height.

WATCH YOUR CURSOR!

Illustrator's cursors change to indicate not only what tool you have selected, but also which function you are about to perform. If you watch your cursor, you will avoid the most common Illustrator mistakes.

If you choose the Pen tool:

- **Before you start,** your cursor displays as the Pen tool with "×" indicating that you're starting a new object.

- **Once you've begun your object,** your cursor changes to a regular Pen. This indicates that you're about to add to an existing object.

- **If your cursor gets close to an existing anchor point,** it will change to a Pen with "–" indicating that you're about to delete the last anchor point! If you click-drag on top of that anchor point, you'll redraw that curve. If you hold the Option (Mac)/Alt (Win) key while you click-drag on top of the point, you'll pull out a new direction line, creating a corner (as in the petals of a flower). If you click on top of the point, you'll collapse the outgoing direction line, allowing you to attach a straight line to the curve.

- **If your cursor gets close to an end anchor point of an object,** it will change to a Pen with "o" to indicate that you're about to "close" the path. If you do close the path, then your cursor will change back to a Pen with "×" to indicate that you're beginning a new object.

- **If you use the Direct-selection tool to adjust the object as you go,** be sure to look at your cursor when

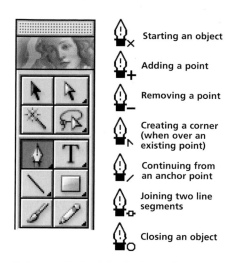

Basic cursor feedback for the Pen tool

Illustrator paths on your screen

Edit: Preferences: General: Anti-aliased Artwork helps paths (including type) appear more accurately drawn to the screen. By default it is on, but it may slow down screen redraws on large files. If you experience problems, try switching it off. Anti-alias Artwork *on* is great for doing screen shots but not so great for thin line weights. These settings only reflect what the artwork looks like on screen—they will print sharp.

Anti-alias Artwork, off

Anti-alias Artwork, on

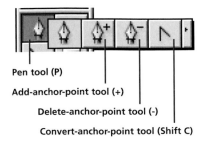

Pen tool (P)

Add-anchor-point tool (+)

Delete-anchor-point tool (-)

Convert-anchor-point tool (Shift C)

you're ready to continue your object. If it's still a regular Pen, then continue to place the next point, adding to your object. If the Pen tool has "×" (indicating that you are about to start a new object), then you must redraw your last point. As you approach this last anchor point, your cursor will change to a Pen with "/"; click and drag over this last point to redraw the last curve. To form a hinged corner on the point as you draw, hold down your Option key (Mac)/Alt key (Win) as you click-drag out a new direction line.

BÉZIER-EDITING TOOLS

The group of tools you can use to edit Illustrator paths are called Bézier-editing tools. To access them, click and hold the Pen, Pencil, or Scissors tool and drag to select one of the other tools. You can also tear off this palette. (To learn about *filters* that edit, see details on Pathfinder filters in the *Drawing & Coloring* chapter.)

- **The Pen tool and Auto Add/Delete** can perform a variety of functions. Auto Add/Delete, when enabled (General Preferences), allows the Pen tool to change automatically to the Add-anchor-point tool when the tool is over a selected path segment, or to the Delete-anchor-point tool when over an anchor point. To temporarily disable the Auto Add/Delete function of the Pen tool, hold down the Shift key. If you don't want the path to constrain to an angle, release the Shift key prior to releasing the mouse.

- **The Convert-anchor-point tool,** found hidden within the Pen tool (default is Shift-C), lets you convert an anchor point on a path from a smooth curve to a corner point by clicking on the anchor point. To convert it from a corner point to a smooth curve, click-drag on the anchor point counterclockwise to pull out a new direction handle (or twirl the point until it straightens out the curve). To convert from a smooth curve to a hinged curve (two curves hinged at a point), grab the direction point and hold Option/Alt as you drag it out to the new position. With the Pen tool selected, you can temporarily access the Convert-anchor-point tool by pressing the Option or Alt keys.

- **The Add-anchor-point tool,** accessible from the Pen pop-up menu or by pressing the + key, adds an anchor point to a path at the location where you click.

- **The Delete-anchor-point tool,** accessible from the Pen pop-up menu or by pressing –, deletes an anchor point when you click *directly* on the point.
  Note: *If you select the Add/Delete-anchor-point tools by pressing + or –, you must press P to get back to the Pen tool.*

- **The Pencil tool** reshapes a selected path when Edit selected paths is checked in the tools preferences. Select a path and draw on or close to the path to reshape it.

- **The Smooth tool** smoothes the points on a path that you trace with the tool by curving corners and deleting points. The Smooth tool attempts to keep the original shape of the path as intact as possible while it goes about smoothing your points and paths.

- **The Erase tool** removes sections of a selected path. By dragging along the path you can erase or remove portions of it. You must drag along the path—drawing perpendicular to the path will result in unexpected effects. This tool adds a pair of anchor points to the remaining path, on either side of the erased section of the path.

- **The Scissors tool** cuts a path where you click by adding two disconnected, selected anchor points exactly on top of each other. To select just one of the points, deselect the object, then click with the Direct-selection tool on the spot where you cut. This will allow you to select the upper anchor point and drag it to the side in order to see the two points better.

Tool tolerance options

Drawing freehand while holding a mouse or even a digital pen can be less than elegant. The Pencil, Smooth, and Brush tools contain options that can help you to create more types of paths, ranging from very realistic to more shapely and graceful ones, without the constant need to adjust anchor points. Double-click on the tool to view the options.

- **Fidelity:** Increases or decreases the distance between anchor points on the path created or edited. The smaller the number, the more points that will make up the path and vice versa.

- **Smoothness:** The smoothness option varies the percentage of smoothness you'll see as you create and edit paths. Use a lower percentage of smoothness for more realistic lines and brush strokes, and a higher percentage for less realistic but more elegant lines.

Note: *Closing Pencil and Brush tool paths is a bit awkward. If you hold down the Option (Mac)/Alt (Win) key when you are ready to close a path, a straight line segment will be drawn between the first and last anchor points. If you hold down the Option/Alt key and extend slightly past the first anchor point, the path will close automatically. Set the tool preferences to low numbers to make closing easier.— Sandee Cohen*

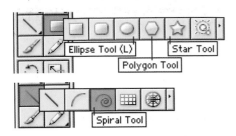

Serious fun with shapes

The Ellipse (or oval, select by typing "L"), Polygon, Star, and Spiral are simple but powerful tools. Used in conjunction with the following key combinations, they are likely to become indispensable:

- **Spacebar-drag** allows you to reposition your object.
- **Shift** constrains the object's proportions.
- **Up-arrow** (↑) increases points on a star, sides on a polygon, and coils on a spiral.
- **Down-arrow** (↓) removes points from a star, sides from a polygon, and coils from a spiral.
- **Option (Mac)/Alt (Win)** increases the angle of the star's points.
- **Command-drag** changes the inside and outside radius of a star, or increases or decreases the decay in a spiral.
- **Option (Mac)/Alt (Win)-click** allows you to create the object numerically.
- **Combinations:** Experiment with all the keys separately and in combination with the other keys. Doing so is the only way to fully understand these fun and powerful tools.

- **The Knife tool** slices through all unlocked visible objects and closed paths. Simply drag the Knife tool across the object you want to slice, then select the object(s) you want to move or delete.

GEOMETRIC OBJECTS

The Ellipse, Rounded Rectangle, Polygon, and Star tools create objects called "geometric primitives." These objects are mathematically-described symmetrical paths grouped with a nonprinting anchor point, which indicates the center. Use the centers of the geometric objects to snap-align them with each other, or with other objects and guides. You can create these geometric objects numerically or manually. Access the tools in the pop-up palette from the Rectangle tool in the Toolbox. (See the *Zen of Illustrator* chapter for exercises in creating and manipulating geometric objects, and Tip at left.)

- **To create a geometric shape manually,** select the desired geometric tool, and click-drag to form the object from one corner to the other. To create the object from the center, hold down the Option (Mac)/Alt (Win) key and drag from the center outward (keep the Option/Alt key down until you release the mouse button to ensure that it draws from the center). Once you have drawn the geometric objects, you can edit them exactly as you do other paths.

- **To create a geometric object with numeric input,** select the desired geometric tool and click on the artboard to establish the upper left corner of your object. Enter the desired dimensions in the dialog box and click OK. To create the object numerically from the object's center, Option-click (Mac)/Alt-click (Win) on the Artboard.

    To draw an arc, select the Arc tool and then click and drag to start drawing the arc. Press the F key to flip the arc from convex to concave, and use the up and down arrow keys to adjust the radius of the arc. Release the mouse to finish the arc.

    To draw a grid, select either the Rectangular Grid tool

or the Polar Grid tool and click-drag to start drawing the grid. Use the up, down, right, and left arrow keys to add or remove sections, and use the Z, X, C, and V keys to skew them. Release the mouse to finish the grid.

SELECTING & GROUPING OBJECTS

Selecting

There are several ways to make selections with this version of Illustrator. You can use the Selection tools to select individual or multiple objects. You can use the target indicators in the Layers palette to select and target objects, groups, and layers. Targeting a group or layer selects everything contained within it. (For more on this, see the *Layers* chapter.)

You can use the Lasso tool to select an entire path or multiple paths by encircling them with the tool. Option (Mac)/Alt (Win) + the Lasso tool subtracts entire paths from a selection. Shift + Lasso tool adds entire paths to a selection.

Use the Direct-select Lasso tool to select individual anchor points or path segments by encircling them with the tool. Option (Mac)/Alt (Win) + Direct-select Lasso tool subtracts anchor points from a selection. Shift + Direct-select Lasso tool adds anchor points to a selection.

Grouping and selecting

Many object-oriented programs (programs that create objects, such as Illustrator and CorelDraw) provide you with a grouping function so you can act upon multiple objects as one unit. In Illustrator, grouping objects places all the objects on the same layer and creates a group container in the Layers palette with a triangle next to it. You don't want to group objects unless you actually need to. (For more on layers and objects, see the *Layers* chapter.)

So, when do you want to group objects? Group objects when you need to select them *repeatedly* as a unit or want to apply an appearance to the entire group. Take an illustration of a bicycle as an example. Use the Group function to group the spokes of a wheel. Next, group the

If you can't group...

If you try to group objects and get the message "Can't make a group of objects that are within different groups":

- Make certain that the objects you wish to group are fully selected.
- Cut the objects.
- Use Paste In Front or Paste In Back to paste the objects back into your image in exactly the same location (see introduction to the *Layers* chapter). While the objects are still selected, select Object: Group.

| Selection tool | Direct-selection tool | Group-selection tool |

Efficient ungrouping

To select an object within a group, you don't need to ungroup it; just use the Direct-selection tool to select it. To group, select the desired objects and ⌘-G (Mac)/Ctrl-G (Win). If you *do* want to ungroup, select the group by using the Selection tool and Ungroup as many times as you wish to remove levels of grouping. For instance, with the example of the bicycle (on the next page), selecting the entire bicycle and pressing ⌘-Shift-G (Mac)/Ctrl-Shift-G (Win) the first time would remove the last grouping applied; typing it four times would remove all the groupings.

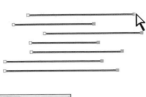

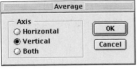

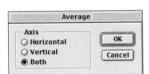

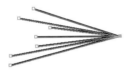

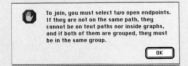

Using the Average command to align selected endpoints vertically, then choosing Both

two wheels of the bicycle, then group the wheels with the frame. We will continue to refer to this bicycle below.

- **With the Direct-selection tool.** Click on a point or path with the Direct-selection tool to select that point or portion of the path. If you click on a spoke of a wheel, you'll select the portion of the spoke's path you clicked on.

- **With the Selection tool.** Click on an object with the Selection tool to select the largest group containing that object. In our example, it would be the entire bicycle.

- **With the Group-selection tool.** Use the Group-selection tool to select subgroupings progressively. The first click with the Group-selection tool will select a single object. The next click will select the entire spoke path. The third click selects the entire wheel, the fourth selects both wheels, and the fifth, the entire bicycle.
  Note: *If you want to grab and move objects selected with the Group-selection tool, you must change to one of the other selection tools or, during a selection, click and drag without releasing the mouse. When you continually click with the Group-selection tool, you're always selecting the next group up.*

- **See the "Finger Dance" lessons in the *Zen* chapter.** This section includes a variety of selection exercises.

JOINING & AVERAGING

Two of Illustrator's most useful functions are Average and Join (both found under the Object: Path menu or in the Context-sensitive menu). Use the Average function to place two endpoints at a single location, averaged between them. Use the Join function to join two endpoints. The Join function will operate differently depending on the objects.

Averaging also allows you to align selected *points*. (To align objects, use the Align palette.) To average, use the Direct-selection tool or Direct-select Lasso tool to marquee-select or Shift-select any number of points belonging to any number of objects. Then use the Context-sensitive menu (for the Mac hold the Control key, use the right mouse button for Windows) to average, aligning the selected points horizontally, vertically, or along both axes.

- **If the two open endpoints are exactly on top of each other,** then Join opens a dialog box asking if the join should be smooth (a curved Bézier anchor with direction handles) or a corner (an anchor point with no handles). Both points will fuse into one point.

- **If the two open endpoints are *not* exactly on top of each other,** then Join will connect the two points with a line. If you try to Join two points to fuse as one but don't get a dialog box, then you've merely connected your points with a line! Undo (⌘-Z for Mac / Ctrl-Z for Windows) and see "Averaging & Joining in one step" below.

- **If you select an open path** (in this case, you don't need to select the endpoints), then Join closes the path.

- **If the two open endpoints are on different objects,** then Join connects the two paths into one.

- **Averaging & Joining in one step.** Hold down Option (Mac)/Alt (Win) and choose Object: Path: Join. The join forms a corner if joining to a line, or a hinged curve if joining to a curve.

WORKING WITH PALETTES

Most of Illustrator's palettes are accessible via the Window menu. Each palette is unique, but share common features:

- **Regrouping tabbed palettes to save desktop space.** Reduce the space that palettes require by nesting the palettes together into smaller groups. Grab the palette tab and drag it to another palette group to nest it. You can also drag a tab to the *bottom* of a palette to dock the palettes on top of one another.

Typing units into palettes

To use the current unit of measurement, type the number, then Tab to the next text field or press Return. To use another unit of measurement, *follow* the number with "in" or " (inch), "pt" (point), "p" (pica), or "mm" (millimeter) and Return. To resume typing into an *image* text block, press Shift-Return. (*Tip from Sandee Cohen:* Type *calculations* in text fields!)

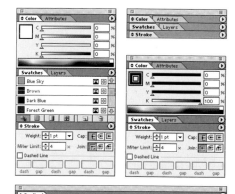

Modes of expansion for docked palettes; lower figure is Gradient palette, alone and expanded

Teeny tiny palettes

Double-click the tab name or the space to the right of the tab, or single-click the double arrows on the tab to cycle through expanded and collapsed views of the palette. Only palettes with more options have double arrows on the palette tab.

Palette be gone!

Press Tab to hide the palettes and Toolbox, then Tab to toggle them into view again. If you'd rather keep the Toolbox and hide the other palettes, just use Shift-Tab.

If you can't see the appearance

If you are trying to alter an appearance but nothing seems to change on the screen, make sure:

• your objects are selected

• you are in Preview mode

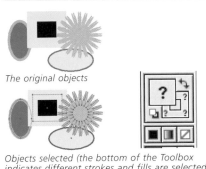

The original objects

Objects selected (the bottom of the Toolbox indicates different strokes and fills are selected)

Objects will remain unchanged unless you actively choose new settings

Typing "1" (Return), or choosing a stroke weight from the pop-up, sets stroke weight for only those selected objects that already have strokes

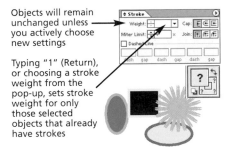

The objects after setting a stroke weight of 1

Easy default styling

Select an object with the appearance you want your next object to have. Illustrator automatically resets the appearance, so the next drawn object will be identical to the last one selected.

Note: *This does not work for type.*

• **You can make most palettes smaller or larger.** If there's a sizing icon in the lower right corner, click and drag it to shrink or expand the palette. Palettes also have pop-up menus offering additional options. If a palette contains more options, it will have an double arrow to the left of the palette name. Click on the arrows to cycle through the various options. Click the square (minimize box), on the top of the title bar to shrink all palettes docked or nested together down to just title bars and tabs. Click the right square again, and the palettes will re-expand. Double-click the title bar to cycle through the states, from maximum to collapsed.

• **You must select your object(s) before you can make changes.** With your objects selected, you can click on the label or inside any edit box in the palette containing text and begin typing. If you're typing something that has limited choices (such as a font or type style), Illustrator will attempt to complete your word; just keep typing until your choice is visible. If you're typing into a text field, use the Tab key to move to other text fields within the palette. **IMPORTANT:** *When you've finished typing into palette text fields, you must press Return (or Enter). This action signals the application that you are ready to enter text somewhere else or to resume manipulating your artwork.*

• **You can edit selective characteristics on multiple objects.** With palettes, you can set one specific style for all selected objects without affecting any other characteristics. For example, your selection might contain multiple objects: one with no stroke, and the rest with outlines of different colors and weights. If, in the Stroke palette, you set the stroke weight to 1 (point) and leave the other choices unchanged, this will set the stroke weight of all objects that have strokes to 1 (point), but it won't add strokes to unstroked objects and won't affect the colors of any strokes. You can use the same technique to change assorted text blocks to the same typeface while maintaining differences in type sizes and other formatting.

- **The many ways to fill or stroke an object.** Focus on a selected object's fill or stroke by clicking on the Fill or Stroke icon near the bottom of the Toolbox, or toggle between them by pressing the "X" key (if you want to set the stroke or fill to None, use the "/" key). Set the color you want by: 1) adjusting the sliders or sampling a color from the color ramp in the Color palette, 2) clicking on a swatch in the Swatches palette, 3) sampling colors from the color picker, or 4) using the Eyedropper tool to sample from other objects in your file. In addition, you can drag color swatches from palettes to selected objects or to the Fill/Stroke icon in the Toolbox.

- **Objects, a group of objects, or a layer can have an appearance associated with it.** Not only can objects have fill and stroke characteristics, they can also have transparency and effects as part of their appearance. Not all objects, groups, or layers have styles applied to them, but most will have an appearance, even if that appearance is only a stroke and a fill (basic appearance).

- **Apply a Style to an object, group of objects, or a layer.** The total sum of applied characteristics can be saved as a style in the Styles palette. Styles are "live" (updatable) combinations of fills, strokes, blending modes, opacity, and effects. For details about working with the Styles palette, see the *Live Effects & Styles* chapter, especially the chapter introduction and the "Scratchboard Art" lesson.

GRAPHING & CHARTING

Through the Graph tool, Illustrator allows you to create charts and graphs in nine different styles. If you're new to charts or graphs, thoroughly read the graph chapter in the *User Guide*. Please keep in mind that the purpose of a chart or graph is clear communication of numeric information as a visual aid. A properly selected chart design will accomplish this. If you create a lot of charts or graphs, look into a specialty graphic application.

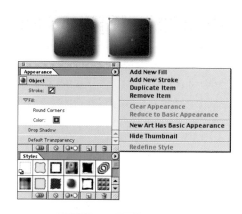

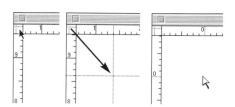

To update or replace a style throughout the entire document, select an object and apply the style you want to modify and update. With the object selected, make changes to it's appearance and choose Replace from the Appearance palette menu. The name of the style will display next to the replace command. This will globally update all objects using this named style. To change the name of the style, double-click on the proxy in the Styles palette and rename it.

Grabbing and dragging the ruler corner to re-center the ruler origin (zero point)

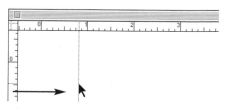

Clicking inside the ruler and dragging into your image to create a vertical or horizontal guide

If you want to continue to work with your graph numerically, *don't*, under any circumstances, ungroup your graph; it will make numerical data changes impossible. To avoid losing the special graph formatting, follow these special precautions:

- Use the Selection tool to select the entire graph for changes in style. Once your graph is selected, 1) Double-click the Graph tool to change the graph style; 2) Choose Object: Graphs: Data to change numeric data; or 3) To apply shaped design elements, see "Customizing graph designs" in this section.
- Use the Group-selection tool to select a category of data, then restyle or recolor as desired.
- Use the Type tool or Direct-selection tool to select and change individual text elements.
- Use the Direct-selection tool to select individual elements to change their styling.

Once you're *completely* finished numerically adjusting a graph, you may wish to delete some objects. Select the graph (with the Selection tool) and Ungroup (⌘-U/Ctrl-U). Once ungrouped, the objects are no longer part of a graph and can be deleted.

Before you begin, set a default chart or graph style by double-clicking on the Graph tool and choosing the style you want. To produce your graph, use the Graph tool as you would use the Rectangle tool: either click-drag to create a rectangular object from corner to corner, or hold down the Option key and click with the tool to numerically specify the dimensions of your graph.

After you establish the dimensions, the Graph dialog box opens, awaiting input of numeric data. Enter labels and numbers by highlighting the desired cell and typing into the entry line along the top. Tab to enter text in the next horizontal cell. See the *User Guide* to determine how you should enter data for the specific graph style you want.

Note: *It's very easy to enter text into the wrong field by mistake; so be meticulous. Mistakes are difficult to correct.*

Alternatively, you can import data that's been saved in *Tab-delineated* text format. Most word processing, spreadsheet, or charting programs let you save or export data and labels as text, separated by Tabs and Returns.

To change the style of an existing graph, select the entire graph with the Selection tool and double-click on the Graph tool in the Toolbox. Choose another style and click OK. Be aware that each type of chart cannot necessarily be translated to all other formats.

To re-access a graph's numeric data, save your graph, then use the Selection tool to select your graph and choose Object: Graphs: Data. There is no Cancel command in data entry, but you can always use Undo (⌘-Z/Ctrl-Z).

Customizing graph designs

Being able to insert design elements into a graph is a snazzy—but overused—aspect of the graphing feature. Illustrator allows you to define graph designs, which can be used as substitutes for rectangular column bars and line markers. For instance, using the "scaling" option, you can take a heart-shaped design and incorporate it into a graph by stretching (vertically scaling) or enlarging (uniformly scaling) the heart to the correct height. A variant of this technique allows you to define a portion of the heart to be scaled (called the "Sliding" Design). By using the "repeating" option, you can stack the hearts on top of each other until they reach the correct height.

Defining a graph design element works much the same way as defining a pattern design (see the *Drawing & Coloring* chapter). After creating the object(s) you wish to use as a design element, place a rectangle to enclose your design (with no fill or stroke) behind that element (choose Arrange: Send To Back), select the rectangle with its design and choose Object: Graphs: Design. In the dialog box, click New and name your design. To apply the design, use the Selection tool to select the graph, choose Object: Graphs: Columns and select the desired method of fitting your design to the column size. You can also use design elements to serve as "markers" (indicating plotted points) for line and scatter graph styles. Follow the above procedure, but choose Object: Graphs: Marker.

Some of the nation's busiest newspapers and periodicals say that even though they often finish their charts and graphs in Illustrator, most use other programs to translate numbers into graphics. Fortunately for those using Mac OS X, documents from other programs (like Microsoft Excel) can be easily converted to Illustrator documents using OS X's built-in support for the PDF format. The Print dialog box in many OS X applications contains a Preview option. Once you generate the preview, it can be saved as a PDF, which can then be opened in Illustrator.

TRANSFORMATIONS

Moving, scaling, rotating, reflecting, and shearing are all operations that transform selected objects. Begin by selecting what you wish to transform. If you don't like the transformation you've just applied, use Undo before applying a new transformation—or you'll end up applying the new transformation on top of the previous one.

In Illustrator, you can perform most transformations manually (see the *Zen of Illustrator* chapter for exercises),

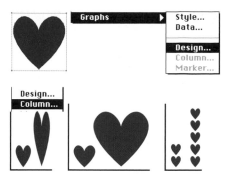

Defining a design; using the heart to create columns vertically scaled; uniformly scaled; forming a repeating design

Using graphs as templates

Designers use the Graph tool to plot points and generate the scale and legend. They create an illustration that uses the placement of the graph as a guide. See the *Brushes* chapter for help in locking the graph for use as a template.

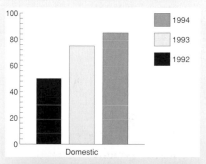

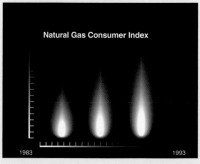

ELBERG

Eve Elberg used this bar graph as a template to plot the basic points in this illustration. For the glowing effect, she used blends and gradients (see the Blends, Gradients & Mesh chapter)

Transform again

Illustrator remembers the last transformation you performed— from simple moves to rotating a *copy* of an object. Use the Context-sensitive menu to repeat the effect (Transform Again).

Moving complex images

If the Transform palette fails, create a proxy rectangle closely surrounding the objects you wish to move. Move the proxy in one motion to the desired location, and delete. To apply the move, select your objects, double-click the Selection arrow, and click OK.

Free Transform variations

With the Free Transform tool you can apply the following transformations to selected objects:

- **Rotate**—click outside the bounding box and drag.
- **Scale**—click on a corner of the bounding box and drag. Option-drag/Alt-drag to scale from the center and Shift-drag to scale proportionally.
- **Distort**—click on a corner handle of the bounding box and ⌘-drag/Ctrl-drag.
- **Shear**—click on a side handle of the bounding box and ⌘-drag/ Ctrl-drag the handle.
- **Perspective**—click on a corner handle of the bounding box and ⌘-Option-drag/Ctrl-Alt-Shift-drag.

through a dialog box for numeric accuracy, with the Free Transform tool (as an effect), or with the Transform palette. In addition, you can select more than one object and choose Object: Transform: Transform Each.

Illustrator remembers the last transformation you performed, storing those numbers in the appropriate dialog box until you enter a new transform value or restart the program. For example, if you previously scaled an image numerically and chose not to scale the line weights, the next time you scale, manually or numerically, your line weights will not scale.

The bounding box

The bounding box should not be confused with the Free Transform tool (which allows you to perform additional functions; see discussion of the Free Transform tool below). The bounding box appears around selected objects when you are using the Selection tool (solid arrow), and can be useful for quick moving, scaling, rotating, or duplicating objects. With the bounding box, you can easily scale several objects at once. Select the objects, click on a corner of the bounding box and drag. To constrain proportionally while scaling, hold down the Shift key and drag a corner. By default, the bounding box is on. Toggle it on/off via the View: Hide/Show Bounding Box, or switch to the Direct-selection tool to hide the bounding box. To reset the bounding box after performing a transformation so it's once again square to the page, choose Object: Transform: Reset Bounding Box.
Note: *Holding down the Option or Alt keys when you transform with the bounding box will* not *create a duplicate, but will instead transform from the center.*

Moving

In addition to grabbing and dragging objects manually, you can specify a new location numerically: Double-click the Selection arrow in the Toolbox or use the Context-sensitive menu to bring up the Move dialog box (select the Preview option). For help determining the distance you wish to move, click-drag with the Measure tool the distance you wish to calculate. Then *immediately* open the Move dialog box to see the measured distance loaded automatically, and click OK (or press Return).

The Free Transform tool

The Free Transform tool (E) can be an easy way to transform objects once you learn the numerous keyboard combinations to take advantage of its functions. In addition to performing transformations such as rotate, scale, and shear, you can also create perspective and distortions (see Tip "Free Transform variations" opposite and the "Dynamics" lesson in the *Drawing & Coloring* chapter). Bear in mind that the Free Transform tool bases its transformations on a fixed center point that can not be relocated. If you need to transform from a different location, use the individual transformation tools, Transformation palette, or the Transform Each command.

The Transform palette

From this palette, you can determine numeric transformations that specify an object's width, height, and location on the document and how much to rotate or shear it. You can also access a palette pop-up menu that offers options to Flip Horizontal and Vertical; Transform Object, Pattern, or Both; and to enable Scale Strokes & Effects. The current Transform palette is a bit odd: You can Transform Again once you've applied a transformation, but the information in the text fields is not always retained. To maintain your numeric input, apply transformations through the transform tool's dialog box, discussed on the next page.

Individual transformation tools

For scaling, rotation, reflection, and shearing of objects with adjustable center points, you can click (to manually specify the center about which the transformation will occur), then grab your object to transform it. For practice with manual transformations see the *Zen* chapter.

Transform palette modifiers

To modify your transformations when you press Return, hold down Option (Mac)/Alt (Win) to transform and make a copy. Click a point in the Transform palette to select a reference point.

An exception to the rule!

Usually, you should scale an image before placing it in a page layout program. However, if your file contains brushes, patterns, gradients, and gradient meshes, you may want to scale the final image after you have placed it.

Scaling objects to an exact size

- *The transformation palette way:* Type the new width or height in the palette and press ⌘-Return (Mac)/Ctrl-Return (Win).
- *The proxy way:* Create a proxy rectangle the size of your image, then from the upper left corner of the proxy, Option/Alt-click to create another rectangle in the target dimensions. With your proxy selected, click with the Scale tool in the upper left and grab-drag the lower right to match the target. (Hold down Shift to scale in only one dimension.) Delete these rectangles, select your objects, double-click the Scale tool and apply settings.

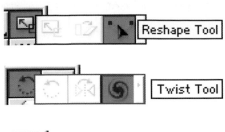

The selected area indicated in red

Direct-selected and dragged wing objects

HESS

For Eric Hess's "Soaring Hearts Futons" logo, he roughly Direct-selected, then with Reshape he marqueed as indicated above, and dragged

Each transformation tool has a dialog box where you can specify: the parameters for the tool, whether to transform the object or make a copy with the specified transform applied, and whether to transform just the objects and/or any patterns they may be filled with. (For more on transforming patterns see the *Drawing & Coloring* chapter.)

Here are three additional methods you can use to apply the individual transformation tools: to objects:

- **Double-click on a transformation tool** to access the dialog box. This allows you to transform the objects numerically, originating from an object's center.

- **Option (Mac)/Alt (Win)-click on your image with a transformation tool** to access the dialog box that allows you to transform your objects numerically, originating from where you clicked.

- **Click-drag on your image with a transformation tool** to transform the selected objects, originating from the center of the group of selected objects.

Reshape, Twist, & Shear

The Reshape tool is quite different from the other transformation tools. Start by Direct-selecting the paths you wish to reshape. If you use the Selection tool by mistake, the entire path will move, and if you haven't made any selection you won't be able to use the tool. Next, choose the Reshape tool from the Scale tool pop-up menu. With this tool, marquee or Shift-select all points you wish to affect, then drag the points to reshape the path. The selected points move as a group.

Using the Twist tool (found within the Rotate tool), click-drag or Option (Mac)/Alt (Win)-click to transform selected objects . For an example of art that used the Twist tool, see Laurie Grace's Gallery in the *Drawing & Coloring* chapter.

You will find the Shear tool hidden within the Reflect tool. It is used to slant objects.

Transform Each

To perform multiple transformations at once, open the Transform Each dialog box (Object: Transform: Transform Each). You can perform the transformations on several objects or on a single one. Additions to this dialog include the ability to reflect objects over the X and Y axis, and to change the point of origin. If you want to apply a transformation, but you think you might want to change it later, try a Transformation Effect (see the *Transparency* chapter).

WORKING SMART
Saving strategies

Probably the most important advice you'll ever get is to save every few minutes. Whenever you make a substantial change to your image, use File: Save As and give your image a new name.

It's much more time-efficient to save incremental versions of your image than it is to reconstruct an earlier version. Back up your work at least once a day before you shut down. Just think to yourself, "If this computer never starts up again, what will I need?" Develop a backup system using CDs, DVDs, Zip or Jaz drives, DATs (digital audio tapes), or opticals so you can archive all of your work. Use a program such as Dantz's Retrospect to automatically add new and changed files to your archives.

Get in the habit of archiving virtually everything, and develop a file-naming system that actually helps you keep track of your work in progress—simplifying your recovery of a working version if necessary. A good system involves three components. First, start with a meaningful description of your current image ("hearts compound"), and second, add a numerical notation of the version ("1.0"). Keep your numbering system consecutive, regardless of the label, throughout the entire project. Keep the number in a decimal sequence when you make an incremental change to your image ("1.1, 1.2, 1.3…"). Change to the next numeric sequence when you make a substantive change ("2.0"). Don't start numbers at 1.0 for each phase of the project or you'll be unable to figure out

Faster Saves

To avoid losing your latest data, you must back up your data often. You may know that Illustrator's native format is PDF, which means you can view native Illustrator files in Acrobat Reader. The PDF content in Illustrator files add to the file size, which means it takes Illustrator longer to save the files and open them. If you're working on a large file and are saving often (as you should), save times might be slow. When you save as an Illustrator 10 file, you now have the option to "Write PDF Compatible file" or turn it off (it's on by default). Turning this option off will reduce file size and make for speedier save times. However, it's important to note that some applications (like InDesign and LiveMotion) read the PDF content in Illustrator files. So if you're going to be importing your artwork into those programs, you'll want to leave PDF compatibility on.

How many Undos are left?

The status line in the lower left corner of your image window is actually a pop-up menu that lets you choose to display Current Tool, Date and Time, Free Memory, Number of Undos, or Document Color Profile.

To make changes to a path, click on the path with the Direct-selection tool. Then make adjustments by selecting and dragging anchor points, direction points, or the curve itself. If you select an object but don't see direction handles:

- Deselect it, then try again.
- If you're in Preview mode, be sure to click on the *path itself* or switch to Outline mode.
- Uncheck Use Area Select in the General Preferences.
- Enable View: Show Edges.

Note: *Only* curves *have handles!*

Interrupting Preview

You don't have to wait for Illustrator to finish redrawing the Preview before you pull down the next menu or perform another task. You can interrupt redrawing the preview and go to Outline mode by typing ⌘ (Mac)/Ctrl (Win)-. *period,* or the Esc key for Windows.

Two views

Illustrator allows you to preview precise anti-aliasing in Pixel Preview mode, and allows you to preview overprints and traps in Overprint Preview mode.

Zoom shortcuts while typing

Press ⌘/Ctrl + spacebar to zoom in or ⌘-Option/Ctrl-Alt + spacebar to zoom out even while typing.

which came first: "Sky 1.0" or "Heart 1.0." Instead, if labels are "Sky 1.0" and "Heart 4.0," then the creation order is self-explanatory. Third, add a suffix to indicate its file type (.ai for Illustrator, .psd for Photoshop, .eps for Encapsulated PostScript file). Also, make sure that you keep all files in a named and dated folder that distinguishes them from other projects. (For saving in other formats see "Image Formats" later in this chapter.)

Multiple Undos

Most programs give you one chance to undo your last move. Illustrator allows up to 200 levels of undo, but will only hold the user-specified number of undos if there is enough memory. When it needs to purge levels of undo to regain memory, Illustrator will remove all levels beyond what you've specified as your minimum. In File: Preferences: Units & Undo you can set the number of levels of undo to a number less than 200. Usually 20 to 30 levels is adequate and keeps you aware that you should still save frequently.

Even *after* you save a file, your Undos (and Redos) will still be available, making it possible for you to save the current version, undo it to a previous stage, and save it, or continue working from an earlier state. Having 20 to 30 undos available in each of multiple documents should come close to the experience of having infinite undos, but remember once you close your file, your undos will disappear.

Note: *Not all operations, are undoable, e.g. Preferences.*

CHANGING YOUR VIEWS
Preview and Outline

To control the speed of your screen redraw, learn to make use of the various Preview and Outline (formerly Artwork) modes (View menu). In Preview mode, you can view the document in full color; in Outline mode you only see the wire frames of the objects.

New View

New View (View: New View) allows you to save your

current window viewpoint, remembering also your zoom level and which layers are hidden, locked, or in Preview mode. Custom views are added to the bottom of the View menu to let you easily recall a saved view (see the *Layers* chapter for more details on views). You can rename a view, but the views themselves are not editable—if you need to make a change to a view, you'll have to make a New View.

New Window

Illustrator gives you the ability to display different aspects of your current image simultaneously. This allows you to separately view different Proof Setups, Overprint or Pixel Previews, and zoom levels. You can resize them, have edges hidden or visible, or hide or lock different *layers* in Preview or Outline (see the *Layers* chapter and "Hide/Show Edges" below). Most window configurations are saved with the file.

Window controls

As in Photoshop, you'll see three small icons at the very bottom of the Toolbox. One is always selected; this is the default in which Illustrator displays your file window. Starting at the far left, choose from Standard Screen mode (desktop showing around the edges of your file), Full Screen mode with menu bar (file window visible, but confined to the center of the screen with no desktop showing; you can access your menu bar) and Full Screen mode (same as above, but you cannot access your menu bar). You can toggle among the views by pressing the "F" key.

ZOOMING IN & OUT

Illustrator provides many ways to zoom in and out.

- **From the View menu.** Choose Zoom In/Out, Actual Size, or Fit in Window.

- **With the Zoom tool.** Click to zoom *in* one level of magnification; hold down the Option (Mac)/Alt (Win)

Where did the window go?

If you have many file windows open, simply select the file you want to bring to the front from the list of files at the bottom of the Window menu.

The Navigator palette & views

The Navigator palette (always in Preview mode) offers many ways to zoom in and out of documents:

- Double-click the mountain icons along the bottom edge of the palette window to increase or decrease the amount of zoom in 200% increments.
- Hold the ⌘ (Mac)/Ctrl (Win)-key and drag to marquee the area in the palette thumbnail that you want to zoom into or out from.
- Enable View Artboard Only to keep your view limited to the Artboard area. This is helpful if you are working on a large document with objects on the pasteboard that are distracting your focus.

Change the color of the border around the thumbnail in the View Options dialog (found in the Navigator palette pop-up menu).

Note: *Navigator might slow down files with a lot of text objects. The Navigator creates a thumbnail view of the document; every time you zoom or scroll, the Navigator must redraw its thumbnail. Unless you need to view the Navigator palette, close it.*

Current magnification is displayed in the bottom left corner of your document. Access a list of percentages (3.13% to 6400%) or Fit on Screen from the pop-up, or simply select the text and enter any percentage within the limit.

Customize your grids in Illustrator. Select a grid style and color.

- View: Show Grid, use the Context-sensitive menu or ⌘ (Mac)/Ctrl (Win)-'apostrophe.
- Toggle Snap To Grid on and off from the View menu or use the shortcut ⌘ (Mac)/Ctrl (Win)-Shift-' apostrophe.
- Set the division and subdivision for your grid in Preferences: Guides & Grid and choose either dotted divisions or lines and the color of those lines.
- To toggle the grid display in front or in back of your artwork, check or uncheck the Grids In Back checkbox (Preferences: Guides & Grid).
- Tilt the grid on an angle by choosing File: Preferences: General and then changing the Constrain angle value.
  Note: *The Constrain angle affects the angle at which objects are drawn and moved. (See the* Drawing & Coloring *chapter on how to adjust it for creating isometrics.)*

key and click to zoom *out* one level. You can also click-drag to define an area, and Illustrator will attempt to fill the current window with the area that you defined.

- **Use the shortcut ⌘(Mac)/Ctrl (Win) for Zoom.** With any tool selected, use ⌘-hyphen (Mac)/Ctrl-hyphen (Win)—think "minus to zoom out"—and ⌘+ (Mac)/ Ctrl + (Win)—think "plus to zoom in".

- **Use Context-sensitive menus**. With nothing selected, Control-click (Mac) or use the right mouse button (Windows) to access a pop-up menu so you can zoom in and out, change views, undo, and show or hide guides, rulers, and grids.

- **Navigator palette**. With the Navigator palette, you can quickly zoom in or out and change the viewing area with the help of the palette thumbnail (see Tip "The Navigator palette & views" later in this chapter).

SHOW/HIDE CHOICES

From the View menu, you can show and hide several combinations of items, such as grids, guides, smart guides, transparency grid, edges, Artboard, and page tilings.

Rulers, Guides, Smart Guides, and Grids

Toggle Illustrator's Show/Hide Rulers, or use the Context-sensitive menu (as long as nothing in your document is selected). The per-document ruler units are set in Document Setup. If you want all new documents to use a specific unit of measurement, change your preferences for Units (Edit: Preferences: Units & Undos).

In some previous versions of Illustrator, the ruler origin (where 0,0 is) was in the lower right corner of the image. In the current version, the ruler origin is in the upper left corner. To change the ruler origin, grab the upper left corner (where the vertical and horizontal rulers meet) and drag the crosshair to the desired location. The zeros of the rulers will reset to the point where you release your mouse (to reset the rulers to the default location, double-click the upper left corner). But beware—resetting your ruler origin will realign all new patterns and affect alignment of Paste In Front/Back between documents (see the *Layers* chapter for more on Paste In Front/Back).

To create simple vertical or horizontal ruler guides, click-drag from one of the rulers into your image. A guide appears where you release your mouse. You can define guide color and style in General Preferences. Guides automatically lock after you create them. To release a guide quickly, ⌘/Ctrl-Shift-double-click on it. You can lock and unlock guides with the Context-sensitive menu in Preview mode. You should note that locking or unlocking guides affects every open document. If you have too many guides visible in your document, simply choose View: Guides: Clear Guides. This only works on guides that are on visible, unlocked layers. Hiding or locking layers retains any guides you have created (see the *Layers* chapter). To learn how to create custom guides from objects or paths, see the "Varied Perspective" lesson in the *Layers* chapter.

Smart Guides can be somewhat unnerving when you see them flash on and off as you work. However, with practice and understanding of each option, you'll be able to refine how to incorporate them into your work flow.

Illustrator also has automatic grids. To view grids, select View: Show Grid, or use the Context-sensitive menu. You can adjust the color, style of line (dots or solid), and size of the grid's subdivisions from File: Preferences: Guides & Grid.

As with guides, you can also enable a snap-to grid function. Toggle Snap To Grid on and off by choosing View: Snap To Grid (see Tip "Glorious grids" opposite). **IMPORTANT:** *If you adjust the x and y axes in File: Preferences: General: Constrain Angle, it will affect the drawn objects and transformations of your grid, as they will follow the adjusted angle when you create a new object. This works out well if you happen to be doing a complicated layout requiring alignment of objects at an angle.*

Understanding Smart Guides

There are a multitude of Smart Guide preferences. Here's what each one does:

- **Text Label Hints** provide information about an object when the cursor passes over it—helpful for identifying a specific object within complicated artwork.
- **Construction Guides** are the temporary guidelines that help you align between objects and anchor points.
- **Transform Tools** help with transformations.
- **Object Highlighting** enables the anchor point, center point, and path of a deselected object to appear as your cursor passes within a specified tolerance from the object. This can be very useful for aligning objects. For best alignment results, select an object's anchor point or center point.

Note: *Smart Guides will slow you down when working on very large files. Also, you can't align using Smart Guides if View: Snap To Grid is enabled.*

Edges and the bounding box

When you toggle to Hide Edges and have Show Bounding Box enabled (both in the View menu), the bounding box will remain visible while the anchor points and paths of objects will be hidden.

Tools: Ellipse, Polygon, Star, Spiral, Rectangle, Rotate, Scale, Shear, and Reflect.

File menu: New, Open, Close, Save, Save As, Save a Copy, Revert, Place, and Export.

Edit: Cut, Copy, Paste, Paste In Front, Paste In Back, Clear, Select All, Deselect All, and the Select pop-up menu items.

Object: Transform Again, Move, Scale, Rotate, Shear, Reflect, Transform Each, Arrange pop-up items, Group, Ungroup, Lock, Unlock All, Hide Selection, Show All, Expand, Rasterize, Blends, Mask, Compound Path, and Crop Marks.

Type: Character, Paragraph, MM Design, Tab Ruler, Block, Wrap, Fit Headline, Create Outlines, Find/Change, Find Font, Change Case, Rows & Columns, Type Orientation, and Glyph Options.

Filters: Colors, Create, Distort, and Stylize.

Guide-related views.

Window: Transform, Align, Pathfinder, Color, Gradient, Stroke, Swatches, Brushes, Styles, Layers, Attributes, and Actions.

Bounding Box transformations.

Selecting objects in an action

When recording an action, use the Attributes palette (Show Note) to name an object, and Select Object (Action pop-up) to type in the object's name (note) to select it.

Transparency Grid & Simulate Color Paper

Now that Illustrator can use transparency, you might want to change the background of the Artboard to the transparency grid, or better yet, to a color. Both the transparency grid and simulated color paper are non-printable attributes.

To view the transparency grid, select View: Show Transparency Grid. Change the grid colors in the Transparency panel of the Document Setup dialog. If you change both grid colors to the same color, you can change the white background to a color (see the *Transparency* chapter).

Hide/Show Edges

If looking at all those anchor points and colored paths distracts you from figuring out what to do with selected objects in your current window, choose View: Hide/Show Edges to toggle them on or off. Once you hide the edges, all subsequent path edges will be hidden until you show them again. Hide/Show Edges is saved with your file.

ACTIONS

Actions are a set of commands or a series of events that you can record and save as a set in the Action palette. Once a set is recorded, you can play back an action in the same order in which you recorded it, to automate a job you do repeatedly (a production task or special effect).

Select the action in the Action palette and activate it by clicking the Play icon at the bottom of the palette, by choosing Play from the pop-up menu, or by assigning the action to a keyboard F-key (function key) so you can play the action with a keystroke. You can select an action set, a single action, or a command within an action to play. To exclude a command from playing within an action, click the checkbox to the left of the command.

In order to play some types of actions, you may have to first select an object or text. Load action sets using the pop-up menu. (You can find sets of actions on the Adobe Illustrator Application CD in the Illustrator Extras folder, as well as in the *Wow! Actions* folder on the *Wow! CD*.)

Since you must record actions and save within an action set, begin a new action by clicking the Create New Set icon or by choosing New Set from the pop-up menu. Name the action set and click OK. With the new set selected, click the Create New Action icon, name the action, and click Record. Illustrator records your commands and steps until you click Stop. To resume recording, click on the last step, choose Begin, and continue adding to the action. When you've finished recording, you'll need to save the action file by selecting the action set and choosing Save Actions from the pop-up menu.

When you are recording, keep in mind that not all commands or tools are recordable. For example, the Pen tool itself is not recordable, but you can add the paths the Pen tool creates to an action by selecting a path and choosing Insert Selected Paths from the pop-up menu. For a more complete list of what is recordable, see Tip "Actions—what's recordable" opposite. Recording actions takes some practice, so don't get discouraged, always save a backup file, and refer to the *User Guide* for more details on Actions.

COLOR IN ILLUSTRATOR

Consumer-level monitors, which display color in red, green, and blue lights (RGB), cannot yet match four-color CMYK (cyan, magenta, yellow, black) inks printed onto paper. Therefore, you must retrofit the current technology with partial solutions, starting with calibrating your monitor.

Some programs (such as the Adobe Gamma utility installed with Photoshop) provide some degree of control over the way your monitor displays colors. ColorSync (Mac) and Kodak Digital Science Color Management (Windows) are the two main systems. The CMS (Color Management System) that ships with this version of Illustrator has been greatly improved. The colors displayed on the screen will be closer to the color you output if you follow a few key steps (see the *User Guide* for more information on using color management).

CMY Color Model   RGB Color Model

CMY (Cyan, Magenta, Yellow) **subtractive** *colors get darker when mixed; RGB (Red, Green, Blue)* **additive** *colors combine to make white*

Whiter whites/blacker blacks

If your whites or blacks seem to be taking on an undesirable color cast, look to your color management system as the possible source of the problem. (See the *User Guide* for more details on color management in this version of Illustrator.) Also, check your Proof Setup or preview modes.

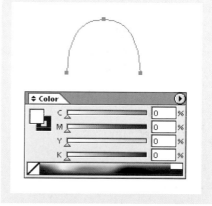

Converting RGB to CMYK

Although Illustrator can make conversions from RGB to CMYK (and vice versa), File: Document Color Mode: CMYK/RGB, such conversions may result in undesirable color shifts. Consult the *User Guide*, your service bureau, and/or printer for detailed directions based on your job specifications.

Continuous-tone, anti-aliased bitmapped images naturally form "traps" to hide misregistration of CMYK inks, but hard, crisp PostScript edges are a registration nightmare. Some products globally trap pages. If you know the exact size and resolution of your final image, you can rasterize Illustrator files (or specific objects) into raster images by using Object: Rasterize and Flatten Transparency or rasterize in Photoshop (see the *Illustrator & Other Programs* chapter).

If your image is not rasterized:

• Construct your images so overlapping shapes having common inks form natural traps (see the *Drawing & Coloring* chapter).

• Set individual colors to Overprint in the Attributes palette.

• Globally set blacks to Overprint (Filter: Colors: Overprint Black).

• See the *User Guide* for details on setting traps in *solid* objects using Pathfinder palette: Trap.

• For trapping patterns and gradients, (see Tip "Manual Trapping…" in the *Drawing* chapter).

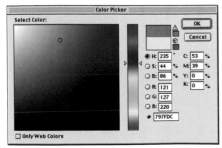

Adobe Color Picker

In addition to software calibration, methods of hardware calibration are available that actually adjust the beams of the cathode-ray tube emitting the RGB lights. Generally, the larger the monitor, the more likely the colors will vary in different areas of the screen. Monitor color is also affected by the length of time your monitor is on and the ambient light in your workroom.

In order to produce an accurate proof (if a printing press is your target), Illustrator needs to support printing profiles for both composite (your printer) and separation (the final printing device) ICC(M) printers. Illustrator now supports ICC(M) profiles for both types of printing, although it is still not possible to emulate the separation printer on the composite printer. It is, however, possible to use Illustrator for proofing directly on your screen and for printing a more accurate proof to your printer when you are not soft proofing to the screen. If you are creating art for placement into QuarkXPress or PageMaker, there is no application-level color management module currently supporting the EPS file format. Always consult with your prepress house and run a proof prior to printing an entire job.

Working in RGB or CMYK

Illustrator offers you the flexibility of working and printing in either RGB or CMYK color. This is a mixed blessing, because the printing environment cannot accurately capture vibrant RGB colors. As a result, the RGB colors are usually muddy or muted when printed. If your final artwork is going to be printed, work in CMYK!

Work in an RGB color space when creating artwork that will be displayed on-screen, or to simulate a spot color (such as a day-glo color) on your printer. (For more on working in RGB, see the *Web & Animation* chapter.)

Single color space

When you open a new document, you select a color model (or color space). Illustrator no longer allows you to work in multiple color spaces at the same time. If you work in print, always check your files to make certain they are in the appropriate color model before you output. The document's color model is always displayed next to the file name, on the title bar.

Opening legacy documents (documents created with older versions of Illustrator) with objects containing mixed color spaces will invoke a warning asking you to decide which color space (RGB or CMYK) the document should open in. Currently, linked images are not converted to the document's color space. If you open the Document Info palette and select Linked Images, the "Type" info is misleading. For example, if you have a CMYK document with a linked RGB image, the linked image type is Transparent CMYK. The linked image has not been converted, but the image preview has been converted to CMYK.

Enabling color management

The default color setting for Illustrator is "Emulate Adobe Illustrator 6.0," which is all color management *off*. To start color managing your documents, select Edit: Color Settings. Choose a setting from the pop-up menu, or customize your own setting. Depending on how you set up color management, you might get several warnings about colors, such as when you open documents or paste colors between documents. The *User Guide* offers detailed explanations about these warnings and what to do.

Color systems and libraries

Besides creating colors in RGB, HSB, or CMYK, you can also select colors from other color matching systems, such as the 216-color "web-safe" color palette or the color picker. You can access Focoltone, Diccolor, Toyo, Trumatch, and Pantone libraries or the web palette by choosing Window: Swatch Libraries, then selecting it from the menu. Keep in mind that color libraries open as separate uneditable palettes, but once you use a color swatch, it will automatically load into *your* Swatches palette, where you can then edit it. The default for the Swatches palette is to open with swatches—*not* view by name. Use the

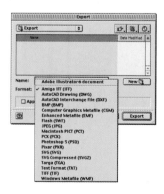

palette menu to change to List View if you prefer. Holding down Option/Alt while you choose a view will set
that view for each of the types of swatches.

To access styles, brushes, or swatches in other documents, choose Window: Style, Brush or Swatch Libraries:
Other Library. Then select the file that contains the item
you want. This opens a new palette with that document's
components. To store a component from an open library
in your current document, just use the style, brush, or
swatch—or drag the swatch from its library palette to the
document's palette.

IMAGE FORMATS

You might need to open a document created in an earlier
version of Illustrator (FreeHand, Canvas, CorelDraw, and
a number of 3D programs allow you to save images in
older Illustrator formats). To open any file saved in an
earlier version, drag it onto an Illustrator alias, or open
the older formatted file from within Illustrator by choosing
File: Open and selecting the document you want to open.
If it's a file you plan to work on or open again, use Save
As to save a copy in the current Illustrator format.

EPS (Encapsulated PostScript)

EPS is a universal format, which means that a wide
variety of programs support importing and exporting
EPS images for printing to PostScript printers. As in most
programs, when saving an image in EPS format you can
choose to include a Preview. This preview is an on-screen
PICT or TIFF representation of your image. When an EPS
image is placed into another program without a preview,
it will print properly, but it cannot be viewed. In order to
import an EPS image into Illustrator, choose File: Place
(see the *Layers* and *Illustrator & Other Programs* chapters
to learn more about EPS).

Other image formats

Illustrator supports many file formats (such as SWF, SVG,
GIF, JPEG, TIFF, PICT, PCX, Pixar, and Photoshop). You

can also open and edit PDF (Acrobat format) documents, and even "raw" PostScript files, directly from within Illustrator. If you place images into a document, you can choose whether these files will remain *linked* (see Tip "Links are manageable" in this chapter) or will become *embedded* image objects (see the *Other Programs* chapter for specifics on embedding, and the *Web & Animation* chapter for details on web-related formats). If you use File: Open, then images become embedded. (See the Adobe *User Guide* and *Read Me* files for lists of supported formats that shipped with this version.) Check Adobe's web site (www.adobe.com) for the latest information on supported formats, as well as other file format plug-ins. (For more on file format issues, see the *Other Programs* chapter.)

POSTSCRIPT PRINTING & EXPORTING

When you're ready to print your image (to a laser or inkjet printer, imagesetter, or film recorder), you should use a PostScript printing device. Adobe owns and licenses the PostScript language, making PostScript printers somewhat more expensive than non-PostScript printers. Some companies produce PostScript-compatible printers or provide PostScript emulation. Although Illustrator images often print just fine to these printers, sometimes you can run into problems. In general, the newer the PostScript device, the faster and less problematic your printing will be. PostScript Level 2 and Level 3 printers provide better printing clarity and even some special effects, such as Illustrator's integration of PostScript Level 3's "smooth shading" technology (which should greatly enhance gradients and reduce banding problems). Finally, the more memory you install in your printer, the quicker your text and images will print. For crucial jobs, develop good relations with your service bureau, and get into the habit of running test prints to identify possible problems. (Also see Tip "Proofing your prints," opposite.)

Correcting and avoiding printing problems

If you have trouble printing, first make sure your placed

Saving time and space

Note: *Before you attempt to minimize the size of your file, make certain that you're working on a copy.* To minimize the size of your file, first remove all your unused colors, patterns, and brushes. Open the Swatches palette, click the All Swatches icon, choose Select All Unused from the Swatches pop-up menu, then click the Trash icon to delete. (You may have to repeat the select and delete process to remove *all* the excess colors.) Next open the Brushes palette, choose Select All Unused from the Brushes pop-up menu. Then click the Trash icon. You should minimize the time it takes to print an Illustrator file, even if it's been placed into another program, such as QuarkXPress or PageMaker (see the *Other Programs* chapter for details on exporting). If you've scaled or rotated an Illustrator image once it's been placed into another program, note the numeric percentages of scaling and the degrees of rotation. Next, reopen the file in Illustrator, perform the identical scale or rotation, then place this pre-transformed version back into the other program. Make sure you reset scaling and rotation to zero. **Note:** *Be certain to scale line weight, objects, and pattern tiles when you perform these transformations in Illustrator.*

Hand tool while typing

First press ⌘/Ctrl + spacebar, then release the ⌘/Ctrl key to access the Hand tool, even while typing.

Cleanup

Select Object: Path: Cleanup and check the items you want to delete from your document. Choose Stray Points, Unpainted Objects, and/or Empty Text Paths. Click OK and all of those items are removed.

In a jam? There's help available

Adobe provides many ways to help you learn Illustrator and troubleshoot problems. Find help under the Help menu (Mac or Windows), along with instant access to Adobe Online. Adobe Online is also accessed by pressing the Venus icon on top of the Toolbox.

The proof is in the Preview

Want the best preview for your art on your screen? Choose View: Overprint Preview for the best way to proof color on your screen and to see how your art will look when printed.

images are linked properly and the fonts needed to print the document are loaded. Second, check for any complex objects in the document. Use Save a Copy (to retain the original file), remove the complex object(s), and try to print. If that doesn't work, make sure File: Document Setup and Separation Setup have the correct settings for your output device. (See the *Blends, Gradients & Mesh* chapter for issues regarding printing gradient mesh objects.) If you are using transparency, or effects that contain transparency, you might want to preview how your art will print using the Flattening Preview plug-in. This is an optional plug-in and can be found in your Illustrator 10 Utilities folder. For more information on the Flattening Preview plug-in, see the Adobe Illustrator 10 Flattening Guide that ships with Illustrator. Printing results will vary depending on these settings. (See the *Transparency & Appearances* chapter for printing and transparency issues.)

More about controlling the size of your files

The major factors that can increase your file size are the inclusion of image objects, path pattern, brushes and ink pen objects, complex patterns, a large number of blends and gradients (especially gradient mesh objects and gradient-to-gradient blends), linked bitmapped images, and transparency. Although linked bitmaps can be large, the same image embedded as an image object is significantly larger. If your Illustrator file contains linked images, and you need to save the entire file in EPS (for placement and printing in other programs), you have the option Include Linked Files. Most service bureaus highly recommend this option, as it will embed placed images in your Illustrator file and make printing from page layout programs and film recorders much more predictable (be sure to see Tip "Proofing your prints" earlier in this chapter). However, since including placed images will further increase the file size, wait until you've completed an image and are ready to place it into another program before you save a copy with placed images embedded.

Whether or not you choose to embed linked images, you must collect all of the files that have been linked into your Illustrator documents and transport them along with your Illustrator file. Illustrator makes your task easier if you choose File: Document Info: Linked Images, which outputs a text file of all images in your document. Press Save to create a text file that you can keep for future reference or give to your service bureau as a record of the images included in your files.

Scripting and Variables

Illustrator supports AppleScript (for Mac), Visual Basic scripting (for Windows), and JavaScript (for both platforms). If you're familiar with any of these scripting languages, you can use them to your advantage to save time in Illustrator. For more information on scripting in Illustrator, see the *Illustrator 10 Scripting Guide*, found on the Illustrator 10 CD.

Illustrator also supports XML variables. You can specify variables using the new Variables palette, found in the Window menu. With variables, you can hook up an Illustrator file to a database, using any of the scripting languages mentioned above, to automatically generate versions of artwork. For example, you can create a business card and then link that card to a database that contains a list of names. A script could then generate a separate card for each name in the database. For more information on this, see the *Illustrator 10 User Guide* on Data-Driven Graphics, and the *Illustrator 10 XML Grammar guide* on the Adobe Illustrator 10 CD.

Data-Driven Graphics

To learn more about the capabilities of data-driven graphics, take a look at the Travel Ads.ai sample file included in the Illustrator 10 Sample Art folder.

Shortcuts setting resolution

If you're saving a batch of documents, and want all to have the same resolution settings, set all settings in the first document and Save your file. Then copy and paste the next image into that document, and Save As with a new name. Repeat for the other images that require that setting. You can also create "stationery" documents for each resolution setting you require, and start new images with these preset resolution documents.

The Zen of Illustrator

2

The Zen of Illustrator

2

Zen: *"Seeking enlightenment through introspection and intuition rather than scripture."*[*] [*]

You're comfortable with the basic operations of your computer. You've read through "An Overview of Adobe Illustrator" in the *User Guide*. You've logged enough hours to Illustrator to be familiar with how each tool (theoretically) functions. You even understand how to make Bézier curves. Now what? How do you take all this knowledge and turn it into a mastery of the medium?

As with learning any new artistic medium (such as engraving, watercolor, or airbrush), learning to manipulate the tools is just the beginning. Thinking and seeing in that medium is what really makes those tools part of your creative arsenal. Before you can determine the best way to construct an image, you have to be able to envision at least some of the possibilities. The first key to mastering Illustrator is to understand that Illustrator's greatest strength comes not from its many tools and functions but from its extreme flexibility in terms of how you construct images. The first part of this chapter, therefore, introduces you to a variety of approaches and techniques for creating and transforming objects.

Once you've got yourself "thinking in Illustrator," you can begin to *visualize* how to achieve the final results. What is the simplest and most elegant way to construct an image? Which tools will you use? Then, once you've begun, allow yourself the flexibility to change course and try something else. Be willing to say to yourself: How else can I get the results that I want?

* Adapted from *Webster's New World Dictionary of the English Language*

The second key to mastering Illustrator (or any new medium) is perfecting your hand/eye coordination. In Illustrator, this translates into being proficient enough with the "power-keys" to gain instant access to tools and functions by using the keyboard. With both eyes on the monitor, one hand on the mouse, and the other hand on the keyboard, an experienced Illustrator user can create and manipulate objects in a fraction of the time required otherwise. The second part of this chapter helps you to learn the "finger dance" necessary to become a truly adept power-user.

The ability to harness the full power of Illustrator's basic tools and functions will ultimately make you a true master of Adobe Illustrator. Treat this chapter like meditation. Take it in small doses if necessary. Be mindful that the purpose of these exercises is to open up your mind to possibilities, not to force memorization. When you can conceptualize a number of different ways to create an image, then the hundreds of hints, tips, tricks, and techniques found elsewhere in this book can serve as a jumping-off point for further exploration. If you take the time to explore and absorb this chapter, you should begin to experience what I call the "Zen of Illustrator." This magical program, at first cryptic and counterintuitive, can help you achieve creative results not possible in any other medium.

Building Houses

Sequential Object Construction Exercises

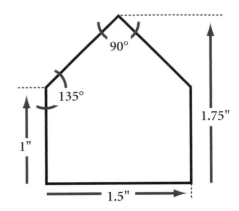

Overview: *Explore different approaches to constructing the same object with Illustrator's basic construction tools.*

1
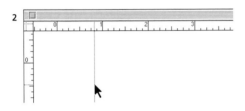

2
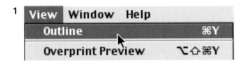

Dragging out a guide from the Ruler, and choosing Window: Info to open the Info palette if it's not open before you begin

3

4
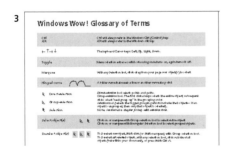

Hint: *Hold down the Shift key to constrain movement to horizontal/vertical direction. For more modifier key help, see the end of this chapter for the "Finger Dance" lesson.*

This sequence of exercises explores different ways to construct the same simple object, a house. The purpose of these exercises is to introduce you to the flexibility of Illustrator's object construction, so don't worry if some exercises seem less efficient than others. In Edit: Preferences: Units & Undo, set Units: General for Inches (so you can use the numbers provided and the measurements above). And read through the recommendations below for preparing your working environment.

1 Work in Outline mode. Doing so keeps you from being distracted by fills or line weights, and lets you see the centers of geometric objects (marked by "×").

2 Use Show Rulers and Show Info. Choose Show Rulers (View menu) so you can "pull out" guides. Use the Info palette to view numeric data as you work, or ignore the numeric data and just draw the houses by eye.

3 Read through the *Wow! Glossary*. Please make sure to read *How to use this book* and the *Glossary* pull-out card.

4 Use "modifier" keys. These exercises use Shift and Option (Opt) or Alt keys, which you must hold down until *after* you release your mouse button. If you make a mistake, choose Undo and try again. Some functions are also accessible from the Context-sensitive menu. Try keyboard shortcuts for frequently-used menu commands.

Exercise #1:

Use Add-anchor-point tool

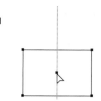

1

1 Create a rectangle and a vertical guide. Create a wide rectangle (1.5" x 1") and drag out a vertical guide that snaps to the center.

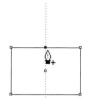

2

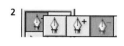

2 Add an anchor point on the top. Use the Add-anchor-point tool to add a point on the top segment over the center guide.

3

3 Drag the new point up. Use the Direct-selection tool to grab the new point and drag it up into position (.75" for a total height of 1.75").

Exercise #2:

Make an extra point

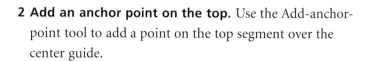

1

1 Create a rectangle, delete the top path and place a center point. Create a wide rectangle (1.5" x 1"). With the Direct-selection tool, select the top path segment and delete it. With the Pen tool, place a point on top of the rectangle center point.

2

2 Move the point up. Double-click on the Selection tool in the Toolbox to open the Move dialog box and enter a 1.25" vertical distance to move the point up.

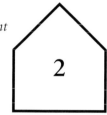

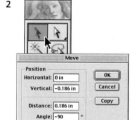

3 Select and join the point to each side. Use the Direct-selection tool to select the left two points and Join (Object: Path: Join) them to the top point. Repeat with the right two points.

3

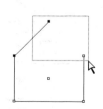

1

2

3

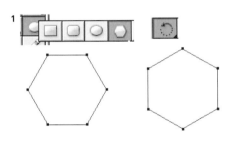

Exercise #3:
Rotate and Add

1 Create two rectangles, one centered on the other.
Create a wide rectangle (1.5" x 1") and drag out a vertical guide, snapping it to the center. Hold down Opt/Alt and click with the Rectangle tool (Opt/Alt-click) on the center guide (on the top segment). Enter 1.05" x 1.05".

2 Rotate one rectangle. Double-click the Rotate tool to rotate the new rectangle around its center and enter 45°.

3 Select and Add the rectangles. Marquee-select both objects, choose Widow: Pathfinder and click the Add icon. Switch to Preview mode to see the single shape!

Exercise #4:
Make a six-sided polygon

1 Create a six-sided polygon. With the Polygon tool selected, click once and enter 6 sides and a .866" Radius. Then double-click the Rotate tool and enter 30°.

2 Delete the bottom point. With the Delete-anchor-point tool, click on the bottom point to delete it.

3 Move the two bottom points down, then the two middle points. Use the Direct-selection tool to select the bottom two points. Then grab one of the points and Shift-drag in a vertical line (down .423"). Lastly, Direct-select, grab and Shift-drag the middle two points down vertically into position (down .275").

Exercise #5:

Use Add Anchor Points filter in a three-sided polygon

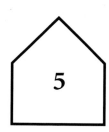

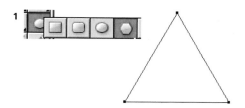

1 Create a three-sided polygon. With the Polygon tool selected, click once, then enter 3 sides and a 1.299" Radius.

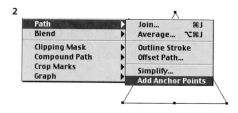

2 Use the Add Anchor Points filter. With the polygon still selected, choose Object: Path: Add Anchor Points (use the default keyboard shortcut, or create your own).

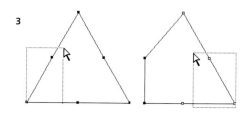

3 Average the two left points, then Average the two right points. Direct-select the two left points and Average them along the vertical axis (Context-sensitive: Average, or Object: Path: Average), then repeat for the two right points.

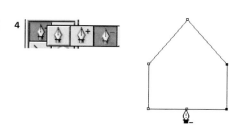

4 Delete the bottom point. With the Delete-anchor-point tool, click on the bottom point to delete it.

5 Move the top point down. Use the Direct-selection tool to select the top point, then double-click on the Direct-selection tool itself in the Toolbox to open the Move dialog box and enter a −.186" vertical distance.

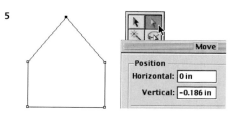

6 Slide in the sides towards the center. Use the Direct-selection tool to click on the right side of the house and drag it towards the center until the roofline looks smooth (hold down your Shift key to constrain the drag horizontally). Repeat for the left side of the house. Alternatively, select the right side and use the ← key on your keyboard to nudge the right side towards the center until the roofline looks smooth. Then, click on the left side to select it, and use the → key to nudge it towards the center. (If necessary, change your Cursor-key setting in Edit: Preferences: Keyboard Increments.)

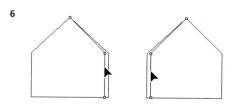

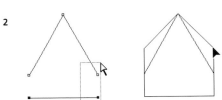

Exercise #6:
Cut a path and
Paste In Front

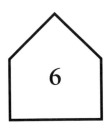

1 Cut, paste, then move the bottom of a triangle. With the Polygon tool selected, click once and enter 3 sides and a .866" Radius. With the Direct-selection tool, select and Cut the bottom path to the Clipboard, choose Edit: Paste In Front, then grab the bottom path and drag it into position (down .423").

2 Create the sides and move middle points into place. Direct-select the two right points and join them, then repeat for the two left points. Finally, select the two middle points, and grab one to drag *both* up (.275").

Exercise #7:
Join two objects

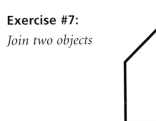

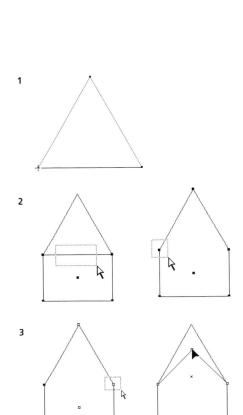

1 Make two objects. Click once with the Polygon tool, enter 3 sides and a .866" Radius. Zoom in on the lower left corner and, with the Rectangle tool, click exactly on the lower left anchor point. Set the rectangle to 1.5" x 1".

2 Delete the middle lines and join the corners. Direct-select marquee the middle bisecting lines and delete. Select the upper-left corner points and Average-Join by either Averaging and then Joining the points (see exercises #5 and #6 above) or by pressing ⌘-Shift-Option-J/ Ctrl-Shift-Alt-J to average and join simultaneously. Select and Average-Join the upper right points.

3 Drag the top point down. Grab the top point, hold the Shift key and drag it into position (down .55").

Exercise #8:

Use Add Anchor Points filter, then Average-Join

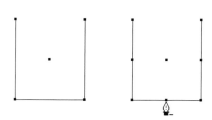

1 Make a tall rectangle, delete top path, add anchor points, remove bottom point. Create a tall rectangle (1.5" x 1.75") and delete the top path. Choose Add Anchor Points (Object: Path) and use the Delete-anchor-point tool to remove the bottom point.

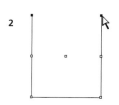

2 Select and Average-Join the top points and move middles into position. Direct-select the top two points and Average-Join (see Exercise #7, step 2). Then Direct-select the middle points, grab one, and with the Shift key, drag them both into position (up .125").

Exercise #9:

Reflect a Pen profile

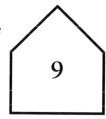

1 Create a house profile. Drag out a vertical guide, then reset the ruler origin on the guide. To draw the profile, use the Pen tool to click on the guide at the ruler zero point, hold down Shift (to constrain your lines to 45° angles) and click to place the corner (.75" down and .75" to the left) and the bottom (1" down).

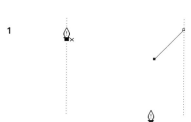

2 Reflect a copy of the profile. Select all three points of the house profile With the Reflect tool, Option/Alt-click-on the guide line. Enter an angle of 90° and click Copy.

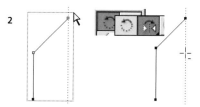

3 Join the two profiles. Direct-select and Join the bottom two points. Then Direct-select the top two points and Average-Join (see Exercise #7, step 2).

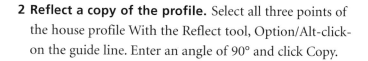

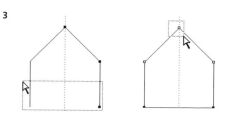

A Classic Icon

Five Ways to Re-create Simple Shapes

Overview: *Finding different ways to construct the same iconic image.*

McSHANE, ADIGARD/M.A.D.

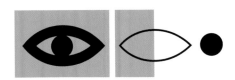

The Artwork view of the original logo

The original logo, constructed from a stroked line and a solid circle

You can construct even the simplest of iconic images in many ways. Patricia McShane and Erik Adigard of the M.A.D. graphics firm designed this classic logo for the *Computers Freedom & Privacy* annual conference. This conference addresses the effects of computer and tele-communications technologies on societal and personal freedom and privacy. This simple iconic representation of an eye is a perfect example of how you can explore different ways to solve the same graphics problem.

1 First, construct your logo in the way that seems most logical to you. Everybody's mind works differently, and the most obvious solutions to you might seem innovative to the next person. Follow your instincts as to how to construct each image. If design changes require you to rethink your approach (for instance, what if the client wanted a radial fill instead of the black fill?), try something slightly, or even completely, different.

Viewed in Outline mode, the original *Computers Freedom & Privacy* logo is clean and elegant with a minimum number of anchor points and lines. The M.A.D. team constructed the eye from a stroked line (made with the Pen tool) and a filled, black circle.

2 Make the outer eye shape. Create the solid black, almond-shaped object in any way you wish: Try drawing it with the Pen tool like M.A.D. did, or convert an oval into the correct shape by clicking on the middle points with the Convert-direction-point tool in the Pen tool pop-up.

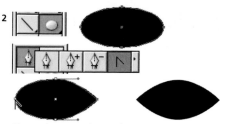

Converting an oval to make the back of the eye

3 Try using solid objects. Starting with your base object, construct the eye with overlapping solid objects. Scale a version of the outline for the green inset and place a black circle on the top.

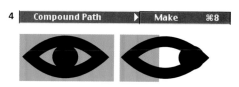

Constructing the logo with three solid objects

4 Try making a compound object. Use the objects that you created in the previous version to make a compound object that allows the inner part of the eye to be cut out. Select the outer black outline and the inner green inset and choose Object: Compound Paths: Make.

Constructing the logo from an outer compound object and an inner solid circle

5 Try using compound shapes. Compound shapes are powerful tools that let you create new shapes by combining and knocking out other shapes from them (see the *Drawing & Coloring* chapter for details). To create the back of the eye, start by creating an ellipse. With the ellipse still selected, hold down the Option-Shift (Mac)/Alt-Shift (Win) keys and drag downward until the center of the new ellipse is at the bottom of the original ellipse. Select both shapes and click on the Intersect button on the Pathfinder palette. To create the shape that will become the white of the eye, select the back of the eye, open the Object: Transform: Transform Each dialog and enter: 70 % H, 50% V, then click Copy. To use this shape to knockout the white of the eye, first put it behind the back of the eye by using Object: Arrange: Send To Back, then select both objects and click on the Exclude button on the Pathfinder palette. Next, create the circle for the pupil over the knocked out eye shape, select them both, and click on the Vertical Align Center and Horizontal Align Center buttons on the Align palette. To finish, click on the Add button on the Pathfinder palette.

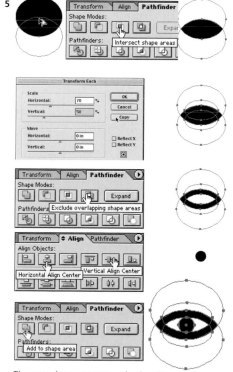

The same logo constructed using Copy, Compound Shape modes, and Transform Each

Zen Scaling ⬚▾

Note: *Use the Shift key to constrain proportions.* **Zen Scaling** *practice is also on the* **Wow!** *CD.*

1 Scaling proportionally towards the top Click at the top, grab lower-right (LR), drag up

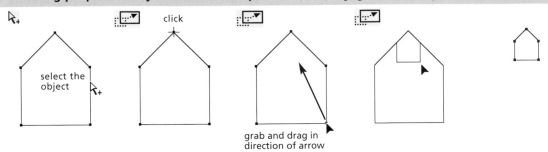

2 Scaling horizontally towards the center Click at the top, grab LR, drag inwards

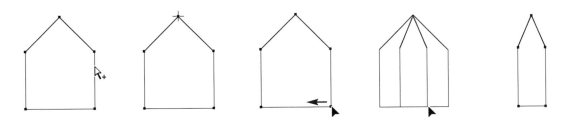

3 Scaling vertically towards the top Click at the top, grab LR, drag straight up

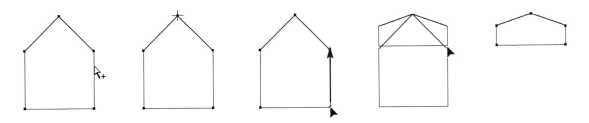

4 Scaling vertically and flipping the object Click at the top, grab LR, drag straight up

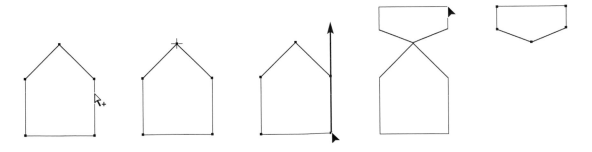

Zen Scaling *(continued)*

Note: *Use the Shift key to constrain proportions.* ***Zen Scaling*** *practice is also on the* ***Wow!*** *CD.*

5 Scaling proportionally towards lower-left (LL) Click LL, grab upper-right, drag to LL

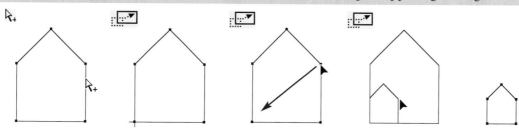

6 Scaling horizontally to the left side Click LL, grab lower-right (LR), drag to left

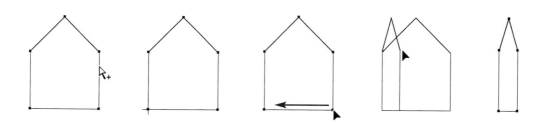

7 Scaling vertically towards the bottom Click center bottom, grab top, drag down

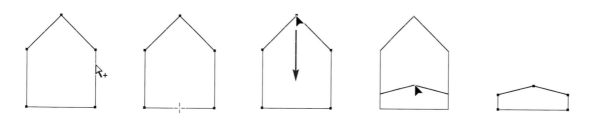

8 Scaling proportionally towards the center Click the center, grab corner, drag to center

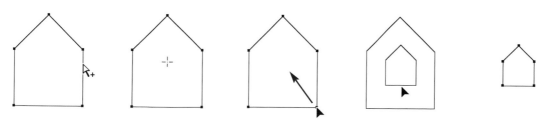

Or, to scale about the center, use the Scale tool to click-drag outside the object towards the center

Zen Rotation ⟳

Note: *Use the Shift key to constrain movement.* **Zen Rotation** *practice is also on the* **Wow!** *CD.*

1 Rotating around the center Click in the center, then grab lower-right (LR) and drag

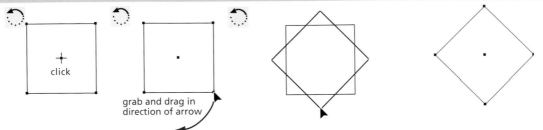

click

grab and drag in
direction of arrow

Or, to rotate about the center, use the Rotate tool to click-drag outside the object towards the center

2 Rotating from a corner Click in the upper left corner, then grab LR and drag

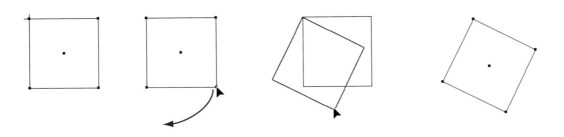

3 Rotating from outside Click above the left corner, then grab LR and drag

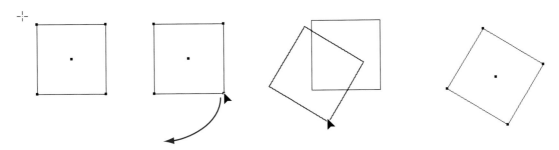

4 Rotating part of a path Marquee points with the Direct-selection tool, then use Rotate tool

Marquee the forearm with Direct-selection tool   *With the Rotate tool, click on the elbow, grab the hand and drag it around*

Creating a Simple Object Using the Basic Tools

Key: *Click where you see a RED cross, grab with the* GRAY *arrow and drag towards* BLACK *arrow.*

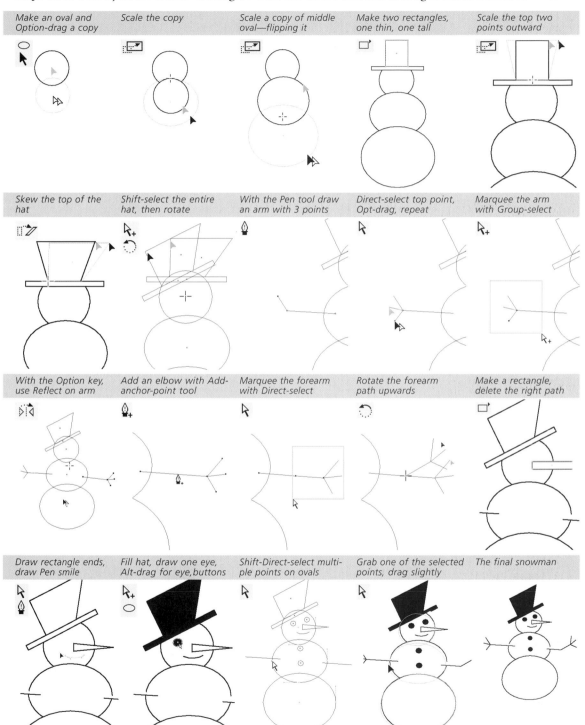

Make an oval and Option-drag a copy	Scale the copy	Scale a copy of middle oval—flipping it	Make two rectangles, one thin, one tall	Scale the top two points outward

| Skew the top of the hat | Shift-select the entire hat, then rotate | With the Pen tool draw an arm with 3 points | Direct-select top point, Opt-drag, repeat | Marquee the arm with Group-select |

| With the Option key, use Reflect on arm | Add an elbow with Add-anchor-point tool | Marquee the forearm with Direct-select | Rotate the forearm path upwards | Make a rectangle, delete the right path |

| Draw rectangle ends, draw Pen smile | Fill hat, draw one eye, Alt-drag for eye, buttons | Shift-Direct-select multiple points on ovals | Grab one of the selected points, drag slightly | The final snowman |

A Finger Dance
Turbo-charge with Illustrator's Power-keys

Overview: *Save hours of production time by mastering the finger dance of Illustrator's power-keys.*

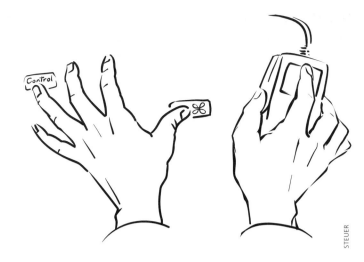

Find a summary of Finger Dance power-keys on the pull-out quick reference card

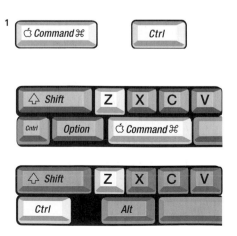

If you are using the mouse to choose your selection tools from the Toolbox, then you need this lesson. With some time and patience, you'll be able to free up your mouse so that practically the only thing you do with it is draw. Your other hand will learn to dance around the keyboard accessing all of your selection tools, modifying your creation and transformation tools, using your Zoom and Hand tools, and last but not least, providing instant Undo and Redo.

This "Finger Dance" is probably the most difficult aspect of Illustrator to master. Go through these lessons in order, but don't expect to get through them in one or even two sittings. When you make a mistake, use Undo (⌘/Ctrl-Z). Try a couple of exercises, then go back to your own work, incorporating what you've just learned. When you begin to get frustrated, take a break. Later— hours, days, or weeks later—try another lesson. And don't forget to breathe.

Rule #1: Always keep one finger on the ⌘ key (CTRL for Windows). Whether you are using a mouse or a pressure-sensitive tablet, the hand you are not drawing with should be resting on the keyboard, with one finger (or thumb) on the ⌘ key. This position will make that all-important Undo (⌘-Z/Ctrl-Z) instantly accessible.

Rule #2: Undo if you make a mistake. This is so crucial an aspect of working in the computer environment that I am willing to be redundant. If there is only one key combination that you memorize, make it Undo (⌘/Ctrl-Z).

Rule #3: The ⌘ (Ctrl) key turns your cursor into a selection tool. In Illustrator, the ⌘/Ctrl key does a lot more than merely provide you with easy access to Undo. The ⌘/Ctrl key will convert any tool into the selection arrow that you last used. In the exercises that follow, you'll soon discover that the most flexible selection arrow is the Direct-selection tool.

Rule #4: Watch your cursor. If you learn to watch your cursor, you'll be able to prevent most errors before they happen. And if you don't (for instance, if you drag a copy of an object by mistake), then use Undo and try again.

Rule #5: Pay careful attention to *when* you hold down each key. Most of the modifier keys operate differently depending on *when* you hold each key down. If you obey Rule #4 and watch your cursor, then you'll notice what the key you are holding does.

Rule #6: Hold down the key(s) until after you let go of your mouse button. In order for your modifier key to actually modify your action, you *must* keep your key down until *after* you let go of your mouse button.

Rule #7: Work in Outline mode. When you are constructing or manipulating objects, get into the habit of working in Outline mode. Of course, if you are designing the colors in your image, you'll need to work in Preview, but while you're learning how to use the power-keys, you'll generally find it much quicker and easier if you are in Outline mode.

Remove "Easy Access"! (Mac)
When you're using Illustrator, you must take the Apple program called *Easy Access* out of the Extensions folder (in the System folder). Although *Easy Access* was developed as an aid to mouse movements for people with limited manual mobility, it interferes with Illustrator's normal functioning. If you have limited manual dexterity, try using QuicKeys to simplify menu selection, keystrokes, and object creation.

Before you begin this sequence of exercises, choose the Direct-selection tool,
then select the Rectangle tool and drag to create a rectangle.

1 Finger Dance (⌘) Grabbing a selected object and moving it

2 Finger Dance (⌘) Deselecting an object, selecting a path and moving it

3 Finger Dance (⌘-Shift) Moving a selected object horizontally

4 Finger Dance (⌘-Shift) Deselecting an object, selecting a path and moving it horizontally

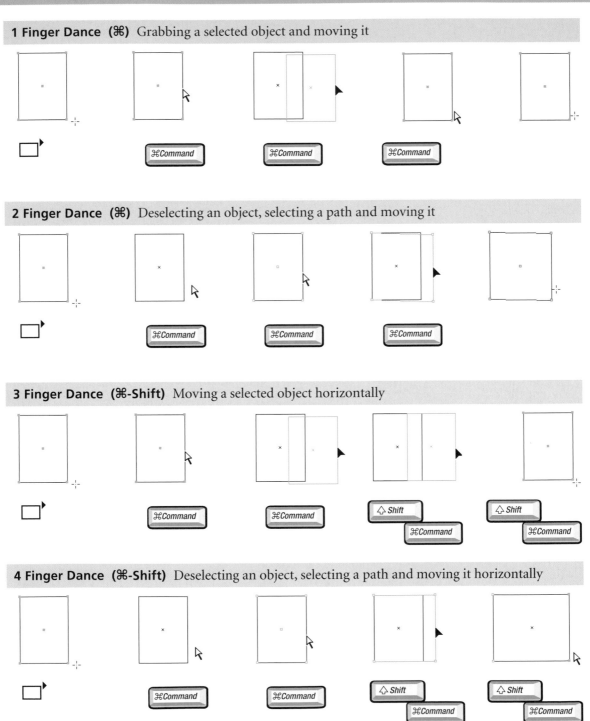

WINDOWS FINGERDANCES

Before you begin this sequence of exercises, choose the Direct-selection tool,
then select the Rectangle tool and drag to create a rectangle.

1 Finger Dance (Ctrl) Grabbing a selected object and moving it

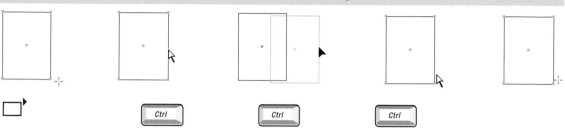

2 Finger Dance (Ctrl) Deselecting an object, selecting a path and moving it

3 Finger Dance (Ctrl-Shift) Moving a selected object horizontally

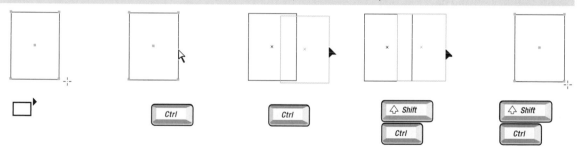

4 Finger Dance (Ctrl-Shift) Deselecting an object, selecting a path and moving it horizontally

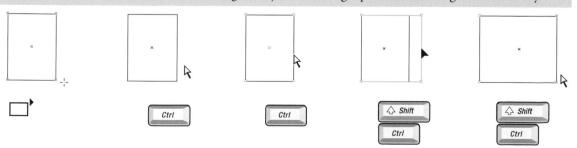

MACINTOSH FINGERDANCES

Before you begin this sequence of exercises, choose the Direct-selection tool,
then select the Rectangle tool and drag to create a rectangle.

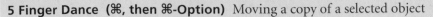

5 Finger Dance (⌘, then ⌘-Option) Moving a copy of a selected object

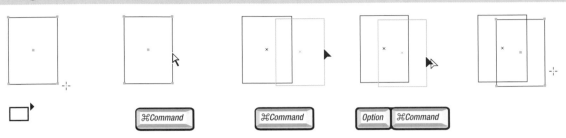

6 Finger Dance (⌘, then ⌘-Option) Deselecting an object, moving a copy of a path

7 Finger Dance (⌘, then ⌘-Shift-Option) Moving a copy of a selected object horizontally

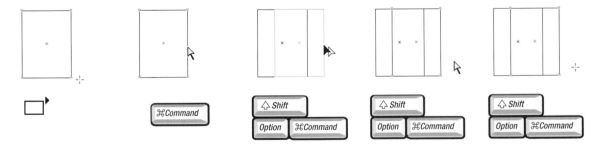

8 Finger Dance (⌘, then ⌘-Shift-Option) Deselecting, moving a copy of the path horizontally

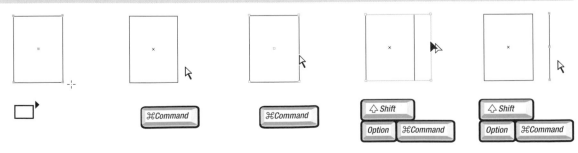

WINDOWS FINGERDANCES

Before you begin this sequence of exercises, choose the Direct-selection tool, then select the Rectangle tool and drag to create a rectangle.

5 Finger Dance (Ctrl, then Ctrl-Alt) Moving a copy of a selected object

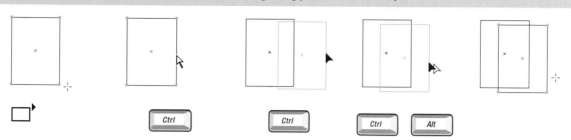

6 Finger Dance (Ctrl, then Ctrl-Alt) Deselecting an object, moving a copy of a path

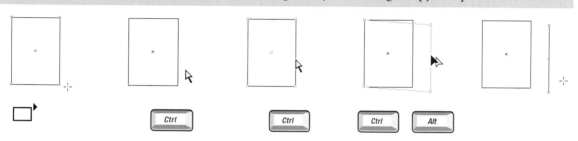

7 Finger Dance (Ctrl, then Ctrl-Shift-Alt) Moving a copy of a selected object horizontally

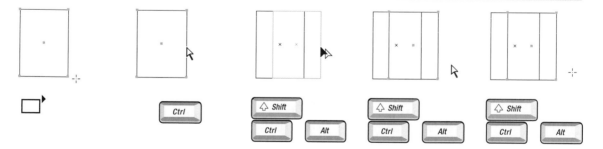

8 Finger Dance (Ctrl, then Ctrl-Shift-Alt) Deselecting, moving a copy of the path

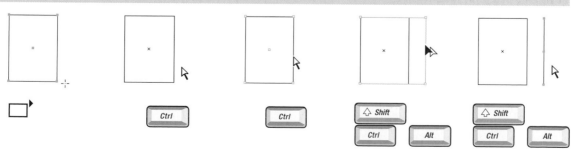

MACINTOSH FINGERDANCES

Before you begin this sequence of exercises, choose the Direct-selection tool,
then select the Rectangle tool and drag to create a rectangle.

9 Finger Dance (⌘-Option, then ⌘-Option) Deselecting, Group-selecting, moving a copy

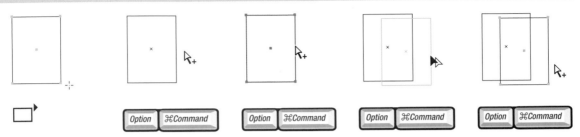

10 Finger Dance (⌘-Option, ⌘-Shift) Group-selecting, moving an object horizontally

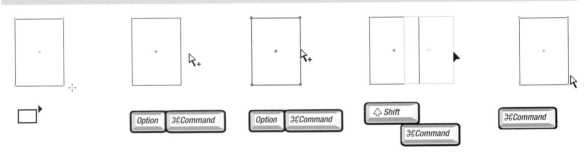

11 Finger Dance (⌘-Option, ⌘-Option-Shift) Moving copies horizontally, adding selections

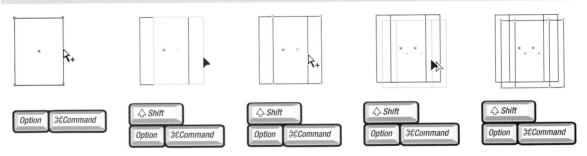

12 Finger Dance (⌘-Option, ⌘-Option-Shift, ⌘) Moving a copy, adding a selection, moving

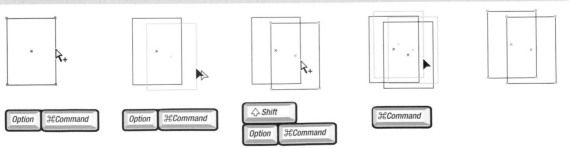

Before you begin this sequence of exercises, choose the Direct-selection tool,
then select the Rectangle tool and drag to create a rectangle.

9 Finger Dance (Ctrl-Alt, then Ctrl-Alt) Deselecting, Group-selecting, moving a copy

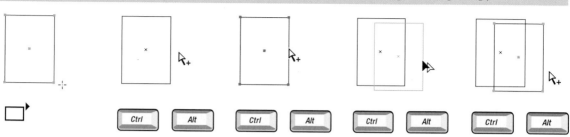

10 Finger Dance (Ctrl-Alt, Ctrl-Shift) Group-selecting, moving an object horizontally

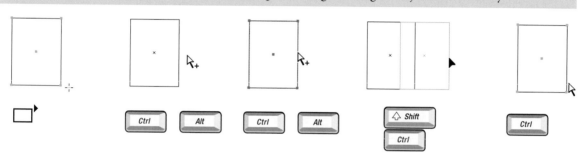

11 Finger Dance (Ctrl-Alt, Ctrl-Alt-Shift) Moving copies horizontally, adding selections

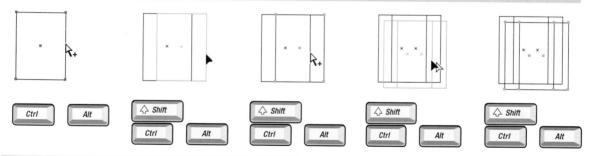

12 Finger Dance (Ctrl-Alt, Ctrl-Alt-Shift, Ctrl) Moving a copy, adding a selection, moving

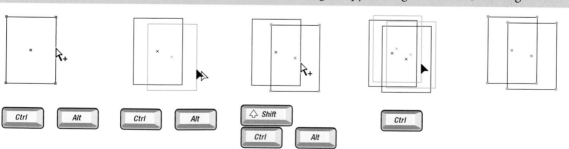

Chapter 2 *The Zen of Illustrator*   57

Drawing & Coloring

3

Drawing & Coloring

Illustrator allows you to fill open paths. When you fill an open path (left) the fill is applied as though the two endpoints were connected by a straight line (right)

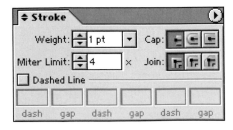

Left, same object as above with Stroke set to None; Right, same object with Fill set to None

Stroke palette

Drawing and coloring are the heart and soul of creating with Illustrator. This chapter continues the discussion of basic techniques that began in the first two chapters, rounding out the essential knowledge you'll need in order to work with Illustrator's drawing and coloring tools.

After reading this chapter, you'll be ready to move on to the more advanced techniques in the chapters that follow. Once you've mastered the techniques in this book, Illustrator offers unlimited possibilities for creating quick, simple, and elegant images.

The first part of this chapter, "Basic Drawing & Coloring," defines the basic tools and terms you'll need in order to understand the material in the rest of the book. You can refer to the "Expanding Your Drawing & Coloring Toolset" section that follows as a resource as you work in Illustrator.

BASIC DRAWING & COLORING

In this section you'll learn the fundamentals of strokes and fills, as well as the ins and outs of the Color palette and the Swatches palette. You'll also learn how to use those handy tools—the Eyedropper and Paint bucket—to pick up and deposit color (plus other functions).

Fill

Fill is what goes inside of a path (hence the name). The fill you choose might be a color, a gradient, or a pattern. You can even choose a fill of None, in which case there will be no fill. When you fill an open path (where the endpoints aren't connected), the fill is applied as though the two endpoints were connected by a straight line.

Stroke

The *stroke* refers to the basic "outline" of your path. While the fill gives you control over the space enclosed by a path, you can think of the stroke as the way you "dress up" the path itself to make it look the way you want. You do this by assigning various attributes to the stroke, including weight (how thick or thin it looks), whether the line is solid or dashed, the dash sequence (if the line is dashed), and the styles of line joins and line caps. You can also assign your path a stroke of None, in which case it won't have a visible stroke at all. (Dashed lines, joins, and caps are covered in the following section, "Expanding Your Drawing & Coloring Toolset.")

The many ways to fill or stroke an object

To set the fill or stroke for an object, first select the object and then click on the Fill or Stroke icon near the bottom of the Toolbox. (You can toggle between fill and stroke by pressing the "X" key.) If you want to set the object's stroke or fill to None, use the "/" key, or click the None button on the Toolbox or the Color palette (the little white box with a red slash through it).

You can set the fill or stroke color you want using any of the following methods: 1) adjusting the sliders or sampling a color from the color bar in the Color palette; 2) clicking on a swatch in the Swatches palette; 3) using the Eyedropper tool to sample color from other objects in your file; or 4) sampling colors from the Color Picker. (To open the Adobe Color Picker, double-click the Fill or Stroke icon in the Toolbox or the Color palette.) In addition, you can drag color swatches from palettes to selected objects, or to the Fill/Stroke icon in the Toolbox.

Color palette

The Color palette is a collection of tools that allows you to mix and choose the colors for your artwork. In addition to the sliders and edit fields for locating precise colors, this palette includes a None button so you can set your Fill or Stroke to no color at all. The Color palette also sometimes displays a Last Color proxy; this allows you to easily return to the last color you used before choosing a pattern, a gradient, or setting None.

Swapping fill and stroke

When you press the "X" key by itself, it toggles the Stroke or Fill box to active (in front of the other) on the Tools and Color palettes. If you press Shift-X it swaps the actual *attributes* or contents of the Stroke and Fill boxes. For example, if you start with a white fill and a black stroke, after you press Shift-X you will have a black fill and a white stroke. **Note:** *Because gradients are not allowed on strokes, Shift-X will not work when the current fill is a gradient.*

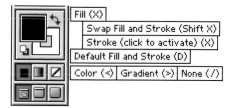

Fill and Stroke section of the Tools palette

The Adobe Color Picker

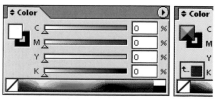

The Color palette. The sliders show the settings of the Fill or Stroke color—whichever is in front. Shown at right is the Last Color proxy (outlined in red); when it appears you can click it to return to the last color used before choosing a pattern or gradient, or setting a style of None

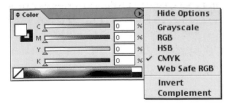

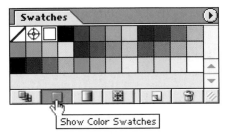

Color palette and pop-up menu

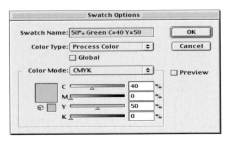

Swatches palette showing only the color swatches

Swatch Options dialog box

When deleting swatches

When you click the Trash icon in the Swatches palette to delete selected swatches, Illustrator does *not* warn you that you might be deleting colors used in the document. Instead Illustrator will convert global colors and spot colors used to fill objects to non-global process colors. To be safe, choose Select All Unused and then click the Trash.

Note: *You are also not warned when you are deleting styles that might be used in the document.*

The Color palette's menu options include Invert and Complement. Invert converts a color to its negative color (as in photographic negative). Complement locates the Adobe color complement of a selected color (the complements don't seem to match art school color wheels).

If you're doing print work in CMYK mode, you'll know you've chosen a non-CMYK color if an exclamation point appears on the Color palette. Illustrator will automatically correct your color to the nearest CMYK equivalent. Click the exclamation point to move the sliders—this will show you the corrected color settings.

If you're creating artwork for the web, you can choose web-safe RGB from the Palette menu, which displays the hexadecimal values for colors in the Color palette. If a non-Web-safe color is selected, an out-of-gamut web color icon displays (it looks like a 3D cube). If you want to stay aware of the CMYK gamut while working in RGB mode, watch for the exclamation point mentioned in the preceding paragraph. It displays when you choose a non-CMYK color, and you can click it to correct the color.

Swatches palette

To save colors you've mixed in the Color palette, drag them to the Swatches palette from the Color palette, the Toolbox, or the Gradient palette. Whenever you copy and paste objects that contain custom swatches or styles from one document to another, Illustrator will automatically paste those elements into the new document's palettes.

The Swatch Options dialog box (which you can open by double-clicking any swatch) lets you change the individual attributes of a swatch—including its name, color mode, color definition, and whether it's a process or spot color. (For pattern and gradient swatches, the only attribute in the Swatch Options dialog is the name.) There's also a checkbox that lets you decide whether changes you make to the swatch will be Global (in which case they'll be applied to all objects using the swatch color throughout the document) or not. The Global checkbox is off by default.

Saving custom swatch libraries

Once you have set up your Swatches palette to your satisfaction, you can save it as a custom swatch library for use with other documents. This can help you avoid having to duplicate your efforts later on.

Here's how to do it: First, name and save your document. Then put the document in the Adobe Illustrator 10: Presets: Swatches folder. The next time you launch Illustrator, the name you gave your file will appear in the Window: Swatch Libraries menu.

This is the most efficient method in most cases, but there are other ways to make your custom Swatches palette accessible to other documents. If you want, you can choose to save the custom Swatches palette into your startup file, in which case it will always be accessible via the Swatches palette in each of your documents. Or, you can simply save your file wherever you'd like, and use the Window: Swatch Libraries: Other Library menu command to open your custom Swatches palette.

Of course, you can always open the original document when you need to access its Swatches palette—but saving it as a custom swatch library, as described above, will save you the trouble.

The Eyedropper and Paint bucket tools

Two extremely useful Illustrator tools are the Eyedropper (which *picks up* stroke, fill, color, and text attributes) and the Paint bucket (which *deposits* stroke, fill, color, and text attributes). These tools allow you to easily borrow color (and styling) from one object and add it to another.

To set the default color for your next object, use the Eyedropper tool to click on an object that contains a color you want to sample. The Eyedropper will pick up the color of the object you clicked on. Then you can apply that color to another object just by clicking on it with the Paint bucket tool.

With one tool selected, you can access the other by holding down the Option key (Mac) or Alt key (Win). In addition to sampling color from objects, the Eyedropper

Eyedropper, Paint bucket, and Measure tools

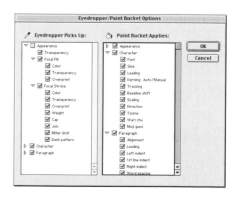

Using the Eyedropper and Paint bucket options, you have complete control over what is picked up and/or deposited. In addition to Stroke, Fill, color, and text formatting, the Eyedropper and Paint bucket tools can also be used to copy styles and type attributes (which are discussed later in the book). See the Adobe User Guide for more about using the Eyedropper and Paint bucket to copy those attributes

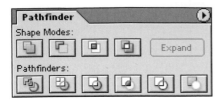

Pathfinder palette

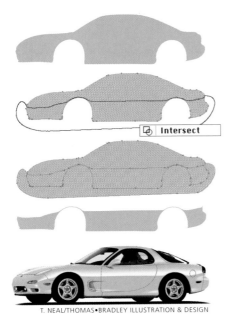

Using the Intersect Pathfinder to cut out the lower part of the car body. Bottom, the finished illustration

T. NEAL/THOMAS•BRADLEY ILLUSTRATION & DESIGN

Tim Girvin used the Divide Pathfinder to create the logo for the film The Matrix. See his Gallery in the Type chapter

Right to left: two ovals (the inner oval has no fill, but appears black because of the black fill of the larger oval behind it); as part of a compound path the inner oval knocks a hole into the outer one where they overlap; the same compound path with inner oval, which was direct selected and moved to the right to show that the hole is only where the objects overlap

can sample colors from a raster image if you hold down the Shift key.

The Pathfinders

It is often easier to create an object by combining two or more relatively simple shapes than it would be to draw the more complex result directly. The Pathfinder operations enable you to easily combine objects to get the result you want. For examples of the Pathfinders in action, take a look at the Pathfinder palette chart on the following pages.

There are two effective ways to combine objects using the Pathfinders: 1) compound shapes, which remain "live" and editable; and 2) Pathfinder commands, which become "destructive" (permanent), and can't be returned to their original editable state except by using Undo.

See the "Add & Expand" lesson for a look at compound shapes in action. The "Divide & Color" and "Cutting & Joining" lessons illustrate some uses of Pathfinder commands.

EXPANDING YOUR DRAWING & COLORING TOOLSET

This section provides more detail about compound shapes and related concepts, and explores some of the technical details involved with creating simple objects in Illustrator. If you're new to Illustrator you'll probably want to experiment a bit with the lessons and Galleries later in this chapter to solidify what you've learned before continuing with this section. Consider "Expanding Your Drawing & Coloring Toolset" a reference section that is available when you're ready to delve deeper into the details of object creation in Illustrator. Topics covered include the Simplify command, color modification filters, and Illustrator's new "Liquify" Distortion tools.

Compound paths

A compound path consists of one or more simple paths that have been combined so that they behave as a single unit. One very useful aspect of compound paths is that a hole can be created where the original objects overlapped. These holes are empty areas cut out from others (think of the center of a donut, or the letter **O**), through which objects below can be seen.

To create a compound path, e.g., the letter **O**, draw an oval, then draw a smaller oval that will form the center hole of the **O**. Select the two paths, and then choose Object: Compound Path: Make. Select the completed letter and apply the fill color of your choice, and the hole will be left empty. To adjust one of the paths within a compound path, use the Direct-selection tool. To adjust the compound path as a unit, use the Group-selection or Selection tool.

In addition to creating holes, you can use compound paths to force multiple objects to behave as if they were a single unit. An advanced application of this is to make separate objects behave as one unit to mask others. For an example of this using separate "outlined" type elements, see Gary Newman's "Careers" Gallery in the *Type* chapter.

Holes and fills with compound paths

For simple holes, the Compound Path: Make command will generally give the result you need. If your compound path has multiple overlapping shapes, or you're not getting the desired holes in the spaces, see "Fill Rules.pdf" on the *Wow! CD*. Or try using compound shapes (described in the next section), which give you complete control. Certain results can be obtained only by using compound shapes.

Compound shapes

As mentioned earlier, sometimes it's easier to create an object by combining simpler objects, rather than trying to draw the complex result directly. A *compound shape* is a live combination of shapes using the Add, Subtract, Intersect, and/or Exclude Pathfinder operations. See the first four rows of the Pathfinder Commands chart (on the following pages) for a look at the various command functions, as well as examples of how they can be used.

Starting objects: the word Sub is a compound shape ("Subtract" is subtracted from "Sub")

The starting objects from above, after Make Compound Shape and the corresponding shape modes have been applied, i.e., "intr" has the Intersect shape mode applied

In a compound shape all the original objects remain editable. Here the word "excl" was expanded to "Exclude," then a gradient and drop shadow were applied to the compound shape as a whole

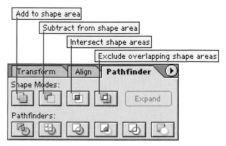

Shape Modes

The default settings for were used unless otherwise noted. Artists' work may use custom settings.

Add
(Unite)

Before and after Unite

MARQUARDT

Subtract
(Minus Front)

Before Minus Front

After Minus Front

Object rendered using Adobe Dimensions

ELBERG

Intersect

Two objects, then overlapping and selected, then after choosing Intersect

Copies of intersection

SHIELDS DESIGN

Exclude

Two objects

Both objects selected

WHYTE

Minus Back

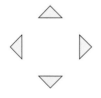

Green objects selected and made compound paths

After Minus Back, objects can then be filled separately

WHYTE

Divide

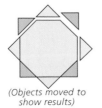

(Objects moved to show results)

Four objects

Objects divided

GROSSMAN

Each newly divided object filled

The default settings for were used unless otherwise noted. Artists' work may use custom settings.

Outline

STEUER

(Objects moved and line weights increased to .5 pt to show results)

Before Outline

After Outline, and resetting line weight

Trim

SHIELDS DESIGN

(Objects moved to show results)

Before Trim; in Preview and Artwork

After Trim; overlaps are reduced, BUT strokes are lost

Merge

STAHL

(Objects moved to show results)

Before Merge in Artwork

After Merge; like fills are united, BUT strokes are lost

Crop

DROBLAS GREENBERG

A copy of the fish in front to use for Crop

After Crop; objects are now separated

Hard Mix

MARGOLIS PINEO (digitized by Steuer)

Note: The Hard Mix filter is available in the Pathfinder Filters action set on the Wow! CD

Same color objects don't mix, so overlapping objects were colored differently

After Hard filter. Each overlap is now a separate object

After using the Eyedropper to switch the colors in the front objects

Soft Mix

FERSTER

Note: The Soft Mix filter is available in the Pathfinder Filters action set on the Wow! CD

Before Soft filter; the blue waves overlap and obscure the detail along the bottom of the rocks

After Soft filter: see "SandeeCs Soft Mix Chart.ai" in SandeeCs Wow! Actions folder on the Wow! CD

Compound shapes can be made from two or more paths, other compound shapes, text, envelopes, blends, groups, or any artwork that has vector effects applied to it. To create a compound shape, choose Window: Pathfinder to display the Pathfinder palette. Then select your objects, and choose Make Compound Shape from the Pathfinder palette menu. To assign a particular Shape Mode, select one of the components of your compound shape and click on the corresponding Shape mode button on the top row of the Pathfinder palette.

Note: *Simply selecting your objects and pressing one of the Shape Mode buttons creates a compound shape and applies the shape mode you've chosen to the objects.*

The pros and cons of compound shapes and paths

Compound paths can be made only from simple objects. In order to make a compound path from more complex objects (such as live type or "envelopes") you have to first convert them into simpler objects (see the *Type* or *Live Effects* chapters for details on how to do this), and you'll only be able to edit them as paths. You can, however, combine complex objects using *compound shapes* and have them remain editable.

As you know by now, compound shapes allow you to combine objects in a variety of ways using Add, Subtract, Intersect, and Exclude. While keeping these Shape modes live, you can also continue to apply (or remove) Shape modes, or a wide variety of effects, to the compound shape as a unit. In later chapters, as you work with live effects such as envelopes, warps, and drop shadows, remember that you can integrate effects into your compound shapes while remaining able to edit your objects— even if your objects are editable type!

The power of compound shapes does come at a cost. Compound shapes require Illustrator to perform many calculations on your behalf, so as a result, too many compound shapes, or too many operations or effects applied to compound shapes, can slow down the screen redraw of your image. Although compound paths are much less powerful or flexible, they won't slow down your redraw. So if you're working with simple objects, it's best to use compound paths instead.

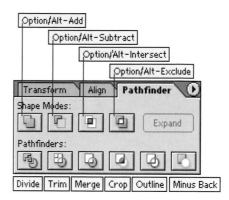

The Pathfinder Commands

Pathfinder commands

The Pathfinder commands consist of Option/Alt-Add, Option/Alt-Subtract, Option/Alt-Intersect, Option/Alt-Exclude, Divide, Trim, Merge, Crop, Outline, and Minus Back, all of which you can use to combine or separate shapes. See the preceding Pathfinder chart for a guide to what the various commands do and for examples of how they can be used.

Unlike objects you create using compound shapes, the results you get when you apply the Pathfinder commands are destructive (alter your artwork permanently). When working with complicated objects, it's best to use compound shapes instead of Pathfinders (see Tip "Compound paths or shapes?" on facing page, and "The Pros and Cons of Compound Shapes and Paths" above.)

The Divide, Trim, Merge, Crop, and Outline Pathfinder commands are used to separate (not combine) shapes—think of them as an advanced form of cookie cutters. The Trim and Merge commands require that your objects be filled before you use them.

The Filter: Colors: Adjust Colors filter

Hard Mix and Soft Mix

You may notice that Hard Mix and Soft Mix are shown on the chart but no longer included on the Pathfinder palette. To restore these Pathfinders, install the *Wow! Actions* "Pathfinder Filters.aia" from the *Wow! CD* (in "SandeeCs Wow! Actions," in the "Wow! Actions" folder), or apply them from Effect: Pathfinder, then choose Object: Expand Appearance (for more on Effects see "Hard and Soft Mix" in the *Live Effects & Styles* chapter).

Color modification filters

Located in the Filter: Colors menu, the Adjust Colors filter lets you adjust the tint of Global colors in selections. Illustrator no longer allows multiple color spaces in a

Expand Compound Shapes?

When would you want to expand a compound shape?

- If a compound shape is so complex that interacting with it is noticeably slow, then expand it.
- Anything that relies on bounding boxes will behave differently on the expanded shape if that shape has a smaller bounding box than the editable compound shape. This affects all the Align commands and certain transformations.
- Finally, you must expand a compound shape before using it as an envelope. For more about envelopes, see the *Live Effects & Styles* chapter.

—*Pierre Louveaux*

The Stroke palette

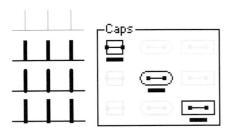

The same lines shown first in Outline, then in Preview with Butt cap, Round cap and Projecting cap

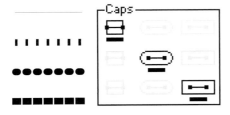

A 5-pt dashed line with a 2-pt dash and 6-pt gap shown first in Outline, then Preview with a Butt cap, Round cap, and Projecting cap

A path shown first in Outline, then in Preview with a Miter join, Round join, and Bevel join

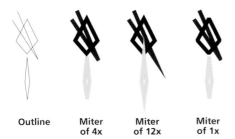

| Outline | Miter of 4x | Miter of 12x | Miter of 1x |

Objects with 6-pt strokes and various Miter limits, demonstrating that the angles of lines affects Miter limits

single document, so some color spaces will be unavailable. The Saturate filter (which integrates Saturate, Saturate More, Desaturate, and Desaturate More filters) lets you adjust the saturation of objects and images either by using sliders or by entering numerical values.

End of Lines

An aspect of Illustrator that often mystifies newcomers is the way endpoints of stroked lines are drawn. You may discover that although a set of lines seem to match up perfectly when viewed in Outline mode, they may visibly overlap when previewed. Solve this problem by changing the end caps in the Stroke palette.

Select one of the three end cap styles described below to determine how the endpoints of your selected paths will look when previewed.

The first (and default) choice is called a Butt cap; it causes your path to stop at the end anchor point. Butt caps are essential for creating exact placement of one path against another. The middle choice is the Round cap, which rounds the endpoint in a more natural manner. Round caps are especially good for softening the effect of single lines or curves, making them appear slightly less harsh. The final type is the Projecting cap, which extends lines and dashes at half the stroke weight beyond the end anchor point.

In addition to determining the appearance of path endpoints, cap styles affect the shape of dashed lines (see illustration at left).

Corner Shapes

The shape of a stroked line at its corner points is determined by the Join style in the Stroke palette. Each of the three styles determines the shape of the outside of the corner; the inside of the corner is always angled.

The default Miter join creates a pointy corner. The length of the point is determined by the width of the stroke, the angle of the corner (narrow angles create longer points, see sidebar) and the Miter limit setting on the Stroke palette. Miter limits can range from 1x (which is always blunt) to 500x. Generally the default Miter join with a miter limit of 4x looks just fine.

The Round join creates a rounded outside corner for which the radius is half the stroke width. Illustrator's Round join option looks like Photoshop's Stroke layer effect. See the *Illustrator & Other Programs* chapter for more about Illustrator and Photoshop.

The Bevel join creates a squared-off outside corner, equivalent to a Miter join with the miter limit set to 1x.

Patterns

The *Adobe Illustrator User Guide* has a very informative section on "Creating and Working with Patterns" (pages 227-231 of the *User Guide*). For an example of working with patterns, see the lesson "Intricate Patterns: Designing Complex Repeating Patterns" later in this chapter.

Distortion tools and filters

You can use Illustrator's Free Transform tool to distort the size and shape of an object by dragging the corner points of the object's bounding box. The shape of the object distorts progressively as you drag the handles.

One of the most exciting additions to Illustrator 10 is the new suite of "Liquify" Distortion tools that allow you to distort objects manually, by dragging the mouse over them. The Warp, Twist, Pucker, Bloat, Scallop, Crystallize, and Wrinkle tools work not only on vector objects, but on embedded raster images as well. Use the Option key (Alt on Windows) to resize the Liquify brush as you drag. These tools are a step beyond the Distort filters Illustrator already had—they're more interactive, more intuitive, and more fun to use.

But you needn't worry that the Distort filters are gone—they can still be found in Illustrator 10 (under the Filter and Effect menus), and they do have their uses. For instance, the ability to control distortion numerically via the filters' dialog boxes can allow for greater precision. They can also be used to create in-betweens for anima-

Creating patterns

To create a pattern from a design you've created, drag the objects to the Swatches palette!

The Free Transform tool

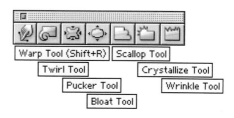

Liquify Distortion tool tear-off palette, see "Tear-off palettes" in the Illustrator Basics *chapter*

The Distort Filter menu

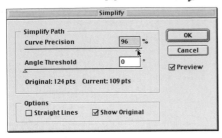

The Object: Path: Simplify dialog can be used to reduce the number of points and to stylize type

More Simplify Commands

- Use Object: Path: Clean Up to remove stray points, unpainted objects, or empty text paths.
- If you want to see the stray points before deleting them, use Select: Object: Stray Points to select them, then press the Delete key to remove them.

Need more points?

Use the Add Anchor Point tool to add points at specific locations along your path. Or use the Object: Path: Add Anchor Points command to neatly place one point between each existing pair of points on your path.

tions in cases where blends might not give the desired results or might be too cumbersome.

The Distort filters include Free Distort, Pucker & Bloat (note that Pucker was called Punk in Illustrator 9), Roughen, Scribble & Tweak, Twist, and Zig Zag. All of these filters distort paths based on the paths' anchor points. They move (and possibly add) anchor points to create distortions. Preview lets you see and modify the results as you experiment with the settings.

Many of the Free Distort functions can also be performed with the Free Transform tool (for a lesson using the Free Transform tool, see the "Distort Dynamics" lesson later in this chapter).

Path Simplify command

More is not better when it comes to the number of anchor points you use to define a path. The more anchor points, the more complicated the path—which makes the file size larger and harder to process when printing. The Simplify command (Object: Path: Simplify) removes excess anchor points from one or more selected paths without making major changes to the path's original shape. You might want to apply this command after using the Auto Trace tool, opening a clip art file, or using Adobe Streamline.

Two sliders control the amount and type of simplification. Enable Show Original and turn on the Preview option to preview the effect of the sliders as you adjust them. The Preview option also displays the original number of points in the curve and the number that will be left if the current settings are applied. Adjust the Curve Precision slider to determine how accurately the new path should match the original path. The higher the percentage, the more anchor points will remain, and the closer the new path will be to the original. The endpoints of an open path are never altered. The Angle Threshold determines when corner points should become smooth. The higher the threshold, the more likely a corner point will remain sharp.

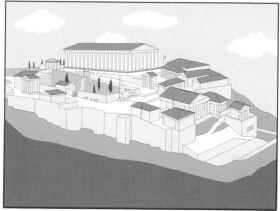
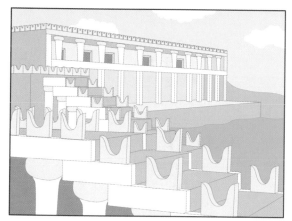
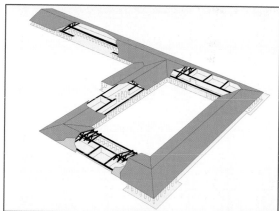
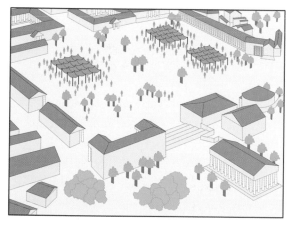
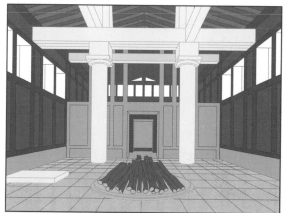

Gary Ferster

Using only simple filled and stroked objects, Gary Ferster was able to create this series of illustrations on Roman life for a children's educational CD-ROM titled "Ancient 2000." For help making perspective guidelines, see "Varied Perspective" in the *Layers* chapter.

Simple Realism

Realism from Geometry and Observation

Overview: *Draw a mechanical object using the Rectangle, Rounded Rectangle, and Ellipse tools; use tints to fill all of the paths; add selected highlights and offset shadows to simulate depth.*

1

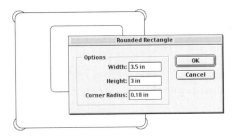

The default Fill and Stroke in the Tools palette; setting the default stroke weight for objects

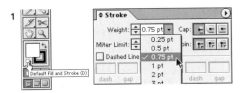

Creating rounded rectangles and ellipses to construct the basic forms

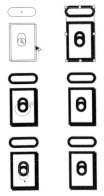

Option-Shift/Alt-Shift dragging a selection to duplicate and constrain it to align with the original; using the Direct-select Lasso tool to select specific points; Shift-dragging to constrain and move the selected points

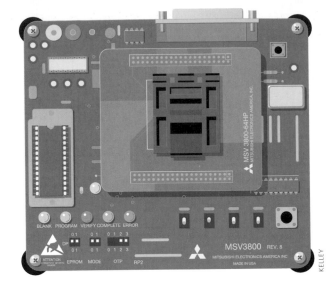

Many people believe the only way to achieve realism in Illustrator is with elaborate gradients and blends, but this illustration by Andrea Kelley proves that artistic observation is the real secret. Using observation and some simple Illustrator techniques, Kelley drew technical product illustrations of computer chip boards for a handbook for her client, Mitsubishi.

1 Recreating a mechanical object with repeating geometric shapes by altering copies of objects. Most artists find that close observation, not complex perspective, is the most crucial aspect to rendering illustrations. To sharpen your skills in observing the forms and details of objects, select a simple mechanical device to render in grayscale. First, create a new Illustrator document. Then experiment with the Ellipse, Rectangle, and Rounded Rectangle tools to draw the basic elements of the device. After you've made your first object—with the object still selected—click on the Default Fill and Stroke icon in the Tool palette, open the Stroke palette (Window: Stroke), and choose a stroke weight of 0.75 pt using the Weight pop-up menu. All objects you make from that point on will have the same fill and stroke as your first object.

Because mechanical and computer devices often have similar components, you can save time by copying an object you've drawn and then modifying the shape of the copy. You can easily align your copy with the original by holding the Option/Alt key while dragging the selected object to the location of your choice.

To illustrate a series of switches, Kelley dragged a selected switch (while holding Option-Shift/Alt-Shift to copy and constrain its movement), stretched the switch copy by selecting one end of the switch knob with the Direct-select Lasso and dragged it down (holding the Shift key to constrain it vertically). She repeated this process to create a line of switches with the same switch plate width, but different switch knob lengths.

2 Using tints to fill the objects. At this point, all the objects are filled with white and have a stroke of black. Select a single object and set the Stroke to None and the Fill to black using the Color palette (Window: Color). Open the Swatches palette (Window: Swatches) and Option/Alt-click on the New Swatch icon to name it "Black Spot," and set the Color Type to Spot Color. Click OK to save your new spot color. Then create a tint using the Tint slider in the Color palette. Continue to fill individual objects (be sure to set their Stroke to None) using Black Spot as the fill color, and adjust the tints for individual objects using the Tint slider until you are happy with their shades. Kelley used percentages from 10–90%, with most of the objects being 55–75% black.

3 Creating a few carefully placed highlights. Look closely at the subject of your drawing and decide where to place highlights. For lines that follow the contour of your object, select part or all of your object's path with the Direct-selection tool, copy (Edit: Copy) and Paste In Front (Edit: Paste In Front) that path or path section. Using the Color palette, change the Fill of your path to None and use the tint slider to change the Stroke to a light value of gray. While the highlight's path is still selected, you can reduce or increase the width of your stroke using the Weight field of the Stroke palette. If you

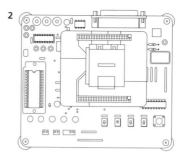

2

The drawn object prior to filling selected paths with gray

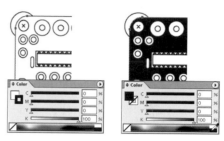

Left, the selected path set to the default stroke and fill colors; right, the selected object set to a fill of Black and a stroke of None

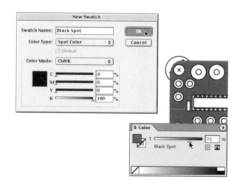

Creating a new custom spot color that will then appear in the Swatches palette; setting the selected path to a fill of 73% Spot Black using the Tint slider in the Color palette

Individual paths filled with tints of Black Spot in a range from 10% to 90%

3

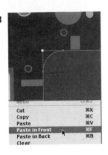
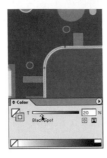

Using Paste In Front on a selected, copied path to duplicate it directly on top; changing the Stroke and Fill of the duplicate path to create a highlighted outline

Using the Stroke palette's Weight field to increase or decrease the width of the highlight path

Placing small circles with a Fill of 0% black (white) and a darker inset curved path to simulate depth; Option-Shift/Alt-Shift dragging a selected path to duplicate the path and constrain its movement

4

Copying a dial and choosing Paste Behind; using cursor-keys to offset the copy; setting the Fill tint to 87% black to create a shadow from the copy

need to trim the length of a highlight, cut its path with the Scissors tool and then select the unwanted segments with the Direct-selection tool and delete them.

For some of the knobs and dials on her chip, Kelley used circular highlights with a value of 0% black (white) and an inset curved path with a darker value to simulate depth. Once you are satisfied with the highlights on a particular knob, select the paths (both the highlights and the knob) and hold down the Option/Alt key while dragging the objects in order to duplicate them (hold down Option-Shift/Alt-Shift to copy and constrain the paths as you drag them).

For her highlights, Kelley used lines that varied in weight from .2 to .57 pt and colors that varied in tint from 10–50%. She also used carefully placed white circles for some of the highlights. Try experimenting with different Cap and Join styles in the Stroke palette; see "The end of the (path) line" section and figures in the beginning of this chapter for more on Caps and Joins.

4 Creating shadows. Follow the same procedure as above, but this time use darker tints on duplicated paths pasted behind in order to create shadows. Select a path to make into a shadow, copy it, and use Paste In Back (Edit: Paste In Back) to place a copy of the path directly behind the original path. Use your cursor-keys to offset the copy, and change the Fill to a darker tint using the Color palette.

Consider using Effects to create shadows and highlights. See the *Live Effects & Styles* chapter for information on building multi-stroke appearances and saving them as styles that you can use on other artwork.

Symbols

Use Symbols instead of copies of artwork if you want to export the illustration as a Shockwave Flash file (Symbols result in a smaller file). See the *Brushes, Symbols & Hatches* chapter to learn more about creating and modifying Symbols, and about the benefits of using them.

FOX/BLACKDOG (Art Director: Neal Zimmermann, Zimmermann Crowe Design)

Mark Fox/BlackDog

Using techniques similar to those shown in the next lesson, Mark Fox redesigned this eagle decal for Bianchi USA—the American branch of the Italian bicycle manufacturer—under the art direction of Neal Zimmermann (Zimmermann Crowe Design).

Cutting & Joining

Basic Path Construction with Pathfinders

Overview: *Design an illustration using overlapping objects; use the Pathfinder palette to join and intersect objects, join lines to circles, and cut objects from other objects.*

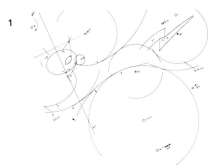

1

Fox's inked sketch drawn with a compass
NOTE: Fox worked on his image in reverse. As a last step, he used the Reflect tool to flip the final image (see the *Zen* chapter for help reflecting).

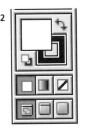

2

Using the Tools palette to set the Fill to None before starting to draw

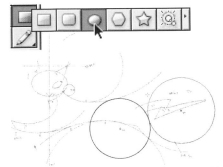

Drawing constrained circles from the center with the Ellipse tool (while holding Option-Shift/Alt Alt-Shift) to trace over the placed template

To redesign the classic "9 Lives" cat symbol that has appeared on Eveready batteries for over 50 years, Mark Fox began with a hand-drawn sketch. Once his sketch was approved, he inked the sketch with a Rapidograph pen and a compass, and then reconstructed the ink image in Illustrator using permanent (destructive) Pathfinder commands. To permanently apply the top row of Pathfinders, you'll have to hold Option (Mac)/Alt (Win) when you click these icons. The bottom row of Pathfinder icons are always permanent. *Especially* when you work with permanent Pathfinders, make sure you save incremental versions of your image as you work.

1 Creating a sketch and placing it as a template. Fox used a compass to create a precise drawing constructed of fluid curves. Using his inked sketch as a template, Fox then used the Ellipse tool to recreate his compass circles in Illustrator. Create your own sketch using traditional materials and then scan it, or sketch directly into a painting program (such as Painter or Photoshop). Save your sketch as a TIFF or your preferred raster format, and place it into a new Illustrator document as a template. To do this, choose File: Place to locate the image you wish to use as a template, then enable the Template option and click Place (see the *Layers* chapter for more on templates).

2 Tracing your template using adjoining and overlapping objects. In order to see what you're doing as you work, use the Fill/Stroke section of the Tools palette to set your Fill to None and Stroke to black before you begin drawing. Now use the Ellipse and Rectangle tools to create the basic shapes that will make up your image. Fox used some circles to form the shapes themselves (like the rump of the cat), and others to define the areas that would later be cut from others (like the arc of the under-belly). To create perfect circles or squares hold the Shift key while you draw with the Ellipse and Rectangle tools. By default, ellipse and rectangles are drawn from a cor-ner—in order to draw these objects from a center point, hold down the Option (Mac) or Alt (Win) key as you draw. To create a circle from its center point, you'll need to hold down the modifier keys Shift+Option (Mac), or Shift+Alt (Win) as you draw —don't release the modifier keys until after you release your mouse button. Because Fox measures everything in millimeters in his inking stage, he creates his circles numerically. With the Ellipse tool, Fox Option-click (Alt click for Win) on each center point marked on his template, entered the correct diame-ter for Width and Height, and clicked OK.

3 Constructing curves by combining parts of different circles. Once your paths are drawn and in position, use the Pathfinder palette (Window: Pathfinder) to combine portions of different circles to create complex curves. After drawing basic circles, use the Line tool to draw a line through the circles at the point where you want to join them, and choose Object: Path: Divide Objects Below. Then select the sub-sections of the divided circles that you don't want and delete. To join separate adjoining curves, select them, hold Option/Alt, and click the Add to Shape Area Pathfinder icon.

4 Constructing objects using the Intersect Pathfinder command. If the area you wish to keep is the portion where objects overlap, use the Intersect command. Fox used Intersect to create the eyes and the nose of the cat. To make the eye shape, he drew a circle and then dragged off a duplicate by holding Option/Alt as he moved it with

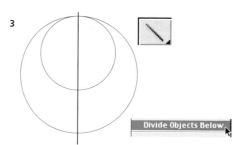

3

Draw a line to mark where objects will be joined and apply Object: Path: Divide Objects Below

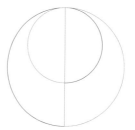

Select and delete unwanted portions of objects that won't be part of the final curve

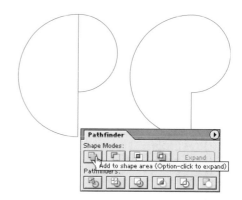

Once only the elements you wish to be joined remain, select them, hold Option/Alt and click on the Add to Shape Area Pathfinder icon

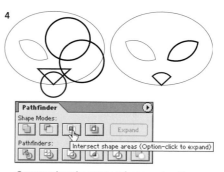

4

Constructing the eyes and nose using the Intersect Shape Areas Pathfinder command

5

Drawing one line from an anchor point on the circle and another angled line slightly removed

Creating a perpendicular copy of the angled line by double-clicking the Rotate tool, specifying a 90° Angle, and clicking copy

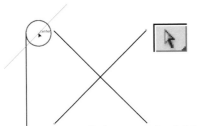

Moving the perpendicular copy to the circle's center and then making it into a guide

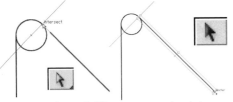

Moving the angled line tangent to the circle using the guide, then lengthening the line

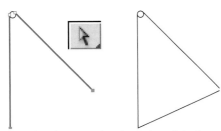

Selecting the two end anchor points of the lines and closing using Join to connect the lines

Using the Add to Shape Pathfinder command to attach the circle to the angled shape, then the completed ears to the cat-head ellipse

the Selection tool. He then positioned the two circles so the overlap created the desired shape, selected both circles, and held down Option/Alt while he clicked the Intersect Shape Areas Pathfinder icon.

5 Attaching lines to circles. Fox connected angled lines to a tiny circle to form the cat's ear. To smoothly attach lines to circles, the lines need to lie "tangent" to the circle (touching the circle at only one anchor point). To work with precision, turn on Smart Guides (View menu).

Start with the Ellipse tool and draw a small circle. To create the first tangent line, choose the Line tool, and place the cursor over the left side anchor-point of the circle. When you see the word "anchor point" click-drag downward from that anchor point to draw a vertical line (hold the Shift key to constrain your line to vertical).

Creating a tangent line that doesn't begin at an anchor point is trickier. Start by drawing another line slightly apart from the circle, but at the angle you desire (holding the Shift key constrains your line to horizontals, verticals, and 45° angles). To help you find the tangent point for this line, you need to create a line perpendicular to it. With your angled line selected, double-click the Rotate tool, enter 90°, and click Copy. Use the Direct-selection tool to grab this perpendicular copy of your line near the middle and drag it toward the center of your circle; release the mouse when you see the word "center." With this line still selected, make it into a guide with View: Guides: Make Guides. Now select your angled line (marquee it with the Direct-selection tool, or click it with the Selection or Group-selection tool). Finally, with the Direct-selection tool, grab the top anchor point and drag it to where the perpendicular guide meets the circle; release the mouse when you see the word "intersect."

To adjust the length of either line, switch to the Selection tool, select the line, and drag the bounding box from the middle end handle at the open anchor point.

The Add to Shape Pathfinder ignores lines, so to attach the lines to the circle, first connect the lines together to form a two-dimensional shape. Using the Direct-selection tool, marquee the two open anchor points and choose Object: Path: Join (⌘-J/Ctrl-J) to connect the points with a line.

Finally, to unite your angled shape with the circle, select them both, hold Option/Alt, and click the Add to Shape Area Pathfinder icon. Fox also used Add to Shape Area to join the ears to the head (he rotated the first ear into position, and used the Reflect tool to create a copy for the other ear—see the *Zen of Illustrator* chapter for help with rotation and reflection).

6 Cutting portions of paths with another object. To create the rear flank of the cat, Fox used a large object to cut away an area (subtract) from another circle. Use the Selection tool to select the path you'll use as the cutter and bring it to the top of the stacking order (in the exact position) either by choosing Object: Arrange: Bring to Front, or Edit: Cut and then Edit: Paste in Front (⌘F/Ctrl-F). Marquee or Shift-select to select the cutter object as well as the objects you want to cut. To apply the cut, hold Option/Alt and click the Subtract from Shape Area Pathfinder icon. If you want a different result—Undo, make adjustments and reapply the Pathfinder.

Joining open paths & closing paths smoothly

Pathfinder: Add to Shape will close open paths, joining them with a straight line. Use the following method to manually join two open paths or to close a path smoothly. Since you can only join two points at a time, start by deleting any stray points (Select: Object: Stray Points). Before you can join points with a smooth curve, you need to ensure the points are exactly on top of each other. Use the Direct-select tool or Direct-select Lasso to select one pair of end anchor points and choose Object: Path: Average (Both) and click OK, then Object: Path: Join and click OK. To Average/Join in one step, press ⌘-Shift-Option-J (Mac/Ctrl-Shift-Alt-J (Win)—there isn't a menu command for this.

Swapping Fill and Stroke

If your objects are styled with  a stroke and no fill, you can swap the Fill and Stroke styling to better see the effects of a Pathfinder command. To do this, with objects selected, click on the Swap Fill and Stroke arrows in the bottom section of the Tools palette. Click again to swap it back.

6

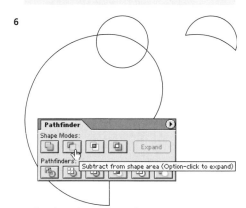
Using the Subtract from Shape Area to cut one object from others

Manually cut with Scissors

Although it's not as precise as using a line and "Divide Objects Below," you *can* use the Scissors tool to cut any path, including open paths. Turn on Smart Guides (View menu) and click with the Scissors tool once the word "Path" appears to place two coinciding points on the path. To separate the points, first deselect the path entirely. Then, with the Direct-selection tool, click on top of the new points to select only the top point. Then you can move or delete the selected point.

Add & Expand

More Pathfinder Palette Basics

KANZLER / THE FUND FOR ANIMALS

Overview: *Create and position overlapping objects; use the Pathfinder palette to unite the paths into an editable Compound Shape, then consolidate the paths with Expand.*

1

Assembling the basic elements for creating the beaver lodge

Positioning the stick paths to overlap the lodge path—the final assemblage

2

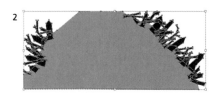

Applying Add in the Pathfinder palette to the selected paths to create a Compound Shape.
Note: The Compound Shape will take on the Fill and Stroke attributes of the topmost object.

The design team of Diane and John Kanzler used the Pathfinder palette to create a logo and vehicle signage for the Urban Wildlife Program of the Fund for Animals. When the illustration was completed and approved by the client, the Kanzlers used the Expand feature of the Pathfinder palette as the final step to prepare the file for sending to the sign company.

1 Creating and positioning overlapping objects. The Kanzlers wanted their logo's final lodge to look like it was made of sticks, like a real beaver lodge. To achieve this effect, begin by using the Pen tool to draw a basic lodge form. Set the lodge path's Fill to Black and the Stroke to None, then adjust the Black to a gray value using the K slider in the Color palette. (For more on using the Color palette, see the "Simple Realism" lesson earlier in this chapter.) Draw a series of jagged logs and branches with a Fill of Black and a Stroke of None; this will make placement of the individual branch and log paths easier to view over the gray lodge shape. Next, use the Selection tool to position the log and branch paths so they overlap the lodge path. When you are satisfied with the placement of the logs and branches, choose Select: All to select all the paths you want to be united.

2 Using the Pathfinder palette to Add. Open the Pathfinder palette (Window: Pathfinder) and click on the

Add button in the top row of palette choices. The result is a fully editable Compound Shape that unites all of the selected paths. You should note that the paths within the Compound Shape will take on the Fill and Stroke attributes of the topmost path. To reposition any path within the Compound Shape, select and move it with the Group-selection tool, or use the Direct-selection tool to click within a filled path to select and reposition it. You can use the Direct-selection tool to edit the shape of any path within the Compound Shape.

The beaver lodge as a Compound Shape

3 Using Expand to convert Compound Shapes into a single path. The Kanzlers maintained the beaver lodge as a "live" editable Compound Shape during the client approval process, which made modifications easier.

When their final sign was approved, the Kanzlers needed to prepare the file to send to the signage contractor. The design was to be output directly to the contractor's vinyl-cutting equipment using an older version of Illustrator on the Windows platform. In order to minimize the possibility of problems in printing their image with an earlier version of Illustrator, and to reduce the potential for their illustration to be inadvertently modified, they chose to apply the Expand command to permanently unite the separate beaver lodge shapes into one continuous path. Once you apply Expand to Compound Shape artwork, the separate paths will be united and you will no longer be able to move the individual stick shapes independently. Therefore, if you think you may need to edit the silhouette sometime in the future, be sure to save a copy of your artwork before you apply Expand.

To Expand your live Compound Shapes (in a copy of your file), use the Selection tool to select your Compound Shape. Then, in the Pathfinder palette, click the Expand button to permanently apply your Pathfinder—in this case, to unite your paths. You can also access Expand by choosing "Expand Compound Shape" from the Pathfinder palette's pop-up menu.

Using the Group-selection tool to move individual paths within the Compound Shape

3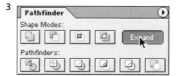

Expanding the Compound Shape to consolidate all of the individual paths into a single path

(Top) The final, expanded path; (bottom) the final logo and signage

Divide & Color

Applying Pathfinder Divide & Subtract

Overview: *Design an illustration using overlapping elements; create individual paths using Divide, and delete unnecessary paths; using Subtract to cut "holes" and create Compound Paths; Divide again and assign colors to divided objects.*

1

Creating the basic elements using the Rectangle and Ellipse tools

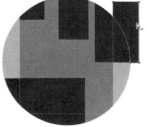

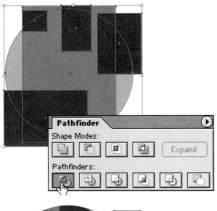

(Top) Selecting all paths and clicking on Divide in the Pathfinder palette; (bottom) selecting and deleting unnecessary paths

Illustrator's Pathfinder palette provides many ways to combine objects. To create this disco clock for a World-studio Foundation's "Make Time" benefit, John Pirman used the Divide and Subtract Pathfinder options to permanently alter his objects. This allowed him to adjust colors within each of the divided areas in his illustration.

1 Creating and positioning paths; dividing overlapping paths. Pirman created a circle and a number of rectangles to serve as the background (and later as the objects to Divide his figure shapes) for his clock face design. In a new Illustrator document, draw a filled circle with no Stroke using the Ellipse tool (hold the Shift key to constrain the ellipse to a circle). Then use the Rectangle tool to draw a few rectangles filled with different gray values, and Strokes of None. Use a selection tool to move the rectangles around until you are satisfied with an arrangement of rectangles in relationship to the circle. Next, choose Select: All, then open the Pathfinder palette (Window: Pathfinder) and click the Divide button (in the palette's bottom row). All overlapping paths will split into separate, editable objects. To delete the extra paths outside of this "divided circle" shape, first choose Select: Deselect, then use a selection tool to select them, and Delete.

2 Using Subtract to create "holes" and Divide again. Next, Pirman drew a series of silhouetted human figures with the Pen and Pencil tools and arranged them in relation to the background. For figures that included enclosed "negative space" (such as an arm partially touching another part of the body) he used Pathfinder: Subtract to cut the areas as "holes," so objects behind would show through. To cut enclosed areas into permanent holes, first make sure that your enclosed paths are on top of the rest of the figure. Next, set solid fills for all the objects, with no strokes. Then select your figure and the enclosed spaces and hold Option (Mac)/Alt (Win) while you click on Subtract in the Pathfinder palette (holding Option (Mac)/Alt (Win) while applying a Pathfinder in the upper row of the palette makes that Pathfinder action permanent). Your figure with holes has now become a Compound Path. Use the Selection tool to reposition the complete figure, the Group-selection tool to reposition the holes, or the Direct-selection tool to edit the paths.

Pirman created a palette of blues, greens, and white to apply to his figures. He then positioned each figure over his "divided circle" background and used his background objects to divide the figures. To do this, choose different color fills for your figures and arrange them in front of your divided background (the stacking order doesn't matter). Next, select all your paths (Select: All) and click Divide in the Pathfinder palette. As before, all of the overlapping paths will now be split into individual paths. Use the Group-selection tool to select and delete paths outside of your background shape, and then to select individual sections of the figures in order to change the fill color. Pirman used colors of similar value to visually integrate the divided figures.

With his figures divided, Pirman then used his palette colors to recolor the various divided sections of the figures and continued to make adjustments to the background. To do this, color all of the paths that make up the fully divided illustration using your color palette. Using the Group-selection tool, click on the individual paths within the circle shape (hold Shift to select multiple paths) and style with any Fill color you like.

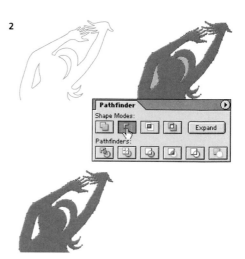

Drawing a figure that includes enclosed objects defining "negative space" (top left), selecting all the objects that create the figure and applying Pathfinder: Subtract while holding Option/Alt (top right), the figure now as a Compound Path

Filled figures; positioning the colored figure paths over the divided circle background

The process of styling individual objects with different colors.

Cubist Constructs

Creative Experimentation with Pathfinders

Overview: *Create objects as the basis for Pathfinder commands; use commands on different sets of objects; make color and object adjustments.*

1

The scanned sketch placed as a template

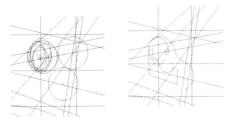

Before and after circles are cut and joined

2

On the left, three objects (shown with different stroke colors); on the right, the objects with colored fills (no stroke) prior to running the Soft Mix command

Soft Mix applied, then objects recolored

To build his geometrically complex style, Ron Chan depends on Illustrator's drawing tools and the Pathfinder palette commands. Many different ways exist to achieve similar effects. Here are some that Chan has perfected.

1 Preparing the basic objects you will work from.

Create the objects that will form the basis for your filtering. Chan used methods discussed elsewhere in the book to prepare the initial objects, including scanning a sketch to use as a template (*Layers* chapter), creating a custom drawing grid (*Type* chapter) in its own layer and making a masking layer (*Advanced Techniques* chapter). He cut and joined circles to form elements such as the head (shown at left). For cutting and joining help, see "Cutting & Joining," earlier in this chapter.

2 Selecting overlapping objects and applying Soft Mix.

After creating a few overlapping objects, you might choose to see how those objects "cut into" each other. First, select the objects with any selection tool. Then use the Pathfinder commands (Window: Pathfinder). The previous lesson "Divide & Conquer" uses the Divide Pathfinder to create separate objects for each area in which the objects intersect. Chan preferred to use the Soft Mix Pathfinder. Soft Mix creates new colors where objects overlap, making the intersections easy to see. In this way, Chan could use the Direct-selection tool to choose particular divided objects for recoloring. (If your version of Illustrator doesn't include Soft Mix and Hard Mix in the Pathfinder palette, see the Tip at right.) To recolor all like-colored objects together, Chan Direct-selected one color and used Select: Same: Fill Color, to select all objects of that color.

3 **Outlining and offsetting paths.** Turning paths into outlined shapes gives you flexibility in styling and aligning lines. Chan stroked the jaw path and then outlined it using Object: Path: Outline Stroke. This allowed him to align the bottom edge of the line to the chin object. If you outline a path, you can fill it with gradients (see the *Blends, Gradients & Mesh* chapter) or patterns (see the last lesson in this chapter). Another way to turn a path into a fillable shape is to offset a copy of a selected path (Object: Path: Offset) and then join the endpoints of the copy and the original.

4 **Cropping copies for an inset look.** To create the look of an inset or lens of your image, first select and copy all the objects that will be affected, and then use Paste In Front and Group on the copy you just made. Using any method you wish, create a closed object to define the inset area. With the object still selected, press the Shift key and use the Selection tool to select the grouped copy and click the Crop icon in the Pathfinder palette. You can then use the Direct-selection tool to choose individual objects so you can change color or opacity, or apply effects from the Effect menu. Also, try experimenting with the Colors: Adjust Colors filter (Filter menu) until you achieve a color change you like.

Where's Soft Mix Pathfinder?
Illustrator 10 deleted Hard Mix and Soft Mix from the Pathfinder palette. To restore Mix functionality, either install the *Wow! Actions* "Pathfinder Filters.aia" from the *Wow! CD* (in "SandeeCs Wow! Actions," in the "Wow! Actions" folder), or apply them from Effect: Pathfinder, then choose Object: Expand Appearance.

3

Selecting a path and then applying Object: Path: Outline Stroke

The outlined path was moved up (Smart Guides are turned on), then recolored

4

Artwork copied and pasted in front, then circle drawn for inset shape

After Pathfinder: Crop, the circle was recolored

Isometric Systems

Cursor Keys, Constrain-angles & Formulas

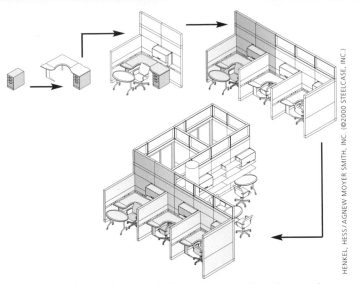

Overview: *Create detailed views of an object from front, top and side; use an isometric formula to transform the objects; set "Constrain-angle" and "Cursor key" distance; use Lasso and cursor keys with snap-to-point to adjust and assemble objects.*

Stubborn snapping-to-point

Sometimes if you try to move an object just slightly, it will annoyingly "snap" to the wrong place. If this happens, move it away from the area and release. Then grab the object again at the point you'd like to align and move it so that it snaps into the correct position. If you still have trouble, zoom in. As a last resort, you can disable "Snap to point" in the View menu.

1

Top, front and side faces with more than one component are grouped

2

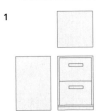

Scaling, skewing and rotating

Technical illustrations and diagrams are often depicted in isometrics, and Adobe Illustrator can be the ideal program both for creating your initial illustrations, and for transforming them into this projection. The artists at Agnew Moyer Smith (AMS) created and transformed the diagrams on these pages using their three-step iso projection. For both the initial creation and manipulation of the isometric objects in space, AMS custom-set "Cursor key distance" and "Constrain angle" (in Edit: Preferences: General) and made sure that View: Snap to point was enabled.

1 Creating detailed renderings of the front, side and top views of your object to scale. Before you begin a technical illustration, you should choose a drawing scale, then coordinate the settings Preferences: General to match. For instance, to create a file drawer in the scale of 1 mm = 2", set the ruler units to millimeters and "Cursor key" distance to .5 mm, and make sure that the "Snap to point" option is enabled. With these features enabled and matching your drawing scale, it's easy to create detailed views of your object. To easily keep track of your object sizing as you work, choose Window: Info. If a portion of the real object is inset 1" to the left, you can use the ← cursor-key to move the path one increment (.5 mm) farther left. Finally, Snap-to-point will help you align and assemble your various components. Select and group all the components of the front view. Separately group the top and side so you'll be able to easily isolate each of the views for transformation and assembly. AMS renders every internal detail, which allows them to view "cut-aways" or adjust individual elements, or groups of ele-ments—for instance, when a drawer is opened.

2 Using an isometric formula to transform your objects, then assembling the elements.

The artists at AMS created and transformed the diagrams on these pages using their three-step process, which is fully demonstrated on the *Wow! CD*. To transform your objects, double-click on the various tools to specify the correct percentages numerically. First, select all three views and scale them 100% horizontally and 86.6% verti-cally. Next, select the top and side, shear them at a −30° angle, and then shear the front 30°. Rotate the top and front 30° and the side −30°. The movement chart shows angles and directions.

To assemble the top, front and side, use the Selection tool to grab a specific anchor-point from the side view that will contact the front view, and drag it until it snaps into the correct position (the arrow turns hollow). Next, select and drag to snap the top into position. Finally, select and group the entire object for easy reselection.

3 Using selection, Constrain-angle and cursor keys to adjust objects and assemble multiple components.

Try using the Direct-selection Lasso tool to select a por-tion of an object (Shift-Lasso adds points to a selection; Option-Lasso/Alt-Lasso deletes points from a selection), setting the Constrain-angle to 30°, then slide your selec-tion along the isometric axes using alternating cursor keys. Select entire objects and snap them into position against other objects. Also, look at the movement chart (top of the page) to determine the direction in which to move, then double-click the Selection tool in the toolbox to specify a numeric movement for selections or objects.

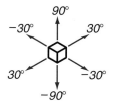

A cursor movement chart based on a Constrain Angle of 30°; a fully transformed and assembled object is then grouped for easy selection; setting Constrain Angle in Edit: Preferences: General

3

You can use the Direct-selection Lasso to select the points you want to move.

To lengthen the cart, select the points indicated and move in the direction of the arrow (−30°)

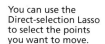

To widen the cart, select the points indicated, and either double-click on the Selection tool in the Toolbox to specify a Move numerically, or use your cursor keys

Transforming one object into the next, by Direct-selecting the appropriate anchor points and using the Move command, or by setting and using a custom Constrain-angle and cursor keys

Automated Isometric Actions!
Rick Henkel of AMS created *Wow! Actions* that automate formulas for isometrics (on the *Wow! CD*).

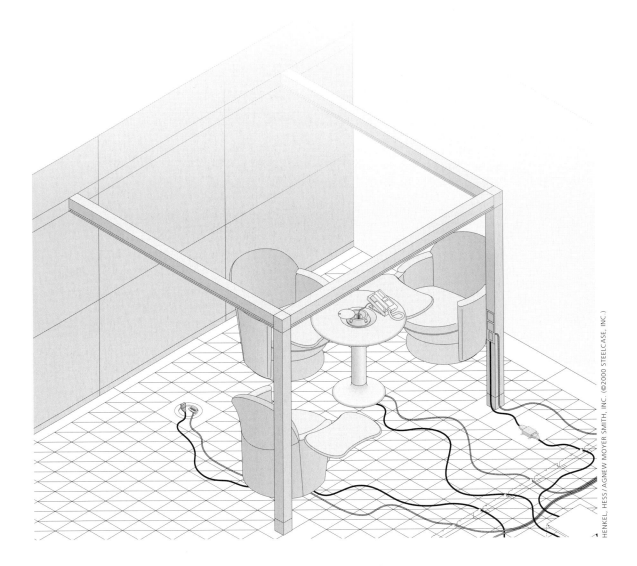

Rick Henkel, Kurt Hess/
Agnew Moyer Smith, Inc.

Agnew Moyer Smith's artists use Illustrator not only to create discrete elements, but also because it provides so much flexibility in composing an environment with those elements. Objects can be saved in separate files by category and used as "libraries" when constructing different scenes.

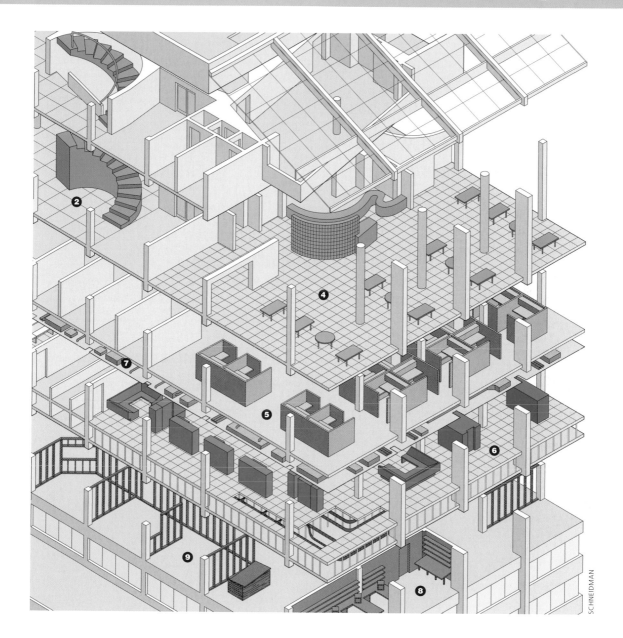

SCHNEIDMAN

Jared Schneidman

Jared Schneidman illustrated this building for a capabilities brochure for Structure Tone, an interior construction company. Schneidman traced a scan of an architectural drawing of the building, rendered originally in an isometric view. While drawing, Schneidman set the Constrain Angle (Edit: Preferences: General) to 30°, so he could edit objects by dragging selected points or lines along the same angles as the isometric view (he held down the Shift key while dragging to constrain movement to the set angles).

Objective Colors

Custom Labels for Making Quick Changes

Overview: *Define custom spot colors, naming colors by the type of object; repeat the procedure for each type of object; use Select filters to select types of objects by spot color name to edit colors or objects.*

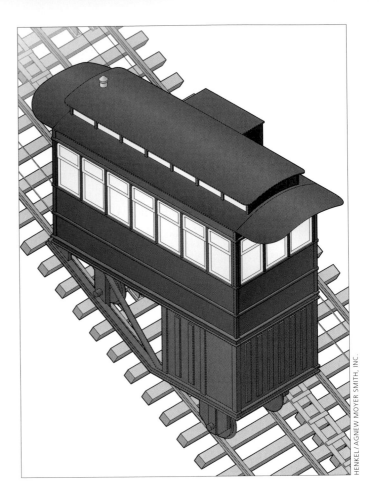

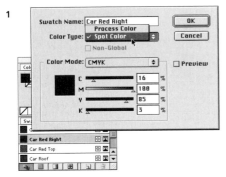

Option-clicking on the New Swatch icon to directly access Swatch Options; naming the color, then setting the color to be a Spot Color, which allows global changes and tinting

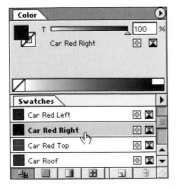

A spot color swatch with its custom label

When you need to frequently adjust the colors of an illustration, it's essential to find a way of organizing your colors. This illustration by Rick Henkel demonstrates how his firm, Agnew Moyer Smith (AMS), uses colors to label different categories of objects, making it simple to isolate and update colors. This method also makes it easy to find all objects in a category in order to apply any other global changes, such as changing the stroke weight or scaling, or adding transparency or effects.

1 Creating custom spot colors. AMS uses spot colors, even for process color jobs, to allow easy access to tints. (You can also use Process colors by checking the Global option in the Swatches palette.) In the Swatches palette,

Option-click/Alt-click on the New Swatch icon. If you have premixed a color in the Colors palette, this color will be loaded in the color mixer. If you are not pleased with the color, then edit it accordingly. Now give your color a name that conveys the kind of object you plan to fill with the color and choose Spot Color from the Color Type pop-up. Rick Henkel used labels such as "CamRight" and "DriveLeft" to label the colors he would use in his illustration of the Duquesne Incline. To help his selection of reliably reproducible colors, Henkel used the Agfa PostScript Process Color Guide to look up the color he actually wanted and then entered the CMYK percentages.

2 Repeating the procedure for all colors and labels, and changing color definitions as necessary. Create colors for each type of object to be styled differently, naming each color for the objects it will fill (to speed creation, see the Tip at the right). Henkel created spot colors, properly labeled, for each type of object included in this incline railroad illustration.

The spot color system makes it easy to change definitions of colors. From the Swatches palette, double-click on the color you want to change in order to open Swatch Options, where you can change the color recipe. Click OK to apply the changes to all objects containing that color.

3 Using the labels to find all like objects. To select all like objects—for example, those colored with "Cam-Right"—click on that color name in your Swatches palette list and choose Select: Same: Fill Color. Once selected, you can edit other attributes besides color (like stroke width, layer position and alignment).

Spot colors for four-color-process jobs

Illustrator's process colors don't update globally by default (as Spot colors do). If you choose to define all swatches as spot colors, be sure to enable "Convert to Process" options in the File: Separation Setup dialog when generating separations.

Creating custom spot color swatches for each category of object to be styled differently

With a color swatch label selected, choosing Select: Same: Fill Color to find the objects filled with that color

After selecting the next color swatch, using the Select Again command to select all objects colored with that swatch

From one swatch to another

When defining swatches with custom parameters in Swatch Options, such as Spot colors or Global process colors, instead of having to continually set similar parameters, simply select a swatch that is close to the color you want, then Option-click/Alt-click the New Swatch icon to redefine and name the Swatch.

Organizing Colors

Arranging an Artist's Palette of Colors

Overview: *Remove default swatches from the Swatches palette; work with printed color swatches to choose initial colors; make a color chart to help organize colors; rename swatches; create color variants and make them into swatches.*

TUTTLE

Show All Swatches icon; the cluttered default Swatches palette of a new Illustrator document

Choose "Select All Unused" from the Swatches palette pop-up menu to select most of the colors in the palette; click on the Delete Swatches icon to delete the selected swatches

As any colorist knows, an organized palette can facilitate the creative process. Artist Jean Tuttle constructs a color chart file that makes it easy to create several illustrations with the same palette and allows her to work with colors in an intuitive manner.

1 Clearing the Swatches palette of unused swatches; using swatches of printed colors to choose base colors with which to work. A new Illustrator document opens with a default set of colors in the Swatches palette. When creating a new palette of customized colors, you'll want to start fresh by removing these default colors. First, choose File: New to create a new Illustrator document. Next, open the Swatches palette (Window: Swatches) and click on the Show All Swatches icon in the lower left corner of the Swatches palette. To select most of the swatches, click on the pop-up menu icon on the upper right corner of the palette and choose Select All Unused. Click the Delete Swatch icon at the bottom of the palette and choose Yes in the dialog box to delete the selected swatches. Your goal is to have just four swatches: None,

Registration, White, and Black. If you have more than those four swatches remaining in your Swatches palette, delete the extra swatches by dragging them to the Delete Swatch icon at the bottom of the palette. To select multiple swatches to delete, hold down the Shift key as you click on each swatch.

If you think you may want to start with a cleaned out Swatches palette in the future, save this blank document and begin with it next time. If you want to start *all* of your new documents with a clear Swatches palette, save a copy of this file as Adobe Illustrator Startup_CMYK (or _RGB) in the Plug-ins folder inside the Illustrator application folder. The next time you start up Illustrator and create a new file, the color palette will have your minimalist color set in the Color palette by default.

As mentioned in *Illustrator Basics*, color on the screen is not a reliable predictor of the color you'll get in print. Therefore, start with a computer-to-print color matching system to choose your initial colors. Tuttle selected tear-out swatches in a Pantone Color Specifier as a starting point in choosing colors to consider for her base palette. Then in Illustrator, she opened the Pantone Process Coated color palette (Window: Swatch Libraries) to access the digital version that included the CMYK breakdown of the colors she had chosen. On the Artboard, Tuttle made a column of 12 rectangles, each filled with a color she wanted in her palette. After choosing and using these base colors, she could close the Pantone palette.

2 **Renaming and reorganizing swatches.** Every time she tried a Pantone color, it added to her Swatches palette, so with her Swatches palette open (Window: Swatches) Tuttle next deleted all the colors except those she actually used in her column of rectangles. After making some slight adjustments to the CMYK mixtures, she renamed each base color in the Swatches palette based on its color. Because Illustrator, by default, lists colors alphabetically by name in List View, Tuttle preceded each color name with a letter and number that would automatically group

To completely clear the Swatches palette, manually drag the extra swatches to the Delete Swatch icon

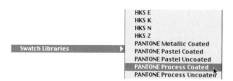
Accessing a Pantone Process color swatch library

The base set of colors used to begin the swatches palette chart

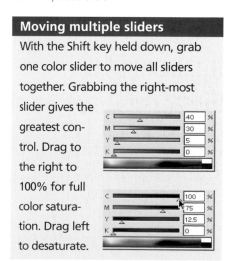
Moving multiple sliders

With the Shift key held down, grab one color slider to move all sliders together. Grabbing the right-most slider gives the greatest control. Drag to the right to 100% for full color saturation. Drag left to desaturate.

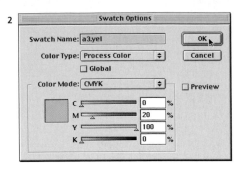

2

Double-click on a swatch in the Swatches palette to rename it and change other properties. Tuttle included a "3" in each name so that she could add two lighter (1 and 2) versions in step 3

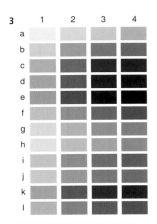

A chart made of custom swatches allows future access to the full palette and helps with naming conventions. Column 3 contains the base set of colors in this palette, columns 1 and 2 contain the lighter variants, column 4 contains the darker variant. The final Swatches palette shows colors falling into place alphabetically in List View (accessed from the palette pop-up menu)

the colors based on her preference. For example, Tuttle used a3.yel for yellow, b3.oran for orange, and so on. To rename a color swatch in the Swatches palette, first deselect all objects (Select: Deselect) then double-click a swatch name in the Swatches palette to display the Swatch Options dialog window. Type in a new name in the Swatch Name field, and make sure that the Color Type is Process Color. Tuttle disables the Global checkbox when creating colors so that editing a swatch's color won't alter the colors in her existing document. (For more on global and spot colors, see the previous lesson.)

3 Creating variant colors and making them into swatches. In the list of colors she was building, Tuttle created two columns of lighter variants to the left and one column of darker variants to the right, renaming each swatch to fall correctly into her Swatches palette. She created the lighter variants by using the Saturation filter on an object filled with a base color (Filter: Colors: Saturate) and moving the Intensity slider to the desired position. She created the darker variants by adding 10–15% black to each base color by moving the K slider to the right in the Swatch Options dialog box. Once you are satisfied with your color variations, select one of the filled objects and Option-click (Mac) /Alt-click (Win) on the New Swatch icon at the bottom of the Swatches palette. Choose a name in the Name field so that it will list alphabetically in the intended position in the Swatches palette, and click OK. Repeat this procedure for each variant-filled object. Save your custom color chart, then use Save As to begin another image with this palette. To access these swatches when the chart isn't open, choose Window: Swatch Library: Other, then locate your chart document.

Accessing tints with "Global" colors

You can specify tints for global colors in the Swatches palette. If you don't see the slider for a color, double-click the swatch and enable the "Global" option. You can then use the Tint slider, or enter a tint numerically.

TATE (©1999 UNITED FEATURE SYNDICATE, INC.)

Clarke Tate

Setting the familiar characters, Woodstock and Snoopy, in famous locations, Clarke Tate illustrated this scene for a McDonald's Happy Meal box designed for Asian markets. Tate produced a palette of custom colors with descriptive names. You can view color names by selecting

Name View from the Swatches palette pop-up menu.

	Bamboo Or Tan 2	☒
	Bamboo Y Hlite 1	☒
	Bamboo Shadow	☒

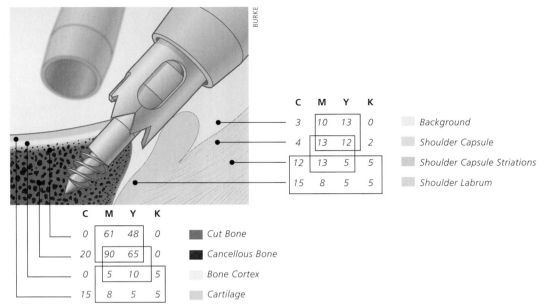

C	M	Y	K	
3	10	13	0	Background
4	13	12	2	Shoulder Capsule
12	13	5	5	Shoulder Capsule Striations
15	8	5	5	Shoulder Labrum

C	M	Y	K	
0	61	48	0	Cut Bone
20	90	65	0	Cancellous Bone
0	5	10	5	Bone Cortex
15	8	5	5	Cartilage

Christopher Burke

When printed in CMYK, Illustrator's smooth, crisp edges can be a registration nightmare. Even the slightest misregistration of inks can create visually disturbing white gaps between colors. So, although you shouldn't have to worry about what happens to your illustration once it's completed, the reality is that in this phase of computer graphics evolution, you still have to help your printer along. "Trapping" is a technique of printing one color over the edge of another—usually achieved by creating overprinting strokes that overlap adjacent objects. Christopher Burke uses a work-around where the colors in his images contain at least one (preferably two) of the color plates in every region of his image. As long as adjacent objects share at least 5% of at least one color, no white gaps can form, and trapping will naturally occur. This technique ensures "continuous coverage" of ink and maintains a full spectrum palette while keeping just enough in common between adjacent colors. (Also see Tip below and Tip "Trapping Issues" in the *Basics* chapter) The background image is a rasterized Illustrator drawing with an applied blur effect; raster images are free of trapping problems (see the *Illustrator & Other Programs* chapter for more on rasterizing Illustrator images).

Manual trapping of gradients and pattern fills

Since you can't style strokes with gradients or patterns, you can't trap using the Pathfinder Trap filter either. To trap gradients and patterns manually, first duplicate your object and stroke it in the weight you'd like for a trap. Then use Object: Path: Outline Stroke to convert the stroke to a filled object, which you should fill in the same style as the object you'd like to trap. Lastly, enable the Overprint Fill box in the Attributes palette. If necessary, use the Gradient tool to unify gradients across objects (see page 228), and manually replicate pattern transformations.

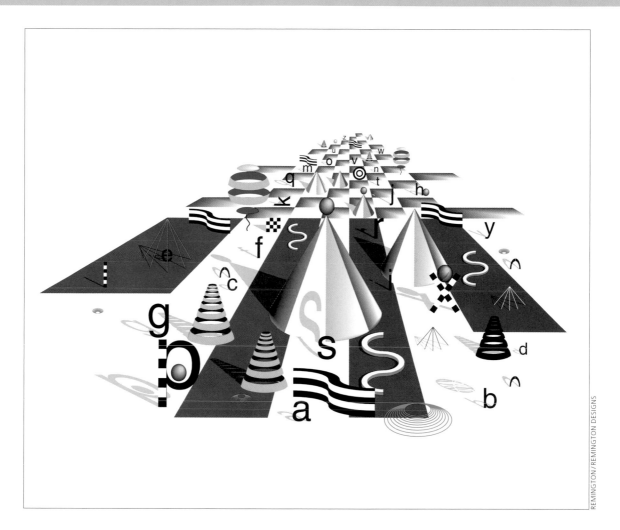

REMINGTON/REMINGTON DESIGNS

Dorothy Remington/Remington Designs

Color printers are notoriously unpredictable in terms of color consistency, so Dorothy Remington developed a method to increase consistency from proof to final output. When Remington constructs an image, she freely chooses colors from any of the CMYK process color models (such as Pantone Process, TruMatch, Focoltone, Toyo, etc.) that come with Illustrator, provided that she has the matching color swatchbooks. When she sends the computer file to the service bureau for proofing, as well as for final output, she also sends along the color swatches representing colors used in the image. Remington asks the service bureau to calibrate the printer to match her swatches as closely as possible. Although requesting such special attention might result in a small surcharge, it can save you an immense amount of time with the service bureau, and expense in reprinting the image because colors did not turn out as expected.

Distort Dynamics

Adding Character Dynamics with Transform

KANZLER

Overview: *Create characters and group them; use the Free Transform tool to drag one corner to exaggerate the character; draw a sun and use the Free Transform tool to add dynamics to circles.*

1

The original bug (top); then with the Free Transform tool the jaw is enlarged, the back is squashed and the entire character is skewed forward

After John Kanzler creates the cast of characters in his scenes, he often uses the Free Transform tool on each of the characters one at a time in order to add energy, movement, dynamics and action.

1 Creating and grouping a character, then applying the Free Transform tool. After building his bug one object at a time, Kanzler thought it needed a more menacing look, and wanted the bug to appear as if it was charging forward. By grabbing and moving various handles, he was able to enlarge the jaws while squashing the body. Then he skewed the bug to the left to give a sense of forward motion and more energy than the original. Select your objects and choose the Free Transform tool (E-key). Now, this is essential throughout this lesson: grab a handle and *then* hold down ⌘ (Mac)/Ctrl (Win) to pull only that selected handle to distort the image.

Look carefully at what results from movement of each of the Free Transform handles. For his hovering wasp, Kanzler used the Free Transform tool to give the wasp a little more "personality" by pulling a corner out to one side. Notice that as you pull a *corner* sideways to expand in one direction, the opposite side distorts and compresses—if you pull a *center* handle, you will merely skew the objects, elongating them toward the pulled side.

The effect of Free Transform on the hovering wasp

2 Applying the Free Transform tool to regularly shaped objects to add perspective and dynamics. In creating an "action line" for his illustration, Kanzler used the Free Transform tool to make an arc of dots skew out of uniformity, while constraining the arc of the skewed path to that of the original, unskewed path. First, he applied a custom dotted Pattern Brush to a curved path (see the *Brushes* chapter for help). Then he chose Object: Expand Appearance to turn the brushed path into a group of oval objects. By carefully tucking and pulling with the Free Transform tool, Kanzler was able to add flair to the arc while keeping the same general size.

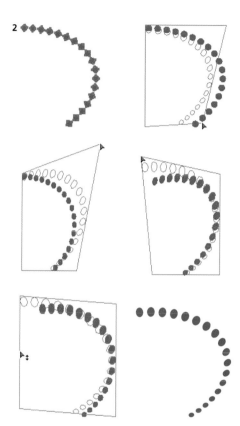

Using the Free Transform tool, pull different handles to create action and perspective effects

3 Making a sun, then creating extreme perspective using the Free Transform tool. To make the sun object, draw a circle (hold Shift as you draw with the Ellipse tool). In Outline mode (View menu), place your cursor over the circle centerpoint, hold Option/Alt *and* the Shift key while drawing a second, larger concentric circle and make it into a Guide (View: Guides: Make Guides). With the Pen tool, draw a wedge-shaped "ray" that touches the outer-circle guide. Select the wedge, and with the Rotate tool, Option/Alt-click on the circle's center point. Decide how many rays you want, divide 360 (the degrees in a circle) by the number of rays to find the angle to enter in the dialog box and click Copy. To create the remaining rays, keep repeating Transform Again, ⌘-D (Mac)/Ctrl-D (Win). Select all sun objects and choose Object: Group. Then choose the Free Transform tool and grab one single corner handle to skew the sun's perspective.

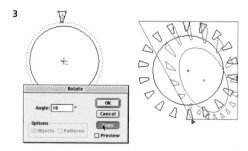

The sun object shown in Outline mode, before the process of Transform Again; and while pulling a Free Transform handle

Distort Filter Flora

Applying Distort Filters to Create Flowers

Overview: *Create rough circles; resize and rotate copies of the circles to construct a rose; fill with a radial gradient; apply the Roughen filter; apply other Distort filters to copies.*

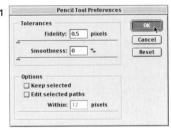
1

Setting the Pencil Tool Preferences; drawing two rough circular paths

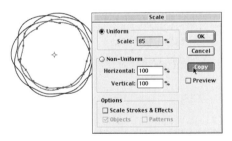

Using the Scale tool dialog window to create a reduced-size pair of circles nested within the first pair of circles

(Left) Using the Rotate tool to rotate the last-created pair of circles; (right) the complete construction of the flower before coloring—the flower center consists of a few small circles

GRACE

Artist Laurie Grace used two roughly drawn circular paths and a series of Distort filters to construct the delicate flowers in her illustration, which she colored with various radial gradients. (See the *Live Effects & Styles* chapter for examples of artwork created using "live" versions of filters, called "effects.")

1 Drawing circular paths; resizing and rotating path copies. Grace drew two rough circular paths, then resized and duplicated the two paths as the first steps in creating each rose. In a new Illustrator document, double-click on the Pencil tool to bring up the Pencil Tool Preferences window. In the Tolerances section, set Fidelity to 0.5 pixels and Smoothness to 0. In the Options section, uncheck "Keep selected" and "Edit selected paths." Using the Color palette, set a Fill of None and a Stroke of Black. Draw a roughly circular path, holding the Option (Mac)/Alt (Win) key as you near the end of the circle to automatically close the path. Then draw another rough circle just within the first circle. Overlapping is okay.

Use the Selection tool or Lasso tool to select the two paths. To create a duplicate pair of circles that is smaller

than and nested within the first pair, double-click on the
Scale tool again (you should note that the previously used
reduction setting is saved) and click the Copy button.
With the last pair still selected, choose the Rotate tool and
click-drag on the image in the direction of the rotation
you want. Continue to resize/copy and rotate selected
pairs of circles until the flower form you are building is
almost filled with circles.

To vary the petal placement in the final rose, you can
continue to rotate some of the pairs after you've created
them. Then, for the center of the rose, click on the Pencil
tool and draw a few small, nested circles. Use the Lasso
tool or the Selection tool to select all the paths that make
up the rose construction, and choose Object: Group, then
deselect all paths by choosing Select: Deselect.

2 Coloring the flower using a radial gradient. To give
the final rose illustration a color effect that mimicked the
petals of real flowers, Grace created a radial gradient
color swatch and applied it to her rose construction.
Open the Swatches palette (Window: Swatches), and click
on the "Show Gradient Swatches" button. Next, click on
the "Black, White Radial" swatch. To change the colors of
the gradient, open the Color and Gradient palettes (Window: Color and Window: Gradient), click once on the
leftmost gradient slider (the beginning point of the gradient) in the Gradient palette, and adjust the color sliders
in the Color palette. Grace chose 100% M for the beginning slider. Next, click on the rightmost gradient slider
(the ending point of the gradient) and adjust the color
sliders; Grace chose 34% M and moved the K slider to
0%. To increase the amount of 100% magenta in your
filled objects, drag the left slider to the right and release it
where you like (Grace used a Location setting of 45.51%).
Finally, create your new Gradient swatch by Option
(Mac)/Alt (Win)-clicking on the "New Swatch" button in
the Swatches palette. Name your swatch (Grace chose
"Pink Flower Gradient") and click OK. Select the rose
illustration and then set the Fill to "Pink Flower

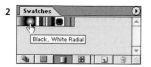

2

Choosing a radial gradient swatch to adjust

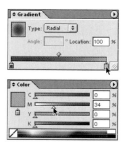

Adjusting the color settings of the beginning point gradient slider

Adjusting the color settings of the ending point gradient slider

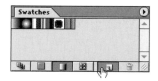

Repositioning the beginning gradient slider

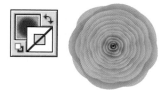

(Top) Creating a new Gradient swatch; (bottom, left and right) setting Fill to the "Pink Flower Gradient" swatch and Stroke to None

3

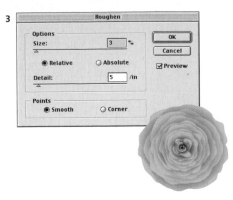

Settings for the Roughen filter; the final rose

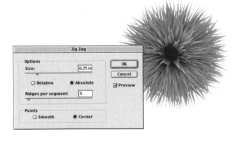

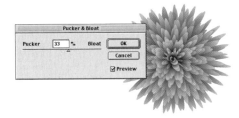

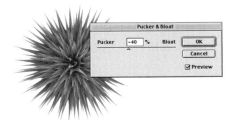

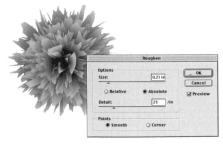

Applying additional distortion filters to copies of the final rose illustration.

Gradient" and the Stroke to None. For more on Gradients, see the *Blends, Gradients & Mesh* chapter.

3 Applying the Roughen filter. To give her rose a realistic rough-edged petal effect, Grace applied the Roughen filter to the illustration. Use the Selection tool to select the rose, then choose Filter: Distort: Roughen. In the Roughen dialog box, enable the Preview checkbox to see the effect of the filter before you apply it. In the Roughen Options, set Size to 3%, Detail to 5/in, and Points to Smooth. Click OK to apply your chosen settings.

Grace used her final rose to create some of the other flowers in her illustration by applying more Distort filters to copies of the rose (be sure to enable the Preview checkbox for each as you work). Select the entire rose and duplicate it by holding down the Option (Mac)/Alt (Win) key as you drag the rose to a new location. With the duplicate still selected, choose Filter: Distort: Pucker & Bloat, enable Preview, and set the Bloat to 33%. Click OK to apply. On another copy of the rose, apply a Pucker & Bloat setting of -40 Pucker. With a third copy of the rose selected, choose Filter: Distort: ZigZag and set Size to ".25" (inch), choose Absolute, set Ridges to 5 and choose Corner in the Points section. With a fourth copy of the rose, apply an additional roughening by choosing Filter: Distort: Roughen. Set Size to ".21 in", choose Absolute, set Detail to 23/in, and select Smooth in the Points section.

You can easily change the colors of the radial gradient for each of your flowers using the three-palette combination of Color, Swatches, and Gradient. Select the flower you want to change and modify the color and positioning of the sliders in the Gradient palette. When you change any attributes of your flower's Fill, it will disassociate from your "Pink Flower Gradient" swatch in the Swatches palette. In order to save any new gradient you create (that you may want to apply later to other flowers), Option (Mac)/Alt (Win)-click on the New Swatch button in the Swatches palette while you have your new gradient-filled object selected, name the swatch, and click OK.

Laurie Grace

Starting with the flowers she created in the previous lesson, Laurie Grace made some adjustments to the colors used for each flower. She created variations on the some the flowers by using Filter: Distort: Roughen. To add to the decorative design for the greenery, she used the Pen and Pencil tools to draw the stems and leaves. She then used Filter: Distort: Zig Zag on some of the pen lines and spirals. To create the star-shaped florals, she used the Star tool (found in Rectangle tool pop-up menu). First, she applied the zig zag filter and then she applied the twist filter. She added another copy by pasting in front and twisting and blending between both copies (see the *Blends, Gradients & Mesh* chapter for help with blends).

GRACE

Vector Photos

Pen and Eyedropper Technique

BRASHEAR

Overview: *Trace object outline using template; create contour paths then divide using Pathfinder; select and fill each object with Eyedropper tool.*

1

The original photographic composite image placed as a template

The Place dialog with the Link and Template checkboxes enabled

2

Brashear's building outline (a closed object) on the left; two open paths drawn on the right (Brashear used the open paths to divide the building outline)

Reproducing a pixel image as a vector composition is usually done by auto-tracing the image in a program like Adobe Streamline. Tracing it manually in Illustrator, however, allows greater control in organizing layers and eliminating unwanted detail. For this scene from Gothenburg, Sweden, artist Bruce Brashear traced shapes from an imported image, used the Pathfinder filters to create the detailed elements of buildings and figures, and sampled image colors with the Eyedropper tool to apply to vector objects he had created.

1 Starting a new document, placing an image, and modifying image visibility. Start your reproduction by creating a new document (File: New). Import the image you'll trace by choosing File: Place. In the Place dialog, select the image and click on the Template checkbox to automatically create a template layer for the image. If you want to change the opacity of the layer, so the image doesn't obscure the vector objects you will create, double-click the template layer's name in the Layers palette and key in a percentage in the Dim Images field. (See the *Layers* chapter for more information on creating and working with the Layers palette and with template layers.)

2 Drawing shapes of buildings and creating compound shapes with the Pathfinder palette. To reproduce the buildings in his image, Brashear drew overlapping paths and relied on the Divide Pathfinder to create adjoining objects (like the sunlit and shadowed parts of a wall) whose edges aligned perfectly (thus alleviating the need to meticulously draw adjoining edges so that there were no gaps between them). To divide a closed path with open paths, first draw a closed path (like the roof of a building) and give it a stroke but no fill. Then draw the line that divides the roof into light and shadow, extending your path beyond the closed object (the roof). Select both the closed object and the open path and click on the Divide icon in the Pathfinder palette. As a result, Illustrator divides the roof object into two closed objects (one representing the sunlit part of the roof and the other the shadowed part).

You may need to divide one closed path with another closed path. To create the building's window balconies, Brashear drew overlapping rectangles, one for the window and one for the balcony. After selecting both objects, he applied the Divide Pathfinder, which created three objects. To remove the object created where the window and balcony overlap, select both objects and Option-click/Alt-click the Add to Shape Area icon in the Shape Modes from the Pathfinder palette. Both objects are then combined into one object. (If you don't remember to Option-click/Alt-click, simply click the palette's Expand button after using the Shape Mode.)

Instead of using the Pathfinders to divide an object, consider using the Knife tool. To access the Knife tool, click and hold the mouse button down on the Scissors tool icon. Select an object and then draw a freehand line with the Knife (press the Option/Alt key *before* you drag it across an object to constrain the direction that the Knife moves). When you release the mouse button, Illustrator will automatically divide the selected object into two separate objects.

Your goal is to make as many closed objects as necessary to reproduce the different shapes you see in the placed image. The more objects you make, the more

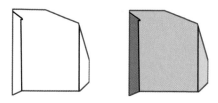

Left, result of using the Divide Pathfinder; right, the three objects (colored for demonstration)

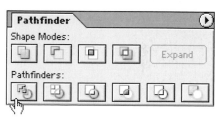

Top left, portion of template image; top right, two rectangles drawn over the template image; bottom, Pathfinder palette with Divide icon being selected

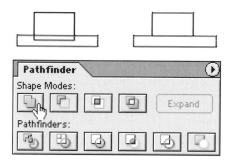

Top left, the result of using the Divide Pathfinder, the two rectangles that need to be merged; top right, the two remaining rectangles after using the Add to Shape Area Pathfinder; bottom, the Pathfinder palette with the Add to Shape Area icon selected

The Knife tool accessed by holding the cursor down on the Scissors icon in the toolbox

Left, the placed image that Brashear sampled with the Eyedropper tool; Right, objects filled with sampled colors (including a radial gradient created from sampled colors)

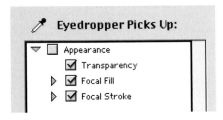

Default Eyedropper tool's options dialog; these settings require a Shift-click to sample an image

By disabling the Appearances checkbox, the Eyedropper tool can be clicked instead of Shift-clicked to sample an image

Changing the shape of a cut

Whether you cut an object with the Divide Pathfinder or with the Knife tool, the result will be two objects that share adjoining edges. While these two edges look like one line, they are two coinciding paths. To change the shape of two unfilled edges at the same time, so that they remain coincidental, be sure to select points using the Direct-selection tool before moving the points. That way you'll move points on *both* of the paths simultaneously.

closely your vector reproduction will match the detail and realism of the image.

3 Using the Eyedropper tool to fill objects with colors selected from the image. After creating his objects, Brashear filled them with colors he sampled from the placed image. First, select an object you want to fill (make sure the Fill icon in the toolbox is active so you color the fill, not the stroke). Next, find a representative color in the placed image and Shift-click on it with the Eyedropper tool to fill the object with the sampled color.

You can create a color gradient with colors that are sampled from the image. To learn about producing a gradient fill, see the *Blends, Gradients & Mesh* chapter. Because a gradient will obscure the image underneath it as you create and edit it, see the *Layers* chapter to learn how to toggle a layer or object from Preview to Outline view before you begin sampling image colors.

From Shift-click to click

Can't remember to Shift-click with the Eyedropper tool when sampling a color from an image? Just change the tool options. Double-click the Eyedropper icon in the toolbox. Then, uncheck the Appearance checkbox in the Eyedropper Picks Up portion of the Eyedropper's options dialog box. Now just click to sample a color from an image.

Two tools at once

You can toggle between a selection tool and the Eyedropper tool using the Cmd/Ctrl key. First, click on the selection tool you'll use to select objects (the Selection, Direct Selection, or Group Selection tool). Then click on the Eyedropper tool. Now, when you're using the Eyedropper and want to select an object, the Cmd/Ctrl key will toggle to the selection tool you clicked on previously. See *The Zen of Illustrator* chapter for additional keyboard shortcuts ("Fingerdances") that can save you time.

HAMANN

Brad Hamann

Brad Hamann created this travel sticker for a Honda Corporation ad campaign for one of its cars (the Passport). He placed a photo of Niagara Falls into his document as a template and then traced over it using the Pencil tool. Using the Eyedropper tool, he held the Shift key to sample color from the photo to fill his pencil-drawn shapes. To finalize his image he create a clipping mask in the shape of a circle and added type (see the *Advanced Techniques* and *Type* chapters for help with masks and type).

Intricate Patterns

Designing Complex Repeating Patterns

Advanced Technique

Overview: *Design a rough composition; define a pattern boundary and place behind all layers; use the box to generate trim marks; copy and position elements using trim marks for alignment; define and use the pattern.*

WEIMER

1

Left, arranging pattern elements into a basic design; right, adding the pattern tile rectangle behind the pattern elements

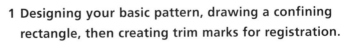

Creating trim marks based on selection of the pattern tile rectangle

Included with Illustrator are many wonderful patterns for you to use and customize, and the *User Guide* does a good job of explaining pattern-making basics. But what if you want to create a more complex pattern?

A simple trick with trim marks can help to simplify a tedious process of trial and error. With some help from author and consultant Sandee Cohen, Alan James Weimer used the following technique to design an intricate tile that prints seamlessly as a repeating pattern.

1 Designing your basic pattern, drawing a confining rectangle, then creating trim marks for registration.
Create a design that will allow for some rearrangement of artwork elements. **Hint:** *You can't make a pattern tile that contains rasterized or placed images, or unexpanded and unmasked patterns, gradients, blends, or brushes.*

Use the Rectangle tool to draw a box around the part of the image you would like to repeat. This rectangle defines the boundary of the pattern tile. Send the rectangle to the bottom of the Layers palette or to the bottom of your drawing layer (Object: Arrange: Send to Back). This boundary rectangle, which controls how your pattern repeats, must be an unstroked, unfilled, nonrotated, nonskewed object. Next, make sure that the rectangle is still selected and select Filter: Create: Trim Marks. Last, Ungroup these marks (in the next step, you'll use the trim marks to align elements that extend past the pattern tile).

2 Developing the repeating elements. If your pattern has an element that extends beyond the edge of the pattern tile, you must copy that element and place it on the opposite side of the tile. For example, if a flower blossom extends below the tile, you must place a copy of the remainder of the blossom at the top of the tile, ensuring that the whole flower is visible when the pattern repeats. To do this, select an element that overlaps above or below the tile and then Shift-select the nearest horizontal trim mark (position the cursor on an endpoint of the trim mark). While pressing the Shift-Option or Shift-Alt keys (the Option key copies the selections and the Shift key constrains dragging to vertical and horizontal directions), drag the element and trim mark upward until the cursor snaps to the endpoint of the upper horizontal trim mark. (For any element that overlaps the left or right side of the tile, select the element and the vertical trim mark and Shift-Option-drag / Shift-Alt-drag them into position.)

3 Testing and optimizing your pattern. To test your pattern, select your pattern elements (including the bounding rectangle), and either choose Edit: Define Pattern to name your pattern, or drag your selection to the Swatches palette (then double-click the swatch to customize its name). Create a new rectangle and select the pattern as your fill from the Swatches palette. Illustrator will fill the rectangle with your repeating pattern. If you redesign the pattern tile and then wish to update the pattern swatch, select your pattern elements again, but this time Option-drag/Alt-drag the elements onto the pattern swatch you made before.

Optimize your pattern for printing by deleting excess anchor points. Select pattern elements and use the Simplify command (Object: Paths: Simplify).

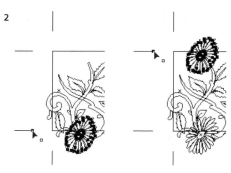

2

Left, selecting the flower blossom and horizontal trim mark; right, after dragging a copy of the flower blossom and trim mark into position at the top of the pattern tile artwork

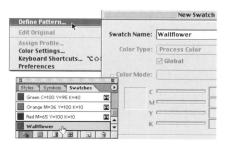

Finished artwork for the pattern tile, before turning into a pattern swatch in the Swatches palette

Making a new swatch using Edit: Define Pattern

Speeding redraw with patterns

After filling an object with a pattern, speed up screen redraw by setting View to Outline mode, or by rasterizing a copy of the object (keep the original object unfilled in case you need to use it later).

Brushes, Symbols & Hatches

4

Brushes, Symbols, & Hatches

Brushes, Symbols, and Hatches blur the boundaries between Strokes, Fills, and Patterns. Using these tools and effects, you can create strokes made of fills or patterns, fills made of strokes and other objects, and patterns that are as regular or as random as you can imagine.

Using Brushes and Symbols, you can create the equivalents of many traditional illustration tools, such as pens and brushes that drip and splatter, colored pencils and charcoals, calligraphy pens and brushes, and spray cans that can spray anything—from single color spots to complex artwork. You can use these tools with a pen and tablet, or with a mouse or trackball.

In this chapter, you will also find a strange set of hybrid filters called Hatch Effects and Photo Crosshatch (Filter: Pen & Ink). These unique filters are part spray can, part pattern fill, and part gradient blend.

These custom brushes created by Lisa Jackmore, as well as others, can be found on the Wow! CD

Find two more brushes lessons in the Transparency chapter: "Transparency 101" (top) and "Transparent Color" (directly above)

BRUSHES

There are four basic types of Brushes: Calligraphy, Art, Scatter, and Pattern. You can use Brushes for everything from mimicking traditional art tools to painting with complex patterns and textures. You can either create brush strokes with the Brush tool, or you can apply a brush stroke to a previously drawn path.

Use Calligraphy Brushes to create strokes that look like they're from a real-world calligraphy pen or brush, or to mimic felt pens. You can define a degree of variation for the size, roundness, and angle of each "nib." You can also set each of the above characteristics to be Fixed, Pressure, or Random. See the "Brush Strokes" lesson, and the "Special Brushes Supplement" later in this chapter for a complete description of the tool and its settings.

Art Brushes consist of one or more pieces of artwork that get stretched evenly along the path you create with them. You can use Art Brushes to imitate drippy, splattery ink pens, charcoal, spatter brushes, dry brushes, watercolors, and more. See the "Building Brushes" lesson, and the "Special Brushes Supplement" later in this chapter to learn how to create your own brushes.

The artwork you use to create an Art Brush can represent virtually anything: the leaves of a tree, stars, blades of grass, and so on. This flexibility is explored in the "Organic Creation" lesson, and in the "Special Brushes Supplement" later in this chapter.

Use Scatter Brushes to scatter copies of artwork along the path you create with them: flowers in a field, bees in the air, stars in the sky. The size, spacing, scatter, rotation, and colorization of the artwork can all vary along the path. See the "Organic Creation" lesson, and the "Special Brushes Supplement" later in this chapter for more examples.

Pattern Brushes are related to the Patterns feature in Illustrator. You can use Pattern Brushes to paint patterns along a path. To use a Pattern Brush, you first define the tiles that will make up your pattern. For example, you can create railroad symbols on a map, multicolored dashed lines, chain links, or grass. These patterns are defined by up to five types of tiles—side, outer corner, inner corner, start, and end—that you create, and one of three methods of fitting them together (Stretch to Fit, Add Space to Fit, and Approximate Path). See the "Pattern Brushes," "Map Techniques," and "Organic Creation" lessons for more on how to create Pattern Brushes.

In addition to the Brushes examples in this chapter, you'll find numerous step-by-step lessons and Galleries involving Brushes throughout the book. In particular, see the "Brushed Type" lesson in the *Type* chapter, and the "Scratchboard Art" lesson in the *Live Effects & Styles* chapter.

Artwork for Creating Brushes

Art, Scatter, and Pattern Brushes can only be made from simple lines and fills, and groups of objects created from them. Gradients, live effects, raster art, and other more complex artwork cannot be used.

Closing a brush path

To close a path using the Brush tool, hold down the Option (Mac)/ Alt (Win) key *after* you begin creating the path, then let go of the mouse button just before you're ready to close the path. Border brushes work best on closed paths.

Constraining a brush

You can't use the Shift key to constrain a Brush tool to draw a straight path, so draw the path first with the Pen tool, *then* select the desired brush in the Brushes palette.—*Robin AF Olson*

Naming Brushes

If you create more than just a few brushes, incorporate the more important brush characteristics into the names of your brushes. This is especially helpful with calligraphy brushes—otherwise you can easily end up with the same icon for different brushes in the palette. Use the List View to group and show the brush names.

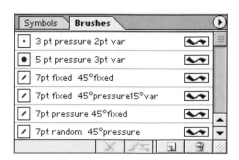

Including brush characteristics in brush name, and using the List View to make brushes easier to find

Brushes to layers

Scatter Brush artwork can be easily separated onto individual layers for use in animation. For details about distributing artwork to layers, see the "Release to Layers" section in the *Web & Animation* chapter introduction.

Scaling brushes

To scale artwork that contains paths with applied brushes:

- Expand the brushed path first (Object: Expand Appearance), then scale the artwork.
- Scale the artwork after placing it into a page layout program.

Note: *When you apply a scale transformation to brushed paths, enabling Scale Strokes & Effects (Edit: Preferences: General) will also scale the brush art.*

More about brushes

- Pasting a path that contains brushes will add them to the Brushes palette.
- Convert an applied brush into editable artwork by selecting the path and choosing Object: Expand Appearance.
- Drag a brush out of the Brushes palette to edit the brush art.
- To create a brush from an applied brush path, blend, gradient, or gradient mesh, expand it first (Object: Expand).

Working with Brushes

Double-click the Paintbrush tool to set application-level preferences for all brushes. When using Fidelity and Smoothness, lower numbers are more accurate, and higher numbers are smoother. Check the "Fill new brush strokes" option if you want the brush path to take on the fill color in addition to the stroke color. When Keep Selected is enabled, the last path drawn stays selected, and drawing a new path close to the selected path will redraw that path. Disabling Keep Selected deselects the last-drawn path. This allows you to draw paths near each other, instead of redrawing the last-drawn path. If left enabled, the Edit Selected Paths slider determines how close you have to be in order to redraw the selected path, as opposed to drawing a new path. The lower the number, the closer you have to be to the selected path to redraw it.

To edit a brush: double-click it in the Brushes palette to change Brush options, or drag it out of the Brushes palette to edit the brush and then drag the new art into the Brushes palette. To replace a brush, press the Option (Mac)/Alt (Win) key and drag the new brush over the original brush slot in the Brushes palette. Then in the dialog, choose either to replace all instances of the applied brush already used in the document with the newly created brush, or to create a new brush in the palette.

There are four colorization methods (None, Tints, Tints and Shades, and Hue Shift) you can use with Brushes. None uses the colors of the brush as they were defined and how they appear in the Brushes palette. The Tints method causes the brush to use the current stroke color, allowing you to create any color brush you like, regardless of the color of the brush depicted in the Brushes palette. Click on the Tips button in the Art Brush Options dialog box for detailed explanations and examples of how all four color modes work.

When drawing with a pressure-sensitive stylus (pen) and tablet, the Calligraphy allows you to vary the stroke thickness according to the pressure you apply to the tablet. For Scatter Brushes there are settings to vary the size, spacing, and scatter of the brush art.

SYMBOLS

Symbols consist of artwork that you create and store in the Symbols palette. From this palette, you then apply one or more copies of the symbols (called *instances*) into your artwork.

Artwork for Creating Symbols

Symbols can be made from almost any art you create in Illustrator. The only exceptions are a few kinds of complex groups (such as groups of graphs) and placed art, which has to be embedded (not linked).

Working with Symbols

There are eight Symbolism tools. Use the Symbol Sprayer tool to spray selected symbols onto your document. A group of symbols sprayed onto your document is called a *symbol instance set* and is surrounded by a bounding box (you cannot select individual instances inside a set with any of the selection tools). Then use the Symbol Shifter, Scruncher, Sizer, Spinner, Stainer, Screener, or Styler tools to modify symbols in the symbol instance set.

To add symbols to an existing instance set, select the instance set. Then, from the Symbols palette, select the symbol to be added—which can be the same as or different from the symbols already present in the instance set—and spray. Additionally, if you are using the default Average mode, your new symbol instances can inherit attributes (size, rotation, transparency, style) from nearby symbols in the same instance set. Use ⌘-click (Mac) or CTRL-click (Win) to add or delete symbols to your current symbol selection in the Symbols palette. See the Adobe User Guide for details about the Average versus User Defined modes.

Similarly, when you want to add or modify symbol instances, be sure you have both the symbol instance set and the corresponding symbol(s) in the

Symbols and the Web

Because Illustrator Symbols are fully supported in SWF and SVG, using multiple instances of symbols in your document will result in file size savings on the Web.

Symbols to layers

Symbol artwork can be easily separated onto individual layers for use in animations. Select and target the Symbol artwork layer, then choose Release to Layers (Sequence) from the Layers palette pop-up menu. For more see "Release to Layers" in the *Web & Animation* chapter introduction.

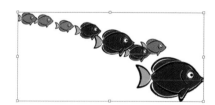

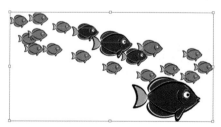

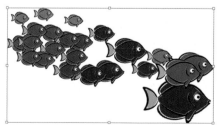

Top, symbols sprayed, sized, and stained.
Middle, symbols added using User Defined mode; new symbols are all same color and size.
Bottom, symbols added using Average mode; new symbols inherit average color and size from symbols nearby (as defined by the brush radius)

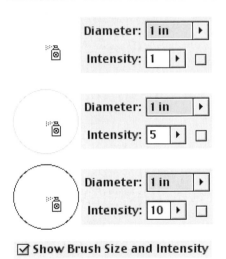

☑ **Show Brush Size and Intensity**

When Show Brush Size and Intensity is enabled, the intensity of the Symbolism tool is indicated by the shade of gray of the brush size circle

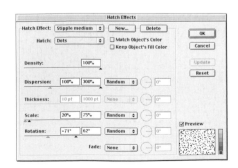

The Hatch Effects dialog box

Symbols palette selected. If you don't, the Symbolism tools can easily appear to be broken.

You can't remove the changes you make using the Symbolism tools, so make sure to save incremental changes as you work! Details on how to create and modify symbols are covered in the "Symbol Basics" lesson later in this chapter.

SYMBOLS VS. SCATTER BRUSHES

In general, Symbols are much more flexible than Scatter Brushes. Symbols can be made from almost anything you can create using Illustrator, whereas brushes are limited to simple lines and fills.

Symbols are also more flexible regarding the types of changes you can make to them after they are applied. Using the Symbolism tools, you can change many attributes (such as size, rotation, and spacing) to individual symbols in an instance set. Using Scatter Brushes attributes will be applied to the whole set—you cannot change attributes for single objects in a set.

With Symbols, you can redefine the original artwork stored in the Symbols palette and have all the instances on the Artboard reflect those changes. Using Scatter Brushes, the original artwork in the Brushes palette cannot be changed.

Using Symbols you can remove individual instances from a symbolism instance set. You cannot delete Scatter Brush objects without first expanding the artwork.

Unlike other types of vector artwork, Symbols are not affected by the Scale Strokes & Effects preference—this option is always enabled for Symbols. Scatter Brush artwork responds in its own unique way, see *Wow! CD*.

PEN & INK: HATCH EFFECTS

Hatch Effects is the strangest hybrid of tools and methods in Illustrator, for which there is no traditional art tool counterpart. Starting with a simple art object, called a Hatch, you can create a wide range of textures, fills, and patterns. After you have experimented with its awkward control panel interface for a while, you will find that you can create nearly any pattern or texture—from regular to random and anything in between. The unique range and control of Hatch Effects will become apparent as you experiment with it.

One of the most powerful features of this tool is the ability to have the artwork change in size along a user-specified axis. This feature can be used to create a variety of perspective and depth effects, from waves on an ocean to scales on the body of a fish.

But hatch and texture marks are just the beginning. The artwork you use to create hatches can represent virtually anything: the leaves of fall, stars and comets, snowflakes, or Christmas ornaments. When hatch artwork is combined with Hatch Effects' unique coloring methods, many striking effects are possible.

See the "Organic Creation" lesson, the Gallery images by Diane Hinze Kanzler & Sandee Cohen, Kevin Barack, and Victor von Salza later in this chapter, and the Gallery by Sandra Alves in the *Transparency & Appearances* chapter for more Hatch Effects examples.

Artwork for Creating Hatches

Hatches can only be made from simple lines and fills. Groups and compound paths get torn apart when a hatch is applied, but don't let that stop you from experimenting. You may find useful textural opportunities in the unexpected results.

Working with Hatch Effects

Despite the awkward interface, using Hatch Effects is really very straightforward. Select the artwork you want to apply the hatch to and choose Filter: Pen and Ink: Hatch Effect. In the Hatch Effect dialog, select the hatch object you want to apply, and set the options by using the controls provided or by selecting from the list of saved settings in the pull-down menu. Then check the Preview, and click OK. If you don't like the resulting effect, immediately Undo and try again.

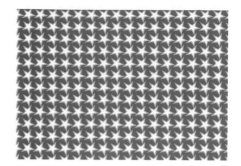

Using Hatch Effects you can create textures as regular as any pattern fill to…

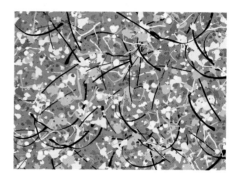

as random as paint on a Jackson Pollock canvas

Hatches changing scale and fading to white from bottom to top

A water effect created by varying the Scale

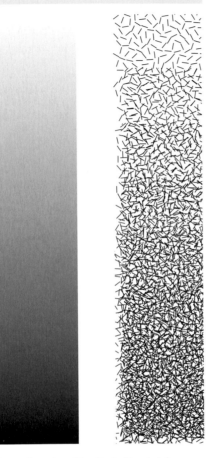

Photo Crosshatch settings

Since there is no way to save settings inside the program, use screen shots to capture your Photo Crosshatch settings.

Grayscale and resulting Photo Crosshatch created using the settings shown below.

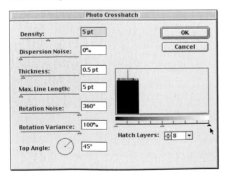

Use grayscale and settings like those shown above as a starting point for your explorations

For a complete description of the Hatch Effects interface, and more about Hatch Effects, see Victor von Salza's "Pen & Ink Hatch Effects.pdf" on the *Wow! CD.*

PEN & INK: PHOTO CROSSHATCH

Photo Crosshatch (Filter: Pen and Ink: Photo Crosshatch) converts rasterized artwork into vectors that simulate grayscale Hatch Effects with black lines. To crosshatch vector art, make a copy and rasterize it first, using Object: Rasterize.

Artwork for Creating Photo Crosshatches

Straight lines are the only kind of artwork allowed by Illustrator. Specify the length and thickness of the lines in the Crosshatch Filter dialog. You may find it easier to understand and predict how Photo Crosshatch works by first changing your original art to grayscale.

Working with Photo Crosshatch

The are no hard and fast rules for using Photo Crosshatch, and you cannot save settings (see Tip at left). Start your Photo Crosshatch explorations by creating a white to black gradient and use the settings shown in the sidebar as a starting point. From there, experiment with each control, one at a time, until you get a feel for what each is doing. Use the histogram sliders to move the shadow and highlight points, and to adjust the density of hatches in specific tonal regions of your image. To get more detail from the filter, start with a larger sized image or lower the Density setting—but remember, the more detail, the more RAM you'll need. Since there are so many adjustments to choose from, and no Preview, much experimentation and heavy use of Undo may be required to find the correct settings in each particular case.

You can find out more about using Photo Crosshatch in the Gallery images by Adam Z Lein on the next page, and in the Gallery images by Daniel Giordan in the *Web & Animation* chapter.

Adam Z Lein

Artist Adam Z Lein used Illustrator's Photo Crosshatch filter (Filter: Pen and Ink: Photo Crosshatch) to convert this grayscale TIFF image to a crosshatched illustration composed of black strokes at a "Max. Line Length" of 24 pt.

Adam Z Lein

After applying the Photo Crosshatch filter in Illustrator, Adam Z Lein rasterized the hatches by placing them in Photoshop and combining them with two copies of the original photo (see the *Illustrator & Other Programs* chapter for more on rasterizing Illustrator artwork).

Ink Brush Strokes

Making Naturalistic Pen and Ink Drawings

Overview: *Adjust the Paintbrush Tool settings; customize a Calligraphic Brush; trace or draw your composition; experiment by using other brushes to stroke the paths.*

1

The digital sketch saved as TIFF and placed as an Illustrator template

---

Maintaining your pressure

Only brush strokes *initially* drawn with pressure-sensitive settings can take advantage of pressure-sensitivity. Also be aware that re-applying a brush after trying another may alter the stroke shape.

It's easy to create spontaneous painterly and calligraphic marks in Illustrator—perhaps easier than in any other digital medium. After creating highly variable, responsive strokes (using a graphics tablet and a pressure-sensitive penlike stylus), you can then edit those strokes as *paths,* or experiment by applying different brushes to the existing paths. This portrait of Devon Rose Jacoby was drawn using one custom Calligraphy Brush and a pressure-sensitive Wacom tablet.

1 If you are working from a source, prepare your template. Although you can draw directly into the application, if you want to trace a sketch or a scan you'll need to prepare an image to use as a template. For her template image, Steuer scanned a red Conté crayon sketch and saved it as TIFF format, then placed the TIFF as a template in Illustrator. To place a TIFF image as a template, choose File: Place, then locate your TIFF file via the Place dialog box, enable the Template checkbox, then click the Place button. Toggle between hiding and showing the template with ⌘-Shift-W (Mac)/Ctrl-Shift-W (Win), or by clicking in the visibility column in the Layers palette (the visibility icon for a template layer is a tiny triangle, circle, and square rather than the normal Eye icon).

2 Setting your Paintbrush tool preferences and customizing a calligraphy brush. In order to sketch freely and with accurate detail, you'll need to adjust the default Paintbrush tool settings. Double-click the Paintbrush tool in the Tools palette to open Paintbrush Tool Preferences. Drag the Fidelity and Smoothness sliders all the way to the left and disable the "Fill new brush strokes" and "Keep Selected" options.

To create a custom brush, select a Calligraphic brush (one of the first brushes in the default Brushes palette). Then click the New Brush icon at the bottom of the palette and click OK to New Calligraphic Brush. Experiment with various settings, name your brush and click OK. For this portrait, Steuer chose the settings of: Angle 60°, Random,180°; Roundness 60%, Pressure, 40%; Diameter 6 pt, Pressure, 6 pt. If you don't have a pressure-sensitive tablet, try Random as a setting for the three Brush Options, since Pressure won't have any effect. The Paintbrush uses your current stroke color—if there isn't a stroke color, it will use the previous stroke color or the fill color. Now draw. If you don't like a mark: 1) choose Undo to remove the mark, or 2) use the Direct-selection tool to edit the path, or 3) select the path and try redrawing it using the Paintbrush (to hide or show selection outlines, choose View: Hide/Show Edges). To edit a brush, double-click it in the Brushes palette, or, drag it to the New Brush icon to duplicate it, then edit the copy.

3 Experimenting with your image. First, save any versions of your image that you are pleased with. Now try applying different brushes to specific strokes and to the entire image. To access more Adobe-made Calligraphic Brushes, choose Window: Brush Libraries: Calligraphic (at right, see two of Adobe's brushes applied to the same strokes).

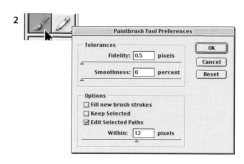

Customizing the Paintbrush Tool Preferences

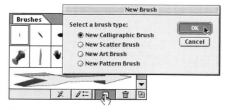

Creating a new Calligraphic Brush

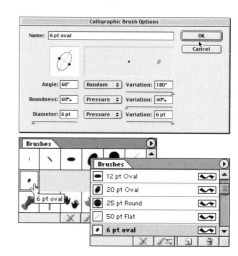

Angle, Roundness, and Diameter can be set to respond to pressure, to vary randomly or to remain fixed; the new brush in the Brushes palette viewed with Tool Tips and in List View

Strokes made with Steuer's customized 6 pt. oval brush (left); applying Adobe's default 3 pt. Oval brush (center), then the 1 pt. Oval brush

STEUER

Sharon Steuer

Using the same Calligraphic Brush as in her preceding lesson, Sharon Steuer drew the seashells in black. On layers below (for help see the *Layers* chapter), she created a background gradient (see the *Blends, Gradient & Mesh* chapter), and then used the Pencil tool to draw enclosed areas of flat color (shown alone below right). On a layer above, she drew a few details in color with the Calligraphic Brush. To create the textured background, she made two copies of the gradient layer, then transformed the first gradient copy into a Gradient Mesh (Object: Expand: Gradient Mesh) so she could select a few interior points and add highlights (see the *Blends, Gradient & Mesh* chapter for more details about mesh). To the other gradient

copy, Steuer applied Filter: Pen and Ink: Hatch Effects, then chose "Stipple light" and "Match Object's Color" (for more on Hatches see the *Advanced Techniques* chapter). She applied this effect to a copy of the shadows as well.

JACKMORE

Lisa Jackmore

Lisa Jackmore often begins her Illustrator paintings by making smaller versions of the default Calligraphic Brushes. Although she often prefers more rounded brushes and draws in black for the initial sketch, sometimes she just makes a variety of brushes, then "doodles until the shape of a line inspires" her. Occasionally Jackmore will even save a doodle and figure out later how to incorporate it into the image.

She constructs her illustration, then colors the brush strokes toward the end of the project. To make a custom charcoal Art Brush, Jackmore used Adobe Streamline to turn a scanned charcoal mark into an Illustrator object. Jackmore opened the object in Illustrator and dragged it into the Brushes palette, then used the new brush to create the marks under the notepaper and in the framed painting.

Chapter 4 *Brushes, Symbols & Hatches*   **125**

ALSPACH

Jen Alspach

Jen Alspach started with a digital photograph of her cat Static, which she placed into a template layer (see the *Layers* chapter). In a new layer above, she traced over the photo, using brushes, with a Wacom "Pen Partner" 4" x 5" tablet. Alspach used darker, heavier brushes to draw the basic outline and the important interior lines like the eyes, ears, and neck (all attributes set to Pressure with a

2–pt Diameter and a 2-pt variation). In another pressure-sensitive brush, she set a Fixed Angle and Roundness (diameter of 6-pt), while in a third brush she set all attributes to Random. Using the Wacom tablet with the pressure-sensitive Calligraphic Brushes, she was able to use very light hand pressure to draw the fine lines around the eyes and the whiskers.

PAPCIAK-ROSE

Ellen Papciak-Rose / In The Studio

In this magazine illustration for *Newsweek International*, Ellen Papciak-Rose used a scratchboard technique to capture the hip-hop feel of Kwaito music, in South Africa. She began by creating several variations of a default charcoal brush found in the Sample Brush Library (Window: Brush Libraries: Artistic Sample). After importing the "Charcoal Rough" brush into the Brushes palette, Papciak-Rose made a copy of the brush by dragging it to the new brush icon. Papciak-Rose double-clicked on the brush copy and opened the Art Brush

Options dialog box, where she altered the new brush by clicking on the direction arrows and entering a percentage to change the width. She then painted the strokes of the drawn objects using various custom-built rough charcoal brushes. Papciak-Rose drew all the letters in her illustration with the Pen tool and applied Styles made of multiple brush strokes. (See the "Scratchboard Art" lesson in the *Live Effects & Styles* chapter for more details about scratch-board technique.)

Preparing Art

Adding Brushes to Existing Artwork

COHEN (from Dynamic Graphics/Designer's Club clip art)

Overview: *Modify existing artwork; change closed paths to open paths; apply Art Brushes to modified artwork.*

1

Red outlines indicate the type of closed paths to change in the original clip art

2

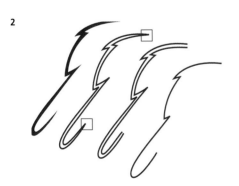

Use the Scissors tool to cut a closed path into two paths, swap the fill and stroke, then delete one path

Sandee Cohen, a vector expert and *Illustrator Wow!* consultant, enjoys working with Illustrator's brushes to modify existing art. This technique shows how Cohen changed ordinary clip art into more sophisticated artwork. Her technique can be used to give both commercial clip art, and any of your own existing artwork, a bit more pizzaz.

1 Examine the clip art shapes. First, Cohen examines the artwork in the Outline mode in order to plot her steps. She typically ignores open paths because they take brush strokes very well. She also does not worry about closed paths if they have large areas. She is most interested in finding thin closed paths that mimic the look of brush strokes. These paths are often found in artwork created by previous versions of Illustrator.

2 Split closed paths and delete segments. So they will accept the brush strokes, Cohen splits thin closed paths with the Scissors tool. She swaps the fill and stroke colors of selected paths by pressing Shift-X to make it easier to see each path. (You can also change from Preview to Outline View to see paths without fills.) After cutting a path, she deletes one of the cut paths, usually the smaller one.

3 Apply natural-looking brush strokes to simplified paths. Once the artwork is cleaned up, the simplified paths are ready to have brushes applied to them. Many different types of looks can be created without moving or deleting any more of the paths in the illustration. Cohen applies her choice of brushes to the simplified, open paths. Among Cohen's favorite brushes is Charcoal, one of the natural-looking brushes found in Illustrator's default set. She also uses brushes found in the Artistic library under Window: Brush Libraries: Artistic Sample.

4 Apply brushes to large closed paths. In most cases, Cohen leaves large, closed paths filled with solid color. Some of the large, closed paths could be made to look more organic by applying Art brushes to their strokes. For instance, Cohen applies natural-media brushes, such as Chalk Scribbler and Fire Ash to the large, closed shapes. Warning: These natural brush forms contain hundreds of points in each brush stroke. While there may be few points in each path, use of these brushes can add dramatically to the file size—a consideration if your computer is slow, or if you need a small file size for storage or to transfer by email.

5 Experiment with Calligraphic brushes. Cohen also uses Calligraphic brushes set to thin roundness and various angles to replicate the feeling of the original artwork. She creates several Calligraphic brushes, each set at a different angle, to apply various appearances to the paths. Cohen accesses the Brush Options in the Brushes palette pop-up menu and chooses the Random setting for the Angle, Roundness, and Diameter options. She then experiments with the numeric settings of each option.

If you alternate between applying a Calligraphic brush with Random settings and another brush, each time you return to the randomized Calligraphic brush the results will be different. Cohen often applies the same brush several times to the same object until she achieves the appearance she likes.

Once the artwork has been cleaned up, you are ready to apply brushes

3

The Charcoal brush (shown in black) gives the art more of a hand-rendered appearance

4

The Chalk Scribbler (top left) and Fire Ash (bottom right) brushes applied to large closed shapes create a more organic look

5

A Calligraphic brush set to an angle of 90 degrees, roundness of 10%, and diameter of 9 points brings back the look of the original art

Pattern Brushes

Creating Details with the Pattern Brush

Overview: *Create interlocking chain links by drawing and cutting duplicate curve sections; select the link artwork and create a new Pattern brush; draw a path and paint it with the new brush.*

At the left, the ring drawn with the Ellipse tool and given a thick stroke; in the middle, the ellipse cut into four curve sections shown in Outline view (sections are separated to show them better); on the right, the four curve sections shown in Outline view, after using the Object: Path: Outline Stroke command

On the left, the two left curve sections copied and pasted, and colors changed to light brown in the middle; on the right, the two sections are slid to the right to form the right half link

*On the left, the half-link selected and reflected using the Reflect tool (the **X** in the middle of the guide ellipse served as the axis); on the right, both half-links in position*

One look at a Bert Monroy image and you will immediately recognize the intricacy and rich realism of his style of illustration. When crafting an image like the Rendez-vous Cafe (see the Gallery image that follows for the complete image), Monroy travels between Illustrator and Photoshop, stopping long enough in Illustrator to construct the intricate shapes and details that turn his scenes into slices of life in Photoshop. The easel chain is one such detail that Monroy created in Illustrator using a custom-made Pattern brush.

1 Drawing, cutting, copying, and reflecting curves. To build a chain-link Pattern brush, Monroy first created one link that was interconnected with half-links on either side (the half-links would connect with other half-links to form the chain once the Pattern brush was applied to a path). To create the pattern unit with the Ellipse tool, begin the center link by drawing an ellipse with a thick stroke. Copy the ellipse, Paste in Back; then turn the ellipse into a guide (View: Guides: Make Guides). You'll use this guide later when making the half-links. Now select the original ellipse and use the Scissors tool to cut the ellipse near each of the four control points (choose

View: Outline to better see the points). Shift-select the four curved paths with the Direct-selection tool and select Object: Path: Outline Stroke. Illustrator automatically constructs four closed-curve objects.

To make the right half-link, select the left two curve objects and duplicate them to make the right half-link by dragging the two objects to the right while holding down the Opt/Alt key; then change the color of the copies. For the left half-link, select the two curves you just dragged and colored, choose the Reflect tool, hold down the Opt/Alt key and click in the center of the ellipse guide (the center point is an **X**). In the pop-up dialog box, click the vertical axis button and click Copy to create a mirror-image of the right half-link for the left half-link. **Note:** *The center link must be aligned exactly in-between the two half-links, so that the half-links join when applied to a path as a Pattern brush.*

2 Finishing the link. The two adjoining half-links should look like they're entwined with the link. Monroy selected the top objects of both the left and right half-links and moved them behind the center link (Object: Arrange: Send to Back). You can create a different look by selecting the top of the left half-link, and the bottom of the right half-link, then move these two curve objects to the back.

3 Making and using a Pattern brush. To make the brush, select the artwork and drag it into the Brushes palette. Choose New Pattern Brush in the pop-up dialog box; in the next dialog box, name the brush and click OK (leave the default settings as you find them). You can now apply the chain pattern to a path by selecting the path and clicking on the brush in the Brushes palette.

Depending on the size of your original links artwork, you may need to reduce the size of the brush artwork to fit the path better. You can do this by reducing the original artwork with the Scale tool and making a new brush, or by double-clicking the brush in the Brushes palette and editing the value in the Scale field of the dialog box.

2

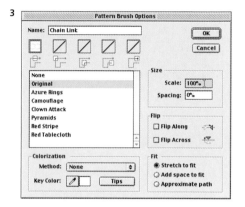

Finished link artwork; at the left, the links as Monroy created them; at the right, an alternative version of the interconnected links

3

The Pattern Brush Options dialog box showing default settings

Original path on top; below, path painted with Chain Link Pattern brush

Drop Shadows

Even if your artwork is destined for Photoshop, you can make a drop shadow for it in Illustrator. Select the artwork, then choose Effect: Stylize: Drop Shadow. Copy the object (which automatically copies all of its appearances) and paste in Photoshop (Edit: Paste: Paste as Pixels). (See *Transparency & Appearances* for more on appearances, and *Illustrator & Other Programs* for more on using Photoshop with Illustrator.)

MONROY

© Bert Monroy 1999

Bert Monroy

Artist Bert Monroy incorporates elements he draws in Illustrator into the detailed realism he paints in Photoshop. In this cafe scene, Monroy used Illustrator Pattern brushes for the sign post and the easel chain. For the leaves in the foreground, Monroy first drew one leaf object and made it into a Scatter brush (he used Random settings for the brush parameters). He brought resulting foliage into Photoshop where he detailed it further. (See the *Illustrator & Other Programs* chapter to learn more techniques for using Illustrator with Photoshop.)

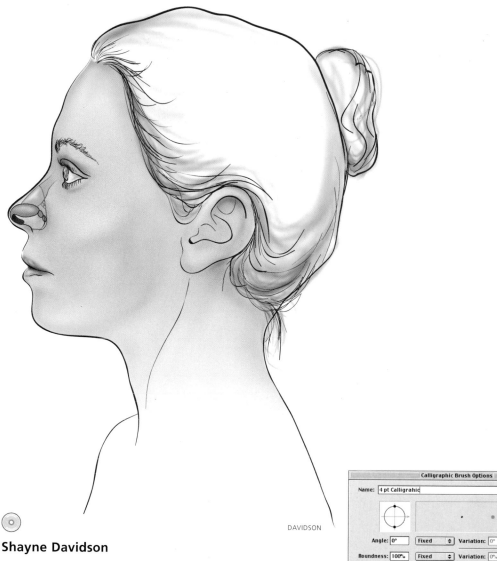

DAVIDSON

Shayne Davidson

Shayne Davidson began this medical illustration by airbrushing the soft background colors in Photoshop. After placing the image in Illustrator, she used custom-made Calligraphic brushes to draw the outlines and details. To create a brush, she opened the Brushes palette, selected New Brush from the palette's menu and picked New Calligraphic Brush from the New Brush dialog. This brought up the Calligraphic Brush Options dialog, where she left the brush Angle at 0° (Fixed), Roundness at 100% (Fixed), and specified a Diameter (she used diameters between 0.8 and 4 points). She also set Diameter to Pressure, and Variation to the same point size as the Diameter (this establishes the maximum width of the stroke on either side of the path), and clicked OK. She repeated this process to create brushes with different diameters.

Chapter 4 *Brushes, Symbols & Hatches* **133**

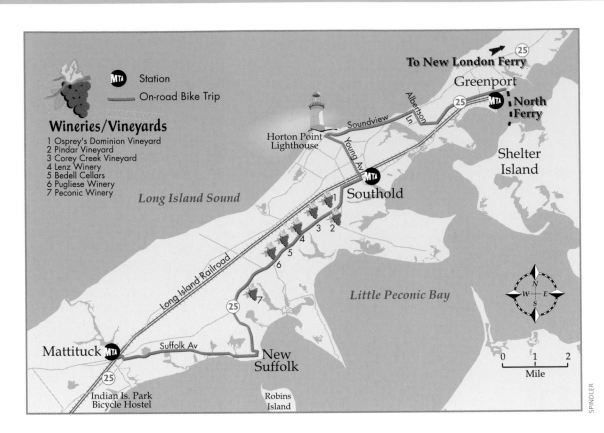

Steve Spindler / Bike Maps

When cartographer Steve Spindler begins using a new version of Illustrator, he quickly adopts its new features to his method of making maps. In this bike map of part of Long Island, New York, Spindler created Art brushes for the bike route and railroad track. He placed scanned photographs on a template layer to draw the vineyard grapes and lighthouse. For the grapes symbol, he used the Tapered Stroke brush for the outlines of the leaves and the Marker brush to draw the stems (both brushes are found on the *Wow! CD*, in Illustrator Extras: Brush Libraries: Artistic: Ink). To create a Scatter

brush from this symbol, Spindler first expanded the artwork (because Illustrator cannot build a brush from artwork that already contains a brush), then dragged the artwork into the Brushes palette. For the compass rose symbol, Spindler imported a custom brush library (Window: Brush Libraries: Other Libraries) containing a collection of his own cartographic Art and Scatter brushes.

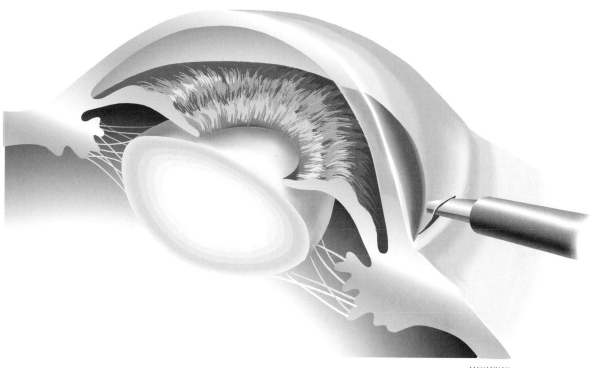

MAHANNAH

Jacqueline Mahannah

Drawing the delicate structure of the iris of the human eye to illustrate glaucoma surgery, artist Jacqueline Mahannah combined Illustrator brushes with the pressure-sensitivity of a Wacom tablet. For the iris structure, Mahannah used the Marker brush from the Ink Brushes library (found on the Adobe Illustrator Application CD, in Illustrator Extras: Brush Libraries: Artistic). She adjusted the width setting of this brush by double-clicking the brush in the palette, then editing the Width field in the Art Brush Options dialog. Mahannah chose a light blue color for the brush and drew the inner-most strokes. Then she chose a darker color and drew the next set of strokes, letting them overlap the first strokes. She continued working outward, sometimes overlapping dark brush strokes with lighter ones to suggest highlights and texture.

Building Brushes

Building Brushes for Lettering

Overview: *Draw and shape letterforms; create and vectorize brush strokes in Photoshop; bring brush paths into Illustrator and edit them; add brushes to the Brushes palette; adjust color and layering, and apply Effects and transparency.*

DONALDSON

1

Hand-drawn letterform paths using Pen and Pencil tools

Donaldson hand-drew two different sets of letterforms and positioned them on two different layers; each was then painted with a different brush (see Step 4 at right)

2

Brush stroke created in Photoshop using the Paintbrush tool; below, brush stroke edited with Eraser and Airbrush tools

Timothy Donaldson's style of abstract calligraphy challenges the lettering artist to look beyond Illustrator's default brushes (like the brushes sets found under Window: Brush Libraries) to paint programs like Photoshop and Painter, where he develops brush strokes with the look of traditional art tools.

1 Drawing, smoothing and shaping letterform paths. Donaldson began the composition "abcxyz" by drawing letterform paths with the Pen and Pencil tools, going back over the paths with the Pencil to smooth them. (Use the Pencil Tool Preferences menu's Smoothness Tolerance to control how the Pencil will simplify and smooth a line you've drawn.) Once you draw the letterforms, refine them further with the Shear and Scale tools until you are satisfied with their shapes.

2 Creating brush strokes in a paint program. To build a custom brush, open any paint program that offers paintbrushes (Donaldson works in Painter and Photoshop). Start a new file in the paint program, specifying a resolution of 72 ppi and a transparent background. Set the foreground and background colors to black and white (this will make it easier when vectorizing the brush stroke in the paint program later). Next, select the Paint brush tool and edit the brush settings or preferences (opacity, blending mode, textures, pressure-sensitivity and others). (See the *Photoshop 6 Wow! Book* by Linnea Dayton and Jack Davis, or the *Painter 7 Wow! Book* by Cher Threinen-Pendarvis for more about painting with brushes.)

Now you're ready to paint a brush stroke. Hold down the Shift key (to constrain the cursor to straight movements) and make a stroke with the brush tool. Modify the look of the brush stroke with the eraser or other painting tools, or with filters (avoid filters that blur or otherwise antialias the brush stroke edge). If your paint program can export vector paths as an EPS or Illustrator file, then select the pixels of the brush stroke with the Magic Wand, or other selection tool, and convert the pixels to paths. Otherwise, save the image as a TIFF.

3 Opening, then editing brush strokes in Illustrator.
Bring your brush stroke into Illustrator by opening the EPS or placing the TIFF image. Use Illustrator's Auto Trace tool to automatically vectorize the raster brush stroke, or manually trace it using the Pen and Pencil tools. You can reshape the brush artwork using the selection tools or the Pencil tool. (See *Drawing & Coloring* for more on modifying paths.) Convert your brush stroke artwork into an Illustrator brush by selecting the artwork and dragging it into the Brushes palette. Select New Art Brush from the New Brush dialog and set various brush parameters in the Art Brush Options dialog box.

4 Applying different brushes. Donaldson created multiple brushed letterforms by duplicating the layer with the paths (drag the layer to the New Layer icon in the Layers palette). For each layer with letterforms, select the paths and click on a custom brush in the Brushes palette. Alter the look of your composition by changing colors or brushes, adjusting the stacking order of layers in the Layers palette, or applying Effects to modify transparency and blending (see *Transparency, & Appearances* and *Live Effects & Styles* for more on transparency and Effects).

3

Top, work path based on selection made in Photoshop before being saved as an Illustrator file; bottom, path in Illustrator after editing and being filled with black

4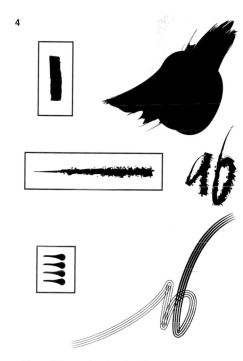

Three different brushes (outlined here in red) applied to the hand-drawn letterforms "ab"

In the background, Feather Effect applied to gray letterforms; in the middle, an 80% transparency and Multiply blending mode assigned to greenish letterforms; in foreground, red letters given a Screen blending mode with 65% transparency

Map Techniques
Simplifying the Creation of Complex Images

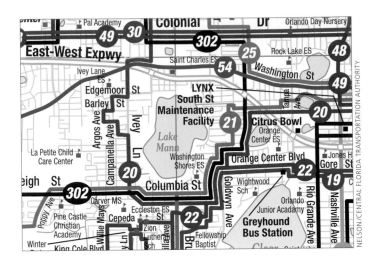

Advanced Techniques

Overview: *Use Simplify to reduce points in paths; create and select Scatter Brushes; create multicolored dashes, tapered lines and self-adjusting scales; import brushes from another document.*

1

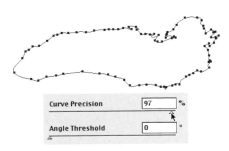

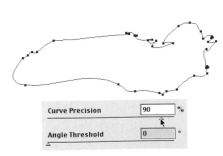

Top, the original lake shape, created from imported geographical data (195 points); middle, using Simplify reduces the lake to 89 points without noticeable distortion of shape; bottom, Simplify reduces the lake to 38 points but with some distortion of shape

From line simplification to brushes that solve many problems, Illustrator now offers professional illustrators and mapmakers many tools and features that help streamline the creation and updating of complex images. In creating a city bus map for Orlando, Florida, cartographer David Nelson was able to take advantage of dozens of recently added Illustrator features.

1 Simplifying paths. When you trace detailed lines such as rivers and roads, or bring clip-art or geographical data into Illustrator, you will likely have paths with too many points. To remove unnecessary points while preserving an accurate path shape, first select a line and choose Object: Path: Simplify. In the Simplify dialog, click to enable Preview and use the Curve Precision control to reduce points (a lower percentage results in fewer points but more distortion to the shape of the path). Use the Angle Threshold setting to make minute changes to some of the curves in the path by smoothing the curve at corner points with angles larger than those specified in the setting.

2 Making, placing and selecting Scatter brush "symbols." Scatter brushes are an ideal way to help manage map symbols. Create symbols for such features as schools, airports, parks, museums, golf courses, and the like. When you've finished making a symbol, drag it into the Brushes palette. In the New Brush dialog, choose New Scatter Brush, then in the Scatter Brush Options dialog, specify 0% Fixed in the Scatter field and select None for the Colorization Method. To place symbols on the map, click once with the Pen tool and select a Scatter brush you made.

While Illustrator doesn't provide a way for you to select all strokes made with a particular Scatter brush, it can locate and select objects by color, so you can "cheat." Simply set a unique color as a Stroke or Fill, then click with the Pen tool to create the points to which you'll apply a particular Scatter brush. If you need to select all of the points you painted with a brush, click on a brush stroke on the map and choose Select: Same: Fill Color. Illustrator will select all brushes whose points have the same Fill or Stroke color as the brush you chose.

3 Creating complex dashed lines. In Illustrator you can even make custom styles for applying complex multicolored dashed lines to paths. Draw stroked paths and color each stroke with a different color. Arrange the paths end-to-end: One way to accomplish this is to make sure you've enabled View: Snap To Point, then position the cursor over the endpoint of one segment and drag it so it snaps on the endpoint of another segment. After you've arranged the colored paths, select and drag them into the Brushes palette. In the New Brush dialog, choose New Pattern Brush. Then in the Pattern Brush Options dialog, choose the "Stretch to fit" option. (See "Pattern Brushes" earlier in this chapter for more about Pattern brushes.)

If your dashes are uneven or gapped when applied to a path, select the path and use the Smooth tool (from the Pencil tool pop-up palette) to "iron out" the problems (see Nelson's "Zooming more means smoothing less" Tip within the "Tracing Details" lesson in the *Layers* chapter).

4 Creating tapered brushes. You can use custom brushes to create elements that taper, like creeks. Draw a color-filled rectangle; Nelson's was about 4 inches long and

On the top and the bottom-left, Scatter brushes representing map symbols and north arrow; on the bottom-right, the New Brush dialog

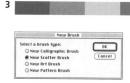

Selecting a Fill color on the left; in the middle, the points created with the Pen tool; on the right, the points after applying a Scatter brush

3

End-to-end strokes (shown enlarged) are made into a Pattern brush

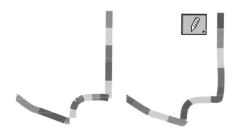

Pattern brush dashes on a path shown before (left) and after being adjusted with the Smooth tool

4

Two of the objects made into tapered brushes

Auto-replacing brush objects
To replace all applications of a brush, hold Option/Alt and drag one brush over another in the Brushes palette (you may wish to duplicate the brush being replaced first!). —*David Nelson*

5

Three "self-adjusting scale" brushes and a map legend that includes a scale drawn with one of the brushes

6

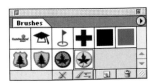

The active document's Brushes palette (top); Window: Brush Libraries: Other Library dialog and the selected document's Brushes palette (middle); the active document's default Brushes palette after importing four new Scatter Brushes

2–3 pts wide. Select the right pair of anchor points and Average (Object: Path: Average), creating a triangle. Drag this path into the Brushes palette and define it as an Art brush, using the point-width in the name of the brush. Select the path that you wish to make into a tapered object and choose your new brush (if the path tapers the wrong way, see "Reversing Brush strokes," at the left). To create a brush that tapers at a different rate, adjust the shape of the triangular object (adding or editing points) and create a new brush with that version.

5 Making a "self-adjusting" scale. Create a scale, using evenly-spaced divisions to represent miles, kilometers or another unit of measure. (One way of creating evenly spaced tick marks is by creating a blend between the two end marks on the scale; see the *Blends, Gradients & Mesh* chapter for more on setting up a blend with the Specified Steps option.) Because you are making a multi-purpose brush that you'll use on different maps, don't add text or numbers to your scale artwork. Now, select your artwork and drag it to the Brushes palette. In the New Brush dialog, choose New Art Brush. On your map, draw a horizontal line whose length represents X units of measure in your document (miles, kilometers, etc.) and apply your new brush—which will adjust proportionately to the length of the line. Add numbers for the units and other necessary text.

6 Sharing custom brushes between documents. You can bring custom brushes into a document by choosing Window: Brush Libraries: Other Library. In the dialog, select a document that contains brushes you'd like to import into your active document. After you select the document and click Open, a palette containing that document's brushes appears with the name of the document in the palette tab. To move brushes, drag from this document palette to your active document's Brushes palette, or apply brushes from the document palette to objects in your active document.

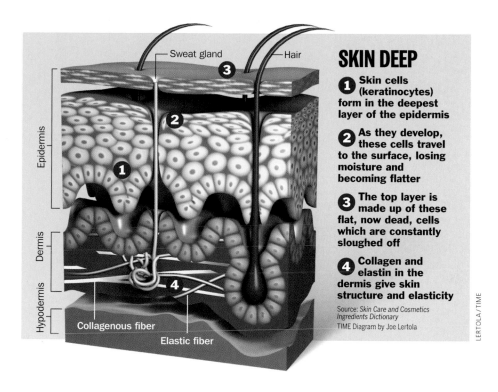

-Sweat gland   ③   -Hair

Epidermis

① ②

Dermis

Hypodermis

Collagenous fiber

Elastic fiber

LERTOLA / TIME

SKIN DEEP

① Skin cells (keratinocytes) form in the deepest layer of the epidermis

② As they develop, these cells travel to the surface, losing moisture and becoming flatter

③ The top layer is made up of these flat, now dead, cells which are constantly sloughed off

④ Collagen and elastin in the dermis give skin structure and elasticity

Source: *Skin Care and Cosmetics Ingredients Dictionary*
TIME Diagram by Joe Lertola

Joe Lertola / TIME

For this medical infographic, artist Joe Lertola relied on the suppleness of Illustrator's Art brushes to show closely packed skin cells. To begin the top layer of cells (**1** and **2** in the illustration above), Lertola built a single cell from two blends, stacking the smaller brown blend on top of the lighter skin-colored blend. Selecting both blends, Lertola chose Object: Expand. Then he dragged the expanded artwork into the Brushes palette and selected New Art Brush from the New Brush dialog. Next, Lertola developed three more cells, varying the oval shape of each cell before turning it into an Art brush.

To make the cells, Lertola drew short paths and painted each with one of the four cell brushes. Lertola finished the illustration by rasterizing the skin cells in Photoshop and exporting a color and grayscale version of the cells. He imported the grayscale cells into the Lightwave 3D modeler software, where he built a model of the cells and applied the color version of the cells as a color map. (To learn more about using Illustrator artwork with other software, see the *Illustrator & Other Programs* chapter.)

Symbol Basics

Creating and Working with Symbols

Overview: *Create background elements; define symbols; use symbolism tools to place and customize symbols.*

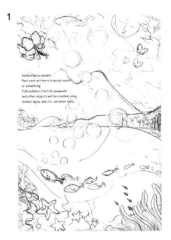

The concept sketch

The background and symbol artwork

Kaoru Hollin created this Tropical Card for Adobe to use as sample art that would show the power and variety of effects possible using the new Symbolism tools. After creating a concept sketch, Hollin defined a library of symbols and then used the Symbolism tools to place and customize the symbols, almost as though they were brushes.

1 Creating the Background art. Based on her sketch, Hollin created the background art using eight simple layered objects, filled with gradients. To create the luminous colors, Hollin applied varying amounts of transparency to each of the objects. Hollin then added depth and richness to the water by applying Effect: Stylize: Inner Glow to the upper water curve, and Outer Glow to the lower water curve. Gradients, transparency, and effects are discussed in detail later in the book.

2 Creating symbols. Hollin created the artwork for each of the 20 symbols that she would use to create the piece. The simplest way to turn a piece of artwork into a symbol is to select the artwork and drag it onto the Symbols palette.

To make your artwork on the Artboard become a symbol instance at the same time you create a symbol, hold down the ⌘ key (Mac) or Ctrl key (Win) as you drag the artwork onto the Symbols palette.

3 Applying symbols. After creating a new layer for the fish, Hollin selected the fish symbol in the Symbols palette and created the school of fish with a single stroke of the Symbol Sprayer tool. You can experiment with the Symbol Sprayer by adjusting the Density and Intensity settings (double-click on any Symbolism tool to access the Symbolism Tool Options), and the speed of your spray strokes. Don't worry about getting an exact number or precise placement for each symbol as you spray; you can fine tune those and other symbol attributes using other Symbolism tools.

4 Resizing symbols. To create a sense of depth, Hollin used the Symbol Sizer tool to make some of the fish smaller. By default, the Sizer tool increases the size of symbols within the tool's brush radius. To make a symbol smaller, hold down the Option (Mac)/Alt (Win) key as you brush over it with the Symbol Sizer tool.

To make the diameter of a Symbolism tool visible, double-click on any Symbolism tool and enable the Show Brush Size and Intensity option. As for brushes, use the "]" key to make the Symbolism tool diameter larger and the "[" key to make it smaller.

5 Modifying symbol transparency and color. To modify the appearance of symbols, use the Symbol Screener,

2

The artwork for the 20 symbols that were used to complete the piece

3

The raw fish after being sprayed on with the Symbol Sprayer tool

The symbolism tools tear-off palette, see "Tear-off palettes" in the Illustrator Basics *chapter*

To access the other symbolism tools, hold down the Control Option (Mac) key or Alt + right click (Win) and drag toward the tool you want to use until the Tool icon changes.—Mordy Golding

4

Hollin used the Symbol Sizer tool to make some of the fish smaller and to add depth

5

The Symbol Stainer tool set to random was used to vary the color of the fish

6

Use the Symbol Spinner tool to adjust the rotation of symbols

7

After using the Symbol Shifter tool with a smaller brush size to adjust the fish positions

8

The final fish after more fine tuning with the Symbol Sizer, Shifter, and Spinner tools

Symbols Stacking Order

To change the symbol stacking order, use the Symbol Shifter tool and:

• Shift-click the symbol instance to bring it forward.

• Option (Mac) or Alt (Win) shift-click to push the symbol instance backward.

Stainer, and Styler tools. The Screener tool adjusts the transparency of symbols. The Stainer tool shifts the color of the symbol to be more similar to the current fill color, while preserving its luminosity. The Styler tool allows you to apply (in variable amounts) styles from the Styles palette. See the *Adobe User Guide* for details about the coloring modes and application methods of these tools.

Hollin used the Symbol Stainer tool, set to Random, to tint the fish a variety of colors with just one stroke. Later, she also used the Stainer tool on the hibiscus and starfish, and the Screener tool on the butterflies.

6 Rotating symbols. To make the first rough adjustment to the orientation of the fish, Hollin used the Symbol Spinner tool set to User Defined (which sets the spin based on the direction the mouse is moved). See "Working with Symbols" in the Introduction to this chapter and the *Adobe User Guide* for an explanation of the User Defined and Average modes.

7 Moving symbols. Hollin used the Symbol Shifter tool with a smaller brush size to adjust the position of the fish.

The Shifter tool was not designed to move symbols large distances. To maximize symbol movement, first make the brush size as large as you can—at least as large as the symbol you wish to move. Then drag across the symbol, as though you were trying to push the symbol with a broom.

8 Deleting symbols. At this point, Hollin felt there were too many fish in the school. To remove the unwanted fish, Hollin used the Symbol Sprayer tool with the Option (Mac)/Alt (Win) key held down. She chose a narrow brush size and clicked on the fish to be removed.

Finally, in order to make the school of fish conform more to the shape of the waves in the background, Hollin used the Symbol Sizer, Shifter, and Spinner tools to make further adjustments.

STEUER / COHEN

Sandee Cohen & Sharon Steuer

Starting with Sharon Steuer's illustration in the "Organic Creation" lesson (later in this chapter), Sandee Cohen created only four symbols to add the grass, stars, and water you see above. After spraying the stars onto the sky, Sandee then used the Symbolism Screener tool to mute the intensity of some stars in order to create a sense of depth. After spraying the foreground grass symbol (which includes the grass shadow), Sandee used the Symbolism Sizer tool to vary the grass heights. Only one symbol was used to create the grass between the dunes. Sandee used the Symbolism Stainer tool to vary the color of the grass, and the Symbolism Spinner tool to vary the angles of some of the grass. For the water, Sandee used one wave of dark blue as the symbol, which she then sprayed over the gradient background, which goes from almost white under the moon to dark blue at the sides of the image. To finish the water, Sandee used the Symbolism Stainer tool to make some of the waves lighter shades of blue.

Diane Hinze Kanzler & Sandee Cohen

Starting with Diane Hinze Kanzler's goldfish illustration (near right), Sandee Cohen used the Pen and Ink filter to add texture. The coral was given a plain pink fill. The Pen and Ink filter was then applied using the "Swash" hatch. The same hatch was also used on the top fin. The body of the fish was created using the "Dots" hatch. The two tail fins were filled with the "Wood grain" hatch. The pectoral fins were filled with the "Vertical lines" hatch, set for different angles. The ventral fins were filled with the "Worm" hatch. Finally, a hatch was defined for the bubble. Then a large rectangle was created over the entire illustration and filled with bubbles. (**Hint:** The bubble could also be a Scatter Brush; see "Organic Creation" in the *Brushes* chapter.)

KANZLER / COHEN

Kevin Barrack

Kevin Barrack began "Batik Dancer" by applying Streamline to his scanned drawing (see the *Illustrator & Other Programs* chapter). In Illustrator, he filled the body shapes with gradients (see the *Blends, Gradients & Mesh* chapter), and on a separate layer, he created blob shapes for the background. In another layer, called "Ink Pen," he created a new blob object with a green fill. To this object he applied Filter: Pen and Ink: Hatch Effects, and set Hatch=Worm; Match Object's Color; Density=75%; Dispersion=Constant 180%; Thickness=Constant 70 pt; Scale=Linear 56–610%, 270°; Rotation=Random 10–180°; Fade=None; and the fourth color square in the indicator scale. Lastly, Barrack added thick strokes to the black solid-filled shapes outlining his figure.

BARRACK

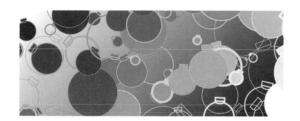
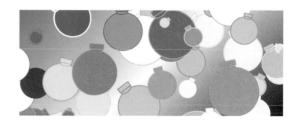

VON SALZA

Victor von Salza

Victor Von Salza creates hatch effects for use as background fills for type, gift paper design, book paper ends, and just for fun. Von Salza created the effects above specifically for the *Illustrator 10 Wow! Book* to demonstrate the rich variety of colorful effects possible. Of the many methods (pattern fills, scatter brush, and symbol sprayer) you can use to create complex textures and fills, Hatch Effects offers a unique

combination of repeatable control and randomness of design. Although you can use Hatch Effects to create fills that look like natural materials, such as stone, wood, and water, you can just as easily use them to fill a sky with fall leaves, or stars and comets, or the rich look of snowflakes etched on glass. See von Salza's "Pen & Ink Hatch Effects.pdf" on the *Wow! CD* for more about Hatch Effects.

Organic Creation

Painting with Brushes, Hatches, and Mesh

Advanced Technique

Overview: *Create Scatter brushes of stars; draw with a "hue-tinted" Art brush; create bark textures with Art brushes; automate drawing of grass with Pattern brushes; add Hatches and Gradient Mesh.*

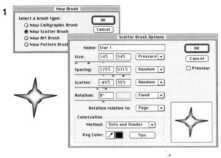

Dragging the star objects into the brushes palette to specify Scatter Brush; the settings for one of the four stars; three selected paths with different star Scatter brushes applied

The leaf Art brush (left) with the Hue Shift Colorization option; the final color strokes for the leaves shown without the Art brush applied

STEUER

Sharon Steuer painted these stars, trees, and grasses using a variety of brushes, with gradients, hatches, and mesh. Please see the *Blends, Gradients & Mesh* chapter for help with the blend, gradient, or mesh portions of this lesson.

1 Defining a star Scatter brush. Create a star. Steuer created her stars using Guilbert Gates's "Glowing Starshine" instructions (*Advanced* chapter), then expanded those blends (Object: Expand). Drag your star to the Brushes palette, and choose Scatter Brush. In Options, name the star and play with various settings, but keep "Rotation relative to" Page. Set Colorization to Tints and Shades. With the Brush tool and new star brush selected, draw some paths—your stroke color will tint the star. For brush variations, drag your brush to the New Brush icon, then double-click that brush to rename and edit it.

2 Drawing leaves. Make a straight leaf. Drag it into the Brushes palette, choose Art Brush, then name the brush and choose Hue Shift for Colorization. With the Brush tool and this brush loaded, choose a stroke color (hue) that this brush will be based on, and draw. Steuer first mixed and stored about a dozen colors, then drew leaves with a Wacom tablet. Though she chose stroke colors as she worked, she also edited the paths (with Direct-selection) and changed stroke colors as the image developed.

3 Creating tree trunks. Create objects to use as a trunk. In order to make a brush of blends or gradients, choose Object: Expand. Drag the trunk into the Brushes palette and choose Art Brush. Apply this trunk brush to a path. If it's too thin or thick for the path, double-click the brush and change the Size %. Steuer made a second trunk brush—slightly narrower and paler—and gave it a different scaling percentage. She applied the thinner trunk to a slightly offset copy of the first trunk path. For texture, draw some strokes and make an Art brush of the strokes with Hue Shift colorization. Selecting a path styled as you want sets the default for the next path.

4 Creating a Pattern brush to generate grass. Design a pattern tile with 20–30 blades of grass. Drag the grouping of grass into the Brushes palette and choose Pattern Brush. Set the direction to be perpendicular to the grass and Tints and Shades Colorization. Draw a curvy path and select the grass Pattern brush to apply it.

5 Creating water, sand and moon effects. To create the water, make an unstroked gradient-filled object on one layer and drag this layer to the New Layer icon to duplicate it (see the *Layers* chapter). Select the top gradient and choose Filter: Pen and Ink: Hatch Effects, choose "Wood grain Light" and enable "Match Object's Color" (see the *Advanced* chapter for Hatches tips). For added texture, offset a copy of the hatches (Option/Alt-drag).

For the sand, Steuer converted a linear gradient into a gradient mesh (Object: Expand). For the moon, she used a gradient mesh circle over the moon-glow gradient.

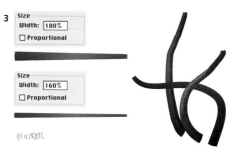

The three Art brushes used in the trunks (the top two with size scaled in Options); the trunks shown (from left to right) with one, two, and all three brushes applied

The Grass objects that make up the Pattern brush; then the brush applied to a path

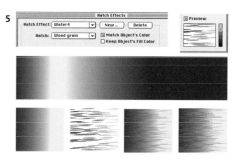

The full two-piece gradient; then the left gradient, turned into Hatches, combined with the original gradient, then Hatches Option-dragged

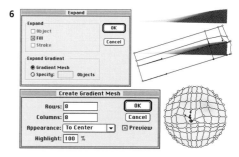

Expanding a gradient-filled object into a mesh (which was then adjusted to curve around the slope of the hill); for the moon, choosing Object: Create Gradient Mesh to convert a circle into a mesh (which was then manipulated using the Direct-selection tool and colored)

Calligraphic brushes allow you to create strokes that resemble those drawn with traditional pen and ink. You can control the angle, roundness and diameter of the brush, and brushes can be set to vary from the pressure of a drawing tablet or "randomly." Multiple calligraphic brushes allow you to create more sophisticated effects. In each of these illustrations, the hair has been changed only by applying different calligraphic brushes. (See the "Brushes Supplement" folder on the *Wow! CD*.)

Calligraphic brush: *0° angle; 100% roundness; 1 pt diameter.*

Calligraphic brush: *0° angle; 100% roundness; 1 pt diameter, 1 pt variation.*

Calligraphic brush: *0° angle, 101° variation; 26% roundness, 14% variation; 3 pt diameter.*

Dark brown calligraphic brush: *-136° angle, 180° variation; 26% roundness 26% variation; 12 pt diameter, 3 pt variation.*
Light brown calligraphic brush: *65° angle; 13% roundness, 3% variation; 2 pt diameter, 2 pt variation.*

Dark calligraphic brush: *0° angle; 100% roundness; 1 pt diameter, 1 pt variation.*
Light calligraphic brush: *0° angle; 100% roundness; .5 pt diameter.*

Dark calligraphic brush: *-90° angle, 180° variation; 10% roundness, 10% variation; 1.5 pt diameter.*
Medium calligraphic brush: *60° angle, 180° variation; 60% roundness, 40% variation; 1.5 pt diameter.*
Light calligraphic brush: *120° angle, 180° variation; 10% roundness, 10% variation; .5 pt diameter.*

Art Brushes can create distortions that can be used in animation. Each original silhouette (the left column) was defined as an art brush. The shape and direction of the brush stroke (gray line) then created different positions of the athlete. (See the "Brushes Supplement" folder on the *Wow! CD*.)

You can start with simple objects and then turn them into natural looking brushes. By applying these brushes to simple artwork, you can give it the feel of art drawn by hand, instead of art created using a computer. (See the "Brushes Supplement" folder on the *Wow! CD*.)

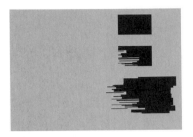

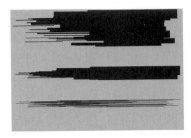

Wispy Brush: *Start with a rectangle and fill it with Pen and Ink Filter Hatch Effects. Use the vertical lines hatch. Release the masking element to see all the lines.*

Use the Scale tool or Bounding Box to make the lines much longer and compact them into a more dense area. Then change the strokes to .25 point and define this as a brush.

The result is a very thin, wispy brush which can be stroked even thinner by changing the Stroke weight after you've applied the brush.

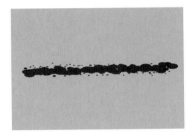

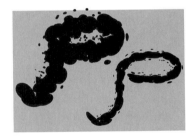

Leaky Pen: *Use the Pen and Ink Hatch Effects with the "Dots" hatch, in the "Scale" pop-up. Choose reflect to create small dots on either side of larger ones.*

Release the mask and apply Unite from the Pathfinder palette. Define this as your brush.

Variation: *Use the Scale tool or the Bounding Box to vertically scale the stroke into a thinner stroke.*
Advantage: *You can't get this ink on your fingers!*

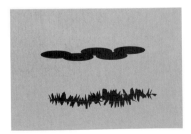

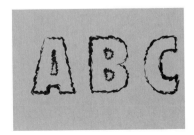

Sketchy line: *Start with a few ellipses. Use Unite from the Pathfinder palette and then apply Filter: Distort: Roughen. Use the bounding box to vertically compress the line into a thinner brush.*

Apply it to all sorts of objects to make a more natural, sketchy look.

Brushes can be used to create textures. The brush strokes (shown in the right corner of each figure), were applied to the outline and stripes of the sweater (original by Lisa Jackmore). None of the artwork was moved or otherwise altered. (See the "Brushes Supplement" folder on the *Wow! CD*.)

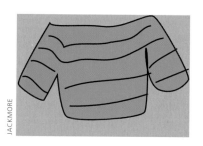

JACKMORE

The original shirt. *Plain green with a black outline and black stripes.*

Sketched shirt. *Art brush of crossed lines was applied to the outline and stripes. Notice that the brush is distorted along the outside path.*

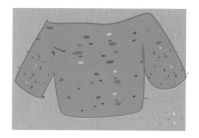

Funky t-shirt. *Art brush of small circles was applied to the stripes.*

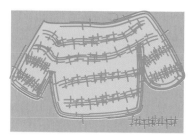

Sketched shirt 3. *An art brush of crossed lines was applied to the outline. This brush was scaled up 150%. The same brush objects, but scaled down 75% with a tighter spacing was applied to the stripes.*

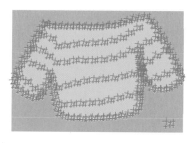

Sketched shirt 2. *Art brush of crosses was applied to the outline and strokes. Notice the distortion along the outside.*

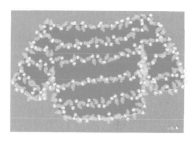

Fuzzy sweater. *Small circles, set with different opacities, were defined as a scatter brush. This brush was then applied to the outline and stripes with varying rotations and spacings.*

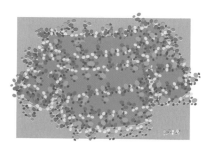

Fuzzy sweater 2. *Small circles were defined as a scatter brush and then applied to the outline and stripes with varying rotations and spacings.*

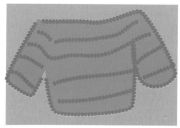

Knitted sweater. *One small circle was defined as a pattern brush, then applied to the outline and stripes.*

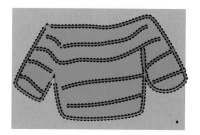

Knitted sweater 2. *One small circle was defined as a pattern brush. Using multiple strokes (see the Transparency chapter), the brush was applied first in black, then in green at a smaller size.*

Layers

5

Layers

Layers palette navigation

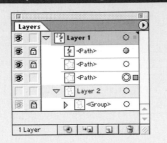

- To hide a layer, click the Eye icon. Click again to show it.
- To lock a layer, click in the column to the right of the eye (a lock displays). Click again to unlock.
- To toggle between locking or showing the selected layer and all other layers, Option (Mac)/ Alt (Win)-click on the appropriate icon.
- To duplicate a layer, drag it to either the *New Layer* or *New Sublayer* icon.
- To select contiguous layers, click one layer then Shift-click the other. To select (or deselect) *any* layer, ⌘(Mac)/Ctrl (Win)-click a layer in any order.
- Double-click on a layer to open Layer Options.

Layer Options (double-click a layer name)

Used wisely, layers can dramatically improve organization of complicated artwork, thereby easing your work flow. Think of layers as sheets of clear acetate, stacked one on top of the other, allowing you to separate dozens of objects and groups of objects. New documents begin with one layer, but you can create as many layers and sublayers as you wish. You can also re-arrange the stacking order of the layers; lock, hide, or copy layers; and move or copy objects from one layer to another.

A few shortcuts will help when you're adding layers to the Layers palette. Click the New Layer icon to add a layer in numeric sequence above the current layer. Hold Option/Alt when you click this icon to open Layer Options as you add the layer. To add a layer to the top of the Layers palette, hold ⌘/Ctrl when you click the New Layer icon. To make a new layer below the current layer and open the Layer Options, hold ⌘-Option/Ctrl-Alt when you click the New Layer icon. Finally, you can easily duplicate a layer, sublayer, group, or path by dragging it to the New Layer icon at the bottom of the Layers palette. To delete selected layers, click on the Trash icon or drag the layers to the Trash. (Make sure to look at the Tip at left for more about palette navigation)

Note: *To bypass the warning that you're about to delete a layer containing artwork, drag the layer to the Trash or hold Option (Mac)/Alt (Win) when you click the Trash. If you're not sure whether a layer has artwork or guides you may need, select the layer and click the Trash so you'll only get the warning if there is something on the layer.*

Sublayers can be very useful. Keep in mind that the sublayers are contained within the layer listed above it. If you delete a container layer, all of the sublayers will be deleted as well.

Maximizing Layer Options

Double-click a layer name to access these Layer Options:

- **Name the layer.** In complicated artwork, naming layers keeps your job, and your brain, organized.

- **Change the layer's color.** A layer's color determines the selection color for paths, anchor points, bounding boxes, and Smart Guides. Adjust the layer color so selections stand out against artwork (see Tip "Color-coding groups of layers" to the right).

- **Template Layer.** There are three ways to create a Template: You can double-click a layer to open the Layer Options and then check Template, select Template from the Layers pop-up menu, or check Template when placing an image in Illustrator. By default, Template layers are locked. To unlock a Template in order to adjust or edit objects, click the lock icon to the left of the layer name.
  Hint: Template layers won't print or export. Make any layer into a Template to ensure that it won't print.

- **Show / Hide layer.** This option functions the same way as the Show / Hide toggle, which you access by clicking the Eye icon (see Tip "Layers palette navigation" on the opposite page). By default, hiding a layer sets that layer *not* to print.

- **Preview / Outline mode.** Controlling which layers are set to Preview or Outline is essential in working with layers. If you have objects that are easier to edit in Outline mode, or objects that are slow to redraw (such as complicated patterns, live blends, or gradients), you may want to set only those layers to Outline mode. Uncheck Preview to set selected layers to Outline mode in Layer Options, or toggle this option on and off directly by ⌘ (Mac)/Ctrl (Win) - clicking the Eye icon in the view column.

- **Lock / Unlock layer.** This option functions the same way as the Lock / Unlock toggle, which you access by clicking the lock column of the layer (see Tip "Layers palette navigation" on opposite page).

Color-coding groups of layers

Select a set of layers and double-click any one of the layers to open the Layer Options dialog. Then set the layer color for all selected layers (see lessons later in this chapter). You can also use this technique to adjust other options globally on a set of selected layers.

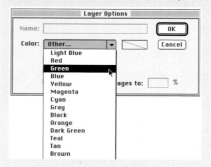

Reordering objects

To change the stacking order of several objects:
- Reorder the layers they are on.
- Move grouped objects from one layer to another.
- Cut the bottom objects, select the topmost object, and Paste In Front with Paste Remembers Layers *off*.
- Drag the selection indicator (large square) from one layer to another, or collapse the disclosure arrow for a container layer and drag the small square.
- If all of the objects are not on the same layer, choose Collect in New Layer (Layers palette menu) and then drag the layer or contents of the layer to the desired location in the layer list.

```
New Layer...
New Sublayer...
Duplicate "Layer 1"
Delete Selection

Options for "Layer 1"...

Make/Release Clipping Mask

Locate Object

Merge Selected
Flatten Artwork
Collect in New Layer

Release to Layers (Sequence)
Release to Layers (Build)
Reverse Order

Template
Hide All Layers
Outline All Layers
Lock All Layers

Paste Remembers Layers

Palette Options...
```

Layers palette pop-up menu

- **Print/Suppress printing.** When you print from within Illustrator you can use this feature to override the default, which sets visible layers to print. If you need to ensure that a layer will *never* print in *any* circumstance (for instance, when placed into a page layout program) make the layer into a Template layer.

- **Dim Images.** You can only dim raster images (not vector Illustrator objects) from 1% to 99% opacity.

You can double-click on any group, path, compound path, clipping path, blend, mesh, object, placed, or raster layer to set Options such as the Name, Show and/or Lock status. If you would like to know what the items are once you've re-named them, retain the name of the subcomponent. For example, you can rename a group to help organize your layer list, but keep the bracket description: *floral <Group>*.

The Layers pop-up menu

You can perform the first six functions in the Layers pop-up menu via the layer palette icons, or Layer Options (see above). With the ability to nest sublayers within other layers and create group objects comes the confusion of how to find objects when they become buried in the layer list. Use Locate Object, or Locate Layer when Show Only Layers is checked in Palette Options, to find selected objects. Merge Selected is available when two or more layers are selected and will place *visible* objects in the topmost layer. An alternative to Flatten Artwork is Select All, Copy and Paste, with Paste Remembers Layers unchecked.

Paste Remembers Layers is a great feature: when enabled, objects retain their layer order (see "Layer Registration" later in this chapter for a lesson using this feature); when unchecked, pasted objects go into the selected layer. If the layers don't exist, Paste Remembers Layers will make them for you! This feature can be turned on and off even after the objects have been copied—so if you paste,

and wish that the toggle were reversed, you can Undo, toggle the Paste Remembers Layers option, then paste again.
Important: *There is one significant problem with this feature. If you target a top-level layer and apply strokes, fills, effects, or transparency and then copy/paste that layer into a new document, all appearance attributes that were applied to that layer will be lost in the new document, even when Paste Remembers Layers is enabled.*

Try this workaround by Jean-Claude Tremblay: Since the attributes of a top-level layer are not retained and you get no warning when pasting into the new document, you need to nest the top-layer into another layer, making it a sublayer. Then copy/paste this sublayer into the new document to retain the appearance attributes.

Collect in New Layer moves all of the selected objects, groups or layers into a new layer. Release to Layers (Build) or Release to Layers (Sequence), allows you to make individual object layers from a group of objects, such as a blend, a layer, or art created by using a brush. (For more on exporting to SWF see the *Web & Animation* chapter.)

Note: *When you're working with blend objects and want to place each object in the blend on a separate layer, you'll need to make sure your blend object is on a top-level layer and* target *the <Blend> layer before you can successfully use Release to Layers.*

Reverse Order reverses the stacking order of selected layers within a container layer. Hide All Layers/Others, Outline All Layers/Others, and Lock All Layers/Others all perform actions on unselected layers or objects.

Last, Palette Options customizes the layer display. This is a great help to artists who have complicated files with many layers. Show Layers Only hides the disclosure arrow so you only see the container layer thumbnail. Adding sublayers reveals the arrow, but you still can't target groups or individual paths in this mode. Row Size defines the size of the thumbnail for a layer. You can specify a thumbnail size from Small (no thumbnail) to Large, or use Other to customize a size up to 100 pixels. Thumbnail

If you can't select an object...

If you have trouble selecting an object, check the following:
- Is the object's layer locked?
- Is the object locked?
- Are the edges hidden?
- Is the Use Area Select box disabled (Edit: Preferences: General)?
- Locate the thumbnail in the layer list and click on the target indicator.

If you keep selecting the wrong object, try again after you:
- Switch to Outline mode.
- Zoom in.
- Hide the selected object; repeat if necessary.
- Lock the selected object; repeat if necessary.
- Put the object on top in another layer and hide that layer, or select Outline for the layer.
- Use the Move command: Option (Mac)/Alt (Win)-click the Selection tool in the Toolbox to move selected objects a set distance (you can move them back later).
- Check for objects with transparency. Overlapping transparency inhibits selection.
- Check if Type Area Select is *on* (Edit: Preferences: Type and Auto Tracing).

Printing issues

In certain situations, hidden selections will print:

- Objects on hidden layers do not print, but hidden objects on visible layers do print once the file is reopened.
- Hidden objects on layers with the print option disabled *will* print if saved as an .eps file and exported into QuarkXPress. There must also be visible art in the file to cause this to occur. To prevent this, save a version of the file without the art you wish to hide and re-export.

Exporting Layers to Photoshop

Export layered Illustrator files as Photoshop (PSD). Select options that allow you to maintain the layer integrity, such as *Point*-type. You can then edit the layers and the type in Photoshop. However, you can't "round trip" text back to Illustrator. (For more on exporting layered files to Photoshop see the *Other Programs* chapter.)

To select *all* objects

First, unlock and show everything in the Layers palette. Click-drag through the Eye and Lock icons or make sure Unlock All and Show All are unavailable in the Object menu. Then choose Edit: Select All (⌘-A for Mac/Ctrl-A for Win).

lets you individually set thumbnail visibility for the Layers, Top Level Only (when Layers is checked), Group, and Object.

CONTROLLING THE STACKING ORDER OF OBJECTS

Layers are crucial for organizing your images, but controlling the stacking order of objects *within* a layer is just as essential. The intuitive layers and sublayers disclose their hierarchical contents when you open the disclosure arrow. Following is a summary of the functions that will help you control the stacking order of objects within layers and sublayers.

Sublayers and the hierarchical layer structure

In addition to regular layers, there are sublayers and groups, both of which act as containers for objects or images. When you click on the sublayer icon, a new sublayer is added inside the current layer. Artwork that you add to the sublayer will be below or underneath the art contained on the main layer. Clicking the New Layer icon with a sublayer selected will add a new sublayer above the current one. Adding subsequent layers adds the contents at the top of the stacking order or puts the artwork above the current layer. Clicking the New Sublayer icon creates a new sublayer level nested within the first one.

Grouping objects together automatically creates a container "layer" named *<Group>*. Double-click the *<Group>* layer to open its options. Group layers are much like sublayers. You can target them to apply appearances that affect all the objects within the group. In some cases, such as when Pathfinder effects are applied, objects have to be grouped and the group layer must be targeted in order to apply the effect. However, group layers cannot be moved in the same way as layers. **Note:** *If you rename your <Group>, you might get confused when it doesn't behave like a regular layer. Instead of removing <Group> from the name appended to it, leave <Group> as part of the renaming of the layer.*

PasteInFront, PasteInBack (Edit menu)

Illustrator doesn't merely reposition an object in front of or behind all other objects when you choose PasteIn Front/Back; it aligns the object *exactly* on top of or behind the object you copied. A second, and equally important, aspect is that the two functions paste objects that are Cut or Copied into the exact same location—in relation to the *ruler origin*. This capability transfers from one document to another, ensuring perfect registration and alignment when you copy and use Edit: PasteIn Front/Back. (See the lesson "Layer Registration" later in this chapter for practical applications of this option, and the *Wow! CD* for exercises in reordering objects using paste commands.)

Lock/Unlock All (Object menu)

When you're trying to select an object and you accidentally select an object on top of it, try locking the selected object and clicking again. Repeat as necessary until you reach the correct object. When you've finished the task, choose Unlock All to release all the locked objects.
Note: *Use the Direct-selection tool to select and lock objects that are part of a group (see the section "Selecting within groups" in the* Illustrator Basics *chapter)—but if you select an unlocked object in the group with the Group-selection or other selection tools, the locked objects can become selected. Hidden objects stay hidden even if you select other objects in the same group.*

Hide/Show All (Object menu)

Another approach for handling objects that get in the way is to select them and choose Hide Selection. To view all hidden objects, choose Object: Show All.
Note: *Hidden objects may print if they're on visible layers and will reappear when you reopen the file.*

Bring Forward/Bring To Front and more

These commands work on objects within a layer, Bring Forward (Object: Arrange) stacks an object on top of the

Drawing under grayscale scans

To place color underneath a black-and-white image, see the "Colors with Layers" lesson later in this chapter. To place color under a grayscale scan, set the Blending mode for the scan to Multiply mode using the Transparency palette (with Multiply mode the white areas of your sketch will become transparent). Be aware however, changing the blending mode invokes Transparency for your image—see the *Transparency* chapter for details on predictable output and transparency.

○	*Target icon for any layer or subcomponent*
◎	*Selection is also currently targeted*
▪	*Selection indicator for a container layer*
■	*Selection indicator when all objects are selected*

Selecting vs. targeting

There are now several ways to make a selection and several other ways to target an object. The main difference between the two is selections don't always target, but targeting always makes a selection. In this example, "Layer 1" contains the selected object but is not currently the target. The circled "<Path>" is the current target.

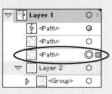

When opening a file created by an older version of Illustrator, it can take a long time for the Layers palette to draw all the thumbnails for each path. Before you attempt to open layers to view their contents, you'll save a lot of time if you choose Palette Options from the Layers palette pop-up menu and uncheck the Object option in the Thumbnails grouping. Once you've reorganized your paths in the Layers palette, be sure to re-enable the Object checkbox in the Palette Options in order to view the thumbnails for your paths.

Problem with new Views

There are unpredictable situations when using sublayers and New Views in which the view doesn't save the state of the sublayer.

Note: *You should think of views as a way to control top-level layers only.*

Making a series of selections

You can use the Unlock or Unhide commands to help make a series of selections. First, make selections and Lock or Hide them. You can make more selections later. Then, when you need to access all selections, choose Object: Unlock or Object: Unhide. Everything you've locked or hidden is now unlocked, visible, and selected.

object directly above it. Bring To Front moves an object in front of all other objects on its layer. Logically, Send To Back sends an object as far back as it can go in its stacking order. Send Backward sends an object behind its closest neighbor.

Note: *Bring Forward and Send Backward may not work on large files. In cases where they do not work, use the layer list to reorder items by moving the selection indicator to the right of the layer name up or down in the layer list.*

MAKING SELECTIONS USING THE LAYERS PALETTE

There are several ways to make selections in this version. Click on the layer's target icon or Option-click (Mac)/ Alt-click (Win) the layer name to select all unlocked and visible objects on the layer, including any sublayers and groups. Click on the sublayer's target icon to select everything on the sublayer, including other sublayers or groups. Clicking on the *group's* target icon will also select all grouped objects. Shift-click on the target icons to select multiple objects on different layers, including sublayers and groups. Always use the *target* icon to make a selection when applying an appearance to a layer, sublayer, or group.

If you have selected artwork on the Artboard, click on the small square to select all of the objects on the layer or in the group. A larger square means that all of the objects on that layer or group are already selected. Clicking in the small space to the right of the target indicator will also make a selection of all objects on the layer, sublayer, or group.

A current bug in the Group command...

A bug in the group command can reorder the relative stacking order of your objects when you group (Object: Group, or ⌘-G/Ctrl-G)! This can occur if you group objects that aren't within any sublayer with objects that are on a sublayer. In order to avoid this, before you group make sure that all of your objects are within sublayers, or that none are in sublayers.

David Nelson/Mapping Services

Cartographer David Nelson uses the Layers palette to its fullest extent in this transportation map of Orlando, Florida. To see more of the Illustrator techniques that Nelson used to create this map, see the "Map Techniques" lesson in the *Brushes, Symbols & Hatches* chapter.

Digitizing a Logo

Controlling Your Illustrator Template

Overview: *Scan a clean version of your artwork; place the art as a template in Illustrator; trace the template; modify the curve of drawn lines to better fit the template image by manipulating points and by using the Pencil tool.*

YIP (SAILOR JACK, BINGO & CRACKER JACK Designs are TMs of Recot, Inc., © Recot 1999.)

A large, clean scan of the artwork

Creating the template and a drawing layer

You can easily use Illustrator's Template layer to re-create traditional line art with the computer—easily, that is, if you know the tricks. San Francisco artist Filip Yip was commissioned to modernize the classic Cracker Jack sailor boy and dog logo, and to digitize the logo for use in a variety of media. Yip scanned the original logo artwork and several sketches he drew and used the scans as sources in developing the new logo.

1 Placing a scanned image as a template and using Filters to modify the image. Select a high-contrast copy of the original artwork that is free of folds, tears, or stains. Scan the image at the highest resolution that will provide the detail you need for tracing. Open a new file in Illustrator (File: New), select File: Place, click the Template option, then choose your scan, thus placing it into a new template layer. Template layers are automatically set to be nonprinting and dimmed layers.

If you need to improve the quality of your scanned image to better discern details, you can edit the image with a program like Photoshop prior to placing it in Illustrator. Alternatively, if you've already brought the image into Illustrator, use the Filter menu to change focus or color. (If you placed the image on a Template layer, you'll need to double-click the layer name in the Layers palette and uncheck Template, which allows the image to be edited.) Select the image and select Filter: Sharpen to make the image more crisp. Choose the Filter: Colors menu and select options like Convert to Grayscale, Saturate, or Adjust Colors to modify image properties.

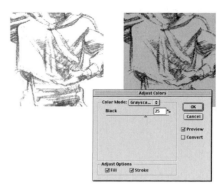

Darkening a scanned grayscale image using the Filter: Colors: Adjust Colors dialog

2 Tracing the template. With the template as an on-screen tracing guide (and the original scanned artwork handy as an off-screen reference), select the Pen or Pencil tool and begin tracing over the scanned image. To reduce visual clutter in small areas of the drawing, try viewing your active layer in Outline mode (while pressing ⌘-D [Mac] or Ctrl-D [Win], click on the visibility icon next to the layer's name in the Layers palette). Don't worry too much about how closely you're matching the template as you draw. Next, zoom close (with the Zoom tool, drag to marquee the area you wish to inspect) and use the Direct-selection tool to adjust corner or curve points, curve segments, or direction lines until the Bézier curves properly fit the template. (See the *Drawing & Coloring* chapter for more on working with Bézier curves.)

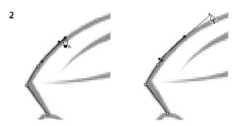

Modifying the fit of a drawn line using the Direct-selection tool to move a direction handle

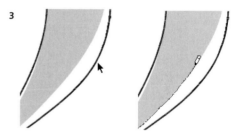

On the left, electing a previously drawn line, and on the right, redrawing the selected line with the Pencil tool

3 Refining lines with the Pencil tool. To modify a line that doesn't follow the template, click the line to select it, then choose the Pencil tool and draw over the template with the Pencil. Illustrator automatically reshapes the selected line (instead of drawing a brand new line). You may need to edit the Pencil tool's settings (double-click the Pencil tool icon and edit the Pencil Tool Preferences dialog) to control the smoothness of the revised line or the pixel distance from the selected line in which the Pencil tool will operate. (Learn more about using the Pencil tool in *Tracing Details* in this chapter.)

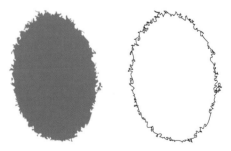

Manually tracing an intricate object may be more tedious and time-consuming than autotracing it; Yip drew the rough-edged parts of the sailor uniform with chalk on watercolor paper, which he then scanned, saved as a TIFF, and autotraced in Adobe Streamline

Tracing Details

Tracing Intricate Details with the Pencil

Overview: *Scan a photo and place it into a Template layer in Illustrator; adjust Pencil Options; trace the photo with the Pencil; create new layers; adjust layer positions and modes.*

Saving images for tracing

While EPS is the preferred format for placed images (see the *Illustrator & Other Programs* chapter), saving images in TIFF format will display more detail for tracing.

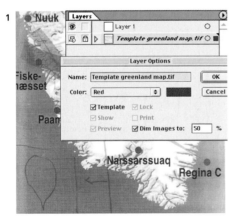

Double-clicking the Template layer to access Layer Options where "Dim Images" percentages can be customized

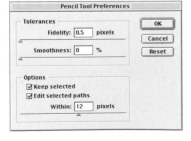

Double-clicking on the Pencil tool to set Options

Laurie Grace loves the way the Pencil tool permits her to trace details with precision. Using the Pencil with custom settings and additional layers, she created this map of Greenland for a *Scientific American* article.

1 Scanning and placing the image into a Template layer. Scan the image you wish to use as a tracing template and save it in grayscale TIFF format. In a new Illustrator document, place your TIFF as a template (see "Digitizing a Logo" in this chapter). Your template will automatically be dimmed to 50%; to customize the percentage at which the template is dimmed, double-click the Template layer.

2 Setting up your Pencil Options for tracing. To draw with precision, you'll need to adjust the Pencil tool's default settings. Double-click the Pencil tool and drag the Fidelity slider all the way to the left, to 0.5 pixels, keeping Smoothness at 0% (higher numbers in Fidelity and Smoothness result in less accurate, smoother lines). For this lesson, keep "Keep Selected" enabled, so you can redraw lines and easily connect a new line to the last.

3 Drawing with the Pencil tool into Layer 1. It's very simple to attach one line to the next, so don't worry about tracing your entire template in one stroke. Zoom in on your work (see the *Illustrator Basics* chapter for Zoom help) and trace one section. When you finish drawing that section (and it's still selected), move the Pencil tool aside until you see "×", indicating that the Pencil would be drawing a new path. Next, move the Pencil close to the selected path and notice that the "×" disappears, indicating that the new path will be connected to the currently selected one, then continue to draw your path. To attach a new path to an unselected path, select the path you wish to attach to first. To draw a closed path with the Pencil (like the islands in Grace's map), hold the Option/Alt key as you approach the first point in the path.

Note: *With the Option/Alt key down, if you stop before you reach the first point, the path will close with a straight line.*

4 Creating and reordering new layers. To add the background water and the coastline terrain details, Grace had to create additional layers. To create additional layers, click on the New Layer icon in the Layers palette. Clicking on a layer name activates that layer so the next object you create will be on that layer. To reorder layers, grab a layer by its name and drag it above or below another layer. Click in the Lock column to Lock/Unlock specific layers.

5 Hiding and Previewing layers. Toggle Hide/Show Template layers from the View menu. To toggle any layer between Hide and Show, click on the Eye icon in the Visibility column for that layer to remove or show the Eye. To toggle a non-template layer between Preview and Outline mode, ⌘-click/Ctrl-click the Eye icon. (To move objects between layers, see Tip "Moving an object from one layer to another" later in this chapter.)

Zooming more means smoothing less...

You can control the amount of smoothing applied with the Smooth tool by adjusting screen magnification. When you're zoomed-out, the Smooth tool deletes more points; zoomed-in, the tool produces more subtle results. —*David Nelson*

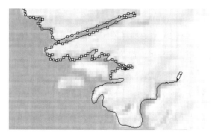

After drawing part of the coastline it remains selected. Moving the Pencil close to the selected path then allows the next path to be connected; continuing the path with the Pencil tool

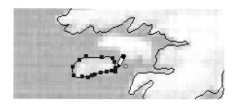

Drawing with the Pencil tool and holding the Option key to close the path

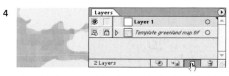

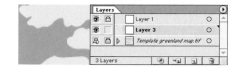

Making a New Layer; a blue object created in the new Layer 3 which is moved below Layer 1; Layer 1 locked with Layer 3 activated

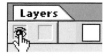

Toggling between Outline and Preview mode for a specific layer by ⌘-clicking the Eye icon

Colors with Layers

Coloring Black-and-White Images with Layers

Overview: *Create a sketch; scan and save it as a bitmap TIFF; set up layers in Illustrator for the TIFF and the colored objects; place bitmap TIFF into the upper layer; color the image; group TIFF with its colors; add background.*

Setting up basic layers in Illustrator

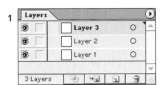

A bitmap outline sketch

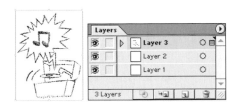

The scanned sketch placed into the top layer

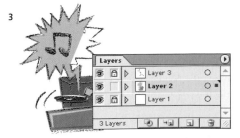

Drawing into layers below the top layer, which contains the scanned sketch

While the most obvious way to trace an image in Illustrator is to place the image on a lower layer and use an upper layer to trace the new Illustrator objects, in some cases you'll want your tracing layer to be *below* a placed image. When creating an illustration for a children's magazine, John Kanzler placed his sketch on an upper layer. This way, he could add color using Illustrator and maintain a hand-sketched look by keeping the scanned sketch in the file.

1 Setting up your Illustrator layers. In Illustrator, create at least three layers for the elements of your image. You'll need to have a top layer for placing your sketches, a middle layer (or layers) for coloring your sketches, and a base layer for background objects. (For help making layers, see "Digitizing a Logo" and "Tracing Details" in this chapter.) Illustrator assigns a different color to each layer name—this helps you keep track of the objects in each layer (selected paths and anchor points will be color-coded to match their layer name).

2 Sketching and scanning a black-and-white drawing; placing the image into the top layer in Illustrator. Scan a hand-drawn sketch as a 1-bit bitmap format (black and white only), or draw directly in a painting program set to a black-and-white (bitmapped) mode. Save your image as a TIFF file. Kanzler sketched his figure with a soft pencil on rough paper, scanned it, then saved it as a bitmap TIFF file.

Next, in the Layers palette of your Illustrator file, make the top layer active (click on the layer name) and use the Place command (from the File menu) to place one of your drawings into the top layer.

The colorized drawing with the sketch visible and the sketch hidden

3 Coloring your drawings. To make coloring your drawings easier, it helps to lock all but the layer in which you will be drawing. You must first unlock and activate the chosen layer (to the left of the layer you should see the Eye icon but no Lock icon; to activate a layer, click on its name in the Layers palette). Then, lock the top layer. Now, using filled colored objects without strokes, trace *under* your placed sketch. To view the color alone, hide the top layer by clicking on the Eye icon in the visibility column for that layer in the left side of the Layers palette.

4

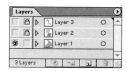

Selected objects that are on different layers, then grouped, automatically move to layer where the topmost selected object resides

4 Grouping your drawing with its colors; adding a background. When you have finished coloring the figure, unlock the top layer, select the placed TIFF with the objects that colorize that figure, and group them together (while selected, choose Object: Group). The grouped figure automatically moves to the top layer.

To add background elements, activate the bottom-most layer and draw on it. Your grouped images can be easily repositioned within your composition by selecting and moving them with the Selection tool.

The background for the illustration, created in the bottom layer

Moving a grouped, colorized figure around the composition

Changing layers by selecting an object

Instead of changing the active layer by selecting a new layer in the Layers palette, let Illustrator make the change for you. When you select an object from an unlocked layer, its layer automatically becomes active. The next object you create will use the same paint style as the last selected object and will be placed on that same active layer.

Overprinting 1-bit TIFF problem

It's usually best to set black TIFFs to Overprint Fill in the Attributes palette. If Overprint is disabled, check www.adobe.com/illustrator for possible corrective updates.

Organizing Layers
Managing Custom Layers and Sublayers

Overview: *Sketch and scan a composition; set up basic, named layers in Illustrator for the objects you will create; place art into temporary sublayers; trace the placed art; delete the temporary sublayers.*

The initial concept for the illustration, used to set up a photo shoot; the assembled photographic collage

Hand-traced sketch scanned

Beginning your illustration with well-organized layers and sublayers can be a lifesaver when you're constructing complex illustrations. Using these layers to isolate or combine specific elements will save you an immense amount of production time by making it easy to hide, lock, or select related objects within layers. When American Express commissioned Nancy Stahl to design a cover for its internal magazine, *Context*, she saved time and frustration by creating layers and using sublayers for tracing and arranging various components of the cover illustration.

1 Collecting and assembling source materials. Prepare your own source materials to use as tracing templates in Illustrator. For the AmEx illustration, Stahl took

Polaroids of herself posed as each of the figures in her planned composition and scanned them into Adobe Photoshop, where she scaled them, composited some elements, and moved them into position. She then printed out the assembled "collage," roughly sketched in the other elements by hand and, with tracing paper, created a line drawing version of the full composition to use as an overall template. She then scanned it into the computer.

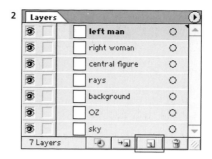

Setting up layers to isolate key elements

2 Setting up illustration layers. Before you begin to import any photos or drawings, take a few moments to set up layers to help you isolate the key elements in your illustration. For the cover illustration, before she actually started drawing in Illustrator, Stahl set up separate layers for the background, the sky, the rays of light, and the building in the background, which she called "OZ," as well as a character layer for each of the figures. Name a layer while creating it by Option-clicking/Alt-clicking on the Create New Layer icon in the Layers palette. You can also name or rename an existing layer or sublayer by double-clicking on it in the Layers palette.

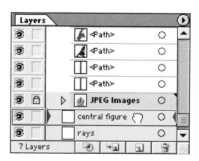

The temporary sublayer before placing the scan

3 Placing art to use as templates. Click on the layer in which you plan to trace your first object, then click on the Create New Sublayer icon in the Layers palette to create a sublayer for your template (Option-click/Alt-click on the icon to name your sublayer as you create it). Use File: Place to select the scan or artwork to be placed into this sublayer. The template sublayer should now be directly below the object layer upon which you will be tracing. Lock the template sublayer and draw into the layer above using the Pen, Pencil, or other drawing tools.

Stahl activated a character layer by clicking on it in the Layers palette, then created a sublayer that she named "JPEG Images". She placed the hand-traced figures image into her sublayer, locked it, and traced her first character into the layer above. Using the Layers palette, she freely moved the locked JPEG Images template sublayer below each character's layer as she drew.

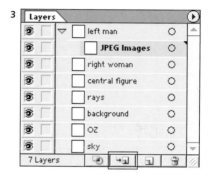

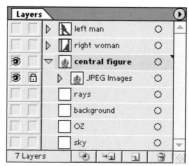

Moving the sublayer and setting up the Lock and Show options for tracing

4

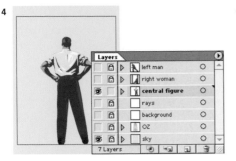

Isolating elements by viewing only the essential layers

5

Clicking on a visible and unlocked sublayer to make it active for placing new art

6

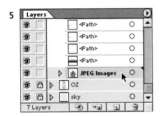

Clicking on or dragging the sublayer to the Trash icon, or choosing Delete from the Layers palette pop-up menu

Changing placed art

Select the image you wish to replace. Next open the Links palette (Window menu) and click on the Replace Link icon (the bottom left icon) or choose Replace from the Links palette pop-up menu. In the dialog box, locate the replacement image and click Place.

4 Drawing into your layers. Now you can begin drawing and tracing elements into your compositional layers and sublayers. Activate the layer or sublayer in which you want to draw by clicking on the layer's name, make sure the layer or sublayer is unlocked and visible (there should be an Eye in the Visibility column and an empty box in the Lock column), and start to work. Use the Layers palette to lock, unlock, or hide layers or sublayers, as well as to toggle between Preview and Outline modes, switch your active layer, or add a new layer or sublayer. By maneuvering in this way, Stahl could easily trace a sketch of basic background elements, create rays against a locked background or develop one character at a time.

5 Adding new placed art to a layer or sublayer. If you need to import art into an existing layer or sublayer, first make sure the layer is visible and unlocked, then make it the active layer by clicking on it. For the AmEx cover, when Stahl needed additional references, she viewed and unlocked the JPEG Images template sublayer, clicked on it to make it active, and then used the Place command to bring the new scan or art into the template sublayer.

6 Deleting layers or sublayers when you are finished using them. Extra layers with placed art can take up quite a bit of disk space, so you'll want to delete them when you are done with them. When you finish using a template, first save the illustration. Then, in the Layers palette, click on the layer or sublayer you are ready to remove and click on the Trash icon in the Layers palette, choose the Delete option from the Layers palette pop-up menu, or drag the layer or sublayer to the Trash icon in the Layers palette. Finally, use Save As to save this new version of the illustration with a meaningful new name and version number (such as "AmEx no JPEG v3.ai"). Stahl eventually deleted all the sublayers she created as templates so she could save her final cover illustration with all the illustration layers but none of the template sublayers or placed pictures.

Nancy Stahl

Using the same techniques as in "Organizing Layers," Nancy Stahl created this image for the interior of American Express's internal magazine, *Context*. When she wanted to move selected objects to another layer, she used the technique shown in the Tip below.

Moving an object from one layer to another

To move a selected object to another layer: open the Layers palette, grab the colored dot to the right of the object's layer, and drag it to the desired layer (see near right). To move a copy of an object: hold down the Option/Alt key while you drag (see far right).

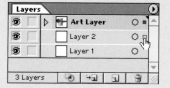

Nested Layers

Organizing with Layers and Sublayers

Overview: *Plan a layer structure; create layers and sublayers; refine the structure by rearranging layers and sublayers in the Layer palette's hierarchy; hide and lock layers; change the Layers palette display.*

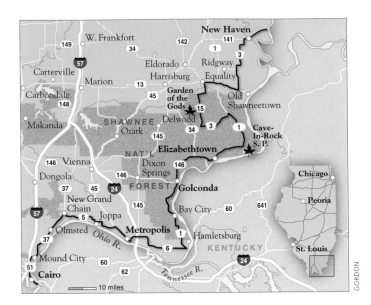

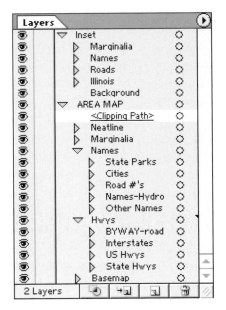

The completed layer structure for the map showing layers and two levels of sublayers

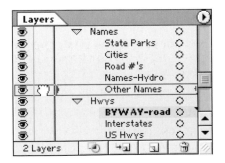

Selecting and dragging the BYWAY-road sublayer up and out of the Hwys sublayer, placing it on the same level in the hierarchy as Hwys

Layers have always been a great way of organizing artwork. With Illustrator 10, you can organize your Layers palette as a nested hierarchy, making it easier to navigate and manipulate. For this map of the Great River Scenic Byway in Illinois, Steven Gordon relied on nested layers and sublayers to organize the artwork he developed.

1 Planning, then creating and moving layers and sublayers. Gordon began by planning a layer structure for the map in which layers with similar information would be nested within several "master" layers, so he could easily navigate the Layers palette and manipulate the layers and sublayers. After planning the organization of your layered artwork, open the Layers palette (Window: Layers) and begin creating layers and sublayers. (Illustrator automatically creates a Layer 1 every time a new document is created—you can use or rename this layer.) To create a new layer, click the Create New Layer icon at the bottom of the palette. To create a new sublayer that's nested within a currently selected layer, click on the palette's Create New Sublayer icon.

As you continue working, you may need to refine your organization by changing the nesting of a current layer or sublayer. To do this, drag the layer name in the

Layers palette and release it over a boundary between layers. To convert a sublayer to a layer, drag its name and release it above its master layer or below the last sublayer of the master layer (watch the sublayer's bar icon to ensure that it aligns with the left side of the names field in the Layers palette before releasing it). Don't forget that if you move a layer in the Layers palette, any sublayer, group, or path it contains will move with it, affecting the hierarchy of artwork in your illustration.

2 Hiding and locking layers. As you draw, you can hide or lock sublayers of artwork by simply clicking on the visibility (Eye) icon or edit (Lock) icon of their master layer. Gordon organized his map so that related artwork, such as different kinds of names, were placed on separate sublayers nested within the Names layer, and thus could be hidden or locked by hiding or locking the Names layer.

If you click on the visibility or edit icon of a master layer, Illustrator remembers the visibility and edit status of each sublayer before locking or hiding the master layer. When Gordon clicked the visibility icon of the Names layer, sublayers that had been hidden before he hid the master layer remained hidden after he made the Names layer visible again. To quickly make the contents of all layers and sublayers visible, select Show All Layers from the Layers palette's pop-up menu. To unlock the content of all layers and sublayers, choose Unlock All Layers. (If these commands are not available, it's because all layers are already showing or unlocked.)

3 Changing the Layers palette display. As you utilize the Layers palette, change its display to make the palette easier to navigate. Display layers and sublayers (and hide groups and paths) in the palette by choosing Palette Options from the palette menu and in the Layers palette Options dialog, clicking Show Layers Only. To view tiny thumbnails of the artwork on each layer or sublayer, select a Row Size of Medium or Large, or select Other and set row size to 20 or more pixels in the dialog.

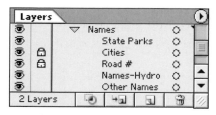

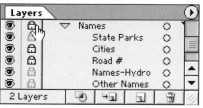

Top, a "master" layer with two sublayers locked; bottom, after the master layer is locked, the two sublayers' edit icons are not dimmed, indicating that they will remain locked when the layer is unlocked

Selecting a row size in the Layers palette Options dialog

Another way to unlock layers

A quick way to unlock all the contents of a layer: Make sure the layer itself is unlocked (the lock icon is gone) and then choose Unlock All from the Object menu.

Let Illustrator do the walking

Illustrator can automatically expand the Layers palette and scroll to a sublayer that's hidden within a collapsed layer. Just click on an object in your artwork and choose Locate Layer or Locate Object from the Layers palette's menu.

Varied Perspective

Analyzing Different Views of Perspective

Advanced Technique

Overview: *Draw and scan a sketch; create working layers using your sketch as a template; in each "guides" layer, draw a series of lines to establish perspective; make the perspective lines into guides; draw elements of your image using the applicable perspective guides.*

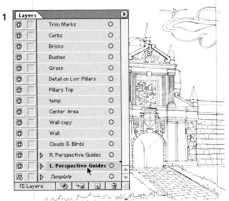

Portion of the original pencil sketch placed on a template layer with a custom layer ready for creation of guides

Top, dragging a perspective line to the uppermost object from the vanishing point; bottom, paths blended to create in-between perspective lines

While any object can be made into a guide, converting lines into guides is indispensable when adding perspective to an image. To illustrate this McDonald's packaging design, Clarke Tate constructed several sets of vanishing point guides, enabling him to draw a background scene (Fort Santiago in the Philippines) that would contrast with the flat cartoon figures of Snoopy and Woodstock.

1 Setting up the layers. Sketch a detailed layout of the illustration on paper, shaping main elements like Tate's brick walk and wall with a perspective view. Scan your sketch and save the scan as a TIFF, then place the TIFF in Illustrator and choose Template from the Layers palette's pop-up menu. Analyze the image to determine the number of vanishing points in your illustration (points along the scene's horizon where parallel lines seem to converge). Create new layers (click the Create New Layer icon in the Layers palette) for compositional elements; add a layer for each vanishing point in the illustration.

2 **Establishing the location of vanishing points.** In the Layers palette, select the first layer you'll use for developing a set of perspective guides. Referring to your template, mark the first vanishing point and use the Pen tool to draw a path along the horizon and through the vanishing point. (Some or all of your vanishing points may need to extend beyond the picture border.) With the Direct-selection tool, select the anchor point from the end of the line that is away from the vanishing point. Grab the point, then hold down Option/Alt and swing this copy of the line up so it encompasses the uppermost object that will be constructed using the vanishing point. You should now have a **V** that extends along your horizon line through your vanishing point, then to an upper or lower portion of your composition.

To create in-between lines through the same vanishing point, select both of the original lines, use the Blend tool to click first on the outer anchor point of one of the lines, and then on the outer anchor point of the other line. (If you need to specify more or fewer steps, you can select the blend and edit the number of steps in the Spacing: Specified Steps field of the Object: Blend: Blend Options dialog box.) For each different vanishing point, repeat the above procedure.

3 **Making and using the guides.** Because Illustrator cannot create guides from blended objects, you must first select each blend with the Selection tool and then expand it (Object: Blend: Expand). Next, transform the blends into guides by choosing View: Guides: Make Guides. Now pick an area of the illustration and begin drawing. You may want to lock the layers containing guides for other vanishing points so you don't accidentally snap objects to the wrong perspective.

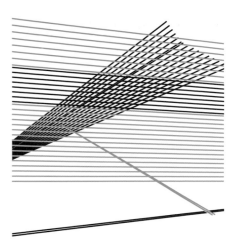

Perspective line blends before being transformed into guides

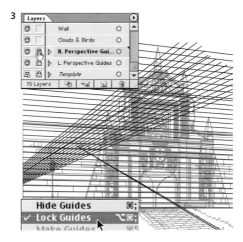

Turning off the "snap to" function for guides by locking the layer (left); locking guides in place by using the Lock/Unlock toggle in the View: Guides submenu

Locking and unlocking guides

- When guides are unlocked (disable View: Guides: Lock Guides), you can select any guide as an object and move or delete it.

- When a layer with guides is locked, the guides lose their "snap to" property—yet another good reason for you to keep guides on separate layers.

Type

6

Type

The Type tool, Area-type tool, Path-type tool, Vertical-type tool, Vertical Area-type tool, and Vertical Path-type tool. Select a Type tool and press Shift to toggle the tool between a horizontal and vertical orientation

One option you may not want

If you keep accidentally selecting type when you're trying to select an object, disable Type Area Select (Edit: Preferences: Type & Auto Tracing). You can still select type by clicking on it with the Direct-select tool or drawing around the baseline with the Lasso tool.

Linking multiple blocks of text

Link multiple text objects so text flows from one to the next: select the desired objects and choose Type: Blocks: Link. Text does not have to be present to do this.

Typographic controls

Set keyboard-accessible typographic control defaults in Edit: Preferences: Type & Auto Tracing, but set units of measurement for type in Preferences: Units & Undo.

Selecting type

Use one of the Lasso tools to easily select type without first selecting the baseline and when Type Area Select is unchecked (Edit: Preferences: Type & Auto Tracing).

Illustrator is a powerful tool for graphically controlling type. Although you're likely to prefer a page layout program such as QuarkXPress, InDesign, or PageMaker for multipage documents like catalogues and long magazine articles, and Dreamweaver or GoLive for web page layout, this chapter will show you many reasons to stay within Illustrator for single-page documents. The Type chapter of Adobe's *User Guide* covers the creation and manipulation of type in great detail, so this introduction will focus on essentials, what's new and production tips.

For creating and manipulating type, there are two palettes you can open from the Window: Type: Character and Window: Type: Paragraph. When you first open these palettes, they may appear in a collapsed view. To cycle through display options for either palette, click the double arrow on the Palette tab.

There are three type options in Illustrator that are accessible through the Type tool: *Point-type*, *Area-type*, and *Path-type*. The flexible Type tool lets you click to create a Point-type object, click-drag to create an Area-type object, or click within any existing type object to enter or edit text. You can gain access to type created in other applications using the File: Open or File: Place commands.

Select letters, words or an entire block of text by dragging across the letters with the Type tool, or use a selection tool to select text as an *object* by clicking on or marqueeing the text baseline (the baseline is the line that the type sits on).

• **Point-type:** Click with the Horizontal-type or Vertical-type tool anywhere on the page to create Point-type. Once you click, a blinking text-insertion cursor called an "I-beam" indicates that you can now type text using your keyboard. To add another line of text, press the Return key. When you're finished typing into one text object, click on the Type tool in the Toolbox to simultaneously select the current text as an object (the I-beam will disappear) and be poised to begin another text object. To just select the text as an object, click on a selection tool.

- **Area-type:** Click and drag with the Type tool to create a rectangle, into which you can type. Once you've defined your rectangle, the I-beam awaits your typing, and the text automatically wraps to the next line when you type in the confines of the rectangle. If you've typed more text than can fit in your text rectangle, you'll notice a plus sign along the bottom right side of the rectangle. To enlarge the rectangle to allow for more text, use the Direct-selection tool to deselect the text block, then grab one side of the rectangle and drag it out, holding down the Shift key to constrain the direction of the drag. To add a new text object that you will link to an existing text object, use the Group-selection tool to grab the rectangle only (not the text), hold down the Option (Mac)/Alt (Win) key, and drag a copy of the rectangle. Text will automatically flow to the new rectangle.
Note: *You can't do this if you're accessing the Group-selection tool by temporarily holding down the Option/Alt key.*

Another way to create Area-type or Vertical Area-type is to construct a path (with any tools you wish) forming a shape with which to place the type. Click and hold on the Type tool to access other tools, or press the Shift key to toggle between horizontal and vertical orientations of *like* tools (see Tip "Type tool juggling" later in this chapter introduction). Choose the Area-type or Vertical Area-type tool and click on the path itself to place text within the path. Distort the confining shape by grabbing an anchor point with the Direct-selection tool and dragging it to a new location, or reshape the path by adjusting direction lines. The text within will reflow.
Note: *If you use the Vertical Area-type tool, you'll see that your text will flow automatically, starting from the right edge of the area flowing toward the left! Those of you who use Roman fonts and typographic standards won't have*

It's Greek to me!
You can set type to be "greeked" on screen (it appears as a gray bar) by choosing File: Preferences: Type & Auto Tracing: Greeking. Greeked text prints normally.

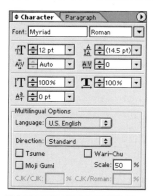

Text different sizes?
To proportionally resize Area-type or Point-type of different sizes, select the text and use ⌘-Shift-> (Mac)/Ctrl-Shift-> (Win) to increase all the font sizes. Use ⌘-Shift-> or Ctrl-Shift-< to decrease the sizes.

Selecting text or objects
Once you've entered your text, use the Type tool to select any text element by clicking and dragging across letters, words, or lines; double-clicking to select a word; triple-clicking to select a paragraph; or Shift-clicking to extend a selection. If the text-insertion I-beam is activated, then Edit: Select All will select all type within that text object. If your text I-beam is not activated, then Select All selects *all unlocked objects* in your image.

Illustrator supports Multinational fonts, including Chinese, Japanese, and Korean. Access the Multinational portion of the Character palette by clicking on the double arrows on the Palette tab to fully expand it. To utilize the multinational font capabilities you must have the proper fonts and character sets loaded on your system, as well as special system software. Some of the multinational options will not work with Roman fonts, such as U.S. and U.K. English language fonts.

The quick-changing Type tool

When using the regular Type tool, look at your cursor very carefully in these situations:

- If you move the regular Type tool over a closed path, the cursor changes to the Area-type icon.
- If you move the Type tool over an open path, the cursor will change to the Path-type icon.

Making a new text object

Reselect the Type tool to end one text object; the next click will start a new text object. Or, deselect the current text by holding down the ⌘ (Mac)/Ctrl (Win) key (temporarily turning your cursor into a selection tool) and clicking outside the text block.

much use for this tool since Roman type flows from left to right (see Tip "Multinational font support" at left).

To set tabs for Area-type, select the text object and choose Window: Type: Tab Ruler. The tab ruler will open aligned with the text box. As you pan or zoom, the Tab ruler does not move with the text box. If you lose your alignment, close the Tab ruler and reopen it. To wrap text around an object, select both the text box and the object and choose Type: Wrap: Make. After paths are wrapped to text objects, reshaping the paths causes text to reflow. To add a new path, Ungroup the current text and path objects, then reselect the text with the old and new paths and choose Type: Wrap: Make. (For more on tabs and wrapping text around objects, see the *User Guide*.)
Note: *You'll have to use Type: Wrap: Release or Ungroup before you can apply some of the filters to the text.*

- **Path-type:** The Path-type tool allows you to click on a path to flow text along the perimeter of the path (the path will then become unstroked or unfilled). To reposition the beginning of the text, use a Selection tool to grab the Path-type I-beam and drag left or right. Drag the I-beam up or down (or double-click it) to *flip* the text so it wraps along the inside or outside of the path.

As with Area-type, use the Direct-selection tool to reshape the confining path; the type on the path will automatically readjust to the new path shape.

MORE TYPE FUNCTIONS (TYPE & WINDOW MENUS)

- **Check Spelling**, **Find Font**, **Find/Change**, and **Smart Punctuation** all work whether anything is selected or not, although some of these functions give you the option to work within a selected text block.

If you try to open a file and don't have the correct fonts loaded, Illustrator warns you, lists the missing fonts, and asks if you still want to open the file. You do need the correct fonts to print properly; so if you don't have the missing fonts, choose Find Font to locate and replace them with ones you do have.

Find Font's dialog box displays the fonts used in the document in the top list; an asterisk indicates a missing font. The font type is represented by a symbol to the right of the font name. You can choose to replace fonts with ones on your system or used in the document. To display only the font types you want to use as replacements, uncheck those you don't want to include in the list. To replace a font used in the document, select it from the top list and choose a replacement font from the bottom list. You can individually replace each occurrence of the font by clicking Change and then Find Next. Otherwise, simply click Change All to replace all occurrences. **Note:** *When you select a font in the top list, it becomes selected in the document.*

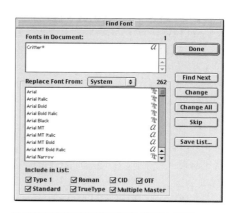

- **Type Orientation** lets you change orientation from horizontal to vertical, or vice versa, by choosing Type: Type Orientation: Horizontal or Vertical.

- **Change Case** lets you change the case of text selected with the Type tool to all upper, lower, or mixed case.

- **Rows & Columns** can be used on Area-type or any selected rectangle. Use a selection tool (not the Type tool) to select the entire text object. You can enter your text first, or simply begin setting up your rows and columns with a rectangle. In the dialog box, specify the number and sizes of the rows and columns and whether you wish to use Add Guides. This creates grouped lines that you can make into Illustrator guides with View: Guides: Make Guides (see the *Illustrator Basics* chapter for more on guides). Keep Preview checked to see the results of your specifications while you work, and click one of the Text Flow options to choose whether text will flow horizontally or vertically from one block to another.

- **MM Design** stands for Multiple Master fonts. There's also a separate MM Design palette, so you can customize Multiple Master fonts (see your font documentation for help).

If you don't have the fonts...

Missing fonts? You can still open, edit, and save the file, because Illustrator remembers the fonts you were using. However, the text will not flow accurately and the file won't print correctly until you load or replace the missing fonts.

Revert Path-type to path

Select the path with the Group-selection tool. Copy the path. Select the path with the Selection tool and delete it. Paste in Front to replace the path.—*Ted Alspach*

Type along the top and bottom

To create type along the top *and* bottom of a path, press the Option (Mac)/Alt (Win) key as you drag the I-beam to flip a *copy* of the type on the path.

Type tool juggling

To toggle a Type tool between its vertical and horizontal mode, first make sure nothing is selected. Hold the Shift key down to toggle the tool to the opposite mode.

Paint bucket and Eyedropper

To set what the Eyedropper picks up and the Paint bucket applies, double-click either tool to open the Eyedropper/Paint Bucket Options dialog box.

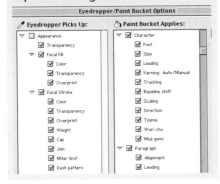

Eyedropper text

To restyle part of a text string or block, pick up a new sample with the Eyedropper tool, hold down the Option (Mac)/Alt (Win) key to select the Paint bucket tool and drag the cursor (as you would with the Text tool) over the text to be restyled.—*David Nelson*

Reflow text as in page layout

Resize a text block by its bounding box handles (see the *Illustrator Basics* chapter) and the text will reflow. —*Sandee Cohen*

The appearance of stroked text

To add strokes to type without distorting the characters: use the Appearance palette to "Add New Stroke," move this new stroke *below* the original, and set the new color and weight.

- **Fit Headline** is a quick way to open up the letterspacing of a headline across a specific distance. First, create the headline within an area, not along a path. Next, set the type in the size you wish to use. Select the headline, then choose Type: Fit Headline, and the type will spread out to fill the area you've indicated. This works with both the Horizontal and Vertical-type tools.

- **Show Hidden Characters** reveals soft and hard returns, word spaces, and an odd-shaped infinity symbol indicating the end of text flow. Toggle it on and off by choosing Type: Show Hidden Characters.

- **Glyph Options** can only be accessed if you have the appropriate Japanese Kanji font loaded. This option is only available for Macintosh users.

CONVERTING TYPE TO OUTLINES

You can now use the Appearance palette to apply multiple strokes to editable type (see the *Transparency & Appearances* chapter for details about working with multiple strokes or fills). You can also reliably mask with live, editable type! So although there are fewer and fewer reasons to convert your type to outlines, there are still some times when converting type to outlines is your best option (see "Why convert type to outlines?" following). As long as you've created type with fonts you have installed on your system (and can print) and you've finished experimenting with your type elements (e.g., adjusting size, leading, or kerning/tracking), you have the option to convert your live type to Illustrator objects. Your type will no longer be editable as type, but instead will be constructed of standard Illustrator Bézier curves that may include compound paths to form the "holes" in objects (such as the transparent center of an **O** or **P**). As with all Illustrator paths and compound paths, you can use the Direct-selection tool to select and edit portions of the objects (see the *Drawing & Coloring* introduction for more about compound paths). To convert type to outlines, select all blocks of type you wish to outline (it doesn't matter if you have non-type objects selected as well) and choose Type: Create Outlines. To fill the "holes" in letters with color, select the compound path and choose Object: Compound Path: Release.

Note: *Outlining type is* not *recommended for small font sizes—see Tip "Don't outline small type" at right.*

Why convert type to outlines?

You might want to outline type:

- **So you can graphically transform or distort the individual curves and anchor points of letters or words.** Everything from minor stretching of a word to extreme distortion is possible. (For examples of this, see the lower right **M** on this page, and Galleries later in this chapter.)

- **So you can maintain your letter and word spacing when exporting your type to another application.** Many programs that allow you to import Illustrator type as "live" editable text don't support the translation of your custom kerning and word spacing. Convert text to outlines before exporting Illustrator type in these instances to maintain custom word and letter spacing.

- **So you don't have to supply the font to your client or service bureau.** Converting type can be especially useful when you need to use foreign language fonts, or when your image will be printed while you're not around. (For an example of this, see the Model United Nations logo at right and lessons and Galleries later in this chapter.)

Don't outline small type

If you're printing to a high-resolution imagesetter or using larger type sizes, you can successfully convert type objects to outlines. However, due to a font-enhancing printing technology (called "hinting"), a *small* type object converted to outlines won't look as good on the computer screen, or print as clearly to printers of 600 dots per inch or less, as it would have if it had remained a font.

Making one text block of many

To join separate Area-text boxes or Point-text objects, select all the text objects with any selection tool and Copy. Then draw a new Area-text box and Paste. Text will flow into the new box in the original *stacking order* that it appeared on the page. (It doesn't matter if you select graphic elements with your text—these elements won't be pasted.) —*Sandee Cohen*

Transporting foreign or unusual fonts (artwork by Kathleen Tinkel)

Filling with patterns or gradients

Masking with type (artwork by Min Wang for Adobe Systems)

Transforming outlines (artwork by Javier Romero Design Group)

Custom Text Paths

Trickling Type with Variations of Type Style

Overview: *Prepare and Place text; create a set of evenly-spaced paths; copy and paste text into appropriate path lines; adjust text baseline paths and placement of text on the paths.*

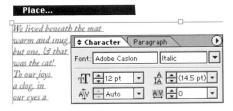

Placed text creates a new rectangle which contains the type; choose a font and size while the text is still selected

Option-drag/Alt-drag to create a second path below the first; use Object: Transform: Transform Again (or ⌘-D/Ctrl-D) to repeat this step

Grab the I-beam to move the text along the path

Adjust curved paths and text placement along those paths using the Direct-selection tool

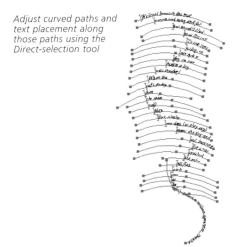

Laurie Szujewska placed type on curved Bézier paths to emulate the shaped lines of Lewis Carroll's original hand-lettered poem from *Alice's Adventures Underground* (an early version of *Alice in Wonderland*).

1 Preparing your type. Use a word processor to proofread and spell-check your text. In Illustrator, choose File: Place and select your text document; this creates a rectangle containing your text. Choose a typeface and size.

2 Creating your baselines and placing your type. Next to your type, draw a curved path with the Pen tool (see "Zen Lessons" in the *Wow! CD* "Tutorial" folder for Pen help). With the Path-Type tool, click on your Bézier path and type a few characters. To determine the spacing between lines, switch to the Selection tool, grab the path, hold the Option/Alt key and drag the selected path downward, until the second path is spaced correctly (release the mouse button while still holding down the key). To duplicate the path and the spacing between paths, press ⌘-D/Ctrl-D (Object: Transform: Transform Again), repeating until you've created the desired number of text paths.

Switch to the Type tool, select the text you want for the top path and Copy. Now click on the top path and Paste. Repeat with the remaining lines.

3 Adjusting the type. With all text placed, use the Direct-selection tool to adjust the curves. If you wish to see all of the text paths at once (whether selected or not), switch to Outline View. To move the starting point for lines of text, click on the path with the Selection tool and drag the I-beam along the path. For downward curving text in her image, Szujewska's adjusted the path, then individually selected the last words, progressively reducing them in size.

We lived beneath the mat
warm and snug and fat
but one, & that
was the cat!
To our joys
a clog, in
our eyes a
fog, on our
hearts a log,
was the dog!
When the
cat's away,
then
the mice
will
play.
But, alas!
one day, (so they say)
came the dog and
cat, hunting
for a rat,
crushed
the mice
all flat,
each
one
as
he
sat underneath the mat, warm, & snug and fat… Think of that!

SZUJEWSKA / ADOBE SYSTEMS, INC. / adapted from Lewis Carroll's *Alice's Adventures Underground*

SZUJEWSKA/ADOBE SYSTEMS, INC.

Laurie Szujewska / Adobe Systems, Inc.

For Adobe's Poetica type specimen book, Laurie Szujewska was inspired by a "love knot" poem from the book *Pattern Poetry* by Dick Higgins, and created a similar spiral path with the Pen tool. She used the Path-Type tool to place the text on the path. She then meticulously kerned and placed spaces along the type path to prevent text overlaps, and to get things just right.

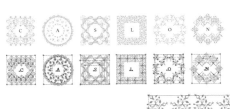

SZUJEWSKA / ADOBE SYSTEMS, INC.

Laurie Szujewska / Adobe Systems, Inc.

For Adobe's Caslon type specimen book, Szujewska created these decorative ornaments by placing, rotating, and reflecting groups of separate Point-type objects filled with a gray color.

WEINSTEIN

Ari M. Weinstein

Ari M. Weinstein developed techniques that allowed this Ketubah, a wedding present for a friend, to conform to traditional scribal standards and appearance. He began by entering text in a calligraphic Hebrew font, line by line, to avoid automatic text wrap. He re-created the traditional scribal method of crafting the length of each line by stretching letter cross-strokes instead of using paragraph justification (which would have created non-uniform word and letter spacing). To accomplish this, Weinstein converted the type to outlines (Type: Create Outlines) and then used the Direct-selection tool to select parts of letter outlines and move them in 1-point increments with the arrow keys.

BURNS

John Burns

Lettering artist John Burns developed this logo for PlanTea, an organic fertilizer for plants that is brewed in water, like tea. He began by typing the name and then converted the letters to outlines (Type: Create Outlines). After drawing a leaf and placing it on the stem of each letter **a**, he selected and copied the artwork, pasted it in back (Edit: Paste In Back) to form the drop shadows, and offset them down and to the right. Burns then filled the copied letterforms with 40% black. To prevent the drop shadows from touching the black letterforms (creating a more stylized look), he selected the black artwork and again pasted it behind (but in front of the drop shadows) and then applied a white fill and thick white stroke to the pasted letterforms. The stages of his process, here applied to the **I**, are shown above left. Finally, Burns used the Direct-selection tool to reshape some of the drop shadow shapes, adjusting the thickness of some of the shadow letter strokes and hiding slivers of shadows that stuck out a little behind the black letters (the **P** directly above shows the shadow before and after reshaping).

HORNALL ANDERSON DESIGN WORKS

Hornall Anderson Design Works /
John Hornall (Art Director)

Designers at Hornall Anderson Design Works set the name "Yves" for this healthy, vegetarian line of foods in Gill Sans and then modified the letterforms to fit the logo design. First, they placed the text along a curve and then converted the font characters to outlines (Type: Create Outlines). To create the shadows on the left side of the name's characters, designers used the Scissors tool to cut the character paths, the Direct-selection tool to move cut pieces, and the Pen tool to connect points and close objects. Another way to accomplish a similar effect is to Copy the original letterforms and Paste in Back twice. Give the top copy a white Fill and a thick white Stroke; while still selected, choose Object: Path: Outline Path and set the new outline stroke to a small width.

Move the bottom copy of the letterforms to the left. Then select the two copies and choose the Minus Front command from the Pathfinder palette. Lastly, delete extraneous objects and use the Scissors and Direct-selection tools to reshape the remaining objects.

Masking Letters
Masking Images with Letter Forms

Overview: *Create a large letter on top of a placed TIF image; convert the letter to outlines; select all and make the letter form into a clipping mask for the placed image.*

THREINEN-PENDARVIS

1

Placing the TIF image; creating Point-type letter

Converting the letter "S" to outlines

2

Selecting both the letter form and the image beneath; making a clipping mask

Selecting an object using the Layers palette, then moving it with the Direct-selection tool

This "**S** is for Surfing" was created by Cher Threinen-Pendarvis for an alphabet poster. Although you *can* mask with "live" type, Threinen-Pendarvis converted her type to outlines. For additional lessons on masking, see the Gallery opposite and the *Advanced Techniques* chapter.

1 Positioning elements and converting a large letter to outlines. Place a TIF image into your Illustrator file by using File: Place. Using the Type tool, click on top of your image to create a Point-type object and type one letter. Choose a typeface with enough weight and a point size large enough for the bottom image to show through the letter form itself. Select the letter with a Selection tool and choose Type: Create Outlines (⌘-Shift-O/Ctrl-Shift-O).

2 Creating the clipping mask and adjusting the image position. The topmost object in a selection becomes the mask when you make a clipping mask. If your letter isn't the top object, select it, Cut, then Edit: Paste In Front. To create the mask, select the outlined letter and the images to be masked and choose Object: Clipping Mask: Make; the mask and masked objects wil be grouped. To adjust the position of an object or the mask, select it from the Layers palette or with the Direct-selection tool, then use the Direct-selection tool to move it. Threinen-Pendarvis ended by applying Effect: Stylize: Drop Shadow (default settings) to a filled copy of the **S** below the mask group, above a TIF background created in Procreate's Painter.

NEWMAN

Gary Newman

Artist Gary Newman combined a compound path and masking to create this title illustration. First, Newman typed the word "Careers" and converted the text to outlines (Type: Create Outlines). Next, he made a single compound path by choosing Object: Compound Path: Make. Newman masked a copy of his background artwork with this compound path. With the compound object on top and all elements selected, he chose Object: Clipping Mask: Make. He then selected the masked background objects and used Filter: Colors: Adjust Colors, increasing the black percentage. Newman added a drop shadow by layering a black-filled copy of the type behind the background-filled type. He set the words "Changing" and "at mid-life" in black type,

and added drop shadows behind them; drop shadows can also be made using the Transparency palette to adjust blending modes and Opacity (for help with blending modes and Opacity, see the *Transparency* chapter).

Bookcover Design

Illustrator as a Stand-alone Layout Tool

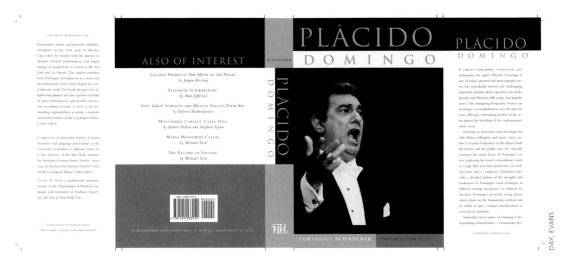

Overview: *Set your document size; place guides and cropmarks; place EPS files and make Area Type for columns and Point-type for graphic type; visually track type to fit.*

Page layout programs such as QuarkXPress and Page-Maker are essential for producing multipage, complex documents. However, Rob Day and Virginia Evans often use Illustrator for single-page design projects such as book jackets.

1 Setting up your page. Choose File: Document Setup to set up the Artboard for your design. Click on landscape or portrait page orientation and enter your Artboard size, making sure it's large enough for crop and/or registration marks (the "Size" parameter will automatically switch to "Custom"). Choose View: Show Rulers and "re-zero" your ruler origin to the upper left corner of where your page will begin (see the *Basics* chapter for more on repositioning the ruler origin), and use View: Outline/Preview to toggle between Outline and Preview modes. Although you can generate uniform grids with Edit: Preferences: Guides & Grid, for columns of varying sizes, Day and Evans numerically created two sets of rectangles: one for bleeds, one for trims. With the Rectangle tool, click to make a box sized for a trim area (see the *Basics* chapter for Rectangle tool help), then immediately Option-click/Alt-click

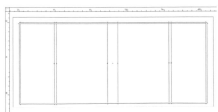

Setting up the Artboard and layout specs

on the center of the trim area box to numerically specify a box .125" larger in each dimension in order to create a bleed area box. Day and Evans made trim and bleed boxes for the front, back, flaps, and spine. To place an overall trim mark, select the boxes that define the entire trim area and choose Filter: Create: Trim Marks.

2 Customizing your guides. Select your trim and bleed boxes (not the trim marks) and create Guides by choosing View: Guides: Make Guides (see the "Varied Perspective" lesson in the *Layers* chapter for more on guides).

3 Placing and refining the elements. Choose File: Place to select an EPS image to import into your layout. Create rectangles or other objects which will define the area for columns of text. Click on the path of one of these objects with the Area Type tool. Once the text cursor is placed, you can type directly or paste text (see "Custom Text Paths" in this chapter). Area Type is used in this layout for columns of type on the flaps. Alternately, click with the Type tool to create Point-type, which is used to place lines of type for titles and headlines, and other individual type elements. To track type visually to fit a space, select a text object and use Option/Alt-←/→. For help with rotating or scaling objects (this applies to text objects as well), see the *Zen* chapter and the *Zen Lessons* on the *Wow! CD*.

Creating "cropmarks," then "trim marks"

Create a rectangle that defines a cropping area, and choose Object: Cropmarks: Make. Cropmarks are visible in Illustrator but become invisible when placed into another program (such as QuarkXPress or PageMaker), except that they will reappear if you position objects beyond the cropmarks. To remove cropmarks, either choose Object: Cropmarks: Release, or make a new rectangle and again choose Object: Cropmarks: Make. Or create always-visible Trim Marks by selecting any object (a rectangle is not required) and choosing Filter: Create: Trim Marks. Files can contain multiple trim marks.

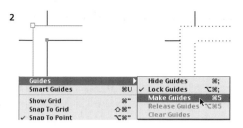

Converting trim and bleed boxes into Guides

All of the elements placed into the layout

Close-ups of an Area-Type object

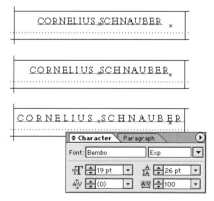

Close-ups of Point-type objects

Tracking a line of Point-type with cursor-keys

JAVIER ROMERO DESIGN GROUP

Javier Romero Design Group

With a client as particular as Disney, Javier Romero needed the flexibility to create many design variations for children's clothing tags. And because the type needed to be fully integrated with the illustrations, Illustrator proved to be the most practical design tool. Of the dozens of designs that Romero presented, Disney selected as finals the designs shown in the photo above and to its right. Shown directly above are three of the comps, which include compositional elements contributing to the final design.

Javier Romero Design Group

Javier Romero Design Group converted the title in this illustration to outlines (Type: Create Outlines) and then manually distorted it. The resulting glowing effect, which the Design Group then applied to the type, can be used on any object—even regular, editable text objects. They filled the letters in a solid color, Copied and chose Edit: Paste In Back to place a copy of the letters behind the original, set the Fill for this copy to None, with a 5.5-pt, medium-colored stroke. They repeated the Copy and Paste In Back step, successively using different colored strokes of 7, 11 and 16 points.

JAVIER ROMERO DESIGN GROUP

GORSKA (design), BALDWIN (illustration)/MAX SEABAUGH ASSOCIATES

Caryl Gorska / Max Seabaugh Associates

After commissioning Scott Baldwin to create a nutcracker illustration (he used Macromedia FreeHand to re-create his linoleum cut), Caryl Gorska scanned a traditional, copyright-free Dover Publications typeface. She saved the scanned typeface to use as a template (see the *Blends, Gradients & Mesh* chapter) and used the Pen tool to carefully trace the letters she needed. She then created the frame into which the type would be placed and, using the Selection tool, she "hand-set" the type by copying and pasting letter forms. Lastly, she fine-tuned the letter spacing, checking herself by printing myriad proofs—both actual size and greatly enlarged. Although her typeface, Newport Condensed, was available as a PostScript commercial font, instead of spending time and money tracking down and purchasing the font, Gorska preferred to spend the time typesetting the letters herself. "It keeps me in touch with the real letter forms and how they fit together, in a way that we often miss, just doing typesetting on the computer."

Brushed Type

Applying Brushes to Letterforms

Overview: *Create centerlines for font characters; customize art brushes and apply brushes to the centerlines and outlines of the letterforms to simulate hand-rendered lettering.*

To convey the variety of museums in Boston, cartographer Steven Gordon wanted a map title that blended the "natural" artistry of pencil and brush with the classicism of serif font characters. Because Illustrator applies brushes as strokes along paths, Gordon drew centerlines for the font characters before painting the centerlines with customized brushes, giving them the look of hand-rendered letterforms.

1

Original font characters filled with 20% black

Black-stroked outlines of font characters on layer above original font characters

The letterform centerlines after drawing with the Pencil tool on a layer above the original font characters; the outline layer is not shown

2

Top, the default Splash brush; below, the edited brush with color fills

1 Creating letter centerlines and outlines. To re-create Gordon's painted lettering, begin by typing text in a serif font (Gordon selected Type: Character and chose Garamond Bold Condensed Italic and 112 pt in the Character palette.) Select the text and give it a 20% black Fill. Copy the layer with the text by dragging it onto the Create New Layer icon at the bottom of the palette. To create the font outline, select the text on the copied layer and convert the characters to outlines (Type: Create Outlines), then change their Fill to None and Stroke to black. Now create a new layer (click the Create New Layer icon in the Layers palette) and drag this layer between the other two. On this new layer, draw centerlines for each font character with the Pen or Pencil tool. The paths don't have to be perfectly smooth or centered inside the letterforms because you will paint them with an irregularly shaped brush later.

2 Creating and applying custom brushes and effects. Gordon looked to Illustrator's brushes to give the letter centerlines the color and spontaneity of traditional brushwork. He opened the Artistic Sample brush palette (Window: Brush Libraries: Artistic Sample) and selected the Splash brush. To customize the brush, first drag the brush from the palette to the canvas. Select each brush object with the Direct-selection tool and replace the gray with a color you like. Next, drag the brush artwork into the Brushes palette and select New Art Brush from the New Brush dialog box. In the Art Brush Options dialog box, further customize the brush by changing Width to 50%, enabling the Proportional brush setting, and clicking OK. (You won't see the change in width displayed in the dialog's preview.) Make several brush variations by copying the brush and then editing brush Direction, Width and other parameters. Now individualize your letterforms by selecting the first centerline and clicking on a brush from the Brushes palette. Try several of the brushes you created to find the best "fit." Continue applying brushes to the remaining centerlines.

To create the look of loose pencil tracings for the font character outlines on the top layer, Gordon edited the Dry Ink brush from the Artistic Sample palette, changing its Width to 10% in the Art Brush Options dialog box. Gordon completed the look by selecting each character outline and applying the Roughen Effect (Size 1%, Distort 10%, Smooth). (See the *Transparency, Styles & Effects* chapter to learn more about applying Effects and using the Appearance palette.)

3 Finishing touches. Gordon selected all the centerlines and offset them up and left while moving the font outlines down and right from the original font characters on the bottom layer, suggesting a loose style. He also simulated the appearance of hand-rendering by adjusting the transparency and blending modes of the brushed letterforms: Gordon selected the centerline objects, and in the Transparency palette, chose Multiply mode and reduced transparency to 75%. This caused the colors of brushed centerline paths to darken where they overlapped, mimicking the effect of overlapping transparent inks.

Experimenting by applying different brushes to centerlines to lend individuality to the letter "s"

On top, the Dry Ink brush; left, the customized brush applied to the font outline; right, the Roughen Effect applied to the brushed outline

Artwork on three layers, from bottom layer (left) to top layer (right)

3

Left, the horizontal and vertical centerlines of the letter "t" with Normal blending mode and 100% opacity; right, strokes placed to form letter "t" and with Multiply blending mode and 70% opacity

Finished lettering on three layers, shown in composite view

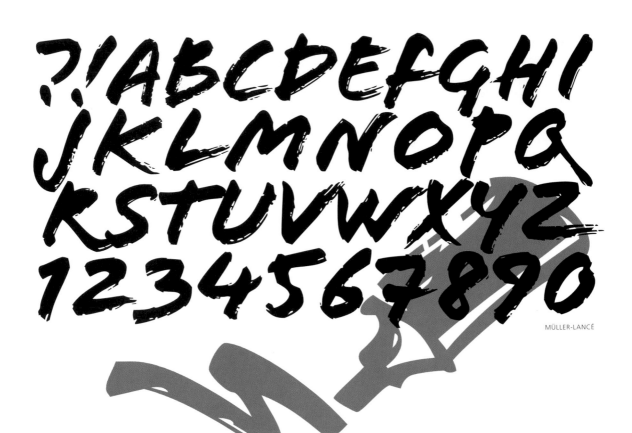

?!ABCDEFGHI
JKLMNOPQ
RSTUVWXYZ
1234567890

MÜLLER-LANCÉ

Joachim Müller-Lancé

The original characters of Joachim Müller-Lancé's Flood typeface were drawn with a worn felt marker during a type seminar hosted by Sumner Stone. Two years later Müller-Lancé rediscovered the drawings when Adobe asked him for new font ideas. Realizing that the original character traces were not of font quality, he redrew all of the characters using Illustrator's Pen and Pencil tools. He composed many of the characters as separate, black-filled objects, which he moved around while also adjusting width, slant, and scale until he got the look he wanted. He used the Merge command from the Pathfinder palette to join the overlapping objects of each character into a single shape. He also drew the holes and streaks as white-filled objects above the black-filled objects and used Minus Front (also from the Pathfinder palette) to knock out the holes and streaks in the characters. Then Müller-Lancé copied the artwork for each character and pasted it directly into the appropriate character slot in Fontographer, where he completed the font.

THE MATRIX

GIRVIN

Tim Girvin /
Tim Girvin Strategic Branding & Design

Designer Tim Girvin began the logo for this futuristic film by setting the title in Times New Roman and converting the type outlines to paths (Type: Create Outlines), He drew objects with the Rectangle and other tools that he used with the Divide command from the Pathfinder palette to break the letterforms into pieces. After modifying some of their shapes with the Direct-selection tool, Girvin repositioned the pieces to form the asymmetrical letterforms of the logo.

BARTLETT

Jennifer Bartlett /
Tim Girvin Strategic Branding & Design

Jennifer Bartlett set this logo using a proprietary Girvin font. To keep the letters of the tagline upright but parallel to the wave of the background banner, Bartlett selected individual characters by dragging with the Text tool and adjusted their vertical positions by entering positive values (to move characters up) or negative values (to move characters down) in the Character palette's Baseline Shift field, accessed by choosing Type: Character and choosing Show Options from the Character palette's pop-up menu.

ICE HOUSE PRESS (AKSELSEN)

Bjørn Akselsen / Ice House Press

For this logo for Private Chef, a gourmet food and catering company, designer Bjørn Akselsen avoided the orderly appearance of calligraphic and script fonts by using Illustrator to distort letterforms. First Akselsen drew the letterforms with traditional brush and ink, then scanned the artwork and placed it in Illustrator, where he traced the letterforms. Next he reshaped their outlines and interiors with the Direct-selection tool to emphasize contrast in the strokes and applied three Distort filters from the top section of the Filter menu (Pucker & Bloat, Roughen, and Scribble and Tweak) to further distort the letter shapes and enhance their individuality. Finally, Akselsen used the Pencil tool to smooth out rough edges.

Pattie Belle Hastings / Ice House Press
(Sharon Steuer illustration and production)

In redesigning the logos for The Traveling Radio Show, Pattie Belle Hastings wanted to convey activity in the title type treatment. Starting with characters from TheSans typeface, Hastings created the title in one line (as it appears on the business cards and brochures) and then outlined the characters (Type: Create Outlines). Zooming in on the characters, she pulled down four guidelines from the horizontal ruler (View: Show Rulers), so she could use them to align the letters. She then selected individual type characters and positioned each vertically, visually aligning it to one of the guidelines. The characters were also individually colored, and then horizontally positioned by Shift-selecting letters, and nudging them

ICE HOUSE PRESS (HASTINGS) / STEUER (Illustration / production)

with the left and right arrow keys. For a sticker design (shown above), the title was split into two lines and enlarged.

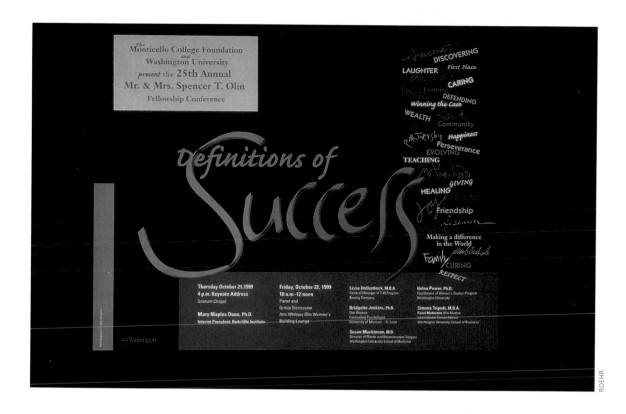

ROEHR

Karen Roehr

In this poster commemorating the 25th anniversary of a women's fellowship conference, artist Karen Roehr mixed computer fonts like Bodoni, Kabel, and Univers with calligraphy she rendered by hand using a Wacom tablet and Illustrator's Pen, Pencil, and Paintbrush tools. To use the Calligraphy brush, Roehr first double-clicked the Paintbrush tool and disabled the "Fill new brush strokes" option in the Paintbrush Tool Preferences. She chose a calligraphy brush (Angle 45°, Roundness 0%, Diameter 30 pt) from the Brushes palette and drew the word "Success." She copied the word and pasted it in back to form both a shadow and letterform gaps. For many of the poster's hand-drawn words, Roehr drew several variations of individual letters using different Illustrator tools, combining the letters that gave the word the appearance she wanted.

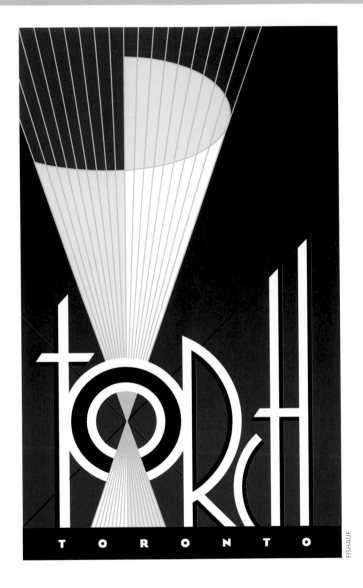

FISHAUF

Louis Fishauf / Reactor Art + Design

Asked to create the visual identity for a proposed news cafe and media tower, designer Louis Fishauf drew the letters for the name with the Pen tool, first assigning a thick stroke to the paths and then outlining the strokes (Object: Path: Outline Stroke). He moved points in the letter tips using the Direct-selection tool, angling the tips parallel to the black lines behind the name. To convey perspective, Fishauf pasted copies of the letters **t** and **H** behind the name, filled them with black, and manually offset each of these shadows to the left or right. For the letters **R** and **c**, Fishauf drew the shadows with the Pen tool, keeping the curves parallel to the white letterforms in front.

PAPCIAK-ROSE

Ellen Papciak-Rose / In The Studio

Ellen Papciak-Rose created the title "Zimbabwe" using geometric objects she drew with the Rectangle, Ellipse, and other tools. She composited the objects and used Minus Front and other commands from the Pathfinder palette to knock out parts of the objects, forming the title letterforms. Papciak-Rose then painted the strokes of the objects with two custom-built variations of a rough charcoal brush found in

the Artistic Sample Brush library (Window: Brush Libraries: Artistic Sample). In the four panels of the poster, Papciak-Rose painted outlines of characters from the Sand font with the two custom-built rough charcoal brushes.

Crunching Type

Transforming Type Using Warps & Envelopes

Overview: *Create and color a title using Appearances; use a warp effect to bow type; create an outline shape to "crunch" type; give the crunched type a dynamic, curved perspective effect using an envelope warp.*

HAMANN

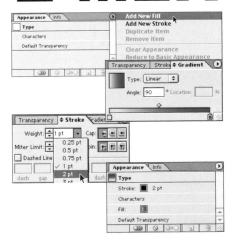

Using Add New Fill in the Appearance palette menu to add a gradient fill to the type

Warps and Envelopes are your superheroes for transforming headline type into any form you wish. No more need to convert type to outlines and laboriously move each anchor point by hand. Using Envelopes, it's literally as easy as drawing an outline and commanding the type to conform. With Warps and Envelopes, the type remains editable no matter how much you "crunch" it. Warps and Envelopes are always on hand to help rescue you from those looming deadlines!

1 Creating and coloring the E-Men title. To create the E-MEN cover title, use 72 point Arial Black font. To add a gradient fill to your type, select the type and choose Add New Fill from the Appearance palette menu. See the *Transparency & Appearances* chapter for more on the Appearance palette.

2 Using a Warp effect to make the E-Men bow. There are 15 standard Warp shapes that can be turned into styles. For "E-MEN," Hamann applied Effect: Warp: Arc Lower. With Preview enabled, he used the Bend slider to bow the bottom of the letters (to 23%), then clicked OK.

Effect: Warp works in many instances, but it didn't warp his gradient-fill along with the type. After applying Undo, Hamann chose Object: Envelop Options, enabled Distort Linear Gradients, then he applied Object: Envelope: Make with Warp, with the Arc Lower option at 23%.

3 Using a path to "crunch" type. To create the "CRUNCH!" Hamann again used the Appearance palette, this time to color "CRUNCH!" with a subtle gradient fill and a strong red stroke. Then, starting with a rectangle, he applied Object: Path: Add Anchor points twice, and then moved the rectangle's anchor points to form a dynamic jagged path. He then placed the path over the type, and with both the path and type selected he chose Object: Envelope Distort: Make with Top Object.

4 Using Envelope Distort: Make with Warp to create a curved perspective effect. To create a curved perspective effect, use Envelope Distort: Make with Warp to warp the "crunched" type. Because you can't nest one envelope inside another, first select your "crunched" type and choose Object: Envelope Distort: Expand. With your expanded type selected, choose Object: Envelope Distort: Make with Warp. Hamann chose Arc from the Style pop-up in the Warp Options dialog, and adjusted the sliders until he had achieved the desired curved perspective look.

5 Adjusting and adding a stroke to the type. To complete the "CRUNCH!" type, Hamann used Object: Envelope Distort: Edit Contents to access the type within the envelope. Using the Appearance palette, he added a yellow gradient fill, a 5 point black stroke, and a 10 point red stroke to the envelope enclosing the type (in that order) to get the desired final effect.

2

With Effect: Warp: Effect: Arc Lower, the gradient fill remains horizontal

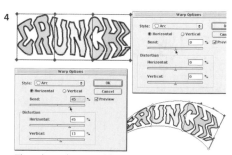

Using Object: Warp: Make with Warp (with Distort Linear Gradients enabled in the Envelope Options dialog), the gradient bends also

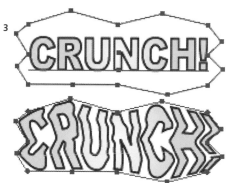

3

The type and path before and after applying Object: Envelope Distort: Make with Top

4

The released type; with Warp sliders set to 0 showing the starting envelope shape; the final Warp option settings; and the resultant envelope

5

The final strokes and the finished type

Blends, Gradients & Mesh

7

Blends, Gradients & Mesh

"W" Blend tool   *"G" Gradient tool*

The speed of the blend

To control the speed of the blend, create the blend and set the number of blend steps as you would normally do. This creates the blend spine, which is editable just like any other Illustrator path. Using the Convert-anchor-point tool, pull out control handles from the anchor point at each end of the blend spine. By extending or shortening these control handles along the spine, the speed of the blend is controlled. This is very similar to how blend speeds are controlled in a gradient mesh.—*Derek Mah*

Recolor after expanding blends

If you've expanded a blend, you can use *filters* to recolor blended objects. Direct-select and recolor the fill for the start and/or end objects, then select the entire blend and choose Filter: Colors: Blend Front to Back. Your objects' fill colors will reblend using the new start and end colors (this won't affect strokes or compound paths). Also try Blend Horizontally or Vertically, Adjust, and Saturate. **Note:** *This doesn't work if your blend includes gradients.*

BLENDS

Think of blends as a way to "morph" one object's shape and/or color into another. You can blend between multiple objects, and even gradients or compound paths, such as letters (see the *Drawing & Coloring* chapter for more on compound paths). Blends are *live,* which means you can edit the key objects by altering their shape, color, size, location, or rotation, and the resulting *in-between* objects will automatically update. You can also distribute a blend along a custom path (see details later in this chapter). **Note:** *Complex blends require a lot of RAM when drawing to the screen, especially gradient-to-gradient blends.*

The simplest way to create a blend is to select the objects you wish to blend and choose Object: Blend: Make. The number of steps you'll have in between each object is based on either the default options for the tool, or the last settings of the Blend Options (details following). Adjust settings for a selected blend by selecting the blend, then double-clicking the Blend tool (or Objects: Blend: Blend Options).

A more reliable method of creating smooth blends in many circumstances is to *point map* between two objects using the Blend tool. First, select the two objects that you want to blend (with the Group-selection tool), then use the Blend tool to *point map* by clicking first on a selected point on the first object, then on the correlating selected point on the second object.

When a blend first appears, it is selected and grouped. If you Undo immediately, the blend will be deleted, but your source objects remain selected so you can blend again. To modify a key object, Direct-select the key object first, then use any editing tool (including the Pencil, Smooth, and Erase tools) to make your changes.

Blend Options

To specify Blend Options as you blend, use the Blend

tool (see the *point map* directions above) and press the Option/Alt key as you click the second point. To adjust options on a completed blend, select it and double-click the Blend tool (or Object: Blend: Blend Options). Opening Blend Options, without any blend selected, sets the default for creating blends *in this work session*; these Options reset each time you restart.

- **Specified Steps** specifies the number of steps between each pair of key objects. Using fewer steps results in clearly distinguishable objects, while a larger number of steps results in an almost airbrushed effect.

- **Specified Distance** places a specified distance between the objects of the blend.

- **Smooth Color** allows Illustrator to automatically calculate the ideal number of steps between key objects in a blend, in order to achieve the smoothest color transition. If objects are the same color, or are gradients or patterns, the calculation will equally distribute the objects within the area of the blend, based on their size.

- **Orientation** determines whether blend objects rotate as the path curves. **Align to Path** (the default, first icon) allows the blend objects to rotate as they follow the path. **Align to Page** (the second icon) prevents objects from rotating as they are distributed along the curve of the path.

Blends along a Path

There are two ways to make blends follow a curved path. The first way is to Direct-select the "spine" of a blend (the path automatically created by the blend) and then use the Add/Delete-anchor-point tools, Direct-selection, Direct-selection Lasso, Convert-anchor, Pencil, Smooth—or even the Erase—tool to curve or edit the path; the blend will redraw to fit the new spine. The second way is to replace the spine with a customized path: select both the customized path and the blend, and choose Object: Blend: Replace

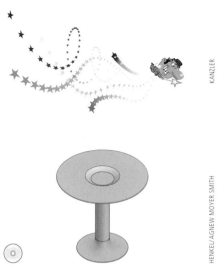

John Kanzler created the fairy (top) with multi-object blends and a replaced spine; Rick Henkel used gradient-to-gradient blends for the pedestal of his table (see his explanation, "Henkel-AMS flared effect," on the Wow! *CD for full details)*

To insert objects into a blend

Direct-select a key object and Option/Alt-drag to insert a new key object (the blend will reflow) that you can Direct-select and edit.

Reverse Front to Back

To reverse the order of a blend with only two key objects, Direct-select one of the key objects and choose Object: Arrange, or with any blend choose Object: Blend: Reverse Front to Back.

Expanding

Items such as gradients, gradient meshes, blends, and patterns are complex and can't be used to define other complex art unless the art is Expanded first using Object: Expand. Once expanded, you can use the objects within the art to define a brush, pattern, or blends.

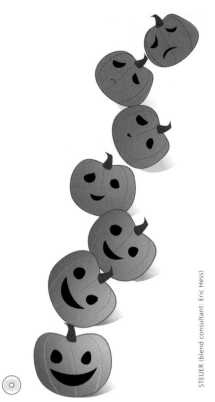

STEUER (blend consultant: Eric Hess)

Groups of objects blended into each other (pumpkins into pumpkins, shadows into shadows) using the Align to Path orientation, Specified Distance, and the "spines" edited into S curves (for more about blends see the Blends folder on the Wow! CD)

Adding color to your gradient

- Drag a swatch from the Color or Swatches palette to the gradient slider until you see a vertical line indicating where the new color stop will be added.
- If the fill is a solid color, you can drag color from the Fill icon at the bottom of the Toolbox.
- Hold down the Option/Alt key to drag a copy of a color stop.
- Option/Alt-drag one stop over another to *swap* their colors.
- Click the lower edge of a gradient to add a new stop.

Spine. This command moves the blend to its new spine.

It's a bit tricky, but you can also blend between multiple objects. Create your first set of objects and Group them (⌘-G/Ctrl-G). Next, select this group and holding Option/Alt, drag off a copy (making sure that you release your mouse button before releasing the keyboard—see "A Finger Dance" in the *Zen* chapter for help). Select both sets of grouped objects, and with the Blend tool, click on one anchor point on the first group, then hold Option/Alt when you click on a correlating point on the second group to specify the number of steps. As long as you maintain the same number of points, you can rotate and scale the objects, and use the Direct-selection tool to edit the objects or the spine. (See "STEUER pumpkin blend.ai" in the "Blends" folder on the *Wow! CD*.)

Reversing, Releasing, and Expanding Blends

Once you've created and selected a blend, you can:

- **Reverse** the order of objects on the spine by choosing Object: Blend: Reverse Spine.
- **Release** a Blend (Object: Blend: Release) if you wish to remove the blended objects between key objects and maintain the spine of the blend (be forewarned—you may lose grouping information!).
- **Expand** a Blend to turn it into a group of separate, editable objects. Choose Object: Expand.

GRADIENTS

Gradients are color transitions. To open the Gradient palette: double-click the Gradient tool icon on the Toolbox, or choose Window: Gradient. Gradients can be either radial (circular from the center) or linear. To apply a gradient to an object, select the object and click on a gradient swatch in the Swatches palette. To view only gradient swatches, click on the gradient icon at the bottom of the Swatches palette.

To start adjusting or creating a new gradient, click on the gradient preview in the Gradient palette. Only after clicking on the preview will you see the color stops and midpoints. Make your own gradients by adding and/or adjusting the stops (pointers representing colors) along the lower edge of the gradient preview, and adjust the midpoint between the color stops by sliding the diamond shapes along the top of the preview.

You can adjust the length, direction, and centerpoint location of a selected gradient. In addition, apply a gradient to multiple selected objects across a unified blend by clicking and dragging with the Gradient tool (see the "Unified Gradients" lesson later in this chapter).

To create the illusion of a gradient within a stroke, convert the stroke to a filled object (Object: Path: Outline Path). To turn a gradient into a grouped, masked blend, use Object: Expand (see the *Advanced Techniques* chapter for more on masks and masked blends).

GRADIENT MESH

You can apply a gradient mesh to a solid or gradient-filled object in order to create smooth color transitions from multiple points (but you can't use compound paths to create mesh objects). Once transformed, the object will always be a mesh object, so be certain that you work with a copy of the original if it's difficult to re-create.

Transform solid filled objects into gradient mesh either by choosing Object: Create Gradient Mesh (so you can specify details on the mesh construction) or by clicking on the object with the Mesh tool. To transform a gradient-filled object, select Object: Expand and enable the Gradient Mesh option. Use the Gradient Mesh tool to add mesh lines and mesh points to the mesh. Select individual points, or groups of points, within the mesh using the Direct-selection tool or the Gradient Mesh tool in order to move, color, or delete them. For details on working with gradient meshes (including a warning tip about printing mesh objects), see Galleries and lessons later in this, and the *Advanced Techniques*, chapter. **Hint:** *Instead of applying a mesh to a complex path, try to create the mesh from a simpler path outline, then mask the mesh with the complex path.*

Reset gradients to defaults

After you make angle adjustments with the Gradient tool, other objects that you fill with the same or other gradients will still have the altered angle. To "re-zero" gradient angles, Deselect All and fill with None by pressing the "/" key. When you next choose a gradient, angles will have the default setting. Or, for linear gradients, you can type a zero in the Angle field.

Super-size gradient palette

Even if the Gradient palette is docked with other palettes, you can make it both taller and wider so you can get a better view of the Gradient bar.

More radial gradients

To learn to create and edit radial gradients, see Laurie Grace's "Distort Filter Flora" lesson in the *Drawing & Coloring* chapter.

Get back your (mesh) shape!

When you convert a path to a mesh, it's no longer a path, but a mesh object. To extract an editable path from a mesh, select the mesh object, choose Object: Path: Offset Path, enter 0, and press OK. If there are too many points in your new path, try using Object: Path: Simplify (for more on Simplify see "Map Techniques" in the *Brushes* chapter).—*Pierre Louveaux and Victor von Salza*

Examining Blends

Learning When to Use Gradients or Blends

Overview: *Examine your objects; for linear or circular fills, create basic gradients; for contouring fills into complex objects, create blends.*

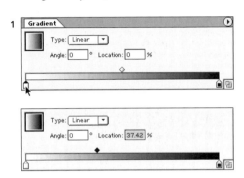

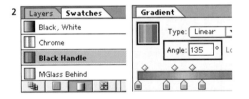

Adjusting the placement of colors, and then rate of color transition in the Gradient palette

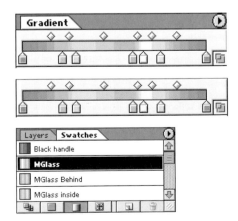

Selecting a gradient from the Swatches palette and setting the gradient Angle

One gradient duplicated and altered for application to different related objects

You need to take a number of factors into consideration when you're deciding whether to create color transitions with blends or gradients. Steve Hart's magnifying glass, created for *Time* magazine, is a clear-cut example that demonstrates when to use gradients or blends.

1 Designing gradients. Select an object you'd like to fill with a linear gradient. Open the Gradient palette. Click on the gradient icon at the bottom of the Swatches palette. Choose Name from the Swatches pop-up menu and click on the "White, Black" gradient. This minimal gradient has two colors: white (at the left) and black (at the right). Click on the left gradient slider to display its position on the scale from 0–100% (in this case 0%). Move the slider to the right to increase the percentage displayed in the scale, and increase the black area of the gradient. Click on the bottom edge of the scale to add additional pointers. Click on a slider to access its numeric position, or to change its color or tint. Between every two pointers is a diamond icon indicating the midpoint of the color transition (from 0–100% between each color pair). Grab and drag a diamond to adjust the color transition rate, or type a new position into the percent field.

2 Storing and applying gradients and making adjustments. To store a new gradient you've made within a selected object, hold Option or Alt and click the New Swatch icon and name your gradient. Hart filled his magnifying glass handle with a gradient set at a 135° angle (in the Gradient palette). He created slightly different variants for gradients representing the metal rings around the outside, along the inside, and inside behind the glass. To create variants of a current gradient, make color adjustments first, then Option-click/Alt-click the New Swatch icon to name your new gradient. Although you can experiment with changing the angle of a gradient, be forewarned that continued adjustments to a gradient in the Gradient palette will not update the gradient stored in the Swatches palette! (See the intro to this chapter.)

3 Using blends for irregular or contoured transitions.
A blend is often best for domed, kidney-shaped or contoured objects, such as shadows (for Gradient Mesh, see later in this chapter). Scale and copy one object to create another and set each to the desired color. With the Blend tool, click an anchor point on one, then Option-click (Win: Alt-click) a related point on the other. The default blend setting, "Smooth Color," often means many steps; however, the more similar the colors, the fewer steps you actually need. You can manually choose "Specified Steps" from the pop-up and experiment with fewer steps. Hart specified 20 steps for the glow in the glass, 22 for the handle knob and 12 for the shadow. To respecify steps of a selected blend, double-click the Blend tool (you may have to uncheck and recheck Preview to see the update). To blend selected objects using previous settings, click with the Blend tool without holding the Option/Alt key.

Automatically updating colors

Changing a spot-color definition (see the *Drawing & Coloring* chapter) automatically updates blends and gradients containing that color. Blends between tints of the *same* spot color (or a spot color and white) will update when changes are made to that spot color, even if the blend isn't "live."—Agnew Moyer Smith, Inc.

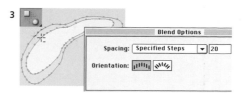

With the Blend tool, clicking first on a selected point of one path, then Option (Alt)-clicking on a selected point of the other to open Blend Options; choosing Specified Steps from the pop-up and entering 20; the blended objects

Selected paths before and after a 22-step blend

Before and after a 12-step blend to create a shadow

The final image as it appeared in **Time**

Shades of Blends

Creating Architectural Linear Shading

Overview: *Create an architectural form using rectangles; copy and paste one rectangle in front; delete the top and bottom paths and blend between the two sides.*

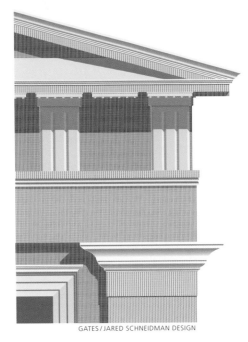

GATES / JARED SCHNEIDMAN DESIGN

A selected rectangle copied and pasted in front in full view, and in close-up

The top and bottom deleted with the sides selected

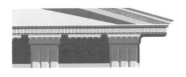

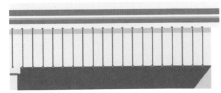

The full blend and a close-up detail

Without much difficulty, Illustrator can help simulate the traditional artistic conventions for rendering architectural details. Jared Schneidman Design developed a simple, but exacting, method to apply vertical line shading.

1 Creating an architectural structure. After establishing the overall form, color and tonality of your illustration, select and copy one rectangle. Choose Edit: Paste In Front to place the copy on top, then set the fill to None and the stroke to .1-pt Black. Choose Window: Info to note the line's width in points (to change your ruler units, see Tip, "Changing measurement units," in the *Illustrator Basics* chapter). Calculate the width of the rectangle, divided by the spacing you'd like between lines. Subtract 2 (for the sides you have) to find the proper number of steps for this blend.

2 Deleting the top and bottom and blending the sides. Deselect the copy, Shift-Direct-select the top and bottom paths and delete, leaving the sides selected. With the Blend tool, click on the top point of each side and specify the number of steps you determined above.

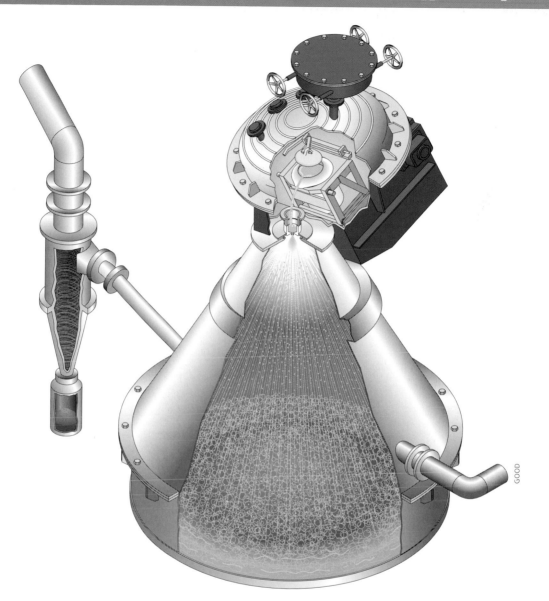

Janet Good / Industrial Illustrators

Illustrator Janet Good's image of the white-hot glow of molten metal spraying inside a chamber of liquid nitrogen is based on a drawing by Crucible Research. For the fiery glow at the top of the chamber, she first drew yellow and orange objects and then blended them. (By making the edge of the orange object jagged,

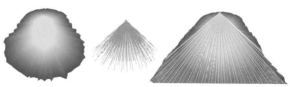

she created a blend that appears to have rays.) On a layer above the blend, Good drew several pairs of yellow and white lines, blending the pairs to form a fan of glowing light rays.

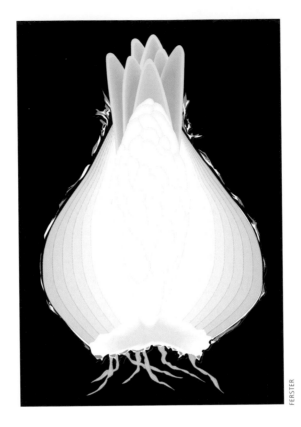

FERSTER

Gary Ferster

For his client Langeveld Bulb, Gary Ferster used blends to create the in-between layers in this flower bulb. He began by styling the outer peel with a .5-pt stroke in a dark brown custom color and filled the object with a lighter brown custom color. He then created the inner layer, filled it with white and gave it a .5-pt white stroke. Selecting both objects, Ferster specified a six-step blend that simultaneously "morphed" each progressive layer into the next while lightening the layers towards white. Blends were also used to create the leafy greens, yellow innards and all the other soft transitions between colors.

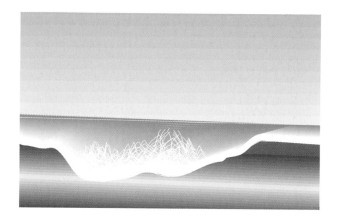

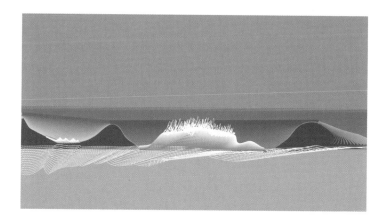

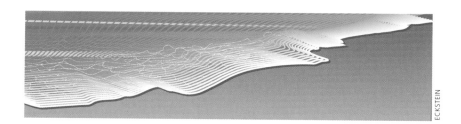

ECKSTEIN

Linda Eckstein

Linda Eckstein used blends in Illustrator to create these beautiful seascapes. In addition to controlling the regularity of blends to depict the ocean, Eckstein needed to control the irregularity of the blends as well. On the bottom layer of her image are blends that establish both the general composition and the broad color schemes. On top of these tonal-filled object blends are irregularly shaped linear blends that form the waves and surf. Using the Direct-selection tool, she isolated individual points and groups of points to stretch and distort the waves.

Peter Cassell

Using the Blend tool is a great way to save time; it lets Illustrator automatically create the intermediate paths between two paths. In this adoption announcement for Morgan Katia Hurt, Peter Cassell drew the two outermost lines of longitude for the globe using the Pen tool. With the two paths selected, he chose the Blend tool and clicked on the end-points of the two paths (to blend properly, be sure to pick two points that have the same relative position on their respective paths). He set the number of intermediate paths by double-click-ing the Blend tool, choosing Specified Steps from the Spacing pop-up menu, and keying in **4** in the Spacing field. To create the bulging effect of a sphere, Cassell wanted to spread out the intermediate paths. To do this, he selected the blend, chose Object: Expand and then Object: Ungroup. After selecting the four inter-mediate paths, Cassell double-clicked the Scale tool and in the Scale dialog, entered **125** in the Horizontal field, while keeping the Vertical field at **100**. He spread the two inner paths far-ther apart by applying horizontal scaling again.

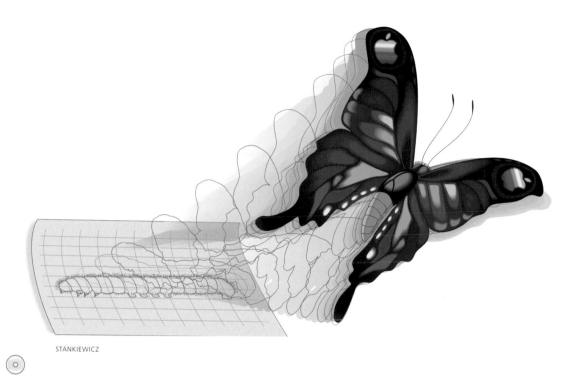

STANKIEWICZ

Steven Stankiewicz

Steven Stankiewicz uses a technique he calls "blends to blends" to smooth one colorful blend with another in his illustrations. To create a butterfly wing, he first drew the wing shape and its spots with the Pen tool and then colored each object. For the wing blend, he copied the wing object, pasted it in front, and scaled it smaller with the Scale tool. After selecting the original and the copy, he used the Blend tool to click on an anchor point on the original wing and Option-click on the corresponding point of the copied (smaller) wing. From the pop-up Blend Options dialog box, Stankiewicz chose the Smooth Color option. Then he performed the same steps to create blends for each of the wing spots. Stankiewicz decided to smooth the color transition between each wing spot blend

and the wing blend behind it. To accomplish this, he chose the Direct-selection tool and selected the outermost object in one of the wing spot blends; then he Shift-selected the innermost object of the wing blend behind it. With both objects selected, Stankiewicz clicked points on both objects that were in roughly the same position on each object. As a result, a new blend was created that smoothly bridged the blend of a wing spot with the blend of the wing behind it.

Unlocking Realism

Creating Metallic Reflections with Blends

Overview: *Form the basic shapes of objects; create tonal boundaries for future blends that follow the contours of the objects; copy, scale, recolor and adjust the anchor points of tonal boundaries; blend highlights and shadows.*

B. NEAL/THOMAS • BRADLEY ILLUSTRATION & DESIGN

1

Designing the basic objects and choosing a base tone (Note: Gray strokes added to distinguish objects)

Creating tonal boundaries for future blends by following the contours of the objects

Achieving photorealism with Illustrator may appear prohibitively complex and intimidating, but with a few simple rules-of-thumb, some careful planning and the eye of an artist, it can be done. Brad Neal, of Thomas•Bradley Illustration & Design, demonstrates with this image that you don't need an airbrush to achieve metallic reflectivity, specular highlights or warm shadows.

1 Preparing a detailed sketch that incorporates a strong light source, and setting up your palette.
Before you actually start your illustration, create a sketch that establishes the direction of your light source. Then, in Illustrator, set up your color palette (see the *Drawing & Coloring* chapter). Choose one color as a "base tone," the initial tint from which all blends will be built, and fill the entire object with that value. After you create the basic outlines of your illustration, work in Outline mode to create separate paths—following the contours of your objects—for each of your major color transitions. After completing the initial line drawing of the lock set, Neal visually, and then physically, "mapped" out the areas that

would contain the shading. He added a few highlights and reflections in the later stages of the project, but the majority of blends were mapped out in advance.

2 Using your color transition paths to create blends.
Next, use the contouring paths you've created to map out your tonal boundaries. Choose one of the objects and fill it with the same color and tonal value as its underlying shape. In the Neal locks, this initial color is always the same color and value selected for the base color. Then, copy the object and Paste In Front (Edit: Paste In Front). Next, fill this copy with a highlight or shadow value, scale it down and manipulate it into the correct position to form the highlight or shadow area. You can accomplish this step by one of two methods: by scaling the object using the Scale tool, or by selecting and pulling in individual anchor points with the Direct-selection tool. In order to ensure smooth blends without ripples or irregular transitions, the anchor points of the inner and outer objects must be as closely aligned as possible and should contain the same number of points. To then complete this highlight or shadow, use the Blend tool to *point map* (see the intro to this chapter for details). The blend in Figure 2 required eight in-between steps. If your blend isn't smooth enough, then use the Direct-selection tool to select anchor points on the key objects and adjust their position or Bézier handles until the blend smoothes.

3 Blending in smaller increments. Some blend situations may require more than two objects to achieve the desired look. For instance, to control the rate at which the tone changes or the way an object transforms throughout the blended area, you may wish to add an intermediate object and blend in two stages, instead of one.

4 Using blends to soften hard transitions. Always use blends when making tonal transitions, even when you need a stark contrast shadow or highlight. A close look at Neal's shadow reveals a very short but distinct blend.

2

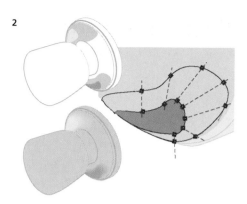

Pasting In Front a scaled down and adjusted copy with the same number of aligned points

3

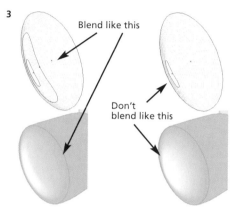

Adding an in-between contour to help control the rate and shape of blends; blending with too few contours flattens the image

4

Long, close-up, and Outline close-up views of highlight and shadow transitions

Blending Realism

Keeping Blends Clean and Accessible

Overview: *Delete the side of a rectangle; offset the top and bottom open ends horizontally; blend this open object with another smaller, darker object; place caps on top and bottom; create contouring blends on the sides.*

The final illustration in Outline mode

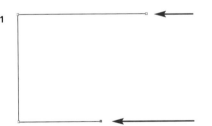

Two copies of a rectangle pasted on top with right side removed and points shifted left

Before and after blending offset objects

KELLEY

A quick look at an illustration in Outline mode usually reveals a lot about how an image is constructed. However, when you look at Andrea Kelley's Apple Computer product illustrations in Preview mode, you would probably mistakenly guess that she uses gradients to create her tonal changes. Actually, since her renderings are used on-screen as well as printed, Kelley often uses blends for more exacting control over her tones (gradients can look banded on the screen even if they print well). Her techniques can help you create a monitor screen with a soft, ambient lighting effect.

1 Creating an "offset" blend. Make a rectangle and fill it with a 35% tint of black. Copy the rectangle, choose Object: Hide Selection, then use Edit: Paste In Front to place the copy on top. Direct-select and delete the right side of the path. Since open objects remain filled in Illustrator, the object looks identical in Preview mode. With the Direct-selection tool, grab the top right point and slide it to the left slightly (about .25"), using the Shift key to constrain movement horizontally. Then grab the lower right point and slide it over to the halfway point on the rectangle (again, use your Shift key). Now select and copy the adjusted object, use Paste In Front to move the copy, and change the tint of this new object to 65%. Use the same technique you did before, but this time slide the bottom right point all the way to the left and the top right point over towards the left corner. (This polygon should look almost like a triangle.) Next, select the top right points of the two objects you just made, click on each point with the Blend tool and use the recommended number of steps. In Outline mode, instead of the expected sea of diagonally blended lines running across the screen, your monitor should appear "clean" and uncomplicated.

2 **Creating the rounded top and bottom.** Choose Object: Show All to reveal your hidden back rectangle. With the Pen tool, draw a bow-shaped "cap" filled with a 35% tint of black that overlaps the top of your blend with a long, almost horizontal curve. Have the points meet beyond the blend on either side, arcing into a bow shape above. To add shadow detail, copy the bottom path of the bow (the long, almost horizontal line) and Paste In Front to place a copy of the path. Change the Fill of this path to None, with a .25-pt stroke weight at a 40% tint of black. Lastly, copy and reflect the full filled cap along the horizontal axis, place it along the bottom of the blended monitor screen and set it to a 10% tint of black.

3 **Contouring the sides.** To create the illusion that the monitor is inset, create three long, overlapping rectangles on the left edge of your blended monitor screen, running from cap to cap. (Adjust the points as necessary so the objects run flush against the cap.) From left to right, make the rectangles 10%, 50% and 45% tints of black. Select the right two rectangles and blend between them, then lock the blend so you can easily blend the left two rectangles. Repeat from the right side of the monitor with rectangles of 5%, 10% and 25% (from left to right). You can make the monitor case the same way as the screen, but shade the case with 10% on the left, blending to 25% on the right. (See the *Advanced Techniques* chapter for blending and masking curved objects.)

2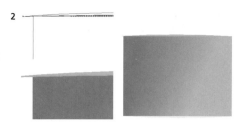

Rounded "caps" put on top and bottom of the blended screen

3

Placing three rectangles of different shades on the left side of the screen (deleting the sides to reduce clutter), then blending the middle object first to the dark, then to the light

Placing three rectangles of different shades on the right side of the screen (again, deleting the sides to reduce clutter), then blending the middle object first to the light, then to the dark

The final monitor screen in Preview

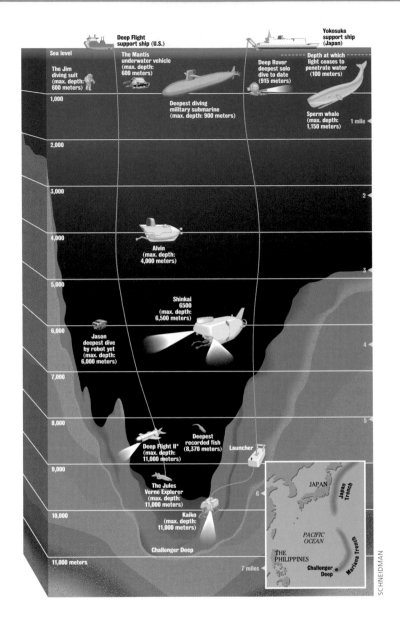

Deep Flight
support ship (U.S.)

Yokosuka
support ship
(Japan)

Sea level

The Jim
diving suit
(max. depth:
600 meters)

The Mantis
underwater vehicle
(max. depth:
600 meters)

Deep Rover
deepest solo
dive to date
(915 meters)

Depth at which
light ceases to
penetrate water
(100 meters)

1,000

Deepest diving
military submarine
(max. depth: 900 meters)

Sperm whale
(max. depth:
1,150 meters)

1 mile

2,000

3,000

2

4,000

Alvin
(max. depth:
4,000 meters)

3

5,000

Shinkai
6500
(max. depth:
6,500 meters)

6,000

Jason
deepest dive
by robot yet
(max. depth:
6,000 meters)

4

7,000

8,000

Deep Flight II*
(max. depth:
11,000 meters)

Deepest
recorded fish
(8,370 meters)

Launcher

5

9,000

The Jules
Verne Explorer
(max. depth:
11,000 meters)

JAPAN

Japan
Trench

6

10,000

Kaiko
(max. depth:
11,000 meters)

PACIFIC
OCEAN

Mariana Trench

Challenger Deep

THE
PHILIPPINES

Challenger
Deep

11,000 meters

7 miles

SCHNEIDMAN

Jared Schneidman / JSD

Illustrator blends helped Jared Schneidman convey the murky depth and bright exploring lights in this *Newsweek* infographic about deep trenches in the Pacific Ocean. Schneidman created the subdued highlights and shadows of the subterranean trench using blended objects.

For the searchlights emanating from the explorer vehicles, Schneidman first made cone objects filled with a pale yellow. He then made companion objects using the dark colors of the ocean and trench. Finally, he made blends between each cone and its companion object.

KELLEY

Andrea Kelley

To illustrate this North Face camping equipment, designer Andrea Kelley carefully analyzed fabric folds, stitched seams, and the play of light and shadow. She began the sleeping bag by drawing the outline of the bag, creating a blend object and masking it with a copy of the sleeping bag outline. She drew each stitched seam as a solid line, and the fabric folds around the seams as jagged, filled shapes. Over the sleeping bag, Kelley drew light-gray-filled objects for the fabric highlights between the seams. Kelley created the tent by first drawing its outline, and then creating a multiple-object blend, which she masked with the tent outline. Kelley created additional masked blends to define other shapes that make up the tent. For the front flap, Kelley created a blend object and masked it with an oval, and then drew light and dark triangles on top of it to show wrinkles in the fabric.

Unified Gradients

Redirecting Fills with the Gradient Tool

Overview: *Fill objects with gradients; use the Gradient tool to adjust fill length, direction, center location and to unify fills across multiple objects.*

The Gradient palette, and the Gradient tool (This tool has the same name and icon as the one in Photoshop, but is completely different.)

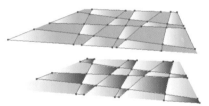

Filling the first group with the cyan gradient, then the other group with the purple gradient

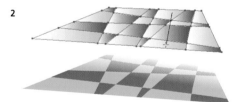

Clicking and dragging with the Gradient tool to unify the gradient fill across multiple objects, and to establish the gradient's rate and direction

How long can a gradient be?

Click and drag with the Gradient tool anywhere in your image window; you don't need to stay within the objects themselves. Also, see the *Wow! CD* for Eve Elberg's "Comet" Gradient tool exercise.

The Gradient tool allows you to customize the length and direction of gradient fills, and to stretch gradients across multiple objects. For this *Medical Economics* magazine illustration, Dave Joly used the Gradient tool to customize each gradient and unify the checkerboard floor.

1 Filling objects with the same gradient. Select multiple objects and fill them with the same gradient by clicking on a gradient fill in the Swatches palette. Keep your objects selected.

2 Unifying gradients with the Gradient tool. Using the Gradient tool from the Toolbox, click and drag from the point you want the gradient to begin to where you want it to end. Hold down the Shift key if you want to constrain the angle of the gradient. To relocate a radial gradient's center, just click with the Gradient tool. Experiment until you get the desired effect. To create his checkerboard, Joly used the Knife tool to segment the floor, grouped every other tile together and filled these with a cyan-to-white gradient fill. He then duplicated the gradient, changed the start color to purple and applied this purple gradient to the remaining tiles. With all tiles selected, he again applied the Gradient tool.

Filip Yip

Filip Yip prefers the simplicity of linear and radial gradients to the photo-realism of blends in creating the stylized look of many of his illustrations. The images above began as pencil sketches that Yip scanned, placed in Illustrator as templates and then traced over to create compositional elements. For the spoonful of vegetables, Yip developed gradients that share similar colors but differ in the number and location of intermediate colors and midpoints along the slider in the Gradient palette. The lobster is more stylized, conveying shadows with color-to-gray gradients. Both illustrations contrast the soft gradient effects with crisp highlights and shadows in strong, solid-filled colors.

WHYTE / LEHNER & WHYTE

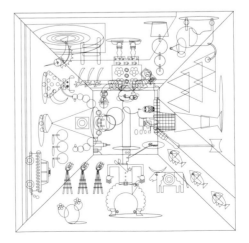

Hugh Whyte / Lehner & Whyte

In this image designed for a promotional poster, Hugh Whyte used gradients and the Gradient tool to create a colorful, cut-out look that is both flat and volumetric. The Outline view at right reveals that Whyte constructed the image entirely of gradients, with no blends.

GORSKA

Caryl Gorska

Caryl Gorska created "Bountiful Harvest" as a package design for Nunes Farms' dried fruits, nuts and chocolates. She used the Gradient tool to customize her radial blends (made of process colors). A scan of parchment paper, saved as an EPS file, is Placed on the bottom layer (see the *Layers* chapter).

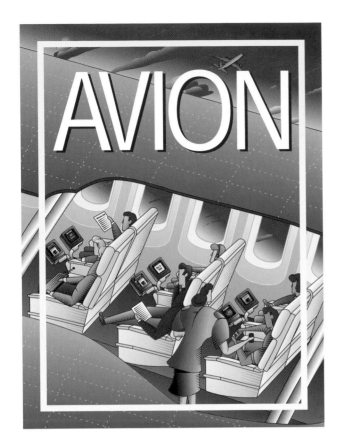

WEBB

Tim Webb

In these two magazine illustrations, Avion (for *Avion* magazine) and Quality Control (for *Field Force Automation* magazine), Tim Webb created a small palette of gradients and varied the gradient angle of the fill to achieve a wide range of color. With an object selected, he clicked and dragged with the Gradient tool from the beginning point to the end point of the area in which he wanted to place the gradient. Webb varied the angle and distance of the gradient to create specific fill colors. The sky, clouds, and windows in Avion are all filled with the same gradient. In Quality Control, the floor and yellow shadows share the same gradient. Using a small palette of gradients allowed Webb to quickly change the color of an object and maintain subtleties of color throughout his illustrations.

Tim Webb

Tim Webb used just a few features of Illustrator to create his Victory Climb and Road lessons illustrations. The crisp woodcut appearance is a result of bold line work layered above gradient fills. Webb began by drawing the image with the Pen tool. Webb then created his color palette by importing colors from a swatch library into the Swatches palette. He then double-clicked the Gradient tool icon to open the Gradient palette and created gradients by dragging colors from the Swatches palette onto the the stops of the Gradient palette. (For more detail on creating a gradient, see the gradients section of the introduction to this chapter).

After he created and saved the gradients in the Swatches palette, Webb drew closed paths and filled them with either a linear or a radial gradient, varying the direction and length of the gradient in order to give volume to the image. The woodcut appearance was created by blending between two triangular shapes on a curved path. Webb created custom art brushes to make the small rocks and the raindrops.

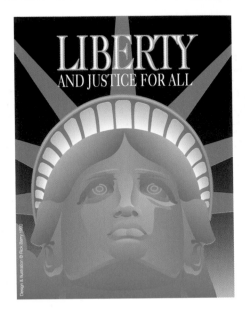

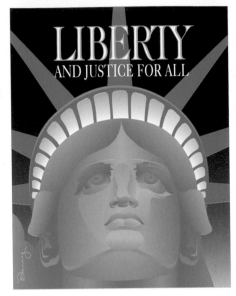

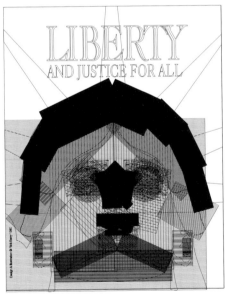

BARRY / DESKTOP DESIGN STUDIO

Rick Barry / DeskTop Design Studio

To demonstrate the difference between blends and gradients, Rick Barry took an image he created in Illustrator (upper left Preview mode, lower left Outline mode), selected the blends (by clicking twice with the Group-selection tool on one of the blend objects) and deleted them.

The objects used to create the blends remained, and Barry filled these objects with custom gradients and then adjusted the rate and range of the gradients with the Gradient tool (upper right Preview mode, lower right Outline mode).

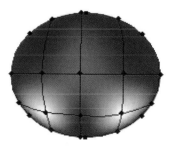

Ellen Papciak-Rose / In The Studio

Gabriella Catches a Star and Her Friends Find Some Stuff in the Sky is the first of four books featuring children who learn about real and abstract environmental topics in a fun way. In this two-page spread, artist Ellen Papciak-Rose filled shapes with soft bright glows she achieved using the Gradient Mesh tool (which gave her more control in placing mesh points, as compared with the uniform grid meshes that she would get from using the Object: Create Gradient Mesh command). To make Gabriella's face, Papciak-Rose drew an oval with the Ellipse tool and then applied a Charcoal brush to it. After filling the oval with a dark brown color, she expanded the object (Object: Expand Appearance), which had to be done in order to fill the brushed object with a Gradient Mesh. She clicked with the Gradient Mesh tool to create the mesh points for the highlights. Then she Shift-selected the two cheek points with the Direct-selection tool and chose white from the Color palette.

Rolling Mesh

Converting Gradients to Mesh, then Editing

Overview: *Draw shapes and fill with linear gradients; expand gradient-filled objects into gradient meshes; use various tools to edit mesh points and colors.*

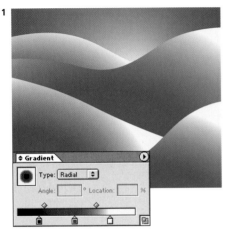

The hills shown filled with radial gradients—although there is some sense of light, it isn't possible to make the radial gradient follow the contours of the hills

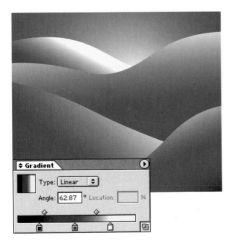

The hills shown filled with linear gradients, which are easier to edit than radial gradients when converted to gradient meshes

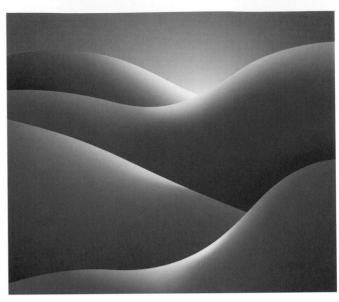

STEUER

For many images, gradients can be useful for showing the gradual change of light to shadow (if you need to learn more about creating and applying gradient fills, first see "Unified Gradients" earlier in this chapter). For these rolling hills, artist Sharon Steuer expanded linear gradients into gradient mesh objects so she could better control the curves and contours of the color transitions.

1 Drawing shapes and then filling them with linear gradients. Begin your illustration by creating closed objects with any of the drawing tools. After completing the objects, select each object with the Selection tool and Fill it with a linear gradient fill. For each linear gradient, adjust the angle and length of the gradient transition with the Gradient tool until you can best approximate the desired lighting effect. Steuer created four hill-shaped objects with the Pen tool, filled them with the same linear gradient, then customized each with the Gradient tool. **Note:** *Although in some objects radial gradients might look better before you convert them, linear gradients create gradient mesh objects that are* much *easier to edit!*

2 Expanding linear gradients into gradient meshes. To create a more natural lighting of the hills, Steuer converted the linear gradients into mesh objects so the color transitions could follow the contours of the hills. To accomplish this, select all the gradient-filled objects that you wish to convert and choose Object: Expand. In the Expand dialog box, make sure Fill is checked and specify Expand Gradient to Gradient Mesh. Then click OK. Illustrator converts each linear gradient into a rectangle rotated to the angle matching the linear gradient's angle; each mesh rectangle is masked by the original object (see the *Advanced Techniques* chapter for help with masks).

3 Editing meshes. You can use several tools to edit gradient mesh objects (use the Object: Lock/Unlock All toggle to isolate objects as you work). The Gradient Mesh tool combines the functionality of the Direct-selection tool with the ability to add mesh lines. With the Gradient Mesh tool, click *exactly on* a mesh anchor point to select or move that point or its direction handles. Or, click *anywhere* within a mesh, except on an anchor point, to add a new mesh point and gridline. You can also use the Add-anchor-point tool (click and hold to choose it from the Pen tool pop-up) to add a point without a gridline. To delete a selected anchor point, press the Delete key; if that point is a mesh point, the gridlines will be deleted as well.

Select points within the mesh using either the Gradient Mesh tool or the Direct Select Lasso tool, using the Direct-selection tool to move multiple selected points. Move individual anchor points and adjust direction handles with the Gradient Mesh tool in order to reshape your gradient mesh gridlines. In this way, the color and tonal transitions of the gradient will match the contour of the mesh object. Recolor selected areas of the mesh by selecting points, then choosing a new color.

If you click in the area *between* mesh points with the Paint bucket tool (from the Eyedropper tool pop-up) you'll add the Fill color to the four nearest mesh points.

By using these tools and editing techniques, Steuer was able to create hills with color and light variations that suggest the subtlety of natural light upon organic forms.

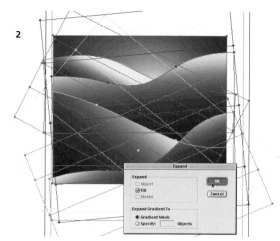

2

After Expanding the gradients into gradient mesh objects

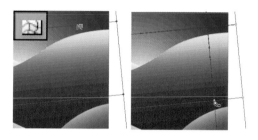

Using the Gradient mesh tool to add a mesh line, then moving the mesh point with the Direct-selection tool

Using the Add-anchor-point tool, using the Direct Select Lasso to select a point, moving selected point (or points) with the Direct-selection tool

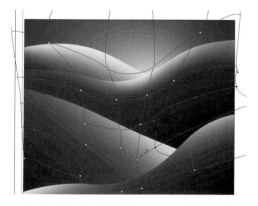

The final rearmost hill, shown after making mesh adjustments

Mastering Mesh

Painting with Areas of Color Using Mesh

Advanced Technique

Overview: *Create simple objects to make into gradient mesh; edit and color mesh objects; create compound-path masks for copies of mesh; make a mesh with no grid to reshape.*

1

The original oval; choosing Object: Create Gradient Mesh; setting the Mesh options

The mesh created; after selecting points and deleting to create a pattern in the mesh

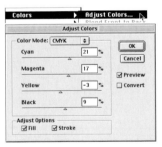

Recoloring selected rows and columns using the Color palette and the Adjust Colors filter

With a background in painting, sculpture and 3D imaging, Ivan Torres knew that the Gradient-mesh tool would allow him to paint in a powerfully unique way. In creating this fish illustration, he demonstrates how, unlike *any* other medium, the mesh allows him to *move a stroke of color* without changing the relationship between colors.

1 Creating the fish's body. Create a solid-filled oval; while it's selected, choose Object: Create Gradient Mesh. Set fairly high numbers for rows and columns; for his fish (shown above at about 30% actual size) Torres set 17 rows, 35 columns. Set Flat for Appearance, 100% Highlight and click OK. Next, to make the base for the fish's stripes, you'll need to create an irregular pattern within the mesh. With the Direct-selection tool, select anchor points and delete—the connected rows and columns will be deleted along with the points. Torres deleted 8 columns and 10 rows. Marquee horizontal anchor points with the Direct-selection tool. For even more selection control, try working in Outline mode, uncheck Use Area Select in Preferences: General, or select points using the Direct-selection Lasso tool. With horizontal rows of points selected (make sure you are now in Preview mode), mix or choose new colors in the Colors palette (use View: Hide/Show Edges to hide/show selection edges). Torres horizontally selected sections of the mesh, changing colors to create a sense of volume. For more subtle color transitions, select an area and choose Filter: Colors: Adjust Colors to adjust the color cast of your selection. Carefully Direct-select points and reposition them to form the fish body.

2 Making the fish's tail and fins. Create several colored rectangles and ovals. Again, convert each object to a gradient mesh, but assign a *low* value for columns. Direct-select sections of each object and use the Adjust Color Filter to create gradual changes in tone (use ⌘-Option-E (Mac)/Ctrl-Alt-E (Win) to reopen the last-used filter). Direct-select points on the objects and adjust them to form tail and fin shapes. Move each object into a separate layer for easy editing (see the *Layers* chapter for help).

3 Creating the fish's eye and lips. Create three circles: one small, one medium and one large. Convert the medium-size circle to a gradient mesh this time by clicking on the circle with the Gradient-mesh tool. Add additional rows or columns by clicking again with the tool; delete by Direct-selecting points, rows or columns and deleting. Torres ended up with unevenly spaced rows and columns (five of each), which he colored to achieve a wet, reflective-looking surface. When you are pleased with the glossy part of the eye, combine all the circles and adjust the outlines of some to be less perfect.

To create the fish's mouth, begin with a rectangle on a layer above the fish. Convert the rectangle to a gradient mesh using Object: Create Gradient Mesh, and enter different low values for rows and columns, maintaining Flat for Appearance. Select areas of the object and use the Eyedropper to load colors from the fish to create smooth color transitions between the mouth and the body. Move this object into position and reshape it to form a mouth.

4 Creating shadows for the fish. Duplicate the layer containing the fish's body by dragging that layer to the

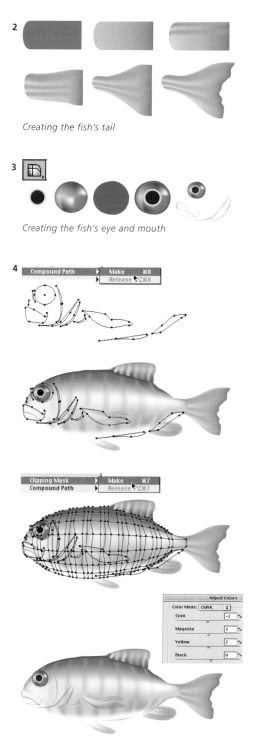

2 Creating the fish's tail

3 Creating the fish's eye and mouth

Drawing objects for shadow areas; making them into a compound path; masking a copy of the fish with the compound path; using Filter: Colors: Adjust Colors to darken a copy of the fish; the final fish shown with completed shadows

5

An oval

After applying a mesh with values of 1, deleting the original oval anchor points (in orange)

The remaining points moved and colored

After reshaping is complete, a copy is created, reflected and sheared, and colors are inverted

Adding to the mesh

To add new rows and columns to your mesh, click on the mesh object with the Mesh(U) tool. To add a new mesh row, click on a column mesh line. To add a new mesh column, click on a row.

New Layer icon in the Layers palette. On a layer above this one, use the Pen tool to draw a contour defining each shadow as a closed object. Select all the shadow objects and choose Object: Compound Path: Make to unite them into one compound object. Use these shadow objects as a mask for the copy of the fish body. Select both the compound path and the copy of the fish body (in the Layers palette, Option-Shift-click/Alt-Shift-click the shadow and fish copy layers to select all objects on those layers) and choose Object: Clipping Mask: Make. To simulate shadow colors, select the masked copy of the fish and use the Adjust Colors filter to darken the area and reduce the contrast. Torres created a shadow that contrasted the cyan color cast of the fish by decreasing cyan and increasing yellow and magenta—each in increments of 2 to 5%. After applying the filter, with selection edges hidden ⌘-H (Mac)/Ctrl-H (Win), he reapplied the filter using ⌘-E (Mac)/Ctrl-E (Win), until he was satisfied.

5 Creating the border "bone" shape. Create an oval; while it's selected, choose Object: Create Gradient Mesh, assigning 1 for rows and columns and "Flat". Using the Delete-anchor-point tool, delete the four original points of the oval, leaving only the mesh points. Reposition the remaining points to create an arcing effect, and assign colors to each point. Next, use the Reflect tool to flip a copy of this object horizontally. With the copy selected, choose Filter: Colors: Invert Colors. Lastly, use the Shear tool to adjust the copied image to touch the original border object (see *Zen* chapter for Reflect and Shear help).

Printing gradient mesh objects

Gradient mesh objects rely on PostScript Level 3 (PS3) to print. Gradient mesh objects printed to older printers will convert to a 150-pixel-per-inch JPEG! If you can't print to a PS3 printer, you may wish to use Illustrator's Rasterize or Export commands, or open the file in Photoshop 5.02 or higher to rasterize it there. *Hint:* See also Tip "Grouping masks" in the *Advanced* chapter.

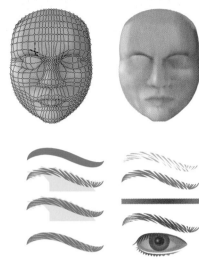

TORRES

Ivan Torres

Ivan Torres began this image by drawing an oval, then choosing Object: Create Gradient Mesh, entering approximately 30 rows, 15 columns and Flat appearance. Working in Outline mode, Torres Direct-selected horizontal rows and moved them closer or farther from other rows to cluster more rows around the eyes, nose and lips (he wanted at least three rows around the lips, for instance). To form vertical structures such as the nose, he used the Direct-selection tool to select and move columns. To create more diagonal lines, he Direct-selected a section of the mesh and used the Shear tool (holding the Shift key). In some cases he used the Convert-anchor-point tool to reset direction handles. He Direct-selected and then colored points using the Color palette. Once he set base colors, he used the Eyedropper tool to transfer color from elsewhere to the selected anchor points. He used the Pen tool to draw the basic eyebrow shape and several overlapping angular objects to represent hair. He

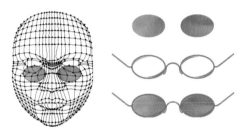

selected all eyebrow objects and cut the angles out of the brow with Effect: Pathfinder: Hard Mix (he selected one cut-out object and used Select: Same: Fill Color to select all of the cut-out objects so he could move them aside). For the glasses he made two ellipses, chose Object: Compound Path: Make and then made this into a mask with a copy of the mesh face, to which he then applied the Filter: Colors: Adjust Colors filter to increase the cyan and yellow (see the preceding technique for details). On layers above and below, Torres created details such as the eyeglass frames, and he used a Charcoal Art Brush (*Brushes* chapter) to add texture to the borders of his final illustration.

MIYAMOTO

Yukio Miyamoto

Yukio Miyamoto combined gradients, gradient mesh, and basic fills to render this photorealistic illustration of a motorcycle for his book, *The Adobe Illustrator Super Guide* (published in Japan). The in-process version above provides an insider's view into his methods for creating the finished piece at right. Miyamoto began by placing a photo as a template. He then traced over the photo using the Pen tool, creating solid black objects. He then systematically began to fill the individual objects with color, gradients, and gradient mesh, using the

Eyedropper tool to pick up color from the photo for his objects, mesh points, and gradients. Miyamoto also combined masking techniques with gradient mesh in the wheels (see the *Advanced Techniques* chapter for more).

MIYAMOTO

Yukio Miyamoto

As with his motorcycle (opposite), Yukio Miyamoto began this illustration of a Yamaha French horn by tracing over a photo with the Pen tool, then filling the objects with solid fills. In layers above the basic tracing, Miyamoto drew the reflections and details of the tubular structure and filled them with linear gradients. He used the Gradient Mesh tool to define several reflections within the horn, with the most obvious on the horn's bell. He then created other areas of reflection with clusters of solid and gradient-filled objects (as on the bell and the valves). Miyamoto made the background out of a large, rectangular, gradient

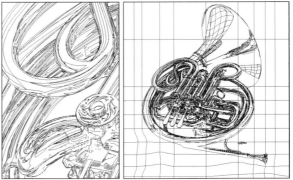

mesh. Within this mesh, he created the horn's shadow. The magnificent level of detail is evident even when the image is viewed in Outline mode (a detail is shown directly above left; the full image in Outline is above right).

Transparency & Appearances

8

Transparency & Appearances

Using transparency with...

- **Fills**—apply an opacity, a blend mode, or an effect that utilizes transparency (e.g., Inner Glow).
- **Strokes**—just as with fills, apply an opacity, a blend mode, or an effect that utilizes transparency (e.g., Outer Glow).
- **Brush Strokes**—scatter brushes, art brushes, and pattern brushes can all be made from transparent artwork. In addition, you can make any brush stroke (including calligraphic brush strokes) transparent by applying an opacity, blend mode, or effect that utilizes transparency.
- **Text**—apply transparency to selected text characters and/or the entire text object.
- **Charts**—apply transparency to the entire chart or the elements that make up the chart.
- **Groups**—select or target the group and apply an opacity, a blend mode, or an effect that utilizes transparency (e.g., Feather). As of Illustrator 10, selecting an entire group automatically targets it.
- **Layers**—target the layer and apply an opacity, a blend mode, or an effect that utilizes transparency. —*Sandee Cohen and Pierre Louveaux*

Transparency is a feature that really sets Illustrator apart from its competitors. Transparency is everywhere—you use it not only whenever you apply an opacity percentage, a blending mode, or an opacity mask from the Transparency palette, but also whenever you apply certain kinds of effects (such as shadows, feathers, and glows) or styles that include those features. Although it's easy to apply cool transparent effects to your artwork, it's important that you understand how transparency works, because this will help you later when you export or print.

If the concepts of Transparency, Flattening, Appearances, Targeting, or Opacity Masks are new to you, it's very important that you take the time to master the lessons in this chapter. Although this is not an advanced techniques chapter, we do assume that by now you have a basic knowledge of Fills, Strokes, and especially layers. If you're unable to keep up with this chapter, please see the *Drawing & Coloring* and *Layers* chapters first.

BASIC TRANSPARENCY

Although the Artboard may look white, Illustrator treats it as transparent. To visually distinguish the transparent areas from the non-transparent ones, choose View: Show Transparency Grid. To set the size and colors of the transparency grid, select File: Document Setup: Transparency. You can check Simulate Paper if you know you'll be printing on a colored stock (click on the top swatch to open the color picker to select a "paper" color). Keep in mind that paper simulation doesn't work while the transparency grid is showing—so it's an either/or situation. Both Transparency Grid and paper color are non-printing attributes and are only visible in on-screen preview.

The term *transparency* refers to any changes in blending modes and opacity. Some masks or Effects, such as Feather or Drop Shadow, use these settings as well. As a result, when you apply these masks or Effects, you're relying on Illustrator's transparency features. To apply transparency to an object or group, make a selection or click on the target indicator in the Layers palette, then adjust the opacity slider in the Transparency palette. (Objects and groups are automatically targeted when you select them; if you want to apply transparency at the layer level, target the layer explicitly.) Completely opaque is equal to 100% opacity and 0% is completely see-through, or invisible. Be careful how you apply transparency; it's easy to get confused—correctly targeting and applying transparency is very important (see the "Basic Transparency" lesson in this chapter).

Blending modes control how the colors of objects, groups, or layers interact with one another. Since blending modes are color mode–specific, they yield different results in RGB and CMYK. As in Photoshop, the blending modes show no effect when they are over the *transparent* Artboard. To see the effect of blending modes, you need to add a color-filled or white element behind your art.

Opacity Masks

Opacity masks allow the dark and light areas in one object to be used as a mask for others. Where the mask is black, you see objects below. Where the mask is white, objects below are hidden. Grays allow a range of transparency. (This works exactly like Photoshop *layer masks*).

The easiest way to create an opacity mask is to first create the artwork you want masked. Next, place the object, group, or raster image you want to use as the mask above it. Select the artwork and the masking element, and choose Make Opacity Mask from the Transparency palette pop-up menu. Illustrator automatically makes the topmost object or group the opacity mask.

To create an empty mask, start by targeting a single object, group, or layer. Since the default behavior of new opacity masks is clipping (with a black background), you'll need to turn off the "New Opacity Masks Are Clipping" option in the Transparency palette pop-up menu or your targeted artwork will completely disappear when

Need more transparency?

Look for more lessons and Galleries that incorporate transparency in the *Live Effects & Styles* and *Advanced Techniques* chapters.

Editing Opacity Masks

- **Disable**—Shift-click the mask thumbnail to turn it off. A red **X** will appear over the preview.
- **Enable**—Shift-click to reapply the mask.
- **Mask View**—Option-click (Mac)/Alt-click (Win) the mask thumbnail to toggle between viewing and editing the masking objects on the Artboard, or to view the mask grayscale values.
- **Release Opacity Mask (palette menu)**—releases the masking effect.
- **Toggle between working on artwork or Opacity Mask**—click the appropriate icon to control what you are editing.
- **Link or unlink the Opacity Mask to artwork**—click between the mask and artwork to toggle the link/unlink option.

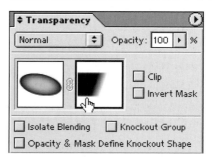

The Transparency palette with all options shown (choose Show Options from the Transparency palette pop-up menu)

Colorize a grayscale image

Creating a monotone image is easy with an Opacity Mask. First, place an image. Next fill a rectangle with a color and send it behind the image. Select the image and the rectangle and choose Make Opacity Mask (Transparency palette menu). To correct for the negative image, check Invert Mask. To print spot colors correctly, be sure to export as an AI10 EPS file or place the native Illustrator file into InDesign 2.0.

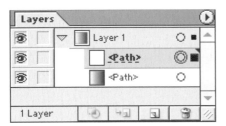

Opacity masks are indicated by a dashed line in the Layers palette

More opacity masks

See the "Opacity Masks 101" lesson in this chapter, and *Advanced Techniques* for more on opacity masks.

Overprint preview

Previewing overprints on your screen has never been easier. Choose View: Overprint Preview to see how your overprints will look when they print. Overprint Preview also provides the best spot color simulations, although editing your file in Overprint Preview mode is slightly slower than in regular Preview mode.

you first create the empty mask. Next, choose Show Thumbnails from the Transparency palette pop-up, and double-click in the right thumbnail area. This creates an empty mask and puts you in mask editing mode; the Layers palette changes to show the opacity mask. Use your drawing and editing tools to create your mask. (For instance, if you create an object filled with a gradient, you'll see your artwork through the dark areas of the gradient.) While the opacity mask thumbnail is selected, you won't be able to edit anything else in your document. Choose to work on your artwork or your opacity mask by clicking on the appropriate thumbnail (the artwork thumbnail is on the left; the opacity mask is on the right).

A few hints can help you with opacity masks. First, the masking objects may display in color, but behind the scenes they're being converted to grayscale. In addition, if you select Invert Mask, the dark and light values of the colors are reversed. To identify which elements have an opacity mask, look for the dashed underline in the Layers palette next to the object or group with the mask.

The link icon in the Transparency palette indicates that the position of the opacity mask stays associated with the position of the object, group, or layer it is masking. Unlinking allows you to move the artwork without moving the mask. The content of the mask can be selected and edited just like any other object. You can transform or apply a blending mode and/or an opacity percentage to each individual object within the mask.

Option-click (Mac) or Alt-click (Win) on an opacity mask thumbnail in the Transparency palette to hide the document's contents and display only the masking element in its grayscale values. Shift-click the opacity mask thumbnail to disable the opacity mask.

Knockout Controls

Choose Show Options from the pop-up menu of the Transparency palette to display the checkboxes that control how transparency is applied to groups and multiple objects.

With a group or layer targeted, check the Knockout

Group option to keep individual objects of the group or layer from applying their transparency settings to each other where they overlap. This is particularly useful for blends containing one or more transparent objects. For this reason, Illustrator automatically turns on the Knockout Group option on all newly created blends.

Check Isolate Blending to limit the effects of a blending mode to the bottom element of a targeted group or layer (see the "It's a Knockout!" lesson later in this chapter).

The final checkbox, Opacity & Mask Defines Knockout Shape, is used in very specific situations to limit the knockout of a color to the area defined by the opacity and the mask. To see any effect, you must use this option on a transparent object inside a knockout group.

This option is most useful on raster images and feathered edges. It's automatically turned on inside the appearance of Drop Shadow, Blur, Feather, and Photoshop effects. If it weren't, putting objects with these effects in knockout groups would produce unwanted results: the entire rectangular bounding box of Drop Shadows, Blurs, and Photoshop effects would knock out, as would the unfeathered outline of Feathered objects.

Document Setup

PostScript printing devices and file formats such as EPS can only reproduce transparent artwork in "flattened" form. Illustrator's flattening process is applied temporarily if you print, and permanently if you save in a format that doesn't support transparency natively. Flattening occurs when areas of transparent overlap are converted into opaque pieces that look the same. Some of your objects may be split into many separate objects, while others may be rasterized. See Tip "The Flattening Preview palette" at right and the section "The last word on transparency" for more information on issues of flattening.

The Raster/Vector Balance setting, found in the Transparency panel of the Document Setup dialog box, determines how much art is rasterized and how much remains vector. In case you're not familiar with the terms,

Transparency is cumulative

The total effect of transparency is determined by the object, group, sublayers, and container layer. **Note:** *There isn't any way to clear all effects for the multiple levels. You have to target each level and click the Clear Appearance icon (see the "Appearances" section later in this chapter).*

Knockout checkbox

The knockout checkbox has a third or neutral state that is indicated by a dash (Mac) or grayed checkmark (Win). Illustrator sets all newly created groups and layers to this neutral state because knockout groups can contain nested groups with different knockout settings. The neutral state prevents the new group from overriding the knockout setting of the enclosing group.

The Flattening Preview palette

Illustrator ships with an optional plug-in called Flattening Preview, which allows you to preview exactly how your artwork will flatten at print or export time. For information on how to install and use this plug-in, read the Adobe Illustrator Flattening Guide, included with your Adobe Illustrator documentation.

rasters are images made up of pixels, while vectors consist of discrete objects. These days, most programs contain aspects of both vectors and rasters, but Photoshop is primarily raster and Illustrator primarily vector.

By default, Illustrator's Raster/Vector Balance setting is 100—which results in the greatest possible amount of art remaining in vector form. At the highest setting, the file contains the most vector objects and may produce longer print times. As you move the slider to the left, toward zero, Illustrator tries to convert vectors (like pure Illustrator files) to rasters (like Photoshop files). At a setting of zero, Illustrator converts *all* art to rasters. Usually you get the best results using the all vector setting of 100, but if this takes too long to print, try the all raster setting of 0. In some cases, when transparent effects are very complex, this might be the best choice. Generally, the in-between settings create awful results.

Because objects are always flattened to a white background, you might see color shifts after you flatten your artwork. To preview the way your artwork would look if flattened, turn on Simulate Paper (in Document Setup) or Overprint Preview (in the View menu).

The last word on transparency

When working with transparency, it is extremely important to know when your files will become flattened. When you print a file, the artwork gets flattened, but your file isn't permanently affected (because the flattening only happens to a temporary *copy* of the file during the printing process). Also, know that there are two kinds of EPS files you can make from Illustrator—Adobe Illustrator 9 (AI9) and newer, and Adobe Illustrator 8 and older—and there's a big difference. When you save an EPS to AI9 or a newer format, two versions of your file actually get saved in the EPS—a flattened version *and* a native unflattened version. This allows you to print the file to a PostScript device (or import it into another application such as QuarkXPress). It also allows you to reopen the file in Illustrator 10 in unflattened form so you can make edits to the file. However, saving as AI8 EPS (or earlier versions) only saves the flattened version of the file. This means that if you reopen the saved AI8 EPS file in a later version of Illustrator, you'll see that all your art is flattened. Reopening a flattened AI8 EPS file in Illustrator results in a loss of spot colors and layer information, and some of your objects may be broken apart or rasterized. In addition, all text and strokes will have been converted to outlines (they become separate objects and will no longer be editable in the same way). Furthermore, if you save as AI9, you'll lose any AI10-specific features (they'll be expanded and lose their editability). So, it's *really* important to save in AI10 EPS format if you need EPS. If you have to save in AI8 EPS or AI9 EPS format, be sure to also save a copy of your file in native AI10 format.

APPEARANCES

Within an appearance are a collection of Strokes, Fills, Effects, and transparency settings. An appearance can be applied to any path, object (including text), group, sublayer, or layer. The specific appearance attributes of a selection are shown in the Appearance palette. Attributes within the appearance are added to the palette in the order they are applied. Changing the order of the attributes will change the appearance. An object and its enclosing groups and layers can all have their own appearances.

To apply an appearance, make a selection or click on a target indicator (Layers palette) and add transparency, effects, multiple fills, and/or multiple strokes (see the "Adding Fills and Strokes" section). When a group, sublayer, or layer is targeted, Strokes and Fills will be applied to the individual objects within the selection, but any effects or transparency settings will be applied to the *target* (see Tip "Selecting vs. targeting" in the *Layers* chapter). Drag the target indicator (in the Layers palette) from one layer to another to move an appearance or Option-drag (Mac) or Alt-drag (Win) the indicator to copy the appearance. To re-use an appearance, save it as a style in the Styles palette.

Rasterization Resolution

When objects are rasterized, they are done so at the Rasterization Resolution. There are some rare cases in which a setting between all raster and all vector will work best. The Rasterization Resolution should be at least twice the linescreen of the final output device. The artwork in "Basic Highlights" later in this chapter required a setting of 80%.

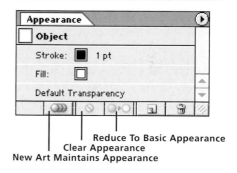

New Art Maintains Appearance
Clear Appearance
Reduce To Basic Appearance

Appearance palette indicators

The appearance indicators for Paint, Effects, and Transparency only show up in the Appearance palette on layers or groups that contain elements with these attributes.

Layers appearance icons

An object has a basic appearance as long as it does not contain multiple Fills or Strokes, transparency, effects, or brush strokes. It is indicated by an open circle in the Layers palette.

More complex appearances are indicated by a gradient-filled icon in the Layers palette.

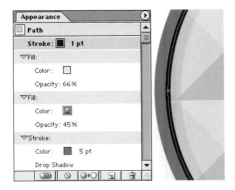

An example of multiple Strokes and Fills, including a 1-pt black stroke, a solid fill at 66% Opacity, a pattern fill at 45% Opacity, a 5-pt green stroke, and a Drop Shadow effect (see the Live Effects & Styles *chapter for more about live effects)*

Move or copy appearances

In the Layers palette, drag the Appearance icon circle from one object, group, or layer to another to *move* the appearance. To *copy* the appearance, hold Option (Mac) or Alt (Win) as you drag the icon.

Why duplicate items?

Why are there duplicate items in both the Filter and Effect menus? Adobe kept duplicates in the Filter menu because they save you a step (namely, the Expand Appearance step) when you don't want them live.

Appearance palette

When an item is selected or targeted, the Appearance palette displays all the attributes associated with the current selection. If there isn't a selection, the palette will display the attributes for the next object drawn. When the current target is an object, the Appearance palette always lists at least one Fill, one Stroke, and the object-level transparency. When the target is a group or layer, no Fill or Stroke is shown unless one has been applied (see "Adding Fills & Strokes" following). "Default Transparency" means 100% opacity, Normal blending mode, Isolate Blending off, and Knockout Group off or neutral.

A basic appearance isn't always a white fill and a black stroke (as suggested by the icon). An appearance is defined as a *Basic Appearance* when it includes one Fill and one Stroke (with either set to None), the Stroke is above the Fill; no brushes or live effects, and it has 100% opacity and Normal blending mode(the defaults).

If the current selection has more than the *basic* attributes you can choose what attributes the next object will have. The first icon at the bottom of the palette is New Art Maintains Appearance (when disabled) and New Art Has Basic Appearance (when selected). For example, if your last object had a drop shadow but you don't want the next object to inherit this attribute, click on the icon and the new object will only inherit the basic attributes.

Click on the Clear Appearance icon to reduce appearance attributes to no Fill, no Stroke, with 100% opacity. Click on the Reduce to Basic Appearance icon to reduce the artwork's appearance to a single Stroke and Fill along with the default transparency. To delete an attribute, drag it to the Trash, or click on it and then click the Trash. **Note:** *Reduce to Basic Appearance removes all brush strokes and live effects!*

THE FINER POINTS OF APPEARANCES
Adding Fills & Strokes

It's not until you start adding multiple Fills and Strokes to an appearance that you completely understand how useful the Appearance palette is. See lessons and Galleries later in this chapter for some great examples of why you would want to use multiple Strokes and/or Fills.

The Appearance palette has a stacking order similar to that of the Layers palette. Items at the top of the palette are at the top of the stacking order. You can click on items in the palette list to select them, and you can rearrange them by dragging them up and down.

Select Add New Fill or Add New Stroke from the palette pop-up menu to add these attributes to an appearance. You can also add effects and transparency attributes to each Fill or Stroke by first clicking on the desired Fill or Stroke line in the palette.

There are several ways to duplicate or delete a Fill, Stroke, or effect. You can select the attribute in the palette list and drag it to one of the icons at the bottom of the palette. You can also select the attribute and click on the appropriate icon at the bottom of the palette. Finally, you can choose the appropriate item from the pop-up menu.

Multiple Fills & Strokes

Create multiple line effects by adding multiple strokes to a path. Select a path, group, or layer and choose Add New Stroke from the Appearance palette pop-up menu. A new stroke is added to the Appearance. In order to see the additional stroke on the path, you must give it different attributes from the initial stroke. Target one stroke (in the Appearance palette) and adjust the color, point size, shape, and/or transparency settings.

To create multiple Fills, target an object, group, or layer and choose Add New Fill. As with multiple strokes, before you can see the effect of the added Fill, it needs a different appearance. To vary the results of additional Fills, apply an effect or different transparency settings.

If you're having trouble seeing the results of your multiple strokes, start with a wider Stroke on the bottom (see the example opposite). To vary the results, try applying dashed lines and/or different end caps. For Fills, try patterns with transparency.

New Art Has Basic Appearance

The New Art Has Basic Appearance button and palette pop-up menu item are the same control, so (for example) when the button is selected, the menu item will be checked, too.

Expandable text shapes

Want to make a text button? Type a word, then select the text object. Choose Add New Fill (in the Appearance palette menu) and drag this new Fill below the Characters line. Click on the Fill line, apply the desired fill color, and then choose a shape from the Effect: Convert to Shape submenu. Set the Relative Extra Width and Extra Height to how far you want the button to extend around the text, and click OK. Each time you edit the text, the button will automatically resize itself.

For a step-by-step lesson applying multiple Strokes, Fills, and brush strokes to "outlined" type, see Steven Gordon's "Brushed Type" lesson in the Type chapter

Target all elements

As of Illustrator 10, when a group or layer is targeted, you can double-click the Contents line in the Appearance palette to target all the individual elements inside the group or layer. —*Pierre Louveaux*

Transparency 101

Assigning Opacity to Default Brushes

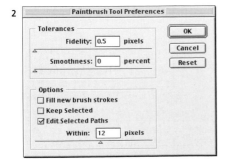

Overview: *Prepare an image for tracing in Illustrator; set Paintbrush preferences; set up the Brush and the level of Transparency; draw, using Layers to save your work in stages.*

1

A scanned sketch, saved as a grayscale TIFF file

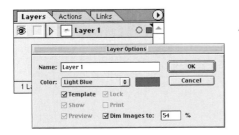

The TIFF in Layer 1; converting Layer 1 to a template layer

2

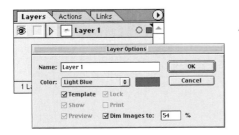

Set the Paintbrush Tool Preferences to prevent new brush strokes from filling and to prevent redraw of marks already made

The most basic use of transparency involves only a drawing tool and the Transparency palette. To create this drawing, Sharon Steuer traced a scanned sketch using Calligraphic brushes set to 45% Opacity. For this lesson, the New Art Has Basic Appearance feature must be off (it's off by default); toggle it on and off in the Appearance palette pop-up menu. All palettes mentioned in this lesson can be accessed from the Window menu.

1 Preparing an image for tracing in Illustrator. Scan a photograph or drawing you want to trace. Save the image in TIFF format. Open it in Illustrator (File: Open). Your scanned image will be contained within Layer 1. In order to be able to draw in great detail without having to resize your brushes, enlarge the image. Click on it with the Selection tool, then Shift-drag a corner to enlarge (Shift-Option-drag/Shift-Alt-drag to enlarge from the image's center). To convert Layer 1 to a template layer in order to prevent your template image from exporting or printing, double-click on Layer 1 in the Layers palette, select the Template option, type in a dimming factor other than the default 50% (if desired), and click OK. (For more about templates and layers, see the *Layers* chapter.)

2 Setting Paintbrush preferences. You'll need to set the Paintbrush Tool Preferences so you can freely make overlapping marks. Double-click on the Paintbrush tool, then uncheck the Options "Fill new brush strokes" (so your marks will be stroked and not filled) and "Keep Selected" (so new marks won't redraw the last drawn mark). With the "Keep Selected" option disabled, you can still redraw a mark by selecting it first with a selection tool, then drawing a corrected mark within the distance specified in the Within field of the Paintbrush Tool Preferences dialog. To create accurate marks, Steuer set the Fidelity to .5 pixels and the Smoothness to 0%. If you want Illustrator to smooth your marks, experiment with higher settings.

3 Setting up the Brush and the level of Transparency. Create a new layer by clicking the New Layer icon in the Layers palette. With the Paintbrush tool selected, open the Brushes palette. The first six default brushes are Calligraphic brushes. Click on one to choose it. Using the Color palette, choose a Stroke color. Next, in the Transparency palette, move the Opacity slider to approximately 50%. To change the opacity of future brush strokes at any point, move the Opacity slider to a new setting.

4 Drawing, and using Layers to save your work in stages. Start drawing. Notice that the opacity you chose will apply after you complete each stroke. Feel free to switch to any of the other Calligraphic brushes; Illustrator will maintain your transparency and color settings. Once you have a group of marks you're satisfied with, make a new layer and begin working into it. Working this way will allow you to easily return to the last stage you were pleased with. Hide and show any layer by clicking on the icon in the leftmost column next to the layer name in the Layers palette. Delete any layer by dragging its name to the Trash icon at the bottom of the palette.

Although your drawing should look as though it were painted with ink washes, real ink was never this flexible or editable. See the next lesson for a more advanced variation of this technique involving Custom brushes, changes in Transparency, and Layers. For more about working with brushes, see the *Brushes* chapter.

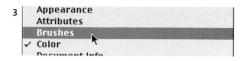

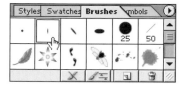

Open the Brushes palette and choose a Calligraphic Brush

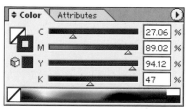

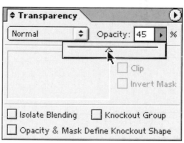

Using the Color palette, set the Fill to None and choose a Stroke color; preset the opacity of future brush strokes using the Opacity slider in the Transparency palette

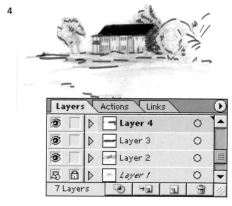

Use the Layers palette to organize groups of brush strokes and save stages of the illustration; you can hide or show layers by clicking on the visibility icon in the left column

Transparent Color
Customizing Transparent Brushes & Layers

Advanced Technique

Overview: *Create custom Calligraphic brushes, setting Paintbrush Tool Preferences and Opacity; create sublayers for categories of objects and for grouping of similar marks; use layers to separate different types of marks and to easily choose brush styles; experiment with Blending modes; add finishing touches and a Clipping Mask to crop the image.*

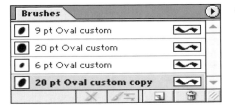

Customize the settings for each new Calligraphic brush using the Brush Options window

Four custom Calligraphic brushes in List view (from the Brushes palette pop-up)

Preset the opacity for future objects by moving the Opacity slider in the Transparency palette to the desired percentage

Illustrator's Calligraphic brushes are among Sharon Steuer's favorite digital tools. For the painting above, she customized Calligraphic brushes, varying the Opacity and colors to achieve a watercolor-like look. For this lesson, the New Art Has Basic Appearance feature must be off (it's off by default); toggle it on and off in the Appearance palette pop-up menu (Window: Appearance).

1 Create custom Calligraphic brushes and set the Paintbrush Tool Preferences and Opacity. You'll first customize a few brushes so you can better control the size of the marks you make. If you have a pressure-sensitive tablet, you can customize brushes so they respond to your touch. To make the first brush, start a new file, then open the Brushes palette (Window: Brushes), click the New Brush icon at the bottom of the palette, select New Calligraphic Brush, and click OK. In the Calligraphic Brush Options window, experiment with various settings, then click OK and make a stroke to test the brush. To try other settings, double-click the desired brush in the

Brushes palette. For her first custom brush, Steuer chose a Pressure setting for Diameter (9 pt with a 9 pt Variation), set the Angle to 60° and the Roundness to 60% with both Fixed, and clicked OK. For greater stroke variation, try choosing a Pressure or Random setting for each option (pressure settings are unavailable or don't work unless you have a graphics tablet installed). To create each of the brush variations, drag the first custom brush over the New Brush icon and adjust the settings.

Once you have created your initial brushes, set the Paintbrush Tool Preferences so you can freely create overlapping marks: Double-click the Paintbrush tool, and uncheck the "Fill new brush strokes" and "Keep Selected" options. (For more on Paintbrush Tool Preferences, see step 2 of the previous lesson.) In order to draw with the maximum amount of detail, Steuer also set the Fidelity to .5 pixels and the Smoothness to 0%.

To paint in transparent color, after you've chosen a Calligraphic brush and a color, open the Transparency palette (Window: Transparency). To set Transparency, click and hold the triangle to the right of the Opacity field to reveal the Opacity slider, which you can adjust.

2 Creating sublayers for categories of objects, then sublayers for each grouping of similar marks. Create sublayers for the major categories of objects within your composition. Whenever you intend to draw a group of marks within a broader grouping (such as Steuer's thicker stalks within the vase), create a sublayer for those (use the New Layer or New Sublayer icons at the bottom of the Layers palette). It's helpful to create nested sublayers because, although you can expand any layer to view the <Path> for each separate object, expanding a layer that contains many objects can slow Illustrator down. It's also helpful to name the layers that contain sublayers so you can identify which layers you can easily expand or collapse. Although she didn't name all of her layers, Steuer named the sublayers that contained further sublayers (flowers and vase). To rename a layer, double-click the

2

The New Sublayer and New Layer icons found at the bottom of the Layers palette

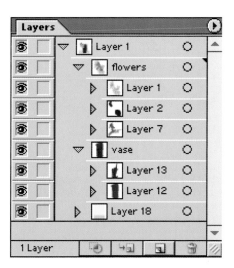

An early stage of the image showing organizational sublayers nested within a master layer (top Layer 1). Steuer custom-named sublayers that contained additional sublayers so she could identify which ones she could easily expand without slowing down Illustrator

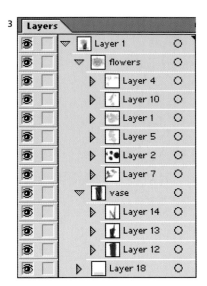

Steuer used Illustrator's built-in layer location and style duplicating features to easily create new sublayers in the desired locations and with the desired styling

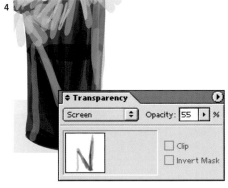

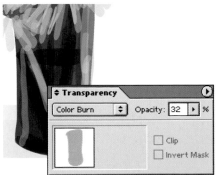

Above, Steuer chose the Screen Blending mode with Opacity set to 55% to achieve a brightening effect on the stem objects. Below, she chose the Color Burn Blending mode with Opacity set to 32% on a duplicate copy of the vase shape layer to achieve a glassy effect

layer in the Layers palette. By holding down Option for Mac or Alt for Windows as you click the New Layer or New Sublayer icon, you can name a new layer as you create it. Drag layers to the trash if you no longer need their contents. Steuer created and trashed many sublayers as she worked, which resulted in some out-of-sequence sublayer names.

3 Using the layers to separate different types of marks and to easily choose the right brush style. One of the wonderful aspects of working with Illustrator is that your last selected object determines the styling and "stacking order" for the next object you draw. For instance, say you select a petal, then deselect it by clicking outside of the image itself (or ⌘-Shift-A for Mac/Ctrl-Shift-A for Win), the next mark you make will match the styling of the last selected object and will be placed at the top of the same layer. If you want the new object to be placed directly above an existing one, click on the existing one in the Layers palette before drawing the new one. If objects on top obstruct your ability to click on the object you want to select, select the problem objects and lock them with Object: Lock: Selection (⌘-2/Ctrl-2). Or expand the layer to find the object in the Layers palette and then select it by clicking to the right of the targeting circle for that <Path>.

4 Experimenting with changing the Blending modes of your marks. In addition to setting the Opacity, you can also adjust the Blending mode for selected objects by choosing from the pop-up menu in the upper left corner of the Transparency palette. For example, after creating a batch of stems on one layer within the vase, Steuer wanted to make them appear brighter, so she changed the mode from Normal to Screen. To adjust the Blending mode for all objects within a layer or sublayer, click to the right of that layer's targeting circle (on the far right side of the layer name) to select all the objects within that layer, and then experiment with different Blending modes. To enhance the effect, you can duplicate the sublayer (by dragging the sublayer to the New Layer icon). If this makes the effect too strong, you can reduce the opacity of the upper sublayer. To enhance the glass vase, Steuer duplicated the sublayer containing the vase shape (by dragging the sublayer to the New Layer icon), and moved the duplicate on top of the other vase objects by dragging its name up in the Layers palette. In the Transparency palette, she chose the Color Burn Blending mode for the duplicate vase sublayer, and reduced the Opacity to 32%. Be aware that custom Blending modes are retained from the last selected object in the same way as the brush style, color, and opacity are retained. You can manually reset your Blending mode to Normal, or any other mode, before or after you create the next object.

5 **Finishing touches, and perhaps a Clipping Mask to crop the image.** For finishing touches, you can work into your layers, adding details. Steuer continued to add sublayers above and below others to add the final details to her still life, and to add a signature.

To neatly trim your illustration, create a Clipping Mask that crops out everything outside the mask. To apply a Clipping Mask across multiple layers, all your objects and sublayers must be contained within one layer (which we'll call the master layer) and the topmost path within your master layer will become your mask. If you haven't been working within a single layer, you'll need to create a master layer. To do this, first select all the layers you want masked by ⌘-clicking each layer for Mac/Ctrl-clicking for Win (you can Shift-click to select contiguous layers) and choose Collect in New Layer from the palette pop-up menu. This converts your layers into sublayers within a new master layer. To make a topmost masking object, first click on the master layer's name to highlight it, then use the Pen tool or Rectangle tool to create a path that will define your mask. With your master layer still highlighted, click the Make Clipping Mask icon at the bottom of the Layers palette.

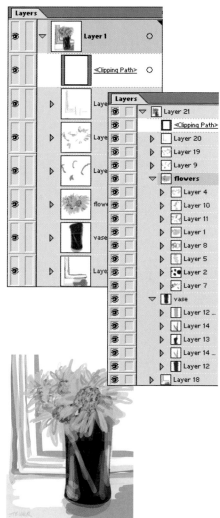

Before and after the finishing touches and cropping, and the final Layers palette shown collapsed (left, with enlarged icons) and expanded (right)

Basic Transparency

Blending Modes, Opacity & Isolate Blending

Overview: *Arrange elements; selectively apply blending modes to objects using Layers, Appearance and Transparency palettes; modify layer opacity; select objects, assign a blending mode, group objects and isolate the blending.*

1

Elements of the final illustration before transparency effects

2

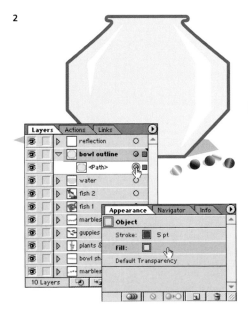

Use the Layers palette to target a path, and the Appearance palette to select the Fill attribute

Once you have mastered selecting and targeting in Illustrator, you can create cool effects using basic transparency. In this illustration, Diane Hinze Kanzler incorporated three aspects of the Transparency palette: opacity, blending modes, and Isolate Blending.

1 Arrange elements of the final illustration on layers.
The logical placement of groups and objects in layers will be helpful as you apply transparency effects to an illustration. In this illustration, for example, all parts of one fish are on one layer, the marbles in the bowl are on a separate layer from the marbles outside of the bowl, etc. (See the *Layers* chapter for help with organizing layers.)

2 Selectively apply a blending mode to an object.
Kanzler wanted the gray fill of her bowl to have a slight deepening color effect on the objects in the layers below. First, she selected the bowl and gave it a fill of light gray and a stroke of dark gray. Next, she targeted the bowl path in the Layers palette. In order to correctly apply a blending mode to the fill of the bowl, Kanzler selected Fill in the Appearance palette by clicking once on the Fill attribute. She chose Multiply from the list of blending modes in the Transparency palette. The light gray fill of the bowl has a blending mode applied to it, but the dark gray stroke of the bowl remains opaque, as intended.

To apply a blending mode to one of the paths in the water layer, Kanzler used the same targeting method. First, she targeted the larger water path (not the splash drops) and selected Fill in the Appearance palette. Then Kanzler chose Multiply as a blending mode in the Transparency palette.

3 Using the Opacity slider. For the reflection effect on the bowl, Kanzler simply reduced the opacity of the white objects. She targeted the "reflection" layer, and in the Transparency palette used the Opacity slider to reduce the opacity of the reflection objects to the desired amount. In this instance, the Appearance palette wasn't even used, as the effect was applied to the entire layer.

4 Isolate the blending. In order to prevent a blending mode from affecting objects beneath a certain point, the blending effect must be *isolated*. With Kanzler's illustration, she wanted the aquatic leaves and stems to be transparent with each other as they overlap, and those plants to show the fish behind them. But she also wanted to prevent the plants from interacting with the bowl shadow which is beneath the plants on a lower layer.

So that the individual paths in the plant group would interact with each other and with the fish, she first *selected* the plant paths by Option (Mac) /Alt (Win)-clicking on the plant <Group>. Then Kanzler chose the Hard Light blending mode in the Transparency palette. If she had *targeted* the plant layer instead, the blending mode would have applied to the plant group as a *whole*, and the overlapping leaves would not blend with each other. To prevent the bowl shadow from showing through the plants, Kanzler selected the plant group and rearmost fishes group and chose Object: Group, which placed all into one new group. She *targeted* that group in the Layers palette, and then selected the Isolate Blending checkbox in the Transparency palette, which maintained the blending mode within the group, but prevented the group from being transparent to layers below.

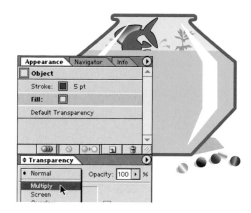

Docking the Transparency palette under the Appearance palette to keep both conveniently available

3

The Opacity slider in the Transparency palette was used to reduce opacity of the reflection highlight shapes

4

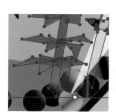

Apply a blending mode to multiple objects individually by selecting rather than targeting before applying the blending mode

Use the Layers palette to target a group of objects that have been assigned a blending mode, then enable Isolate Blending (in the Transparency palette) to prevent that blending mode from affecting objects outside the group

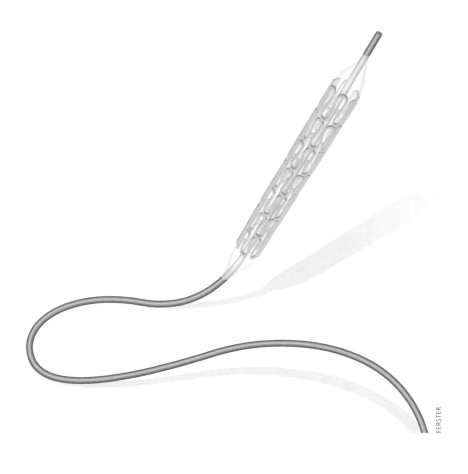

FERSTER

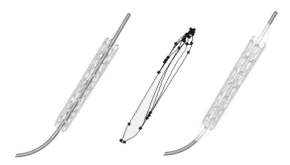

Gary Ferster

A product illustration for a catheter for Medtronic AVE challenged Gary Ferster to combine a subtle gradient mesh with transparency effects. To create a semi-transparent catheter balloon (positioned inside the lattice-like "stent" near the top of the catheter), Ferster drew a balloon object with the Pen tool and then created a mesh with the Gradient Mesh tool. After choosing subtle colors for the mesh intersection points, Ferster used the Transparency palette to specify a 65% Opacity value (and Normal blending mode) for the object.

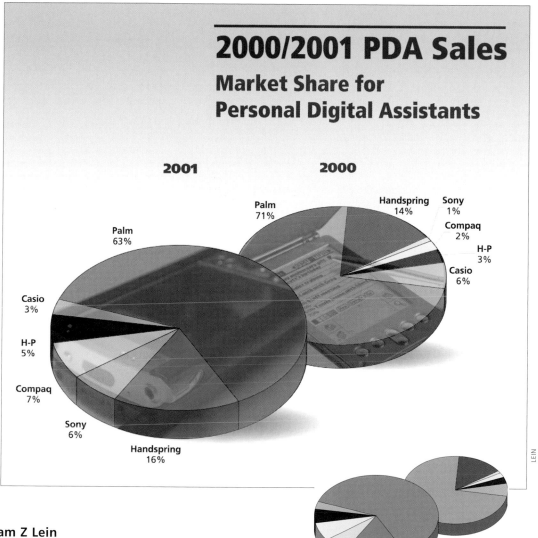

2000/2001 PDA Sales
Market Share for
Personal Digital Assistants

2001

2000

Adam Z Lein

Adam Z Lein began this pie chart in Microsoft Excel by selecting data and using Excel's Chart Wizard to turn the data into a chart tilted in a perspective view. Lein used the Acrobat 5 PDF maker to create a PDF of the graph. When he opened the PDF in Illustrator, the graph retained all of the shapes as vector objects and the type as outlines. Lein then placed a photographic image on a layer below the pie chart artwork and used the Transparency palette to set the Blending mode to Luminosity and the transparency to 30%. To fit the image within the pie chart, Lein created a clipping mask from the circle and edge of the pie chart. (See the *Advanced Techniques* chapter for more about clipping masks.)

Basic Highlights

Making Highlights with Transparent Blends

Overview: *Create your basic objects and a light-colored highlight shape; use blends to make the highlights; scale the highlights to fit.*

Using transparency, highlights are now as simple as creating a blend in the correct highlight shape. For help creating smooth contoured blends, see "Unlocking Realism" in the *Blends, Gradients & Mesh* chapter.

The original objects (locked in the layers palette) shown with the basic highlight shape

1 Creating your basic objects and determining your basic highlight shape and color. Artist Sharon Steuer created this "Bubbles" image using overlaying transparent radial gradients (to see how she created the hill, see "Rolling Mesh" in the *Blends, Gradients & Mesh* chapter). She modified an oval with the Direct-selection tool to create her basic highlight shape. After creating your main objects, make a light-colored highlight object on top. Use the Layers palette to lock everything except the highlighted object (see the *Layers* chapter for help).

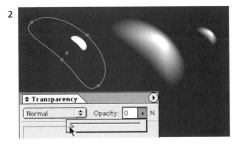

The highlight objects before blending (the outer object is set to 0% Opaque in the Transparency palette); after blending in 22 steps; the blend shown at actual size

2 Creating the highlight. Select the highlight shape and Copy, choose Edit: Paste In Back, then Object: Lock. Now, select and shrink the front copy (for scaling help see the *Zen* chapter). Choose Object: Unlock All, then set the Opacity of this selected outer object to 0% in the Transparency palette. Select both objects, then with the Blend tool, click on one anchor point of the outer object, then Option/Alt-click on the corresponding anchor point of the inner object and specify the number of blend steps (Steuer chose 22 steps). Steuer scaled copies of her highlight blend (with a "registration circle") for each bubble.

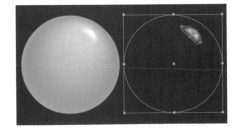

The final blend in place and shown in a "registration" circle for easy scaling on other bubbles

Nancy Stahl

Nancy Stahl created a soft, airbrushed look throughout her illustration for *The Illustrator 10 Wow! Book* cover by using opaque-to-transparent blends, as described in the "Basic Highlights" lesson opposite. Shown bottom left are the steps Stahl used in creating the hat band: the first two figures in the first diagram show her custom Pattern Brush and that brush applied to a path (see the *Brushes, Symbols & Hatches* chapter for brushes help), third down shows the opaque-to-transparent blends on top of the brushed path, next are the brush and blends masked, at bottom is that masked group on the hat colors, with the brushed path set to a Multiply mode with a 65% Opacity (Transparency palette).

At bottom right is the gondolier with and without the opaque-to-transparent blends.

Basic Appearances

Making and Applying Appearances

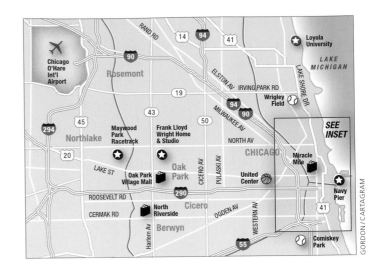

Overview: *Create appearance attributes for an object; build a three-stroke appearance, save it as a style, and then draw paths and apply the style; target a layer with a drop shadow effect, create symbols on the layer, then edit layer appearance if needed.*

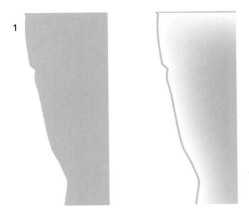

1

On the left, the lake with blue fill and stroke; on the right, the lake with the Inner Glow added to the appearance attribute set

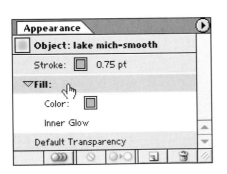

Appearance palette displaying the finished set of attributes (Gordon used the Appearance palette so that he could create a single path for the lake that contained a fill and the coastline stroke above it)

Complexity and simplicity come together when you use Illustrator's Appearance palette to design intricate effects, develop reusable styles and simplify production workflow. In this location map of Chicago, cartographer Steven Gordon relied on the Appearance palette to easily build appearances and apply them to objects, groups and layers.

1 Building an appearance for a single object. Gordon developed a set of appearance attributes that applied a coastline, vignette and blue fill to a path symbolizing Lake Michigan. To begin building appearance attributes, open the Appearance palette and other palettes you might need (Color, Swatches, Stroke, and Transparency, for example). Gordon began by drawing the outline of the lake with the Pen tool and giving the path a 0.75 pt dark blue stroke. In the Appearance palette, he clicked on the Fill attribute and chose the same dark blue he had used for the stroke. To give the lake a light-colored vignette, he applied an inner glow to the Fill attribute (Effect: Stylize: Inner Glow). In the Inner Glow dialog box, Gordon set Mode to Normal, Opacity to 100%, Blur to 0.25 inches (for the width of the vignette edge), and enabled the Edge option. He clicked the dialog's color swatch and chose white for the glow color.

2 Creating a style. Until Illustrator 9, you created a "patterned" line like an interstate highway symbol by overlapping copies of a path, each copy with a different stroke width. Now you can use the Appearance palette to craft a multi-stroked line that you apply to a single path. First, deselect any objects that may still be selected and reset the Appearance palette by clicking the Clear Appearance icon at the bottom of the palette (this eliminates any attributes from the last selected style or object). Next, click the Stroke attribute (it will have the None color icon) and click the Duplicate Selected Item icon twice to make two copies. Now, to make Gordon's interstate symbol, select the top Stroke attribute and give it a dark color and a 0.5 pt width. Select the middle attribute and choose a light color and a 2 pt width. For the bottom attribute, choose a dark color and a 3 pt width. Because you'll use this set of appearance attributes later, save it as a style by dragging the Object icon at the top of the palette to the Styles palette. (Double-click the new style's default name in the palette and rename it in the dialog box if you want.)

3 Assigning a style to a group. Draw the paths you want to paint with the new style you created above. Then choose Select All and Group. To get the three levels of strokes to merge when paths on the map cross one another, click on Group in the Appearance palette and then apply the interstate style you just saved.

4 Assigning appearance attributes to an entire layer. By targeting a layer with appearance attributes, you can create a uniform look for all the objects you draw or place on that layer. Create a layer for the symbols and click the layer's target icon in the Layers palette. Then select Effect: Stylize: Drop Shadow. Each symbol you draw or paste on that layer will be automatically painted with the drop shadow. Later, you can modify the drop shadows by clicking the layer's targeting icon and then double-clicking the Drop Shadow attribute in the Appearance palette and changing values in the pop-up Drop Shadow dialog box.

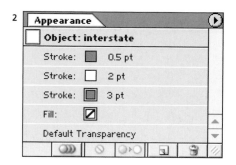

2

Appearance palette for Gordon's interstate highway symbol

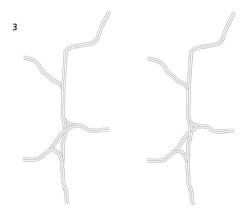

3

On the left, the interstates with the Style applied to the individual paths; on the right, the interstate paths were grouped before the Style was applied

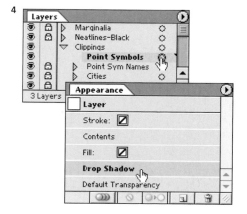

4

Top, targeting the layer in the Layers palette; bottom, the Appearance palette showing the Drop Shadow attribute (double-click the attribute to edit Drop Shadow values)

Tinting a Scan

Using Transparency Effects & Simplify Path

Advanced Technique

Overview: *Place an EPS image and its clipping path; tint the image using the clipping path, Blending Modes and Opacity; reduce a path's anchor points using Simplify; use Isolate Blending to prevent double shadows.*

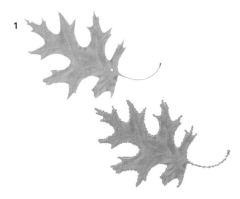

1

The grayscale leaf scan; the outline selection converted to a path in Photoshop and designated as a clipping path (the small hole in the leaf has been included in the path, making it a compound clipping path in Illustrator)

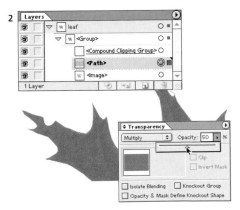

2

Drawing the russet-colored rectangle into the compound clipping path group; targeting the rectangle path and specifying a Multiply blending mode and opacity of 50%

Diane Hinze Kanzler enhanced her original salamander illustration using transparency effects and Simplify to make her image more unique and naturalistic.

1 Scanning and placing an image and its clipping path.
If you don't have access to Photoshop, place a grayscale image with a simple outline shape and manually create your own clipping path (see the *Advanced Techniques* chapter for help). To add a bit of nature to her illustration, Kanzler scanned a real oak leaf in grayscale mode in Photoshop. To create a clipping path for the leaf, she used Photoshop's Magic Wand tool to select everything except the leaf (using the Shift key to add the hole to her selection) then chose Select: Inverse. To convert the leaf selection into a clipping path, Kanzler chose from the Path pop-up menu (in order): Make Work Path (with .5 Tolerance), Save Path, and Clipping Path (with a 4 Flatness). To preserve the clipping path, she used Save As and chose Photoshop EPS format, then in Illustrator she chose File: Place to place the EPS leaf, unchecking the Link option to embed the scan and its clipping path.

2 Tinting the scan in Illustrator. Kanzler used the leaf's clipping path to tint her scan. First, in the Layers palette she located the scan's <Group>, expanded it and clicked the scan <Image>. She then drew a russet-colored rectangle above the scan (bigger than the leaf) and targeted this object. In the Transparency palette she set a Multiply blending mode and 50% Opacity for her targeted object.

3 Adding a shadow. To create a shadow, Kanzler began by copying her clipping path (use the Group-selection tool to select your clipping path and then copy). She then clicked the New Layer icon, and moved this new layer below the leaf's layer. After moving your new layer below your image, paste your copied outline in proper registration by first turning off Paste Remembers Layers (from the Layers palette pop-up menu), then choose Edit: Paste in Front (⌘-F/Ctrl-F). Kanzler then chose a new fill color for the outline and used cursor keys to offset its position.

4 Creating a simpler shadow. In order to minimize the overall size of her file, Kanzler wanted to create a simplified shadow for her salamander. In the Layers palette, she selected the salamander outline path by clicking to the right of the target circle. She then made a copy of the selected outline to a layer below by dragging the colored square to the layer below while holding Option/Alt. After choosing a color for the shadow, Kanzler simplified the shape by choosing Object: Path: Simplify, and set the Curve Precision to 82%, thus reducing the path from 655 to 121 path points, while still maintaining the shape's overall look. She then offset the salamander's shadow.

Kanzler selected all the objects in the leaf file, copied, and switched to her salamander illustration. Then she turned on Paste Remembers Layers (in the Layers palette pop-up menu) and pasted. Using the Layers palette, she moved the leaf layers below the salamander layers, and targeted her salamander shadow object. In the Transparency palette, she chose a Multiply blending mode.

To prevent a "double shadow" effect where shadows overlapped, Kanzler used Isolate Blending. She selected and grouped (Object: Group or ⌘-G/Ctrl-G) the salamander shadow and the leaf group—but *not* the leaf shadow. She *targeted* this *new* group in the Layers palette, then clicked Isolate Blending in the Transparency palette.

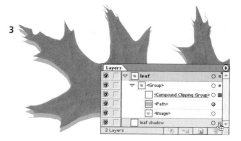

3

Using a copy of the leaf's clipping path to create an offset shadow on a layer below the leaf scan

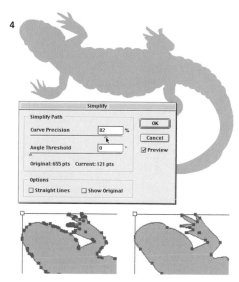

4

Simplifying the salamander's shadow object path (left: before; right: after Simplify)

Assigning a blending mode to the salamander's shadow in the final, combined illustration

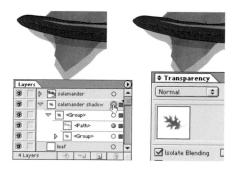

Using the Transparency palette's Isolate Blending feature to prevent an overlapping shadow effect

It's a Knockout!

See-through Objects with a Knockout Group

Advanced Technique

Overview: *Arrange elements in layers; apply a gradient fill and solid stroke to text; modify opacity and use a blending mode; create a Knockout Group; adjust transparency effects.*

KANZLER

1

All elements of the final illustration, before applying blending modes and Knockout Group

A copy of the gradient-filled "Organic" is pasted behind and given a 6-pt stroke of dark blue and a fill of None

2

Detail of the rainbow <Group> after reducing opacity in the Transparency palette

For this sign, Diane Hinze Kanzler used Illustrator's Knockout Group feature to allow woodgrain to show through text while blocking out other elements.

You may already be familiar with the concept of knockout from darkroom or film prepress work. A knockout film is typically used to "punch a hole" in an illustration or photograph, thus revealing images, text, or even the paper color below.

The Knockout Group feature in Illustrator (found in the Transparency palette) works according to the same principle as prepress knockout film, yet it is much more powerful because it also allows transparency effects to be applied with the knockout. The real trick to controlled use of the Knockout Group feature is the proper use of the Layers palette to correctly select or target objects.

1 Arrange elements of the final illustration on layers, convert text to outlines, and apply a gradient fill. It is important, particularly when you're planning to use a Knockout Group, that all of your illustration's elements be placed on layers in a logical fashion (see "Organizing Layers" in the *Layers* chapter) and grouped (Object: Group or ⌘-G/Ctrl-G) when appropriate. This will make selecting or targeting groups much easier.

Create some text using a font bold enough to fill with a gradient, and convert the text to outlines using Type: Create Outlines (converted text is automatically grouped). Next, select the group and click on a Gradient-fill swatch to apply the fill to each letter of the text.

To add a stroke to her text without distorting it, Kanzler selected "Organic," copied it, deselected the text, created a new layer below the filled text layer and chose Edit: Paste In Back with the Paste Remembers Layers toggle off (see the Layers palette pop-up). She gave that copy a fill of None and a thick stroke of dark blue.

2 Apply transparency effects to chosen objects.

Kanzler wanted her rainbow to be transparent, so she targeted the layer of her rainbow group and set the Opacity slider to 75% in the Transparency palette. She also wanted the woodgrain of the background to show through "Organic" while still being affected by the gradient fill. In order to do this Kanzler targeted the gradient-filled text group in the Layers palette, then chose a blending mode of Hard Light in the Transparency palette. At this point, all the objects below the gradient-filled "Organic" showed through, including the thick strokes from the copy of "Organic."

3 Grouping objects and creating a Knockout Group.

Kanzler controlled which objects showed through the topmost "Organic" with the Knockout Group feature. First, she Option-Shift-clicked (Alt-Shift-click for Win) each of the layers containing objects she wanted to select, including the layers containing the filled "Organic" text, the stroked "Organic" text, the corn, and the rainbow, and Grouped (Object: Group, or ⌘-G/Ctrl-G). Next, she targeted the group (in its new position in the Layers palette), and clicked on the Knockout Group box in the Transparency palette until a ✔ appeared (you may have to click more than once to get the ✔). With a Knockout Group applied, each object knocks out all the objects below it within the group. In this case all objects within Kanzler's group were knocked out by the shape of her topmost object. This allowed the woodgrain (which was not part of the Knockout Group) to show through and be affected by the blending mode of the filled "Organic" text.

With a blending mode applied to the gradient-filled "Organic," all lower layers to show through and can be affected by the blending mode (also shown enlarged)

3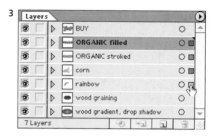

Option-Shift-click /Alt-Shift-click on layers to select objects within multiple layers. Object: Group will move all selected objects into a new <Group> on the topmost selected layer.

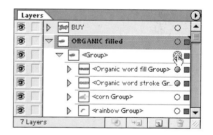

Target the new group, now composed of all objects to be included in the Knockout Group

Knockout Group applied to targeted group; the topmost object's shape "punches a hole" through the rest of the objects in the group and reveal lower objects not included in the group

Opacity Masks 101

Applying Glows and Using Opacity Masks

Advanced Technique

Overview: *Scan sketched artwork, place it as a template, and draw objects; apply Inner Glow; blend one object into another using an Opacity Mask.*

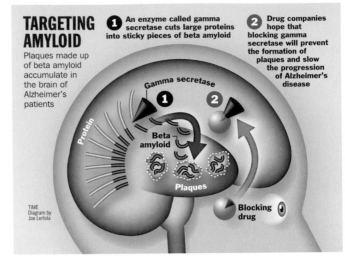

1

Pencil sketch layout of the illustration

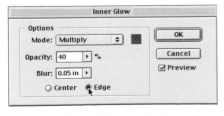

2

Top, head before and after applying Inner Glow; bottom, the Inner Glow dialog box

Blending complex shapes and achieving contoured glows and shadows can be daunting tasks—unless you know how to use Illustrator's Transparency palette and Effect menu. Joe Lertola makes the most of glows and opacity masks in this *TIME* magazine illustration, enjoying the convenience of applying raster effects in Illustrator.

1 Sketching and scanning, then drawing. Draw the objects to which you want to add a glow. Lertola placed a scan of a rough pencil layout in Illustrator as a tracing template (File: Place, and check the Template box) and drew the brain, lobes, arrows, and other elements.

2 Creating Inner Glows. Heighten the visual drama of the objects you've drawn by applying glows, shadows, and other effects from the Effect menu. For example, Lertola selected the outline of the head and choose Effect: Stylize: Inner Glow. In the pop-up dialog, he selected Multiply for Mode, entered 40% for Opacity, and set the Blur. Next, he clicked the color icon to bring up the Color Picker dialog and chose a dark color. To start the Inner Glow color at the edge so it fades inward to the object's center, Lertola selected Edge. (To create the glow with a color chosen in the Color Picker dialog at the center of an object—and fading outward to the edges—you would select Center.)

Similarly, you can add a drop shadow to a selected path by choosing Drop Shadow from the Effect: Stylize menu and specifying Opacity, Offset, and Blur in the Drop Shadow dialog.

3 Applying an opacity mask. Making an object appear to blend into another object may seem difficult. Using an opacity mask, you can perform this trick easily. First, make sure the object that will be blended into another is in front (in Lertola's illustration, the lobe was moved in front of the brain by dragging it in the Layers palette).

To make an opacity mask, draw a rectangle (or other shape) in front of the object you want to fade. Fill with a black-to-white gradient, placing the black where you want to fully hide the top object and the white where you want that object fully revealed. (See the *Blends, Gradients & Mesh* chapter to learn how to create and modify gradients.) Next, select both the rectangle and the object to be masked (Shift-click the outlines of both objects to select them). Make sure the Transparency palette is open (display the palette by selecting Window: Transparency), and choose Make Opacity Mask from the palette's pop-up menu.

Once you've made the opacity mask, the object and its mask are linked together (moving the object will move the mask with it). To edit the object's path, click on the artwork thumbnail in the Transparency palette and use any of the path editing tools; to edit the mask, click on the mask thumbnail. Edit the gradient using the Gradient palette or the Gradient tool.

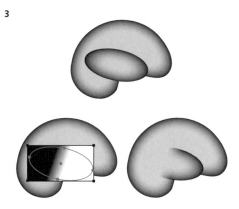

3

Top, brain with overlying lobe; bottom left, lobe and opacity masking object (black-to-white gradient fill) selected; bottom right, lobe following Make Opacity Mask

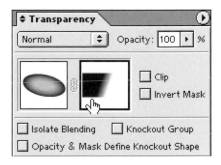

Entering mask-editing mode by clicking on the mask thumbnail in the Transparency palette

Opacity Masks—source materials

You do not have to limit yourself to using a single vector object in constructing an opacity mask. Any artwork will do. Experiment with placed images, gradient meshes, and even objects that contain opacity masks of their own. Remember that it's the grayscale luminosity of the masking artwork that determines the opacity of the masked artwork, not its color or vector structure.

Why can't I draw now?

You may be in mask-editing mode and not know it if:

- You draw an object, deselect it, and it seems to disappear
- You fill an object with a color, but the color doesn't display

If you are in mask-editing mode, the Layers palette tab will read Layers (Opacity Mask). To exit mask-editing mode, click on the artwork thumbnail in the Transparency palette.

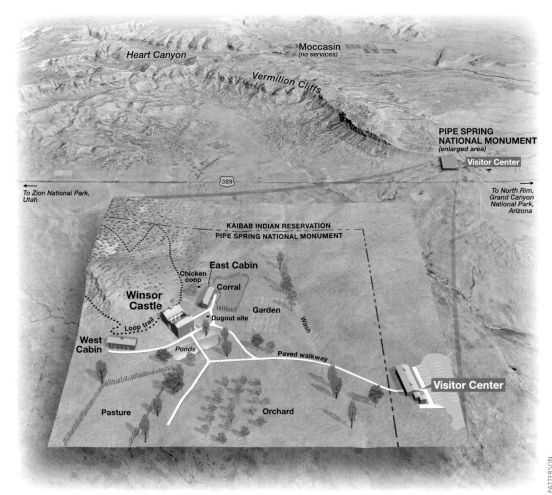

PATTERSON

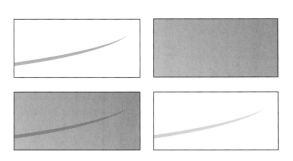

Tom Patterson / U.S. National Park Service

After building the map background in Bryce and Photoshop, cartographer Tom Patterson applied Illustrator transparency to create special effects. He drew each tapered "zoom" line with the Pen tool, connecting the inset map with the background map. He filled the zoom lines with red-brown and applied 40% opacity using the Transparency palette. To make the lines appear more transparent as they zoomed down into the background, Patterson drew a large rectangle that overlapped them, and filled the rectangle with a black-to-white gradient. Then he selected the gradient-filled rectangle and the two zoom lines and chose Make Opacity Mask from the Transparency palette.

ALVES

Sandra Alves

Sandra Alves created this interior using a variety of transparency and Effects features. The flowers in the vase were created using gradient meshes; the petals and buds are each made of multi-colored gradient meshes (see the *Blends* chapter for gradient and mesh help). Alves created a couple of flowers, then rotated, skewed, and scaled each of them (for transformation help see the *Zen* chapter). The stems were 2-pt strokes converted to outlined paths (Object: Path: Outline Stroke) so that they could be filled with gradients (gradients can't be applied to strokes). The vase itself was a gradient mesh

with 50% opacity. She created the drapes with gradient mesh and gradient-filled objects set to various opacities. To add depth to the image, Alves applied the drop shadow effect to a number of objects (Effect: Stylize: Drop Shadow), including the drapes. The clouds outside the window were created in Photoshop and placed in Illustrator (File: Place). She created the floor and the room in this illustration using the default Wood grain light Hatch Effect setting (Filter: Pen & Ink: Hatch Effects) with Keep Object's Fill Color option checked (for more on hatches, see the *Advanced Techniques* chapter).

CASSELL

Peter Cassell / 1185 Design

As a kind of artwork not normally associated with Illustrator's hard-edged vector tools, Peter Cassell's fluffy cumulus clouds comprised one of the packaging illustrations created for Adobe Illustrator 9 (see Cassell's cityscape Gallery opposite). Cassell began by placing a photographic image on a template layer in Illustrator. Next, he created a gradient mesh with the maximum number of rows and columns (50). To color the clouds, he first chose View: Outline (so he could see the cloud image on a layer below the mesh). Next, he selected the Direct-selection tool, clicked on a mesh point, selected the Eyedropper tool, and then clicked in the cloud image to sample its color. He repeated this process to color the rest of the mesh to match the cloud image. To reshape parts of the grid to follow the contours of the clouds, Cassell clicked mesh points with the Mesh tool and dragged them. Where he needed more detail,

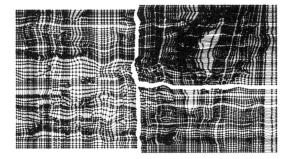

Cassell added rows and columns to the mesh by clicking on a mesh line or in an empty space in the mesh with the Mesh tool. As the composition became unwieldy with detail, Cassell selected overlapping sections of the mesh and copied and pasted each section into a separate file. Once he finished with a section, Cassell copied and pasted it into the final, composite file. He was careful not to adjust mesh points where sections overlapped, so he could maintain a seamless appearance where the separate sections he had worked on overlapped.

CASSELL

Peter Cassell / 1185 Design

Peter Cassell's European cityscape, commissioned for the Adobe Illustrator 9 packaging illustration, was built with mists he created using a gradient mesh as an opacity mask. After drawing the rough shapes of reflections in the water, Cassell drew a rectangle on a layer above the water and filled the rectangle with white. He copied the rectangle, pasted it in front, filled it with black, and then selected Object: Create Gradient Mesh to turn it into an 18 x 15 mesh. He edited the mesh by selecting mesh points with the Direct-selection tool and filling the points with gray values varying from 30%

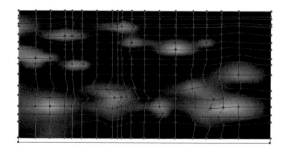

to 50% black. To shape a mist, he selected and moved mesh points. To mask the white rectangle with the gradient mesh above it, Cassell selected the mesh and the rectangle and chose Make Opacity Mask from the Transparency palette's pop-up menu.

Live Effects & Styles

Live Effects & Styles

TARGETING AMYLOID

Plaques made up of beta amyloid accumulate in the brain of Alzheimer's patients

1 An enzyme called gamma secretase cuts large proteins into sticky pieces of beta amyloid

2 Drug companies hope that blocking gamma secretase will prevent the formation of plaques and slow the progression of Alzheimer's disease

TIME Diagram by Joe Lertola

LERTOLA

See Joe Lertola's "Opacity Masks 101" lesson in the Transparency & Appearances *chapter*

Transform effects!

This one is a gem! Any transformation can be applied as an *effect* (Effect: Distort & Transform: Transform). Know exactly how much you've rotated, skewed, or scaled an object and you can completely undo or adjust it.

Some effects do not scale

Layer and *group* effects do not scale with objects. To get around this, save as *.eps* and then place the artwork back into Illustrator.

Applying effects

Once an effect has been applied to an object, double-click the effect in the Appearance palette to change the values. If you reselect the effect from the Effect menu, you will apply a second instance of the effect to the object, not change it.

The effects that Illustrator offers us get better with each release. Illustrator 9 brought us live effects, and now Illustrator 10 has expanded its repertoire to include two powerful new tools: warps and envelopes. This chapter will bring you up to speed on Illustrator's various effects and will also acquaint you with the eminently useful Styles palette.

EFFECTS VS. FILTERS

Illustrator provides a variety of methods for altering or enhancing paths. The *Drawing & Coloring* chapter introduces you to some basic methods, from manual adjustments to Pathfinder filters. This chapter focuses on *effects*. Effects are similar to filters, with one exception—effects are live. While filters permanently change your artwork, effects alter the appearance of your work without permanently changing the base art—and they can be removed at any time. When an effect is applied to an object, group, or layer, it will display as an attribute in the Appearance palette. The effect's position in the palette indicates which element it will modify.

Effects are organized in the same manner as filters, with those that modify but retain the vector characteristic of the artwork at the top of the menu, and those that require rasterization (including the Photoshop-compatible filters) on the bottom. Like their filter counterparts, most of the effects in the lower part of the Effect menu can be applied only when your document is in the RGB color mode (space).

EFFECT PATHFINDERS

The effects listed on the Effect: Pathfinder menu are effect versions of the Pathfinders described in the *Drawing & Coloring* chapter. To apply a Pathfinder effect, you must either group the objects and make sure that the group is also targeted (see Tip "Pathfinder Group Alert"

---

at right), or target the layer with the objects (which will apply the effect to *all* the objects on that layer). Then, select Effect: Pathfinder and choose an effect.

Hard Mix and Soft Mix

Hard Mix and Soft Mix change the color of the areas where the objects overlap, in order to simulate transparency (see tip at right). Also see "SandeeC's Soft Mix Chart" on the *Wow! CD*, and see the Pathfinder Palette chart in the *Drawing & Coloring* chapter for examples of how Hard Mix and Soft Mix can be used.

Filter versions of these effects are no longer available on the Pathfinder palette. To obtain the equivalent result, apply the effect, then choose Object: Expand Appearance; or use the *Wow!* Pathfinder Filter actions available on the *Wow! CD*. When you expand, or use the action versions of Hard and Soft Mix, the objects get divided just as though you had first applied the Divide command from the Pathfinder palette.

Pathfinder effects vs. compound shapes

With live Pathfinder effects, you create a container (group or layer) and then apply one effect (Add, Subtract, Intersect, or Exclude) to the container. But in a compound shape, *each component* independently specifies whether it adds to, subtracts from, intersects with, or excludes from the components below it.

In general, when you use more than one or two shape modes you'll find it simpler to work with compound shapes. One of the great benefits of compound shapes over Pathfinder effects is that compound shapes behave much more reliably when the objects being combined aren't simple.

Compound shapes can be exported live in PSD (Photoshop) files, or copied in Illustrator and pasted into Photoshop as shape layers. Compound shapes can also be used as clipping paths.

See the *Drawing and Coloring* chapter for much more about Pathfinders and compound shapes.

Hard/Soft Mix & Transparency

You can obtain the same color effect as the Hard Mix Effect by setting the Transparency Blend Mode to Darken and Opacity to 100%. There is no Transparency equivalent for Soft Mix.

Pathfinder Group Alert

Even if your objects were already grouped, you may still get the following warning when you apply a Pathfinder Effect:

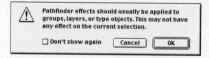

This happens if you Direct-select the objects and miss some of their points, causing the objects to get targeted.

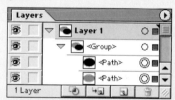

To fix this, target the group

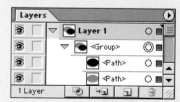

the objects are in, then apply the Pathfinder effect. To avoid the problem and ensure that the group gets selected, hold down Option (Mac)/Alt (Win) to switch from the Direct-selection tool to the Group-selection tool while selecting your grouped objects.

STYLES IN ILLUSTRATOR

If you plan on applying an appearance more than once, you might want to save it as a style in the Styles palette. Once saved, a style can be applied to objects (including text objects), groups, and layers. A style provides a recipe, or formula, for producing a predictable appearance. The default style is a white fill and a 1-point black stroke.

To apply a style, simply select an object—or target a group or layer—and click on a thumbnail in the Styles palette. You can also sample a style from another object using the Eyedropper tool. Alternatively, you can drag a style from the Styles palette directly onto an object.

To create a new style, choose the desired appearance attributes (with or without an object selected), then either click the New Style icon on the bottom of the Styles palette or drag the appearance thumbnail from the Appearance palette to the Styles palette. Styles are saved with the color mode (color space) in which they were originally created.

If you want to separate a style from an object, click on the Break Link to Style icon at the bottom of the palette, or select the item from the Styles palette pop-up menu. You might want to do this when you are replacing a style but don't want to change all the objects using the current style to the updated or replaced version (see the Tip "Replace styles" at left).

WARPS AND ENVELOPING

It's often said that the anticipation of something is better than the actual thing itself. Such is not the case with warps and envelopes—which have finally been added to Illustrator 10. These tools are robust and very powerful, offering much more than just simple transformations.

Warps and envelopes may look similar at first, but there's an important difference between them. Warps are applied as live effects—meaning they can be applied to objects, groups, or layers—and can be saved within a graphic style. Envelopes, on the other hand, are actual objects that contain artwork—if you edit the envelope shape, the contents inside the envelope will conform to the shape.

Warps

Applying a warp is actually quite simple. Target an object, group, or layer and choose Effect: Warp: Arc. It really doesn't make a difference which warp effect you choose, because you'll be presented with the Warp Options dialog box where you can choose from any of the 15 different warps. While the warp effects are "canned" in the sense that you can't make adjustments to the effects directly, you can control how a warp appears by changing the Bend value, as well as the Horizontal and Vertical Distortion values.

Once a warp is applied, you can edit it by opening the Appearance palette and double-clicking on the warp listed there. Like any other effect, a warp can be applied to just the Fill or just the Stroke—and if you edit the artwork, the warp updates as well.

Since warps are effects, you can include them as a style. This style can then be applied to other artwork.

Envelopes

While warp effects do a nice job of distorting artwork, there are times when you need more control. That's where Illustrator's envelopes come in—offering more control than you can imagine.

There are three ways to apply envelopes. The simplest way is to create a shape you want to use as your envelope and make sure it's at the top of the stacking order—above the art you want to place inside the envelope. Then, with the artwork and the shape you created both selected, choose Object: Envelope Distort: Make with Top Object. Illustrator will create a special kind of object—an envelope. This object is a container in the shape you chose and it appears in the Layers palette as an <Envelope>. You can edit the path of the envelope as you would any other, and the artwork inside will update to conform to the shape. To edit the contents of the envelope, you need

Four's company

"Stylize" is listed twice in the Filter menu and twice in the Effect menu. The Filter: Stylize commands change the paths of the objects to which you apply them. The Effect: Stylize commands produce "live" effects, altering the appearance of objects but leaving the paths unchanged and available for editing. Note that the bottom Stylize choices in each menu always require an RGB color space.

"Crunching Type" lesson in the Type *chapter*

These warps look familiar

If you've used Photoshop 6 or 7, you'll recognize that Illustrator's Warp feature looks much like Photoshop's Text Warp feature. The difference? While Photoshop's warps work on text only, Illustrator's warp effect can be applied to anything—text, vectors, and even rasters!—*Mordy Golding*

Smart people use Smart Guides

Although they can sometimes be annoying, Smart Guides can be quite helpful when you work with Warps or Envelopes, as it may become difficult to edit artwork that has an appearance applied to it. With Smart Guides turned on, Illustrator will highlight the art for you, making it easier to identify where the actual artwork is (and not the appearance). Make good use of the ⌘-U/Ctrl-U keyboard shortcut to turn Smart Guides on and off. —*Mordy Golding*

Editing envelopes

Remember that you can edit the contents of any envelope by selecting the envelope shape and choosing Object: Envelope Distort: Edit Contents. See Sandee Cohen's "Warps & Envelopes" lesson later in this chapter for examples on how to combine meshes with envelopes to create realistic shading effects. —*Mordy Golding*

Envelope distort options

If your artwork contains pattern fills or linear gradients, you can have envelopes distort them by choosing Object: Envelope Distort: Envelope Options and checking the appropriate items in the dialog box.—*Mordy Golding*

to choose Object: Envelope Distort: Edit Contents. If you then look at the Layers palette, you'll notice that the <Envelope> now has a disclosure triangle that reveals the contents of the envelope—the artwork you placed. You can edit the artwork directly or even drag other paths into the <Envelope> in the Layers palette. When you're finished editing the contents, choose Object: Envelope Distort: Edit Envelope.

There are two other types of envelopes, and they are closely related. Both of them use meshes to provide even more distortion control. One of them is called Make with Warp and it's found in the Object: Envelope Distort submenu. This technique starts off by displaying the Warp dialog. When you choose a warp and press OK, Illustrator converts that warp to an envelope mesh. You can then edit individual mesh points with the Direct-selection tool to distort not only the outer edges of the envelope shape, but also the way art is distorted within the envelope itself. To provide even more control, use the Mesh tool to add more mesh points as desired.

The third way to create an envelope is to start from a rectangular mesh. Select artwork and choose Object: Envelope Distort: Make with Mesh. After you've chosen how many mesh points you want, Illustrator will create an envelope mesh. Use the Direct-selection tool to edit the points and use the Mesh tool to add mesh points.

Ted Alspach

Ted Alspach used the Flare tool to create an air of mystery in this mock movie poster. The Flare tool simulates a lens flare in a photograph by creating a halo, rays, and rings around an object. Alspach selected the Flare tool (found in the Rectangle tool pop-up menu), clicked and dragged to set the halo size, then click-dragged again to set the distance and direction of the rings, while using the cursor-keys to adjust the number of rings. He colored some elements (such as the type) a light shade of gray to give the flare an illusion of greater brilliance. In addition to the click-drag method, components of the flare can be modified using the Flare Options dialog box. Here, you can adjust the diameter, opacity, and brightness of the flare's center, as well as the fuzziness of the halo, the number of rays, and the flare's crispness.

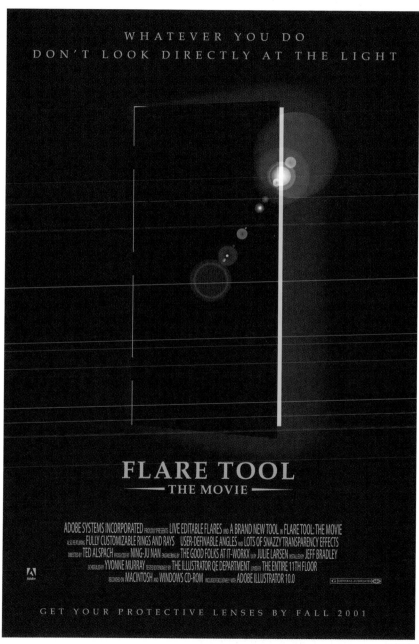

ALSPACH

Scratchboard Art

Using Multiple Strokes, Effects, and Styles

Overview: *Apply multiple strokes to simple objects; offset strokes; apply effects to strokes; create and apply styles.*

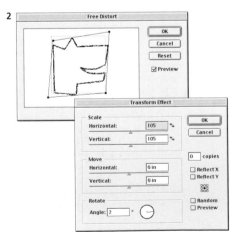

The original scratchboard art consists of simple primitive shapes

To offset a path's Stroke from its Fill, select the Stroke in the Appearance palette and apply Free Distort and Transform from the Effect: Distort & Transform menu

Artist Ellen Papciak-Rose asked consultant Sandee Cohen if there was a way to simulate scratchboard art in Illustrator. Cohen devised a way to transform Papciak-Rose's artwork using Art Brushes, multiple strokes, and stroke effects, which were then combined and saved as styles. Once a series of effects is saved as a style, you can easily apply that style to multiple objects to create a design theme. Art directors may find this method helpful for unifying and stylizing illustrations created by a number of different artists.

1 Applying Art Brushes and Fills. To create a more natural-looking stroke, Cohen applied Art Brushes to simple objects supplied by Papciak-Rose. Cohen used Charcoal, Fude, Dry Ink, Fire Ash, and Pencil Art Brushes (included on the *Wow! CD*). Select a simple object, then click on your choice of Art Brush in the Brushes palette or in a Brush Library. (For more on Art Brushes, see the *Brushes* chapter.) Next, choose basic, solid fills for each object.

2 Offsetting a stroke. To develop a loose, sketchlike look, Cohen offset some of the strokes from their fills. First, highlight a stroke in the Appearance palette and apply

Effect: Distort & Transform: Free Distort or Effect: Distort & Transform: Transform to manually or numerically adjust the position of the stroke so that it is not perfectly aligned with the fill. This gives the stroke a different shape than the fill without permanently changing the path. (You can further reshape the stroke by double-clicking the Transform attribute in the Appearance palette and manually or numerically adjusting the offset of the Stroke attribute.)

3 Adding more strokes to a single path. To add to the sketchlike look, Cohen applied additional strokes to each path. First, she chose a Stroke attribute in the Appearance palette and clicked the Duplicate Selected Item icon at the bottom of the palette. With the new Stroke copy selected, she changed the color, as well as the choice of Art brush. She also double-clicked the stroke's Distort & Transform effect in the Appearance palette and changed the settings to move the Stroke copy's position. Cohen repeated this until she had as many strokes as she liked.

To make a stroke visible only outside its Fill, make sure that the object is still selected, and simply drag the stroke below the Fill in the Appearance palette.

4 Working with styles. To automate the styling of future illustrations, Cohen used the Appearance and Styles palettes to create a library of styles. Whenever you create a set of strokes and fills you like, click the New Style icon in the Styles palette to create a new style swatch.

Once Cohen had assembled a palette of style swatches, she could alter the look and feel of the artwork by simply applying a variety of styles to selected paths. Using new colors sent by Papciak-Rose, Cohen's styles from an earlier scratchboard project were re-colored to create the styles used here. The use of styles allows the artist or designer to create a number of overall themes in a style library, and then apply them selectively to illustrations or design elements. This work flow can also be used to keep a cohesive look throughout a project or series.

3

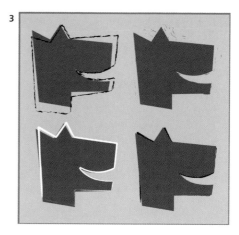

This graphic illustrates the individual strokes that Cohen combined to create the multiple strokes for the face object in the final illustration

4

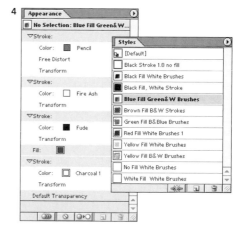

Multiple Strokes applied to an object shown in the Appearance palette; appearance attributes saved in the Styles palette by clicking the New Style icon

Applying different styles to objects can give the same artwork several different looks

Embossing Effects

Building 3D Appearances

Overview: *Apply object-level effects for highlights and shadows; build appearances, save as styles and apply to layers.*

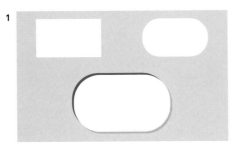

At the top, making the screw slots (on the left, the rectangle and on the right, the rectangle with Round Corners Effect): at the bottom, an enlarged view of the composite appearance

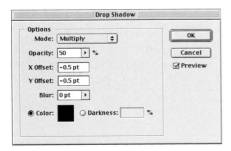

The Drop Shadow options pop-up dialog box; edit the X and Y Offset fields to adjust the position of the shadow and highlight (check the Preview box to see the effect as you work)

Resizing appearances

If you plan to resize an Illustration that contains appearances with stroke values, be sure to apply the appearances to objects, not to layers. Illustrator may fail to rescale stroke values in layer-targeted appearances.

Ted Alspach, Senior Product Manager for Adobe Illustrator, choose the embossed letters, numbers and lines of a license plate to demonstrate the ease and flexibility of using Illustrator's effects and appearances. In this memorial to French mathematician Pierre Bézier, inventor of the original Bézier curve, Alspach simulated the look of embossing by applying a drop shadow effect and by building a sophisticated style.

1 Applying the drop shadow effect. Start the license plate by drawing the background shape, circles, curves and other linework. While technically not a raised surface, the four screw slots still require highlights and shadows to convey the impression of dimension. To create a slot, draw a rectangle and then Fill with White and Stroke with None. Use the Round Corners Effect (Effect: Stylize: Round Corners) to give the object a more oval shape. To cast the plate's shadow on the edge of the slot, select the slot rectangle and apply the Drop Shadow Effect (Effect: Stylize: Drop Shadow). In the Drop Shadow dialog box, choose black for color, Blur 0, and Offset up and to the left (using negative numbers for "X" and "Y" offsets). Then click OK. Repeat the drop shadow effect to make the highlight, except choose a light color and Offset down and to the right (using positive numbers). To further tweak the drop shadows (modifying their color or width, for example), simply double-click the attribute name "drop shadow" in the Appearance palette (Window: Appearance) and edit the values in the dialog box.

2 Building multiple appearances. Alspach took another approach to embossing by building a sophisticated style in which transparency and multiple offset strokes simulate highlights and shadows.

To make the license plate lettering, type the characters in a sans serif font and convert them to outlines (Type: Create Outlines). Ungroup the characters, select a character and set its Fill to orange. To make the first embossing highlight, select the orange Fill appearance attribute in the Appearance palette (Window: Appearance) and copy it by clicking the Duplicate Selected Item icon at the bottom of the palette. Now, select the lower Fill attribute in the palette, choose white from the Color palette and, in the Transparency palette, set Opacity to 25% and blending mode to Screen. Then, choose the Transform Effect (Effect: Transform: Distort & Transform) to offset it up and to the left by editing the Move fields (negative Horizontal and positive Vertical). Make two more copies of this white Fill attribute by once again clicking the Duplicate Selected Item icon. Offset each copy farther up and and to the left by double-clicking the Fill's Transform attribute and editing the Move values in the Transform dialog.

To start the shadows, first duplicate the lowest white Fill. Now select the bottom white Fill and set its color to black, Opacity to 50%, and blending mode to Multiply. Double-click the Fill's Transform attribute and edit the Move values to offset it down and to the right. Copy this shadow and offset it farther down and to the right. When you have finished, the Appearance palette will display six Fill attributes for the object.

3 Creating and applying a Style. Alspach turned the appearance set into a style by dragging the Appearance palette's preview icon and dropping it in the Styles palette. He then applied the style to the layer with the number characters. You can achieve the same embossing look by applying the style to selected character outlines or to a group composed of the character outlines.

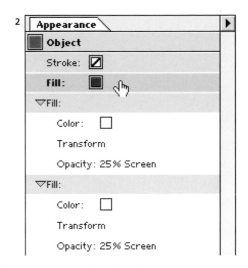

2

Appearance palette showing the appearance preview icon (top left), and the target of the appearance (Object)

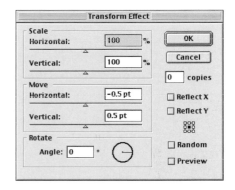

Move values in the Transform Effect dialog box to offset Fill attribute up and left

Close-up view of the embossed letter characters with the multiple highlight and shadow strokes that progressively hide the background artwork

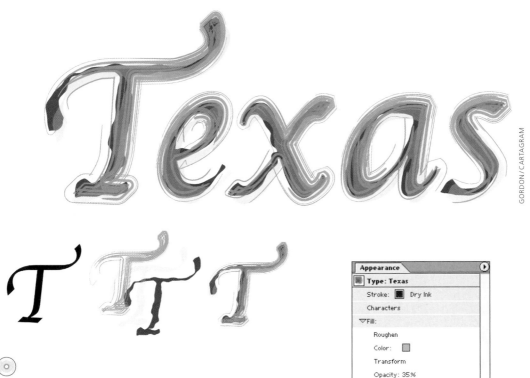

GORDON / CARTAGRAM

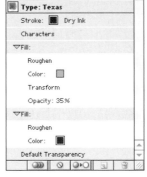

Steven Gordon / Cartagram

Illustrator's brushes and effects can transform the lettering of a calligraphic font into art that suggests a more hand-rendered appearance. To begin this map title, Steven Gordon typed "Texas" and then chose a calligraphic font that included swash capital letters (Apple Chancery). He adjusted kerning to fine-tune the spacing between characters. With the text object selected and the Appearance palette open, Gordon selected Add New Fill from the palette's options menu and gave the new fill a purple color. He duplicated the fill by clicking on the Duplicate Selected Item icon at the bottom of the palette, and gave the duplicate a pale blue color. Next, he clicked on a brush in the Brushes palette (Gordon chose the Dry Ink brush that comes with Illustrator 10's default

Brushes palette). Selecting the stroke in the Appearance palette, he chose a dark blue color. To further customize the title, Gordon selected the pale blue fill in the Appearance palette, offset the fill and distorted the fill's edges using the Transform and Roughen commands from the Effect: Distort and Transform menu. He also made it transparent by moving the slider in the Transparency palette. To finish, Gordon selected the bottom fill and applied the Roughen command from the Effect: Distort and Transform menu. (For a similar technique, see "Brushed Type" in the *Type* chapter and see the *Transparency* chapter for more on Appearances.)

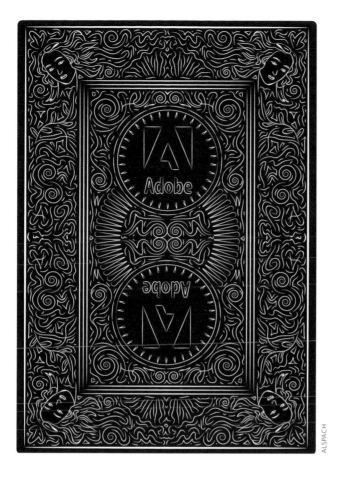

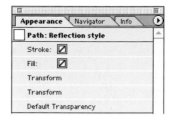

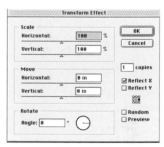

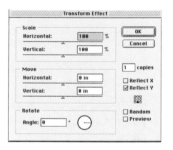

ALSPACH

Ted Alspach, Adobe Systems, Inc.

Inspired by the classic Bicycle brand playing card, Ted Alspach incorporated Adobe imagery into the backside of a deck of cards he designed to give his Adobe Illustrator 10 team. Alspach used the Transform Effect (Object: Transform: Transform Each) to simplify the process of drawing this complex maze of lines by applying an Appearance that used the Transform Effect twice. As he drew the upper left corner of the card, the other three corners were automatically created. The Adobe medallions in the middle of the card were added after the corners were completed. Alspach placed an

invisible rectangle one quarter the size of the card on the layer the effects were applied to, to be sure the effects were applied consistently. In the Transform dialog box (Effect: Distort & Transform: Transform) he chose 1 copy, Reflect X (to reflect the corner across the top of the card), and set the reflect origin to the middle right (he clicked on the middle square on the right side of the icon that represents the corner art's bounding box). For the second Transform Effect, he clicked 1 copy, Reflect Y (to reflect the top half of the card vertically), and set the reflect origin to the middle bottom position.

Warps & Envelopes

Using Warping and Enveloping Effects

Overview: *Group clip art for use with Warp; apply Warp; save Warp effect as a Style; apply Envelope using a shaped path; add a shading effect using a mesh.*

1

Making sure that the flag artwork is grouped. Note: The Appearance palette shows information for the currently targeted (not just selected or highlighted) object in the Layers palette

The Flag Warp applied to a not-fully-grouped flag artwork. The stripes are grouped, but the stars and the union (blue field) are separate objects

2

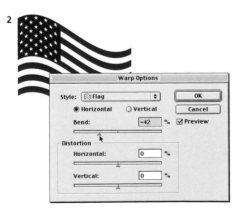

With Preview enabled, experiment with the Warp Options settings

After the tragic events of September 11, 2001, consultant Sandee Cohen wanted to make some flag decorations for her web site. She used Illustrator's Warping and Enveloping effects to mold copies of a basic rectangular flag into a waving flag and a bow tie.

Warps are the easier of the two methods to understand and use. Simply choose one of the 15 preset shapes from the Warp menu and adjust the shape using the sliders in the Warp Options dialog box.

Envelopes let you use any path, warp preset, or mesh object to shape and mold your artwork into almost any form imaginable. You can further manipulate the shape using the envelope's anchor points.

Although Warps and Envelopes both leave original artwork unchanged, only Warps can be saved as Styles.

1 Group clip art for use with Warp effects. Cohen started with a standard United States flag from a clip art collection. First, she made sure that the flag artwork was a grouped object by selecting the flag artwork (which also targets it in the Layers palette) and checking its description in the Appearance palette. If the artwork is not a grouped object, then the effects will not be applied to the artwork as a whole, but rather to each of the paths individually (as shown in the sidebar).

2 Make a copy of the flag artwork and apply a Warp effect. Next, Cohen made a duplicate copy of the flag by selecting it and, while holding down the Option/Alt key, dragging it to a position below the original. While the duplicate was still selected, Cohen chose Effect: Warp: Flag to bring up the Warp dialog box. She enabled the Preview checkbox in the Warp dialog box so she could preview the effect her settings would have on the artwork. Cohen set the Horizontal Bend slider to -42% to create the first stage of her waving flag effect, and clicked OK to apply the Warp. She then applied a second Warp effect to the flag artwork, to complete her waving flag. With the artwork still selected, she chose Effect: Warp: Arc and, with Preview enabled, set the Horizontal Bend slider to 40%.

Note: *In the Warp dialog box, you have access to the full library of Warp shapes no matter which warp you chose from the Effect: Warp menu. Simply click and drag on the Style pop-up menu in the Warp dialog box to access any of the Warp shapes. As long as Preview is enabled, you can then experiment with each Warp shape and settings to see how each will affect your artwork before you apply one.*

To remove a Warp effect, target your artwork. Then, in the Appearance palette, select the Warp (or Shift-click to select multiple Warps) and either click on, or drag your selection to, the Trash button.

3 **Save your Warp effect as a Style.** Once you are pleased with a particular Warp effect or effects that you have achieved, you can easily save the effects as a Style for application to other artwork. Begin by targeting the artwork that you applied your warp(s) and other effects to in the Layers palette. Then Option-click/Alt-click on the New Style button at the bottom of the Styles palette to create and name your new style. If the appearance you save as a style has no fill or strokes, the thumbnail for the style you created will be blank. When this happens, choose either the Small or the Large List View (from the Style palette pop-up menu) to view the Styles by name. To apply a style, simply target the object, group, or layer, and then click on the style in the Styles palette.

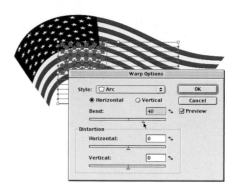

Applying a second Warp effect. Because Warps are live effects, the original flag artwork (seen here as an outline in light blue because the artwork is still selected) remains unchanged

Removing Warp effects from the artwork by highlighting the effects in the Appearance palette, and then clicking on the Trash button to delete them

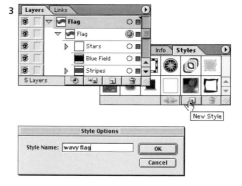

To create a new style, target your artwork, then Option-click/Alt-click the New Style button, and give your new style a name

Applying a Warp effect style to a grouped object

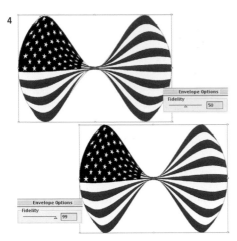

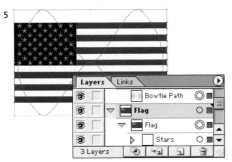

With Envelope Options fidelity set too low, red color in the lower right corner of the upper figure spills outside the bow tie shape. When the fidelity is set to 99% the artwork conforms much more closely to the envelope shape.

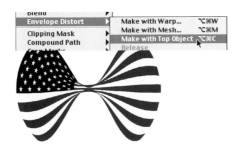

Bow tie path positioned above the flag artwork, and selected, just before making the envelope

Applying the envelope, and the resulting artwork

Using Edit: Paste in Front to create a duplicate positioned directly over the original artwork

4 Use Envelope Options to maximize Envelope fidelity. Envelopes are more versatile in the ways you can shape and manipulate them, but sometimes (especially when the shape you use to create the envelope is kinked or makes sharp changes in direction) the artwork may not conform tightly to the envelope. To minimize this problem, set the Object: Envelope Distort: Envelope Options Fidelity to 99%. Note: Setting Fidelity to 100% creates many more intermediate points along the deformed path, and is usually not necessary.

Cohen used an Envelope to give her flag the shape of a bow tie, and added some shading using a mesh.

5 Apply Envelope using a shaped Path. Cohen added points to a circle and then distorted it into a bow-tie-shaped path. To apply a shaped path of your own, place it above your flag artwork, select both the flag and your shaped path, and choose Object: Envelope Distort: Make with Top Object.

6 Add a shading effect with a mesh. Next, Cohen added a shading effect by using a mesh object on top of her bow tie flag. Begin by creating a duplicate of the bow tie flag (Edit: Copy), then paste it in front of the first one using Edit: Paste in Front to exactly align it over the original. With the duplicate still selected, choose Object: Envelope Distort: Reset with Mesh. In the Reset Envelope Mesh dialog box, make sure that Maintain Envelope Shape and Preview are both enabled. Increase the number of Rows and Columns until you are satisfied with the mesh grid in terms of how you intend to shade it. For her mesh, Cohen used 6 rows and 6 columns. Click OK, and with the mesh artwork still selected, choose Envelope: Distort: Release to free the mesh from the flag. Delete the flag artwork and keep the mesh object. When a mesh object is released from an envelope, it is filled with 20% black. Select the mesh object, then with a Direct-select tool, select points on the mesh grid and change their fill to a shadow color. Cohen selected interior grid points and gave them a value of white until she was satisfied with the mesh's shading.

Note: *Multiple contiguous points and large areas in the mesh are most easily selected using the Direct-select Lasso.*

To see the effect of the shading on the original bow tie flag beneath the mesh, Cohen (with the mesh selected) set the Blending Mode in the Transparency palette to Multiply. This applied the Blending mode only to the selected mesh object, and not the whole layer.

Finally, using the same enveloping and mesh techniques described above, Cohen created a center for the bow tie using a copy of some of the stripes and an elongated rounded rectangle path.

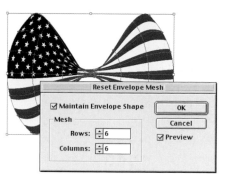

Creating a mesh object using a duplicate of the bow tie flag envelope artwork

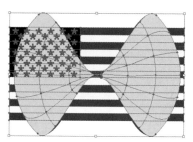

Using Envelope: Distort: Release to free the mesh from the flag artwork

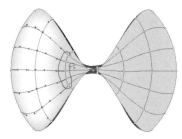

Using the Direct-select Lasso to select multiple mesh points

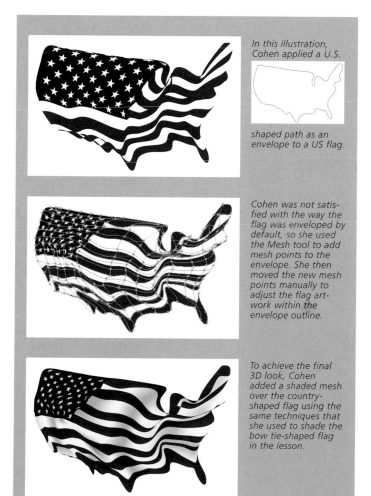

In this illustration, Cohen applied a U.S. shaped path as an envelope to a US flag.

Cohen was not satisfied with the way the flag was enveloped by default, so she used the Mesh tool to add mesh points to the envelope. She then moved the new mesh points manually to adjust the flag artwork within the envelope outline.

To achieve the final 3D look, Cohen added a shaded mesh over the country-shaped flag using the same techniques that she used to shade the bow tie-shaped flag in the lesson.

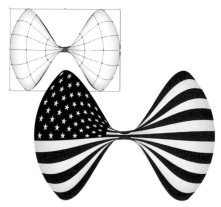

Before and after applying a Blending Mode of Multiply to the shaded mesh object

Enveloping Magic

Using Envelopes to Shape Meshes

Advanced Technique

Overview: *Create and color a gradient mesh; deform the gradient mesh into a bottle shape; use the control points and handles of an envelope mesh to form the straight-sided mesh into the final tapered bottle shape.*

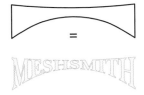

Typical use of an envelope to distort objects. Type (at top) is placed under desired shape (middle), selected, and Object: Envelope Distort: Make with Top is used to create tapered type (bottom)

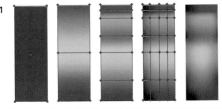

1

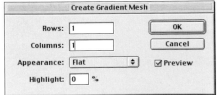

Creating a colored mesh for the bottle. Starting with a rectangle, Torres created a mesh, then added rows with color, and columns (without adding colors)

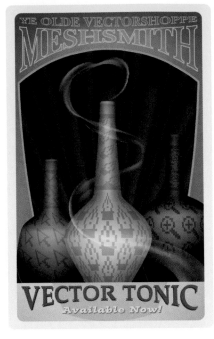

TORRES

Ivan Torres used meshes, enveloping, and his knowledge of 3D techniques to create and form these fanciful bottles etched with patterns made up of Illustrator tool icons. Typically enveloping is used to make artwork or type fit into specific shapes—as in the type in the label above. Envelopes can also be used to directly manipulate and form complex objects, such as meshes, into new shapes. Starting with one gradient mesh in the shape of a straight-sided bottle, Torres used the control points and handles of a simple rectangular envelope to form the straight-sided mesh into the final tapered bottle shapes.

1 Create and color the starting mesh for the bottle.
Draw a rectangle, fill it with color, and convert it to a mesh object (Object: Create Gradient Mesh; Rows: 1, Column: 1, Appearance: Flat). Using the Mesh tool, click along the edges to add rows, Direct-select a row, and adjust the color of the row using the HSB sliders (accessed via the Color palette pop-up menu) as you go.

When your rows are complete, use the Mesh tool (while holding down the Shift key) to add three equally spaced columns to the mesh without adding color.

To complete the coloring of the mesh, select vertical sections of the mesh using the Direct-select tool, and use the Filter: Colors: Adjust Color filter to darken colors that will be near the edge of the bottle, and lighten those that will be near the center (doing so helps make it look 3D).

2 Deform the mesh into a straight-sided bottle shape.

Starting with your colored mesh in Outline mode, Direct-select the top half and use Object: Transform: Scale (or the Scale tool) to pull the points closer together to create a neck for the bottle. Next, using the Mesh tool, add rows to the mesh just below where the bottle widens and at the top. Direct-select all the points in the lower, wider area of the bottle and use the Scale tool to widen that section. Then Direct-select the topmost row, and use the Scale tool to pull the points slightly closer together to form the tapered lip at the top of the bottle. You may have to adjust some anchor point handles to keep the mesh lines straight. Direct-select the points on the upper straight portion of the neck. While holding the Shift key down drag them upward to lengthen the neck as pictured.

3 Use an envelope mesh to complete the bottle.

Torres wanted to create a bottle with a long tapered neck. To do this by manipulating the mesh's many rows of anchor points would be difficult and time consuming. Instead, he put the bottle in an envelope and used the anchor points of the envelope to do the final shaping.

To put your bottle into an envelope, select your straight-sided bottle mesh, and choose Object: Envelope Distort: Make with Mesh; specify 2 rows, 1 column, and click OK.

To lengthen the neck of the bottle, Direct-select the two middle points of the envelope and Shift-drag them down. To taper the top of the bottle, Direct-select the top two points on the envelope and use the Scale tool to narrow the neck of the bottle. To complete the shape, Direct-select the bottom two points and use the Scale tool to narrow the bottom of the bottle.

2

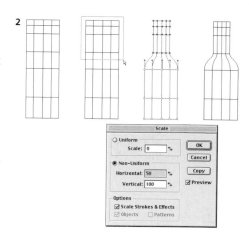

Creating a neck for the bottle by Direct-selecting the upper portion and using the Scale dialog

From right to left: after adjusting the row positions; after adding some rows and creating a taper at the top of the bottle, after widening the bottom of the bottle and narrowing the neck; turning Preview on to see the finished mesh

3

Using Make with Mesh to create a simple envelope around the bottle mesh

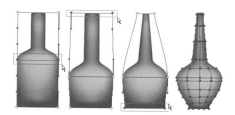

Forming the bottle using the envelope's anchor points, and the final bottle shape expanded to show how the points of the original straight sided mesh have been tapered

Blurring The Lines

Photorealism with Blends and Effects

Overview: *Trace a placed image; draw objects and fill them with colors sampled from the image; create blends; rasterize objects and apply Gaussian Blur.*

1

The original composite photograph (made from separate images in Photoshop) placed on a template layer

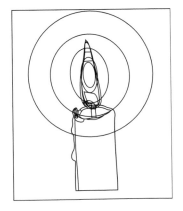

All of the objects Brashear drew for the illustration, displayed in Outline View

Using a technique he calls "Pen and Eyedropper," artist Bruce Brashear reproduces photographs in Illustrator by tracing a placed image and filling objects with colors sampled from the image (see Brashear's Vector Photos in the *Drawing & Coloring* chapter to learn about this technique). In this illustration, Brashear expands his technique by employing blends and Gaussian blurs to capture the subtleties of candlelight and reflections.

1 Placing an image, and drawing and coloring objects. After beginning a new file, Brashear placed an image of a candle and flame on a template layer (File: Place). He traced the shapes for the candle, wick, flame and halo using the Pen tool. For a complex object like the candle flame or the candle wick, you may need to create several objects or blends to completely illustrate its different colors or shapes (Brashear created 11 objects for his candle flame). To fill your objects with colors from the image on the template layer, select the Eyedropper tool, select an object, and Shift-click in the image to sample its color.

2 Making a halo from blends, rasterizing it, and applying a blur to it. Brashear's soft, round halo behind the flame was created with blends and several effects. To begin a halo, draw at least two objects to blend (Brashear made five objects to serve as transitional color blends in the image's halo). Next, fill each object with a color sampled from the placed image using the Eyedropper tool. Then, select the objects and choose Object: Blend: Make. To set the complexity of the multi-step blend that Illustrator creates, choose Object: Blend: Blend Options (or double-click the Blend tool icon in the Tools palette). In the Blend Options dialog, click the pop-up menu, select Specified Steps and key in a high enough number to provide a sufficient transition of shapes or colors (the number you choose sets the steps between each pair of objects, not the total steps for the whole multi-step blend). If you need to reshape the halo, click on anchor points with the Direct-selection tool and move the points or their Bézier handles. Finish by drawing a background rectangle and filling it with a color that will contrast with the colors in the halo blend.

While blends can soften the shape and color transitions between objects, you can further soften the appearance of your halo by applying a Gaussian Blur. Because applying a raster effect to a complex blend can tax your computer's processor, consider rasterizing the blend before applying the blur. (Note: because rasterizing artwork will prevent it from being further edited, save a copy of it in case you need it later.) To rasterize, select the black background rectangle and the multi-step blend you created previously and choose Object: Rasterize. In the pop-up Rasterize dialog, set Resolution to a value that suits the size or medium of your illustration's display or publication; also, set Anti-aliasing to None. Be sure to review the Illustrator Basics chapter for guidance on settings that affect the quality of exported Illustrator files with raster objects and effects.

When you're ready to apply the blur, select the rasterized object and then choose Effect: Blur: Gaussian Blur. In the Gaussian Blur dialog, move the slider to the right or key in a number in the Radius field (Brashear applied

2

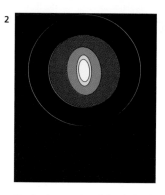

The background and five halo objects (each halo object shown here with magenta stroke for demonstration)

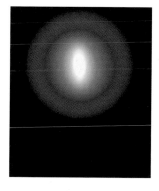

The multistep blend with 12 blend steps between each of the five original component objects

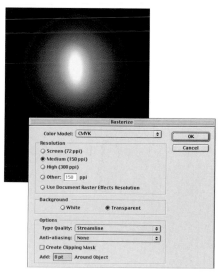

Above, the rasterized object created from the multi-step blend; below, the Object: Rasterize dialog

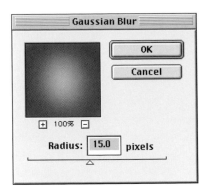

Top, the Gaussian Blur dialog box; bottom, the rasterized object following blurring

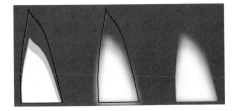

The original yellow candle flame tip on the left; on the right, the original flame tip and a copy that was scaled smaller and filled with yellow-white

On the left, an elongated copy of the original candle flame tip in front of the yellow and white tips; in the middle, the yellow and white tips are blurred; on the right, the blurred flame tips after being masked

a blur with a 20-pixel radius to his halo's blend). If you want to change the blur later, simply select the blurred object and double-click Gaussian Blur in the Appearance palette. Then, key-in another number in the Radius field.

3 **Blending, blurring and masking the flame.** Brashear observed that the orange tip of the flame in the photographic image was hard-edged along the sides but gradually blurred near the tip. You can achieve this visual effect in Illustrator with a blur and a clipping mask. Start by selecting the object you drew as a triangular flame tip. Then select the Scale tool and click on the bottom-left point of the tip, then click on a point or line on the other side of the tip and drag inward while pressing the Option/Alt key to create a smaller copy of the object. Fill the copy with a yellow-white color. With the copied object still selected, click on the bottom-left point with the Scale tool, click on a point or line opposite it and Option-drag/Alt-drag a new outline that is taller but not wider than the other tip objects. Next, select the first two tip objects and choose Effect: Blur: Gaussian Blur; in the pop-up Gaussian Blur dialog, set the Radius to 1.0 pixel. To finish, select the blurred tips and the unblurred tip (the second copy you made) and choose Object: Clipping Mask: Make. As a result, the blur is confined to the edges of the clipping mask (but spreads through the empty area at the top of the masking object).

The two faces of Rasterize

When you apply Effect: Blur: Gaussian Blur to a vector object, Illustrator automatically rasterizes the paths "live" (using the parameters found in the Effect: Document Raster Effects Settings dialog). This doesn't happen with the Filter version of the Gaussian Blur, however. You need to convert your vector object to a raster object using Object: Rasterize before you can apply the Gaussian Blur filter. Remember that unless you undo the rasterization, your vector object will be permanently changed to raster—so make a copy first!

Advanced Techniques

10

Advanced Techniques

Choose Clipping Mask: Make from the Object menu or use the Make Clipping Mask button on the Layers palette

This chapter builds upon techniques and exercises covered in earlier chapters and combines techniques found in different chapters. With masking effects in particular, the techniques will be easier to follow if you feel comfortable with layers and stacking order (*Layers* chapter), as well as blends and gradients (*Blends, Gradients & Mesh* chapter), and are willing to experiment with Pathfinder filters (*Drawing & Coloring* chapter).

CLIPPING MASKS

There are two kinds of masks in Illustrator: Clipping Masks and Opacity Masks. This chapter will discuss the use of Clipping Masks in a variety of techniques. Opacity Masks are made using the Transparency palette and are discussed in the *Transparency & Appearances* chapter.

Choosing Object: Clipping Mask: Make puts all of the masking objects into a group with the masking element at the top of the group

Illustrator's Clipping Mask command converts the topmost object in your clipping group into a mask, which hides portions of your image that extend beyond the mask boundaries. After you've applied a Clipping Mask, you can easily adjust the contour of the masking object itself as well as the objects within the mask using the Lasso or any path-editing tools. Use the Direct-selection tool to edit paths, the Group-selection tool to isolate objects within a group or to select entire objects, or the Selection tool to work with groups of objects.

Clicking the Make Clipping Mask button at the bottom of the palette turns the first item below the highlighted group or layer into a clipping path, without creating a new group

In order to use multiple objects as a mask, you'll need to first select the objects and convert them to a Compound Path (Object: Compound Path: Make), or a Compound Shape (choose Make Compound Shape from the Pathfinder palette pop-up menu, or use the *Wow!* Action loaded from the Compound Shape Commands group of actions in *Wow! Actions* on the *Wow! CD*). In either case, your multiple objects form one compound object that can then become a single masking object (see the Tip "Compound Paths or Shapes" opposite for more on this).

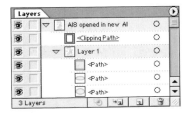

When you open a legacy file with layer-masks, the masked layers become sublayers of the masking layer, because all masking objects must be on the same container layer

Two indicators in the Layers palette can tell you that you have an active Clipping Mask. First, your Clipping Mask path will be underlined and will remain underlined even if you rename it. Second, with an active Clipping Mask, you'll see dotted lines between the clipped items in the Layers palette instead of the standard solid lines.

Once you've created the object or Compound object you wish to become your mask, you can convert it into a Clipping Mask using either the Make Clipping Mask button of the Layers palette, or the Object: Clipping Mask: Make command. The Layers palette commands maintain your layers' structure as they mask, whereas the Object menu command gathers all the selected objects into a new group. See below for details on both methods.

Masking technique #1: The Layers palette options

To mask unwanted areas of artwork within a container (*container* refers to any group, sublayer, or layer), create an object to use as your mask and make sure it's the topmost item within your container. Next, highlight the container that has the object that will become your mask, and click on the Make Clipping Mask button on the bottom of the Layers palette. The result is that the topmost object within the container you selected becomes the Clipping Mask object (which hides all elements that extend beyond the mask) within that container.

Once you've created a Clipping Mask, you can move objects up or down within the layer or sublayers to change the stacking order. However, if you move items out of the container that has the Clipping Mask, they will no longer be masked (see the *Layers* chapter for more on Layers). Moving the clipping path itself out of the container it was created within releases the mask completely. To release a Clipping Mask without reordering objects or layers, highlight the mask's container in the Layers palette and click the Make/Release Clipping Mask icon.

Before Illustrator 9, if you selected objects on different layers and chose to Make Mask, you'd be creating a "layer-mask" that would hide all objects between the selected

Clipping Mask icon disabled

The container (layer, sublayer, or group) that holds your intended clipping object must be highlighted in the Layers palette before you can apply Make/Release Clipping Mask. Also, in order for the button to be enabled, the top item inside the highlighted container must be something that can be turned into a clipping path (or container full of clipping paths). Possible items are a path, a compound path, a text object, a compound shape, or a group or sublayer containing only items in this list.

Compound Paths or Shapes?

When creating masking objects, use Compound Paths to combine simple objects. Use Compound Shapes for more control over the "holes" in overlapping objects or to combine more complex objects, such as live type or envelopes. Convert selected objects into a Compound Shape with Make Compound Shape from the Pathfinder pop-up menu, or the Make Compound Shape *Wow! Action* (in the "Compound Shape Commands" in *Wow! Actions* on the *Wow! CD*). For more about Compound Paths and Shapes, and Pathfinders, see the *Drawing & Coloring* chapter.

Inserting objects into a mask

To insert objects into a Clipping Mask, make sure that Paste Remembers Layers (in the Layers pop-up menu) is off, then Cut or Copy the objects you wish to insert. Next, select an object within the mask and use Paste In Front or Back to place the copied object into the mask. Alternatively, you can drag the new object into the mask using the Layers palette (see the *Layers* chapter).

Magically move a Clipping Path

Once an object is a Clipping Path, you can move it anywhere *within* its layer or group in the Layers palette and it will still maintain its masking effect!

Figuring out if it's a mask

If you're not sure whether a current selection contains a mask or is being masked, for:

- The <Clipping Path> entry in the Layers palette. Even if the entry has been renamed, it will remain underlined if it is a mask. All clipped objects will be in the same layer or group as the mask.
- Object: Clipping Mask: Release being enabled indicates that a mask is affecting your selection.
- An Opacity Mask is indicated with a *dotted* underline.

An example of how type can be used as a masking object

objects, with the topmost object becoming your mask. If you open one of these files in your current version of Illustrator you'll see that all your layers are now contained within a new layer called a "master layer."

In order to mask across layers in the current version of Illustrator, you'll have to manually create your own "master layer" into which you'll place everything you want to mask. To do this, first select all the layers that you wish to mask (click on the first layer you want masked, then Shift-click on the bottom layer) and choose Collect in New Layer from the Layers pop-up menu—this places all of your layers within a new "master layer." Although any topmost object can now become your mask (including an entire group or sublayer), it's probably easiest to create or move a masking object in the "master layer" itself. Make sure the element to be used as a mask is at the top of the contents within the master layer; then select the master layer in the Layers palette, and click the Make/Release Clipping Mask button at the bottom of the palette, or choose Make Clipping Mask from the Layers palette pop-up menu. For practice applying a Clipping Mask across multiple layers, see step 5 in the "Transparent Color" lesson in the *Transparency & Appearances* chapter.

Masking technique #2: The Object menu command
You can also create masks for objects and groups of objects that are independent of layers and sublayers. Use this method when you want to confine the masking effect to a specific object or group of objects that you can easily duplicate and relocate. Since this method modifies your layer structure, don't use it if you need to maintain objects on specific layers.

As before, start by creating a topmost object or compound object that will become your Clipping Mask. Next, select *all* the objects you want to be masked (the topmost object will become the mask). Now, choose Object: Clipping Mask: Make. When you use this method, all the objects, including the new Clipping Path, will move to the layer that contained your topmost object and will be contained within a new <Group>. The masking effect will be restricted to only those objects within the group, and you can easily use the Selection tool to select the entire clipping group. If you expand the <Group> in the Layers palette, you will be able to move objects up or down within the group to change the stacking order. Expanding the <Group> will allow you to move objects into or out of the clipping group. This chapter includes many examples that show how to use this command to create intricate contours by masking complex groups, such as blends.

MASK PROBLEM-SOLVING STRATEGIES
Using type or type outlines as a mask

You can use editable type as a mask to give the appearance that the type is filled with any image or group of objects. Select the type and the image or objects with which you want to fill the text. Make sure the type is on top, then choose Object: Clipping Mask: Make. To use separate type characters as a single Clipping Mask, you have to first make them into a Compound Shape or Compound Path. You can make a compound shape from either outlined or live (i.e., non-outlined) text. You can make a compound path only from outlined text (not live text). Once you've made a Compound object of your separate type elements, you can use it as a mask. (See the Tip "Compound paths or shapes?" earlier in this introduction for more. See the *Type* chapter for examples of masking with text.)

Mask error message

If you've tried to make a Clipping Mask, but you get the message "selection cannot contain objects within different groups unless the entire group is selected," the objects you've chosen to mask are part of a subset of a group of objects. To create a mask with these objects, Cut your selected objects, then Paste In Front (⌘-F for Mac/Ctrl-F for Win). Now you'll be able to apply Object: Make Clipping Mask.

Colorful Masking

Fitting Blends into Custom Shapes

Advanced Technique

Overview: *Create a complex blend; mask it with a custom masking object; create a second mask-and-blend combination; make a two-object mask using compound paths.*

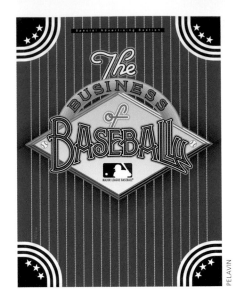

The best way to learn how to mask is to make some masked blends. With Laurie Grace's pencils, you'll learn how to mask complex blends to fit into custom shapes. And with the patriotic corners of Danny Pelavin's baseball illustration, you'll learn how to mask one blend into two different objects by using compound paths.

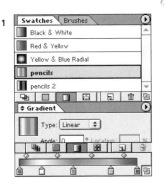

The gradient for a pencil body

1 Creating the basic elements not requiring masking. Create your basic objects. For her pencils, Grace created the long barrel of the pencil with a gradient fill.

Creating objects and blending them in pairs, then creating an object to use as a mask

Selecting the blends with an overlying object designed as a mask; the blends masked

2 Creating the first mask-and-blend combination. To prepare a mask for the pencils, create a closed object outlining the shaved wood and pencil tip, and Lock it (Object menu). To ensure that your blend will completely fill the mask, make sure that each created object extends beyond the mask. Then select and blend each pair of adjacent objects (see the *Blends, Gradients & Mesh* chapter). Grace created the slanted outside objects first and the center object last so the blends would build from back to front towards the center. Unlock your pencil-tip object, choose Object: Arrange: Bring to Front, select the blends with the mask object and choose Object: Clipping Mask: Make. Then Group the mask and the blend (Object menu).

3 Preparing the next masking objects and mask. Select and copy your mask, then select and lock the mask with the masked objects to keep from accidentally selecting any of them as you continue to work. Next, use Paste In Front to paste a copy of your previous mask on top, and make any adjustments necessary to prepare this object as the next mask. Grace cut and reshaped a copy of the full pencil-tip mask until it correctly fit the colored lead at the top. Hide this new mask-to-be (Object: Hide Selection) until you've completed a new set of blends.

4 Creating a new mask that overlays the first. Create and blend new pairs of objects as in Step 2. When your blends are complete, reveal (Object: Show All) your hidden masking object and Bring to Front to place the mask on top of these latest blends. Then select the colored-tip blends with this top object, make a mask as in Step 2 and, as before, Group them together for easy reselection. Finally, Unlock the first blends (Object: Unlock All), select the entire piece and Group it all together.

5 Making a mask from a compound path. Create a blend to be masked by two objects. As Pelavin did for his patriotic corners, start with a circle as a template. Turn on View: Smart Guides and use the Pen tool to draw a straight line from the circle's center point to its bottom edge. With the Rotate tool, Option-click/Alt-click on the circle center to specify an 11.25° rotation and click Copy. Then choose Object: Transform: Transform Again seven times to repeat the rotated copy a full quarter of a circle. Recolor every other line and blend from one to the next, as above. Next, create two paths for a mask (Pelavin cut and joined quarters of concentric circles) and choose Object: Compound Path: Make. Place the compound path on top of the blends, select them all and choose Object: Clipping Mask: Make to see your blend show through both paths. Pelavin recolored a copy of the red blend with a range of whites, masked the white blend with a larger arc and placed it behind the reds.

3

Completed objects selected and locked, then a copy of the last mask made into a new mask

4

New objects before and after blending, and after being masked

5

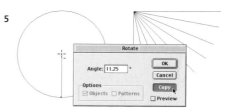

Rotating a copy of a line about a circle's center 11.25°, then applying Transform Again 7 times

Coloring every other line and blending in pairs

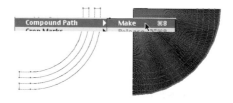

Compounding paths and getting ready to mask

Blends masked by compounds and a final corner (shown here also with a masked white blend)

Contouring Masks

Using Masks to Control Realistic Tonality

Advanced Technique

Overview: *Create the full outline for your image; copy an object representing a surface; create a blend and mask it with the copy of the surface object; use simple lines as accenting details.*

1

Many of the shapes would serve as masks for blending

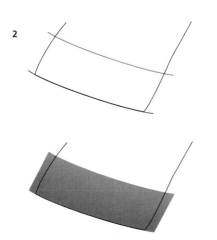

2

Two stroked paths (top) were blended (bottom) to create shading for part of the front surface of the PDA

For some purposes, gradients can make the smooth color transitions of light and shadow needed for a photo-realistic image. But many of the shapes you will model will have complex or curved surfaces that can best be modeled with masked blends. Andrea Kelley used masked blends to define the gentle curves, smooth edges and tapered sides of this Apple Computer PDA.

1 Creating outlines. Draw an outline version of your image, constructing each surface as a single closed object. You can draw all of the objects on a single layer, then use the Release to Layers option in the Layers palette menu to automatically distribute each object to its own separate layer. For each shape that requires a masked blend, select its layer and lock the others (see the *Layers* chapter if you need help with basic layer functions covered here).

2 Making blend objects. To create the blend, draw two objects whose shapes follow the contours of the surface object; alternatively, copy the object and use the Scissors or Knife tool to cut the copy into the pieces (open paths) you need as blending objects. Now, select the two paths and blend (Object: Blend: Make).

3 Masking and editing blends. To mask the blend inside the surface, select the surface object in the Layers palette and drag it above the blend object (but keep it on the same layer as the blend object). Select the layer in the Layers palette (it will highlight) and then click the Make/Release Clipping Mask icon at the bottom of the palette; Illustrator automatically masks the blend with the top object on the layer (in this case, the surface). If the blend doesn't fill the surface object, reshape the blend by Direct-selecting and adjusting points in one of the original blend objects.

When you create blends that lie in front of or next to other objects (for example, the highlight blend on the side of the stylus is positioned on the barrel), you can smooth the transition between the blended object and a neighboring object by matching the ending color of your blend with the color of the neighboring object. To do this, select the blend object and then click on the neighboring object with the Eyedropper tool.

When working on an illustration where many of the objects lie close together, use the Layers palette to lock and hide objects (by clicking on the palette's lock and eye icons) when you have finished masking their blends.

4 Accenting details. Carefully analyze the surfaces of your object to identify shape and lighting details. Kelley often uses thin lines in dark or light colors to create simple contrasting highlights and shadows.

Transform gradients into masked blends

To transform a gradient into a masked blend, expand the gradient (Object: Expand) and specify the number of steps; the gradient will be replaced by a masked blend.

3

The Layers palette showing the masking object (<Path>) above the blend object

The Layers palette after clicking the Make/Release Clipping Mask icon

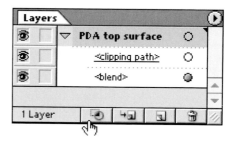

The masked blend

4

Before and after: light stroke added to show reflection on stylus tip and thin dark stroke added to show groove on stylus barrel

Dark and light strokes defining edges of the PDA's surfaces around the icon panel

Reflective Masks

Super-Realistic Reflection

Advanced Technique

Overview: *Move a copy of a blend area; if you're using type, convert it to outlines; skew and adjust it to the right shape; use filters to make an offset; recolor and remask blends; move blend back into position.*

Two techniques in earlier chapters demonstrated how Thomas • Bradley Illustration & Design (T•B I&D) used the Pathfinder palette to generate its basic objects for blending, and how the blends themselves are formed (see "Unlocking Realism" in the *Blends, Gradients & Mesh* chapter). This technique focuses on replicating contouring blends to create reflectivity and surface variation.

1

A blended area selected and a copy moved off the image area 5" (using Shift-Option/Shift-Alt and cursor-keys set to .5" increments); and type converted to outlines

1 Replicating an area of your image for placing new details. This process can be used to create color or surface variations, but we'll use the application of type detailing as a demonstration. After you've outlined your image and filled it with contouring blends, choose an area for detailing. With the Shift key down, use Selection and Group-selection tools to select all blends and originating objects for the blends that exist in that area. To move a copy of these blends out of the way, set the Cursor-key distance to .5" in Edit: Preferences: General. Now hold Shift-Option/Shift-Alt and press the → key to pull a copy of the selected blends 5" to the right (10 times the cursor-key distance). To move this copy further, use Shift → to move the selected blends in 5" increments, or use → alone to nudge in .5" increments. With the Type tool, place a letter or number on top of the moved blend (see the *Type* chapter for help). Click a Selection tool to select the type as an *object* and choose Type: Create Outlines.

2

Skewing outlined type, then adjusting and coloring it to fit the blend contour

Creating reflections for an "outline" by copying the outlined type object, then stroking and choosing Object: Path: Outline Stroke and then Unite in the Pathfinder palette

2 Reshaping type to fit your blended contours and creating an offset. Working from templates, references or just your artistic eye, use the Rotate, Scale and Shear tools with Direct-selection to adjust various anchor points until the type fits the contour. For the type on the race car, T•B I&D skewed the letters (by clicking first in the center of a baseline, grabbing above right, and Shift-dragging to the right). Then they Direct-selected individual points and groups of points, moving them into the visually correct positions.

To create the outlining effect, first copy a solid-filled version, then set the stroke in the desired weight and color. While this object is still selected, choose Object: Path: Outline Stroke, then Unite in the Pathfinder palette.

3 Pasting the original back on top, designing new colors for copies of the older blends and masking the new versions. First, Paste In Front the original, unstroked type element. Next, select and Lock blends or objects that won't fall within the detail (Object: Lock), but that you want to keep for reference. Copy and Paste In Front each of the source (key) objects for new blends and recolor them for your detailing. To recolor a blend, Direct-select each key object you want to recolor and choose a new color—the blend will automatically update! As necessary, recolor each pair of key objects using the same procedure (bear in mind, blending between *Spot* colors results in *Process* in-between colors). T•B I&D recolored the car blends for the red **3**, then added a tear-shaped blend for more detail. Select and copy (in Outline mode if necessary) the original **3**, use Paste In Front, press the Shift key and click to add the new grouped blends to the selection, then choose Object: Clipping Mask: Make. Group and Hide these finished masked objects and repeat the recoloring of copied blends, masked by a top object for any additional highlights and shadows. Choose Object: Show All when these masks are complete, group all the masks together and use the cursor-keys to snap this group of reflective details into position. T•B I&D created one more version of the **3** for a dark offset. For areas requiring more reflections, they constructed even more masks upon masks, as well as occasionally applying compound-masks (see "Colorful Masking" earlier in this chapter).

3

Re-creating blends in new colors and preparing to mask them with a copy of the "3" on top

With the red, reflective blends masked, creating a darker, offset "3"

The dark "3" and the entire group of objects complete, before and after being moved back into position with cursor-keys

Other elements require more stages of blending (see "Colorful Masking" in this chapter for compounding multiple objects, like type elements, to apply as a single mask)

FERSTER

FERSTER

Gary Ferster

In creating a product illustration, Gary Ferster strives to combine realism with a dramatically appealing view of the product. For the Jeep and the sneaker, Ferster began by scanning photographs of the products and placing these grayscale TIFFs on template layers (see "Digitizing a Logo" in the *Layers* chapter). On layers above the templates, he drew the objects' outlines with the Pen tool and then drew blending objects, created blends, and masked them with copies of the outlines. For each sneaker lace, Ferster created several dark-colored blends overlaying a light background. Then he masked each of the blends and background with the lace outlines.

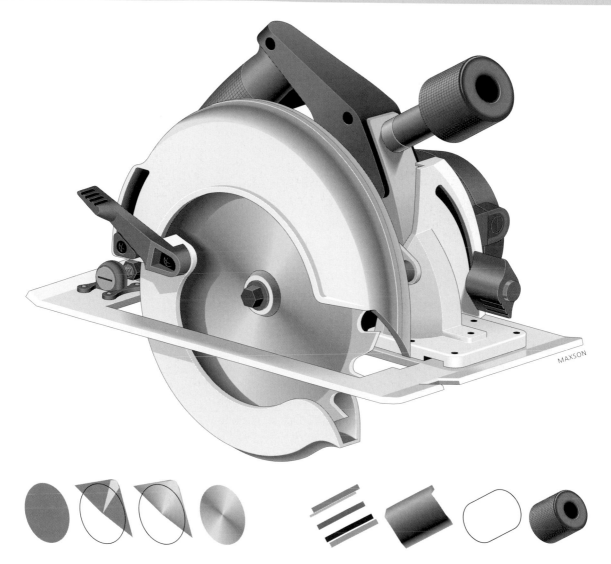

MAXSON

Greg Maxson / Precision Graphics

Illustrating the metal surfaces of this circular saw required Greg Maxson to create overlapping blends. For the blade, Maxson began with an ellipse filled with a dark gray. Next, he created two blending objects, one filled with the same dark gray as the ellipse and the other (on top) filled with a light gray. Maxson blended these to create the highlight and shadow. He used the Reflect tool to create a copy of the blend for the bottom half of the blade. He copied the dark gray ellipse and used the ellipse to mask both blends. For the round grip, Maxson created five blend objects, and blended between them to form the grip's surface. He masked these blends with an object built by connecting ellipse shapes (the cylinder and the circular face at the end of the cylinder) to form the grip.

Glowing Starshine

Blending Custom Colors to Form a Glow

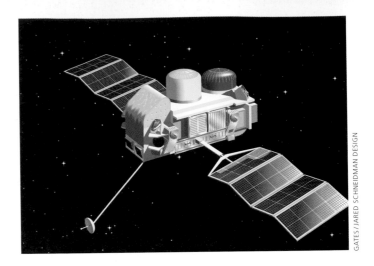

Advanced Technique

Overview: *Create a custom color for the background and the basic object; scale a copy of the object; make object adjustments and blend a glow.*

The background spot color; dragging a guide to the center of a circle, drawing a center line and rotating a copy of the line

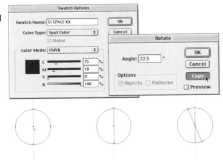

After pressing ⌘/Ctrl-D six times, making guides and adding anchor points at guide intersections

After Shift-Option/Shift-Alt scaling the circle smaller and changing the center to 0% tint; Direct-selecting and moving top, bottom and side points outward

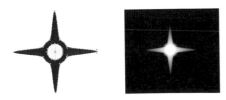

Before and after a 12-step blend

Illumination is the key to creating a realistic nighttime sky. This variation on a technique by Guilbert Gates and Jared Schneidman Design (JSD) will help you create glowing lights, not just stars, simply and directly.

1 **Creating a custom color and the basic object.** Create a background rectangle filled with a dark, spot color. JSD's background was 25% C, 18% M and 100% K. In Outline mode, make a circle, then drag a guide from the ruler until it "snaps" to the circle's center (the arrow turns hollow). With the Pen tool, click on an edge of the circle where the guide intersects, hold Shift and click on the other edge. Select this line, double-click the Rotate tool, specify 22.5° and click Copy. Press ⌘/Ctrl-D to repeat the rotate/copy six times, then select only the lines and choose ⌘/Ctrl-5 to make the lines into guides. Use the Add-anchor-point tool to add eight points, one on each side of the circle's original points at guide intersections.

2 **Creating the glow.** With the circle selected, use the Scale tool to make a smaller copy of the circle (hold the Shift and Option/Alt keys) and specify a 0% tint fill in the Color palette. Direct-select the top point and Shift-drag it outward. Repeat with the bottom and two side points. With the Blend tool, click on corresponding selected points from each circle and specify 12 steps.

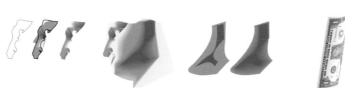

Kenneth Batelman

Kenneth Batelman used masks to constrain the blends that composed the shapes of his Liberty illustration. First, Batelman constructed blends for Liberty's arm, eyebrows, and jaw. Once the blends were completed, Batelman drew paths for the outlines of the arm, eyebrows, and jaw. He selected these paths and turned each into a clipping mask by choosing Object: Clipping Mask: Make (see the *Layers* chapter to learn how to arrange artwork or layers for masking). For the curved surface of the dollar, he drew the bill in Illustrator and mapped it onto a curved surface in Adobe Dimensions (see the *Illustrator & Other Programs* chapter for more on Dimensions). Batelman then imported the curved dollar bill back into Illustrator and placed it into Liberty's hand by layering it under the thumb and over the fingers.

Chapter 10 *Advanced Techniques*   315

WEIMER

Alan James Weimer

Alan James Weimer achieved the detailed symmetry in the above design using Illustrator's Rotate and Polar Grid tools. After selecting the Polar Grid tool, he clicked where he wanted to position the grid. Within the dialog box, Weimer entered the width and height of the circle, as well as the number of concentric and radial dividers. (The Polar Grid tool can also be clicked and dragged to create the grid. Use the arrow keys on the keyboard to adjust the concentric circles and dividers.) The grid was then made into a guide (View: Guides: Make Guides). Alan created the individual elements

of the design, such as the the pink flower petal, by drawing half of the petal with the Pen tool and creating a copy for the other side using the Reflect tool. Next, Weimer positioned the petal on one of the guides, selected the Rotate tool, and Option-clicked (Alt-click for Win) the cursor once on the centerpoint of the circle. In the dialog box, he entered "360/8" (in order to have Illustrator calculate 360°÷8, the total number of petals he wanted), and clicked Copy. He then pressed ⌘-D (Ctrl-D for Win) to continue copying and rotating six more petals around the circle.

WEIMER

Alan James Weimer

To make the two medallions for a horizontal "tile" (right), Alan Weimer used the circle-and-guides technique described on the opposite page. After arranging the medallions and other elements to form the tile, he Option-dragged/Alt-dragged the tile to the right to form the first row. To create the repeating pattern, Weimer diagonally Option-dragged/Alt-dragged copies of the first tile row onto a grid of guidelines to form rows above and below the first row. To "crop" the design, he drew a rectangle on the same layer as the tiled design,

and, at the bottom of the Layers palette, clicked the Make/ Release Clipping Mask icon. On a layer above the mask he added a border composed of blended, stroked rectangles.

Masking Opacity

Making Transparency Irregular

Advanced Technique

Overview: *Draw an object outline and convert it to gradient mesh; duplicate the mesh and convert it to grayscale; make a copy of the grayscale object; rasterize, "reverse" and blur it; then add it to the grayscale mesh and create an opacity mask.*

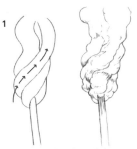

Original sketches of the movement of the flame

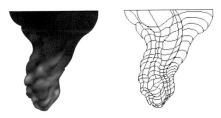

Flame mesh in Preview and Outline modes

Rasterization resolution

If you're using live Effects and the screen redraw is too slow, set the Resolution in Effect: Rasterize: Raster Effects Settings to Screen (72ppi). But don't forget to reset this to the correct output (typically twice the line screen), and adjust each Effect setting, before saving for print!—*Ivan Torres*

TORRES

Ivan Torres found that Illustrator's gradient mesh and opacity mask provided the perfect solutions for creating the light-and-dark, opaque-and-translucent character of a match flame, while allowing him to do all of his work within Illustrator rather than moving artwork between Illustrator and a bitmap program like Adobe Photoshop.

1 Drawing the gradient mesh. Torres began his flame by placing a scan of a sketch into Illustrator to use as a tracing template. He drew a filled outline of the flame and converted it to a gradient mesh (Object: Create Gradient Mesh). See the *Blends, Gradients & Mesh* chapter to find out more about creating and editing gradient meshes. Torres edited the mesh to color the flame.

2 Making an opacity mask and modifying its opacity.
As Torres observed, a flame can contain transparent and opaque parts. To achieve irregular transparency, you can build and apply a customized opacity mask. First, select the gradient mesh object you made, Copy, and then Paste In Front. Next, convert the color mesh to grayscale by selecting Filter: Colors: Convert To Grayscale. Now use the Direct-selection tool to click on intersection points in the grayscale mesh and change their gray values in the Color palette. (The darker the point's gray value, the more transparent the object will be when the mesh is made into an opacity mask and applied to the object.)

3 Adding a blurred outline, then completing the opacity mask. Torres added a blurred outline to the grayscale mesh, so that when applied later as an opacity mask it would soften the edge of the flame. To create a blurred edge, begin by duplicating the grayscale mesh (Copy, then Paste In Front). In the Object menu, select Rasterize, and in the Rasterize dialog, click to enable Create Clipping Mask. Next, release the mask you just made (Object: Clipping Mask: Release) and Ungroup; select the square (which is the rasterized grayscale copy) and delete it. This leaves the mask object, an exact duplicate of the flame outline. Give this mask object a black stroke.

Next, create a "reverse" version of the mask using drawing tools or the Pathfinder functions (see the *Drawing & Coloring* chapter for more on creating and modifying paths). Fill this reverse object with black, and blur the object by selecting Effect: Blur: Gaussian Blur and assigning a blur radius that is wide enough to create the look you want.

To finish constructing the opacity mask, select the blurred object and the grayscale gradient mesh you created earlier and group them (Object: Group).

4 Applying the mask. Select the mask artwork and the original color gradient mesh and choose Make Opacity Mask from the Transparency palette's pop-up menu.

2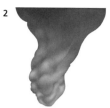

At the left, color mesh converted to grayscale; at the right, the edited version of the grayscale mesh made by changing the gray values of individual mesh intersection points

3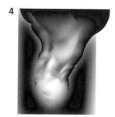

In Outline View, the rasterized grayscale gradient mesh (with the mask outline and the raster rectangle) on the left; on the right, the "reverse" object Torres created by cutting the top line with the Scissors tool, deleting the top segment, and then joining the remaining segments

The filled "reverse" object of the rasterized mask on the left, and the same object on the right after blurring

4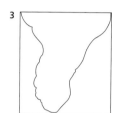

On the left, the composite artwork of the opacity mask (the grayscale gradient mesh and the blurred "reverse" object); on the right, the opacity mask applied to the flame

Wrapping Textures

Creating Meshes for a True 3D Look

Advanced Technique

Overview: *Extract an outline from a enveloped mesh; create a specially shaped mesh for use with enveloping to distort pattern; overlay the pattern onto a bottle.*

1

A close up of the Pen tool pattern as applied to the center bottle on the label. The pattern is applied in two parts—diagonally on the top half of the bottle, and vertically on the bottom half

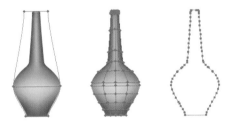

The original bottle in its envelope (left), the resulting mesh after expanding it (center), and the final outline derived from the mesh (right)

Dividing the outline into two sections corresponding to the upper and lower pattern areas

Ivan Torres used meshes for the bottles, background curtains, and smoke in his self promotion piece above. Torres created a specially shaped mesh, which he used together with enveloping, to distort the label and tool patterns. He then laid the mesh on top of the bottle shapes.

1 Create an outline of the bottle. To create an outline of the bottle using enveloping, choose Object: Envelope Distort: Expand, followed by Object: Path: Offset Path, 0", and Ungroup to access the path.

The Pen tool pattern on the bottle consists of two parts (see detail at left). To create outlines for those two pattern sections, divide the outline by drawing a line across the bottle where you want to cut it, and use Object: Path: Divide Objects Below. Since the patterns do not go all the way to the top or bottom of the bottle, use the same technique to clip off a little from the top and bottom of each of those outlines (as shown at left).

2 Create a mesh for the Pen tool pattern. To make the Pen tool pattern appear to conform to the curved surface of the bottle, Torres created a specially designed mesh that mimicked the foreshortening that occurs at the points where the sides of the pattern disappear around the edges of the bottle. On this special mesh, the columns are spaced closer together near the edges of the bottle and farther apart in the middle.

To create the mesh, use Object: Create Gradient Mesh with 6 columns and 4 rows. Use the Direct-select tool to select and respace the columns to match the 3D mesh pictured in the sidebar. Watch Torres's Flash Animation on the *Wow! CD* to learn how to accurately create the correct spacing using simple Illustrator commands.

3 Make the mesh conform to the outline. Place your mesh over the outline. Direct-select each row of your mesh, one at a time, and use the Scale tool to shrink the row until the outer points of the mesh conform to the outline. Then adjust each anchor point's handles so the lines of the mesh follow the contours of the outline.

4 Use the mesh to distort the pattern. With the mesh placed over the pen pattern, and both objects selected, choose Object: Envelope Distort: Make with Top, and click OK. If your pattern is made from a pattern filled shape (not multiple copies of art, like the Pen tool pattern used in this lesson), be sure to enable the Distort Pattern Fill option in the Object: Envelope Distort: Envelope Options dialog before applying the envelope.

5 Color and apply the pattern onto the bottle. Use Object: Envelope: Edit Contents to access the pattern inside its envelope. Use the Eyedropper to pick up a shade of green from the bottle and apply it to the mesh. Place the mesh over the bottle, and then using the Transparency palette, set the Blending Mode to Multiply and lower the opacity until the desired look is achieved.

For the neck of the bottle, use the same techniques; simply rotate the pattern before applying the mesh in Step 4. Similarly, the label was applied as shown at right.

A failed envelope distort using the outline; the Envelope tool doesn't know that the outline is of a 3D object. Compare result with step 4 below

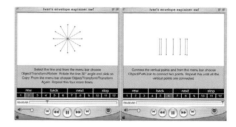
Two screen shots from Ivan Torres's Flash Animation on the Wow! CD showing how the spacing is determined for the mesh

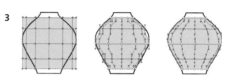
Conforming the mesh to bottle outline; after moving the points the diection handles are incorrect; the final properly shaped mesh

Using the mesh as the top object of an envelope distort to shape the pen pattern

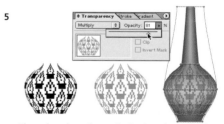
The colored mesh, applied using the Multiply Blending Mode with Opacity set to 81%

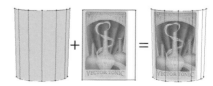
Distorting the label for the bottle. The label is offset in a rectangle, which offsets it in the final envelope for overlaying on the bottle

Modeling Mesh

Shaping and Forming Mesh Objects

Advanced Technique

Overview: *Create an outline for smoke; create a simple rectangular mesh; bend the mesh using the Rotate and Direct-selection tools; align the mesh to your outline; add columns to lend a 3D effect; color your mesh; use the Screen Blend mode to make the smoke transparent.*

1

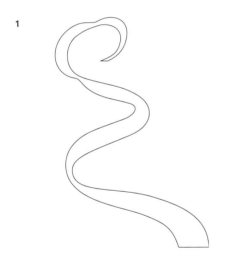

Create an outline of the desired final smoke form

Smoke outline locked on a layer, with the starting mesh above

Ivan Torres molded a mesh as though it were a piece of clay to form the smoke in his art piece "Meshsmith." One of the highlights of this lesson is Torres's use of the Rotate tool to bend *portions* of a mesh (as opposed to using it to rotate *whole* objects).

1 Setting up your artwork. Start by using the Pen or Pencil tool to create an outline of a smoke form. Lock the smoke outline in a layer, then place a rectangle at the base of the smoke. Convert the rectangle to a mesh, using the Object: Create Gradient Mesh command, with 1 column and 3 rows. Keep your starting mesh simple, it is easier to add rows as needed later.

2 Making the rough bends. Make your first big bend using the Rotate tool. Start by Direct-selecting all but the bottom two points of the mesh. Next with the Rotate tool click on the inside of the first curve of the smoke outline to place the center for rotation, and then grab the top of your mesh rectangle and drag it around the center of rotation to form the first curve (see images at right).

At each bend or pinch in the smoke, you will need a row in order to make the next bend. If an existing row of your mesh is nearby, Direct-select it and move it over the bend or pinch. To add a row, click with the Mesh tool on the edge of the mesh outline, at the bend or pinch. Once you have placed or added a mesh row at a bend or pinch, leave those points out of the next selection as you work your way up the smoke. Repeat this step until you reach the top of your smoke outline.

3 Aligning and straightening the mesh rows. Once you have the mesh roughly aligned, zoom in at each pinch and bend where you placed a mesh row and make it straight and perpendicular to the curve. Straightening out the mesh rows is essential for your final smoke to look correct and work smoothly.

4 Aligning the mesh curves with the smoke. With the Direct-selection tool, start at the bottom and click a section of the mesh curve. Adjust the direction handles so they align with the smoke outline. You may have to go back and forth between the next and previous sections of the curves in order to properly adjust the sides of the mesh to fit the smoke outline.

5 Adding columns to lend a 3D effect. The final 3D form of the mesh will be defined by where the highlight and shadow colors are placed on the mesh. If you were to draw evenly spaced columns around the actual smoke and photograph it, the columns in the photograph would appear to be closer together near the edges of the smoke outline and farther apart in the middle of column. To

2

Selecting top portion of mesh. After clicking on inside of the first curve to set the rotation point (blue crosshair in lower right), clicking the top of the rectangle, and dragging to left and down

Working up the smoke, rotating the mesh at each major bend; placing mesh rows at pinches and using the Direct-select tool to adjust

3

Aligning the rows with the pinches in the outline, making them straight and perpendicular to the sides of the curve

4

Starting from the bottom, using the Bézier handles to align the curves of the mesh to the outline of the smoke

5

Adding columns to the smoke mesh using the Gradient tool and spacing them closer at the edges to create a rounded 3D look

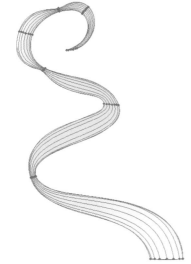

The completed smoke mesh

Creating a highlight at a mesh point

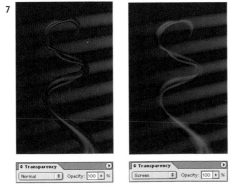

The smoke before and after setting the Blend Mode to Screen on the Transparency palette

create this 3D effect, use the Mesh tool to add a first column by clicking on the center of the bottom edge of the smoke. Next, add two more columns close to each outside edge of the smoke. Then, place two columns between the center and the next closest columns on each side—not exactly in between, but closer to the outside edge.

Because of your careful work in steps 3 and 4 above, your new columns will be parallel to—and flow smoothly through—the pinches and bends of your smoke outline.

6 Coloring the mesh. Torres chose a dark blue color for his smoke (if you want to use a different color you will have to adjust the color choices in the steps below). To see where the mesh points are as you work, turn on Smart Guides from the View menu, or ⌘-U/Ctrl-U. In order to make the selection line color interfere less with the mesh color as you work, use a dark shade of blue for the selection line color (choose Dark Blue from the Layer Options Color menu). Also, learn to use the single-key navigation shortcuts to quickly switch between the Mesh (U), Paint bucket (K), and Direct-selection (A) tools.

Start by adding a middle blue value to the whole mesh. Next, from the Color palette pop-up menu, choose HSB, and then use the Brightness ("B") slider to create lighter highlight or darker shadow tints of your starting color. At the center of where highlight or shadow areas should be, use the Paint bucket to apply your highlight or shadow color. If there is no mesh point there, use the Mesh tool to add one. Because the point where you click with the Mesh tool remains selected, you can easily adjust the fill color using the HSB sliders. For final tweaking of the highlights and shadows, use the Direct-selection tool or Direct-selection Lasso tool to select areas, and then make adjustments using the HSB sliders.

7 Making the smoke transparent. Select your smoke and on the Transparency palette, experiment with various combinations of the Screen Blend Mode and Opacity settings until you get the desired effect.

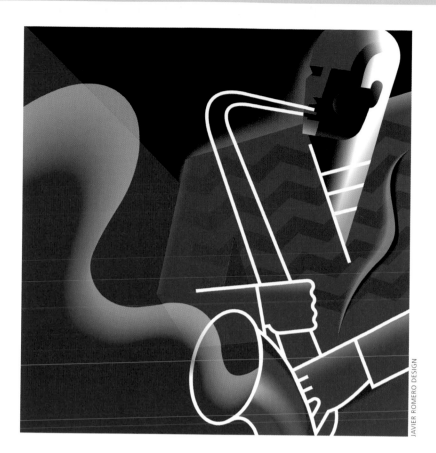

JAVIER ROMERO DESIGN

Javier Romero / Javier Romero Design Group

Throughout this illustration for the *Illustrator 10 Wow! Book* cover, Javier Romero adjusted the Opacity and blending modes of his objects to soften the transitions and overlaps, and to create a glowing look. To create the wavy lines in the shirt he filled several wavy shapes with a black to white linear gradient. He then used the Gradient tool to adjust the angle of the gradient uniformly across all the shapes (see the "Unified Gradients" lesson in the *Blends, Gradients & Mesh* chapter for help with this). Romero then applied a 30% Opacity and a Multiply Blending mode to the wavy shapes. To confine the waves to the shirt, Romero masked the waves by transforming a copy of the shirt path into a clipping mask (see earlier in this chapter for help with clipping masks). To make these lines slightly lighter on the sax player's left shoulder, he made a duplicate of the wavy lines, adjusted the Opacity to 25% and masked that set with a narrow shape defining the left shoulder. To create the swirl of sound coming from the horn, Romero created a blend from a light yellow object set to 50% Opacity, to a dark red object set at 100% (directly above, right). Another of the blends forms the orange glow on the shoulder; the top orange object is set to Lighten 66%, and the dark object below is set to Multiply at 18% (shown in Normal mode at 100% Opacity, top right).

Web & Animation

11

Web & Animation

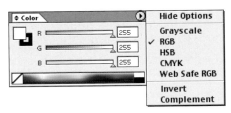

Choosing color models from the Color palette's pop-up menu. You can also cycle through color models by Shift-clicking on the Color Spectrum. Selecting a different color model to mix colors does not change the color mode of the file

This chapter focuses on how you can use Illustrator to prepare artwork for on-screen display. Nearly every aspect of the application has been enhanced to produce better web graphics. Although everything in this chapter relies heavily on Illustrator, some of the techniques also involve working with other applications (see the *Illustrator & Other Programs* chapter).

The actual assembly of animations and web graphics in this chapter was produced using a number of other programs, including Macromedia's Director; Adobe's Premiere, After Effects, and GoLive; Yves Piguet's GIF Builder; Thorsten Lemke's GraphicConverter; and Bare Bones Software's BBEdit. Also, check the *Wow!* web site for animations and links to related sites (www.peachpit.com/books/wow.html).

Web designers will find that Illustrator 10 supports a wealth of file formats, and that the work flow for creating web graphics has been simplified. Save for Web in the File menu makes it easy to optimize graphics for the web, by letting you visually compare examples of different quality settings and file compression options side by side, in a multi-view dialog. And Pixel Preview allows you to view precise antialiasing right in Illustrator.

WORKING IN RGB IN ILLUSTRATOR

To create artwork in RGB, first start with a new RGB file (File: New and Color Mode: RGB Color in the dialog). Choose a Web-safe RGB palette of colors if you want to create colors that are never dithered when viewed on 8-bit monitors.

A FEW THOUGHTS ON RGB AND CMYK COLOR

- **You should work in the RGB color mode (space) if you're creating graphics for *on-screen* display.** If you're designing for the web, it's particularly important to keep file sizes to a minimum, and the final files must be in RGB (see "The Web Swatches palette" below).

- **Don't convert the same artwork repeatedly between RGB and CMYK.** Converting RGB to CMYK forces one range of colors (a gamut) into a smaller range of colors. This process involves either clipping or compressing certain colors, and can make the colors in your file appear muddy or muted. If you absolutely need both CMYK and RGB versions of your artwork, maintain two versions of your art—one in RGB and one in CMYK. To experiment with clipping or compressing colors between gamuts, see the *Illustrator User Guide* on choosing the appropriate rendering intent in the Color Settings dialog.

- **If you're going to use your artwork for both print and on-screen viewing, create in CMYK and then export the art to RGB.** With the CMYK color space's smaller color gamut, and with the control available to produce predictable color for print, it makes sense to create your artwork in CMYK color mode *before* exporting it to RGB for display on a monitor. RGB has a wider gamut, so it won't clip or compress the colors of your CMYK document.

The Web Swatches palette

Illustrator includes a noneditable Web-safe swatches palette. Its 216 RGB colors are common to both Mac and Windows platforms, and are the most reliable colors for creating web artwork when you don't know the color depth or platform your audience will be using. To access this palette, choose Window: Swatch Libraries: Web, or open the file directly (Window: Swatch Libraries: Other). To create a smaller custom palette from the Web-safe palette, simply drag the desired color swatches to the Swatches palette for storage and save the file. (Remember to clear the Swatches palette before you build your custom palette—see "Setting up your palettes" in the *How To Use This Book* section.)

If you already have artwork prepared in CMYK and you need to change the color mode for on-screen RGB viewing, make sure you first save a copy of your file, then choose File: Document Color Mode: RGB Colors. Remember, try not to convert your artwork back and forth between color spaces, because your colors can become muddy or muted (see text at left for more details).

The process of turning vector art into a pixel-based image is called *rasterizing*. Anyone creating artwork for the web or for multimedia applications might, at some point, need to rasterize vector art, with the exception of SWF and SVG (see "SVG" later in the chapter). The Rasterize dialog (Object: Rasterize) makes it easy to control the rasterization of artwork. You can also rasterize artwork if you apply any of the Photoshop filters or effects.

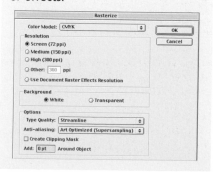

ASSIGNING URL'S AND SLICING

Illustrator's Attributes palette lets you create an image map area and assign a URL (Uniform Resource Locator) to any object, group, or layer in your artwork. Creating image maps is an essential tool for web designers because it allows them to create links to other web pages by defining clickable parts of the artwork. Illustrator creates a separate HTML (HyperText Markup Language) file containing the URL information, which can be imported into an HTML editor such as Adobe GoLive, Macromedia Dreamweaver, or BareBones Software's BBEdit.

To assign a URL to a selection, open the Attributes palette (Window: Attributes), select the type of image map from the Image Map pop-up, and type the URL into the URL text field (see the Gulf Shores web page Gallery later in this chapter for more information on making image maps). If you need to verify whether your URL is correct, simply click the Browser button in the Attributes palette. This will launch your default web browser and automatically open the link. You can export the file by using Save for Web and choosing Save as Type: HTML and Images (*.html).

Illustrator also provides another way for you to assign URLs or links to objects—by using web slices. Web slicing is a way to divide a large image into several smaller pieces that are displayed in HTML as a table. This allows you to optimize individual parts of your artwork in different formats (e.g., GIF, JPEG, SVG), and helps the files download faster to a web browser. To assign a URL to a web slice, apply a slice to an object by selecting the object and choosing Object: Slice: Make, and then with the object still selected, choose Object: Slice: Slice Options. In the URL field, enter the correct link information. You can also get to the Slice Options dialog box by double-clicking on a slice with the Slice Select tool in the Save for Web dialog box.

When you apply a slice to an object, group, or layer using the Object menu, you've actually assigned a slice as an "attribute." This means that if you update your artwork, your slice will update automatically. So, once you make a slice, you never have to recreate it.

If you want to create a slice whose position remains unchanged when you update the artwork from which the slice was originally generated, choose Object: Slice: Create from Selection, or draw the slice using Illustrator's Slice tool. (In ImageReady, this kind of slice is called a *user slice*.) Slices applied as attributes are exported as *layer-based slices* when you choose File: Export: Photoshop (*.PSD) and you select the Write Slices option. If you edit the exported layers in Photoshop or ImageReady, the corresponding slices will reshape themselves just as they would have done in Illustrator. This PSD export option only works on slices attached to elements that are not contained inside any groups or sublayers. All other slices are exported as user slices.

RELEASE TO LAYERS

Illustrator gives you the ability to take multiple objects or blended objects and distribute each onto its own layer. For example, having the objects on separate layers makes it easier to develop animations. *Highlight* a layer, group, or live blend in the Layers palette by clicking on it—if you merely select or target the artwork, this will not work. Next, choose Release to Layers (Sequence) from the palette pop-up menu. Each new layer is created within the current layer or group and consists of a single object. To perform an additive effect, choose Release to Layers (Build). Instead of containing a single object, each new layer is generated with one more object. You end up with the same number of layers, but what appears on those layers is very different.

When releasing objects to separate layers, keep in mind that their stacking order in the Layers palette can affect the final animation. With brush art, it's sometimes hard to predict the order in which the individual objects will be released to the layers: the stacking order is dependent on the direction of the path. You can reverse the direction of a path by clicking on an end anchor

- **Color Table:** 8-bit images have a maximum of 256 colors. The Perceptual table is more sensitive to colors that can be differentiated with the human eye. Selective gives more emphasis to the integrity of the colors and is the default setting.

- **Colors:** You can have up to 256 colors in a color table. However, the image might not need that many. Select a smaller number of colors when you optimize by adjusting the number of colors in the color table. The fewer colors, the smaller the file.

- **Dither:** Blends colors in a limited color palette. Diffusion dither is usually best. Vary the amount of dither to reduce banding of solid-color areas by adjusting the Dither slider. Leave it off for clean-edged vector graphics.

- **Transparency:** Choose this for non-rectangular artwork that you want to put over multicolored backgrounds. To reduce edge artifacts, choose a color to blend with the transparent edges from the Matte pop-up.

- **Interlacing:** Allows viewers to see a low resolution version of the image as it downloads, which continues to build until the image is at full resolution. A non-interlaced image draws one line at a time.

point with the Pen tool. You can reverse blends by choosing Object: Blend: Reverse Front to Back.

EXPORT FILE FORMATS
Save for Web

An important feature for web designers is the ability to export optimized files from the Save for Web dialog. GIF is the most widely used image format on the web. GIF compression works well with vector-based images or files that have large areas of solid color (see the Tip "GIF or JPEG?" in this chapter). GIF files support transparency and interlacing (whereas JPEG only supports interlacing).

JPEG provides a variable level of compression and works best for images with gradients or photos that have continuous tones. Although JPEG is a "lossy" format (because when you optimize the file size you lose image detail), this trade-off still tends to result in good-quality images, making JPEG a particularly useful format for web designers. It can also be a useful alternative to a PDF file. For example, a JPEG file can be used to transfer a layout for client approval. JPEGs are much smaller than PDFs while sacrificing very little image detail, and smaller files transfer more easily (and sometimes more reliably) via the Internet. Other JPEG options include progressive and optimized. A progressive JPEG is similar to an interlaced GIF—it first appears blurry, then builds up with increasing clarity until the image is fully displayed.

Note: *If Progressive is checked, checking Optimized will not make the file any smaller.*

To save a version of your artwork for use on the web, choose File: Save for Web and adjust the various optimization settings (see the Tip "Save for Web" in this chapter for more). If you've defined slices in your file, use the Slice Select tool to click on and select the slice you want to optimize, then select a file type from the Optimized file format pop-up. If you want to compare the compression of two or more settings, click on one of the other views, either 2-Up or 4-Up. The final file format, size, download time, and specifics about the compression are listed under each preview panel. Finally, if you want to export your artwork now, click the Save button to specify how you want your files saved. If you have slices, you can choose to export the images and the HTML as well. If you opened Save for Web only to define the optimization settings for your slices, you can press the Done button and Illustrator will take you back to your file, while remembering all the settings you just applied. Refer to the *User Guide* for a more complete description of all the format options.

Note: *PNG, SWF, and SVG are available file formats in the Save for Web dialog, but these formats may require browser plug-ins in order to be viewed on the web.*

Macromedia Flash (SWF) export

Although many multimedia artists and designers use Illustrator with Macromedia Flash to create web pages and animations, there is no completely foolproof method for bringing artwork from one program to the other. Illustrator now comes with a Flash export module, but as of this writing it has some significant problems, ranging from poor rendering quality to the creation of extra frames and symbols. If you want to create Flash files from Illustrator artwork, your best bet is to import the Illustrator file into Macromedia Flash and create the animation there. If you have very simple artwork, you can also use the Flash Export dialog in Illustrator. Here are some strategies for maximizing the quality and usefulness of your Illustrator files in Flash:

- **Use Illustrator symbols to represent repeating objects.** With Illustrator 10, you can convert artwork (both raster and vector) into *symbols* that you can *place* multiple times, instead of using multiple copies of the original artwork. Each time you place an instance of a symbol, you are creating a *link* to the symbol stored in the palette, rather than duplicating the symbol artwork. This reduces the size of your Illustrator file and of any SWF files you export from Illustrator.

SVG and alpha channels

Illustrator 10 ships standard with (and installs by default) the SVG 3.0 browser plug-in. If you're creating SVG graphics, make sure that whoever is viewing them also downloads the free SVG 3.0 viewer that's available from the www.adobe.com/svg web page.

Transparency and web colors

Even if you've been working in RGB mode with Web-safe colors, if you've used Illustrator's transparency in your file, you will end up with out-of-gamut shades when the artwork is rasterized or flattened. Files with extensive transparency use should be saved as JPEG, not as GIF, to avoid excessive dithering.

Web-safe RGB

The Web Safe RGB Color palette will not display the Out of Gamut warning for CMYK colors, but the RGB color palette will.

LiveMotion 2 support

LiveMotion 2 can read native Illustrator 10 files and even understands Illustrator's native transparency. To use Illustrator art in LiveMotion 2, simply save the file as an Illustrator file. Make sure the Create PDF Compatible File option is checked when you save.

- **Use Save As to convert the Illustrator file into the version 7 format.** This converts most artwork that Flash doesn't understand, such as brushes, into discrete objects that it does understand. Artwork from later versions, particularly art with gradients, doesn't maintain all of its attributes. Don't forget to save a copy of your document in AI10 format before you quit Illustrator, or you'll be left with only the less editable AI7 version.

- **Use flat colors rather than blends, gradients, or gradient mesh objects.** You'll make smaller SWF files if you use Flash to add gradient colors. If you must use gradients or gradient mesh objects, recognize that you'll be creating bitmapped images that result in larger file sizes.

- **If you import or create rasterized art for the Internet,** rasterize at 72 ppi, not the default of 150 ppi, to keep file sizes small.

- **To export a file's layers or paths selectively,** hide the ones you don't want before exporting.

- **If the object you want to export to Flash contains a dashed stroke,** expand it using the Tip "Outlining Dashed Strokes" in the *Drawing & Coloring* chapter. Or you can use the operating system clipboard to copy the stroke from Illustrator and paste it into Flash. To preserve the dash and gap pattern of the Illustrator object, choose Preferences: File & Clipboard and then select PDF as the Copy As option. Otherwise, the dash and gap pattern will be converted to the default pattern in Macromedia Flash.

- **Choosing Export AI Layers to SWF Files turns each Illustrator layer into a separate Flash file,** which is the preferred method of exporting elements for animation.

SVG

Illustrator supports the export of Scalable Vector Graphics (SVG). SVG is an emerging standard for a web graphic format that contains a combination of elements such as vectors, gradients, type, raster effects, and JavaScript events, all based on the popular XML standard. SVG is also a text-based format, which means it can be easily edited even after the file has been uploaded to a web server. We'll talk more about this later when we discuss data-driven graphics. SVG is potentially a very exciting file format, because it combines very small file sizes with crisp artwork that, like Illustrator vector art, can be zoomed into and scaled up or down with no loss of quality. As with Flash, in order for exported SVG files to be viewed in a browser, a special viewer (plug-in) is required. The SVG plug-in is automatically installed in your browser when you install Illustrator.

The SVG format supports JavaScript interactivity as well as static image display. To add a JavaScript event to your artwork you must know JavaScript! Open the SVG Interactivity palette (Window: SVG Interactivity); then, with an object selected, choose an event from the pop-up menu, and type a JavaScript command in the JavaScript text field.

DATA-DRIVEN GRAPHICS

Illustrator has a new palette called the Variables palette. With this palette, you can create artwork in Illustrator that can automatically be updated or replaced using a script you write. For example, you can create a template for a news headline where the actual word *headline* is defined as a text variable. With the use of a script you can retrieve a news headline from a database and automatically update the text of your headline with the current news item. The real time saver here is that your template can be used over and over again for each new headline—all by simply running the same script again.

There are four different kinds of variables you can define in Illustrator: text, linked images, graph data, and visibility. When text is defined as a variable, you can apply any attributes to the text and they will stick with the variable (for example: font, color, style information),

Pixel preview

Choose View: Pixel Preview and zoom in to 200% or more to display a rasterized preview of your vector artwork.

No more SVG export?

Illustrator 10 now lets you save as SVG directly from the Save and Save As dialog. If you check the Preserve Illustrator Editing Capabilities option, a native version of the AI file will be included in the SVG file, allowing for complete editability in Illustrator.

Go, Go Dynamic!

You can take dynamic graphics a step further if you're using Adobe GoLive 6.0, which understands Illustrator's variable content. Simply save your file in SVG format and import it into GoLive as an Illustrator Smart Object. The variables you defined in Illustrator can then be changed in GoLive.

CSS Layers

Illustrator allows you to export CSS (Cascading Style Sheets) layers. Newer browsers take advantage of DHTML, which allows you to overlap artwork layers. Top level layers can be converted to CSS layers on export from the Save for Web dialog, and you can specify what layers to export from the Layers tab there.

and the text string will be replaced (as in the headline example we mentioned above). A linked image variable means that one linked image is replaced by another. If scaling or effects have been applied to a linked image, then any image that replaces it will also have the scaling or effects applied to it. Graph variables allow you to design a graph using Illustrator's graph tools and link the graph to a database; when data changes, the graph is automatically updated. The final variable type is visibility, which allows you to show or hide artwork. You define whether artwork is visible or not simply by showing or hiding the layer or sublayer for that artwork in the Layers palette.

To define a variable, open the Variables palette (Window: Variables). Type some text on the Artboard and click on the Make Text Dynamic button on the Variables palette. (The same button changes to Make Graph Dynamic or Make Linked File Dynamic depending on your selection.) Use the same technique to define other kinds of variables. For visibility variables, use the Make Visibility Dynamic button.

You can also store multiple data sets in Illustrator—which almost makes Illustrator itself into a database. Once you've defined your variables, click on the Capture Data Set button (or choose Capture Data Set from the Variables palette menu). You can then change the data of your variables, capture another data set, and repeat. At that point, you can use the Previous Data Set and Next Data Set icons to step between data sets and see the data update on your screen. This is a great technique for seeing how multiple versions of data will look when you design your template.

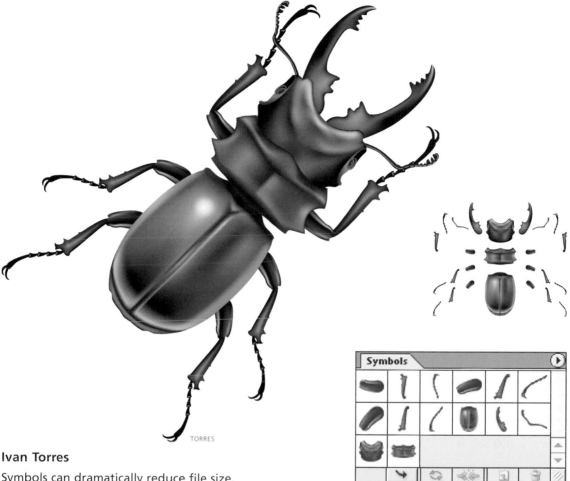

TORRES

Ivan Torres

Symbols can dramatically reduce file size, especially in art destined for the web. Artist Ivan Torres began this beetle by first creating individual body parts, many of which were complex gradient meshes. (To learn more about creating and editing gradient meshes, see the *Blends, Gradients & Mesh* chapter.) Then he converted the parts into symbols by dragging and dropping each onto the Symbols palette. To assemble the beetle from body part symbols, Torres dragged the parts from the Symbols palette and dropped them on the Artboard, creating instances of the symbols. To create the body parts with mirrored twins on opposite sides of the beetle body, he used the Reflect tool, chose Vertical and clicked Copy. When he had completed the illustration, Torres chose File: Export and selected Macromedia SWF format. In the pop-up dialog, he picked Export As: AI File to SWF File. After opening Macromedia Flash (SWF), Torres imported the Illustrator Flash file (File: Import) and then used Flash's tools to manipulate the body part symbols to create an interactive animation.

Off in a Flash
Making Artwork for a Flash Animation

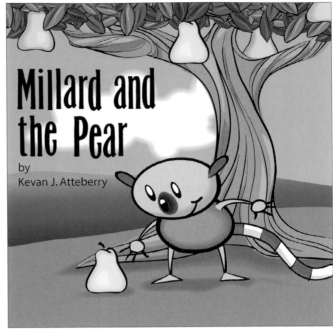

Overview: *Sketch character artwork; create brushes and blend objects for moving parts in the animation; export the artwork as a static Macromedia SWF file and a SWF animation; preview animations in Illustrator.*

Character parts sketched with a custom calligraphic brush (see the Brushes chapter for help with brushes)

	Symbols ▸
	left ear
	right ear
	eye
	head
	body
	nose

Symbols palette displayed in Large List View

Seattle artist and animator Kevan Atteberry knows how to get the most from Illustrator when preparing artwork for animation in Macromedia Flash. Besides making his Illustrator file a sketchpad filled with the eyes, ears, arms, and legs of the character he will animate later in Flash, Atteberry uses the Layers palette to preview parts of the animation. He also exports a Flash animation from Illustrator to view as a draft version as he works on the final animation in Flash.

1 Sketching characters, drawing body parts. Atteberry began with a custom calligraphic brush, sketching a series of facial expressions and figure poses, honing the visual character of a lemur until he was satisfied with the characterization and ready to construct the lemur's body parts. Once you're done drawing your character's parts, you can keep your artwork as Illustrator objects or turn the artwork into symbol instances. It takes fewer steps to convert your artwork to symbol instances in Illustrator than to bring your artwork into Flash and make symbols there. Also, if you plan to export a Flash movie from Illustrator, turning your character parts into symbol instances results in a smaller and faster-loading Flash file.

To make symbol instances, select the artwork for each part body you drew and Shift-drag it into the Symbols palette. After you release the mouse button, Illustrator adds the artwork as a symbol in the Symbols palette and replaces the selected artwork with an instance of the symbol that was just made. (See the *Brushes, Symbols & Hatches* chapter for more on symbols and instances).

2 Making brushes, creating blends for objects, expanding blends, and creating symbols. For any part you animate, you will need to create a sequence of parts—for example, a leg that moves from straight to bent. Atteberry created art brushes for the lemur's moving parts, so he could paint each part in the motion sequence with the brush. (This saved the effort of creating separate art for each part in the sequence.) First, draw a straight version of the part. When you have the look you want, drag and drop it on the open Brushes palette. In the New Brush dialog, choose New Art Brush.

Next, you'll create artwork for the two extremes in the motion sequence. Draw the straight part, and a few inches away draw the bent part. Select both paths and apply the art brush for the part that you created previously. Now, to make other parts in the movement sequence, make sure both paths are selected and choose Object: Blend: Make; then choose Object: Blend: Blend Options and key in the number of steps in the Spacing: Specified Steps field. Consider using a small number of blend steps—Atteberry uses three or four—so that if used as frames in a Flash animation, your SWF file will have a smaller number of frames and a smaller file size. Finally, expand the blend (Object: Blend: Expand) and ungroup it so you have separate objects to use in constructing poses for the motion sequence.

3 Exporting an SWF animation. Once your artwork is complete, you can export the file as a draft or final animation that you can view in a browser or in the Flash

2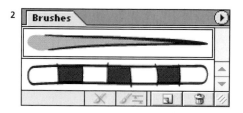

Two of the brushes Atteberry created for the moving parts

The straight and bent lemur legs representing the extremes of a motion sequence that Atteberry used to create a Blend

A blend using three steps created between the straight and bent lemur legs

AI instances to Flash symbols

If you make symbols in Illustrator and want to import them into Flash, be sure to make instances of your symbols first. When you export an SWF file from Illustrator, the Symbols palette is not exported with the SWF file. Flash will recognize Illustrator's instances in the SWF file, however, and add them as symbols to its own Library.

Exporting an SWF file

Illustrator's three Export As options for exporting an SWF file produce files you can import into the Macromedia Flash application.

Previewing a motion sequence using Illustrator's Layers palette as a crude film projector

player. To prepare your file for animation, first add as many layers as frames needed to show the motion sequence. Treating each layer as an animation frame, assemble the artwork for a particular pose or step in the motion sequence on each layer. Move from layer to layer, creating renditions of the character on each layer until the character has performed all of the poses or movements you want to preview. When you have completed all the layers, select File: Export. From the Format pop-up, select Macromedia Flash (SWF) and in the Format Options dialog, choose Export As: AI Layers to SWF Frames. If your animation will use a lot of frames, or will include complex motion sequences that require many intermediate poses or steps, create the final animation in Flash instead of in Illustrator. Flash's tweening commands automatically create many of the intermediate poses you would otherwise assemble manually in Illustrator.

There is another animation technique you can use to preview motion—from within Illustrator itself. Atteberry constructed a draft version of part of the animation to preview the look of objects and of the motion sequence. To do this, you can construct a preview by first following the steps described above for positioning poses on successive layers. After you've filled all your layers with artwork, select Palette Options from the Layers palette menu. Click on the Show Layers Only checkbox to enable this option and key in 100 pixels in the Other field. To preview the animation, position the cursor over a Layers palette scrolling arrow and press the mouse button to cause the layer thumbnails to scroll like frames in a projector.

4 Exporting an SWF file to import into Macromedia Flash. Another use of your artwork is to export it as an SWF file and then import the SWF into Flash to develop the finished animation. To export, choose File: Export and from the Format pop-up, choose Macromedia Flash (SWF). Then, in the Format Options dialog, choose the Export As option that saves the SWF in the format (single frame file, animation file, or multiple files) that you need.

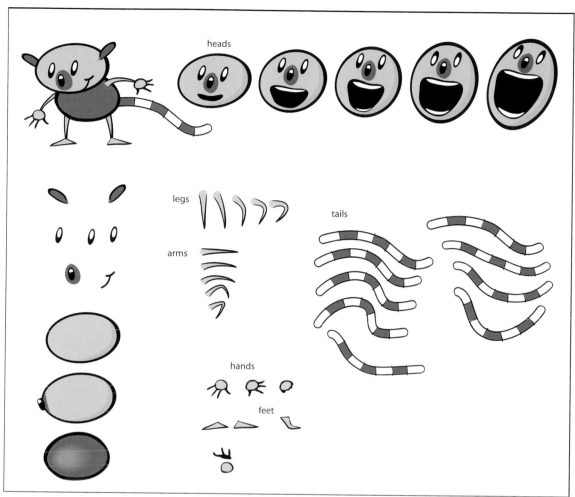

ATTEBERRY

Kevan Atteberry

To assist in constructing his animation "Millard and the Pear," which is described in the previous lesson, artist Kevan Atteberry developed a file of recyclable parts—a cartoon "morgue"—from which he copied parts and pasted them in the file in which he created the animation. To trim the file size of the animation, Atteberry converted the artwork for parts into symbol instances by Shift-dragging them to the Symbols palette. When he needed to edit a symbol,

Atteberry selected the instance and chose Object: Expand. After editing the artwork, Atteberry selected the artwork and Shift-dragged it to the Symbols palette to automatically convert it back into a symbol instance.

Symbol Flashes

Creating a Shockwave Flash Animation

NEWMAN

Overview: *Create Illustrator artwork and paste in Adobe Dimensions; make an animation sequence and save as an Illustrator file; expand artwork to separate layers; turn artwork into a symbol and position on each layer; export as a Shockwave Flash file.*

Artist Gary Newman began his animation, Peace, by using Adobe Dimensions and Illustrator, and then returned to Illustrator to create a multiple-layer file that he exported as a 24-frame Shockwave Flash animation.

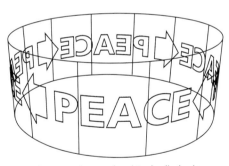

Text and arrow created in Illustrator

Artwork wrapped around a virtual cylinder in Adobe Dimensions

One of 24 overlapping artwork groups positioned on single layer in Illustrator file exported from Dimensions

1 Building the artwork in Illustrator and creating the animation sequence in Adobe Dimensions. Newman began his animation by typing "Peace" and drawing an arrow in Illustrator. He made three copies of the text and arrow and arranged them in a line. After copying the artwork, Newman pasted it in a new Dimensions document. Using Dimensions' Operations: Generate Sequence command, he made the artwork rotate 90° around a virtual cylinder (which, with 4 repetitions of the text and arrow, simulated 360° of rotation), and specified a sequence of 24 frames. Then Newman saved the animation sequence as an Illustrator file, which automatically groups the artwork in each frame and places everything on a single layer in the Illustrator file. (For more on Adobe Dimensions, see the *Illustrator & Other Programs* chapter.)

2 Expanding the artwork to multiple layers. Before exporting the artwork as a Shockwave Flash file (using the AI Layers to SWF Frames option), Newman repositioned the artwork groups on separate layers. You can do this by first making sure that Show Layers Only is unchecked in the Palette Options dialog from the Layers palette pop-up menu. Then, distribute the artwork groups by choosing Select All from the Edit menu and selecting Release to Layers (Sequence) from the palette menu. Because the Flash export converts layers (not sublayers) to animation frames, you'll need to turn the sublayers into layers. Shift-select the sublayers and drag and drop them above the layer under which they were located. Finally, delete the now-empty Layer 1 so that it doesn't become an empty animation frame. (For more on working with the Layers palette, see the *Layers* chapter.)

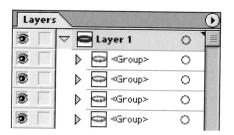

Artwork groups in Layers palette in the Illustrator file exported from Dimensions

3 Creating a symbol and positioning it among the artwork. Newman used globe artwork he had created previously for the center of his animation. To conserve file size, Newman created a symbol from his globe artwork and pasted a symbol instance on each of the 24 layers. You can do this by selecting your artwork, clicking the New Symbol icon on the Symbols palette, and deleting the selected artwork (you're going to replace it with a symbol instance). Next, select the lowest layer in the Layers palette and then drag the symbol you just created from the Symbols palette, drop it on your artwork, and position it where you'd like it. Because Newman's design had artwork in front of the globe and behind, Newman expanded the layer in the Layers palette and dragged the globe sublayer so that it was vertically positioned between the front and back artwork in the palette. Next, he expanded each of the remaining layers and then Option-dragged the globe sublayer from the layer below to copy it to the layer above. When he finished, there were 24 vertically registered copies of the globe symbol.

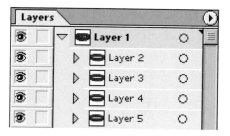

Artwork groups released to layers using the Release to Layers (Sequence) command

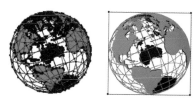

Selected globe artwork on left and symbol on right

4 Exporting the artwork to a Shockwave Flash animation. Newman selected File: Export and picked Macromedia Flash (SWF) from the pop-up menu. In the Export Options dialog, Newman chose AI Layers to SWF Frames and specified a Frame Rate of 24 fps. Then he tested the animation by running it in several web browsers.

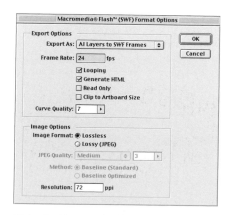

Dialog for Macromedia Flash (SWF) export

Making Waves

Transforming and Blending for Animation

Advanced Technique
Illustrator with Photoshop
Overview: *Create "key" frames with transformation tools; blend to create steps; transform your steps; bring the steps into Photoshop.*

MONROY

1

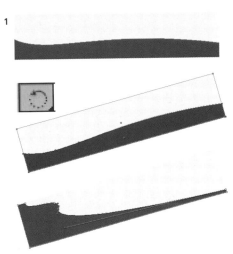

The first key frame; next, Rotating a copy; then using the Add-anchor-point and Direct-selection tools to transform the copy into the next frame

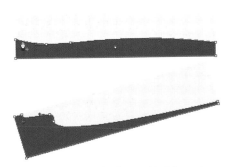

Making certain that the first and last frame have the same number of anchor points in similar alignment for smooth blending (see "Unlocking Realism" in the Blends chapter for more on preparing objects for smooth blending)

Illustrator's transformation tools, used in combination with the Blend tool, are wonderful animation timesavers. Commissioned by Adobe Systems for a special promotion, Bert Monroy used these techniques to prepare many of the objects within a room for animation.

1 Establishing the "key" frames. To create an animation, you must first establish the "key" character positions. How many key frames you'll need will depend on the character, and how it will be animated. Create a character in a neutral position, and if you'll need help maintaining registration, draw an unstroked, unfilled bounding rectangle, amply surrounding the character. Select the objects making up the character and the bounding rectangle and Option-drag/Alt-drag a copy to the side of the original. On the copy of the character (*not* the bounding box), use the transformation tools and Direct-selection editing to create the next extreme position (for more on transformations, see the *Basics* and *Zen* chapters). In Monroy's animation, the characters were: fan, clock second hand, clock pendulum, plant, and the "wave." He first drew the wave in horizontal position using a gray rectangle and a second object for the blue liquid. To create the left-tilted position, he rotated a copy of these two objects, then used the Add-anchor-point and Direct-selection tools to adjust the liquid anchor points manually.

2 Using the Blend tool to generate the in-between steps.

Also called "tweening," the secret to smooth animation is to create the correct number of steps between the key frames. For video animations, smooth illusion of motion is achieved with 24 frames per second (fps) of animation; for film it's 30 fps; for on-screen animation it's simply as many frames as is needed for your animation to run smoothly. To make the steps between your first two key frames, select each pair of like objects and blend between them (for help with blends, see "Examining Blends" in the *Blends* chapter); you can only apply a blend reliably between two objects, so you'll have to apply the blend separately for each pair of like objects (including your bounding rectangle), making sure that each pair has the same number of anchor points, and that you select the correlating anchor point in each object when blending. For the wave, Monroy first blended in 12 steps from box to box, and then from liquid to liquid. Since the same number of steps was chosen for each transition, the liquid blends were perfectly registered within the box blends.

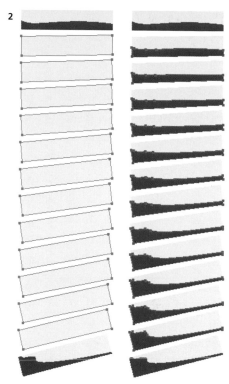

The outer objects after blending (left column), then blending the inner wave (right column)—
Note: Selecting the upper right point on the wave gives the smoothest blend

3 Transforming blends to extend the animation.

Rather than continually starting from scratch, it's often easier to rotate, scale, skew or reflect your blends to extend your animation. Monroy selected the blended boxes and waves, and Reflected them vertically as copies (see the *Zen* chapter, Exercise #9) to create the right-side rocking motion.

4 Pasting it into Photoshop.

With Illustrator still open, launch Photoshop and create an RGB document larger than your biggest key frame. In Illustrator, copy each character frame and bounding box, and then moving to the Photoshop file, paste "As Pixels" to create a new layer with that step. While that object is still in memory, *also* paste "As Paths" for easy reselection (see the *Illustrator & Other Programs* chapter for more about Photoshop). Monroy used his paths to make selections for applying special effects locally—using Alpha Channels to create effects such as the darkening and bubbles in the liquid.

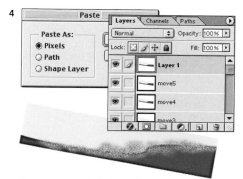

The option to "Paste As Pixels" or "Paste As Paths" when pasting from Illustrator to Photoshop; the frames after pasting into layers; the wave after effects using Alpha Channels

d'JAXN

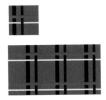   

d'JAXN

Artist d'JAXN began this teddy for the PrintPaks "KidGear" CD by taping his sketch to a Wacom tablet and tracing it with the Pencil tool. After converting those objects into Guides (View: Guides: Make Guides), in a new layer (see the *Layers* chapter) he outlined each of the shapes as separate closed objects with the Pen tool. The floor and the wall were filled with radial gradients (see the *Blends, Gradients & Mesh* chapter) and overlaid with objects representing wallpaper pattern and floor texture. d'JAXN separately rasterized (Object menu) at 72 ppi, then filtered each with various Photoshop filters to create texture. All background objects were then merged using Rasterize again, and filtered together. Teddy was rasterized, filtered, and then masked using a copy of the original

paths (for masking help see the *Advanced Techniques* chapter). d'JAXN created a plaid pattern for the footpads, which were rotated and scaled individually (enable "Transform pattern tiles in Preferences). To create Teddy's fuzz, he created a Pattern Brush using irregular hatch shapes, then applied it to copied sections of the outline (see the *Brushes* chapter for help). d'JAXN then exported the image as an anti-aliased JPEG (File: Export) at 180 ppi, as specified by the client (in the JPEG Options dialog box choose Custom from the Resolution: Depth pop-up to enter a custom resolution, and check Anti-Alias in the Options section). He used LemkeSoft's GraphicConverter to Trim (crop) the image. You can also crop in Illustrator using Object: Crop Marks: Make.

GIORDAN

Daniel Giordan / DigiRAMA Studios

Daniel Giordan began this illustration, and the subsequent animation, with a digitized photograph. He placed the image on a layer in Illustrator, and duplicated the layer three times (for a total of four aligned layers, each with the same image). Giordan applied the Photo Crosshatch filter (Filter: Pen and Ink: Photo Crosshatch) separately to each layer, adjusting the filter each time to emphasize a different part of the tonal range. By adjusting the midtone slider of the filter's histogram control, Giordan controlled what portions of the image were filtered. Together, the four layers were filtered to emphasize line distribution in the shadows, midtones, quartertones and highlights. In addi-

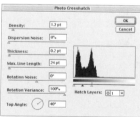

tion, Giordan varied the thickness of the lines on each layer to emphasize specific tonal areas. Once he achieved a balanced tonal range, Giordan selected the hatch lines on each layer and applied a stroke color. To animate the design, Giordan opened the file in Adobe Live Motion and selected Object: Convert Layers Into: Objects. This placed each layer as a separate object in the timeline. To finish the animation, he modified the layer's position and opacity.

Chapter 11 *Web & Animation*   **347**

Webward Ho!

Designing a Web Page in Illustrator

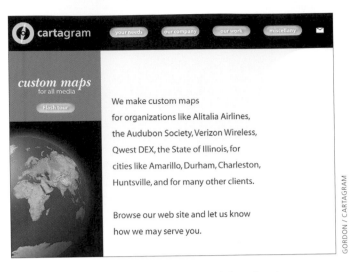

Overview: *Set up a document for web page design; use layers to structure artwork for pages and frames; save layouts as template images; slice text and artwork and save an HTML file and sliced image files.*

Gordon constructed the Cartagram web site around a two-frame design; the black rectangle represented the top frame's web page, used for the logo and main navigation controls; the other colored rectangles served as a design grid for dividing areas of the web pages that would load in the bottom frame

216 colors, or millions?

The palette of 216 non-dithered, Web-safe colors was designed for text and graphics displaying on 8-bit monitors. But how many people are restricted to 8-bit color anymore? Not many. Most computers are now equipped with 24- or 32-bit video boards, rendering Web-safe colors unnecessary. So you can choose from millions of colors, not just 216.

If you are comfortable designing and drawing in Illustrator, why go elsewhere to design your web pages? Steven Gordon uses Illustrator to design and preview web pages, create comps for client approval, export a layout as a template for use in Adobe GoLive, and slice and optimize artwork before saving it for use on web pages.

1 Choosing document settings. With Illustrator, you can draw and organize artwork to design a simple web page or a more complex page with multiple frames. To start your page, create a new document (File: New). In the New Document dialog, set Units to pixels, specify an Artboard size in pixels equal to that of your intended web page size, and choose RGB Color for Color Mode. You may want to create a grid (File: Preferences: Guides & Grid) that will help you align and constrain artwork.

Also, if your artwork will be exported in a bitmap format like GIF or JPEG, consider turning on pixel preview (View: Pixel Preview)—this lets you see the antialiasing of your artwork. (See Tip, "Anti-antialiasing," for a technique that helps you reduce the amount of blurring that affects artwork when it is antialiased.)

2 Structuring pages with layers and adding artwork. Let the Layers palette help you organize the layout and content of your web page. (See "Nested Layers" in the

Layers chapter for more on making and manipulating layers.) Gordon created separate layers for the top and bottom frames of his page, and sublayers for multiple pages he designed for the bottom frame. He toggled layer visibility on to preview the layout and content of different pages in the bottom frame of his page design.

Once you've set up the layer structure of your document, you're ready to add content to your page design. As you create text and graphics, and import images, use familiar Illustrator tools and palettes to help make and arrange objects. Gordon relied on the Align palette to easily align and distribute navigation buttons in the top frame and to center or justify colored background rectangles for both frames (using the Align to Artboard option in the Align palette).

3 Saving a web page design and importing it into GoLive. Once your page design is complete, export it as a GIF or JPEG and import the file into Adobe GoLive as a "tracing image" to help you construct a finished HTML page. If you set up the Artboard to match the dimensions of the web pages you'll construct in GoLive, you can crop your Illustrator artwork so that it matches those dimensions when exported as a bitmapped image. To do this, either create cropmarks from the Artboard (see the *Type* chapter for instructions on making cropmarks) and then use File: Export, or skip the cropmarks and choose File: Save for Web (which automatically crops artwork to the Artboard).

When you begin working in GoLive, import the image you just exported from Illustrator and use it as a template to guide you in building the page. First, choose Window: Tracing Image; then, in the Tracing Image palette, click the Source checkbox and the Browse icon to select your Illustrator-exported image. Next, adjust the HTML page's frame widths, and create text boxes and other objects in GoLive that match the Illustrator image. Repeat these steps with other exported images when building other pages in GoLive.

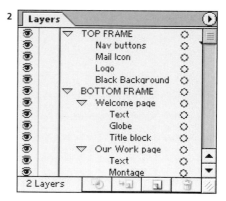

The layer structure for the web page design, showing the top and bottom frames, and two sublayers representing separate pages designed to load in the bottom frame

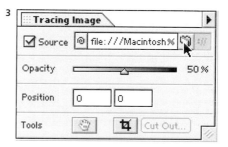

The Tracing Image palette in Adobe GoLive5; Gordon clicked the Browse icon to locate the layout image file he had exported previously using Illustrator's Save for Web command

Anti-antialiasing

When artwork is saved as a bitmapped image, straight lines and other objects may be antialiased (blurred). To minimize this, first set Keyboard Increment to 0.5 pixels in the Edit: Preferences: General dialog. Then make sure both View: Pixel Preview and View: Snap to Pixel are turned on. Next, draw and position your objects. Finally, turn off View: Snap to Pixel, and nudge aliased objects in 0.5 pixel increments as needed, using the arrow cursor-keys.

—*Mordy Golding*

4 Slicing artwork. Instead of using your Illustrator artwork as a template in GoLive, consider using Illustrator's slices to turn text, artwork, and placed images into elements you can use when building your HTML pages. Slices also let you divide a large image or layout into smaller areas that you can save as separate, optimized images. These images will load simultaneously, and usually faster than a single large image in a web browser.

You can use artwork selections, guides, or the Slice tool to divide your Illustrator design into slices. Gordon's design was divided by colored backgrounds and a masked image. (You can use non-contiguous objects for slicing; Illustrator will add slices to fill in any gaps between objects.) To make the slices, first choose Object: Slice: Clip to Artboard, then select an object and choose Object: Slice: Create from Selection. Repeat these steps until you've created all of the slices you need. If you need to remove a slice, select and delete it; or in the Layers palette drag its name (<Slice>) to the palette's trash icon.

4

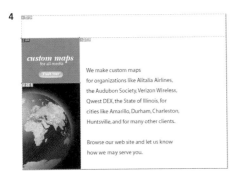

The numbered slices created after using the Object: Slices: Create from Selection command

5

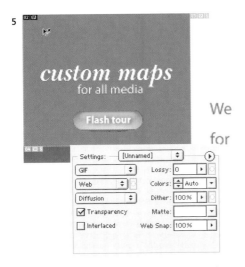

In the Save for Web dialog box, a preview of the slices is displayed; Gordon clicked in a slice with the Slice Selection tool to select it and then specified settings related to file format and other image characteristics in the Settings portion of the dialog box

5 Saving slices, and using and previewing the HTML page. When you've finished slicing your artwork, you can save the slices as text and images. Choose File: Save for Web; in the dialog box, click on the Slice Select tool and click one of the slices. Pick the settings that you want to use in saving the selected slice. Gordon set GIF as the file format for the two blocks with solid color fills and text. For the globe image, he chose JPEG as the file format and enabled Optimized to make the file size smaller. After clicking on Save, Gordon entered a file name for the HTML file (which automatically became the root name of each of the sliced image files), and made sure that HTML and Images were selected in the Format pop-up menu. After Illustrator saved the HTML file and the sliced image files, Gordon opened the HTML file in GoLive to add head tags (like meta tags) and then previewed the file in a web browser.

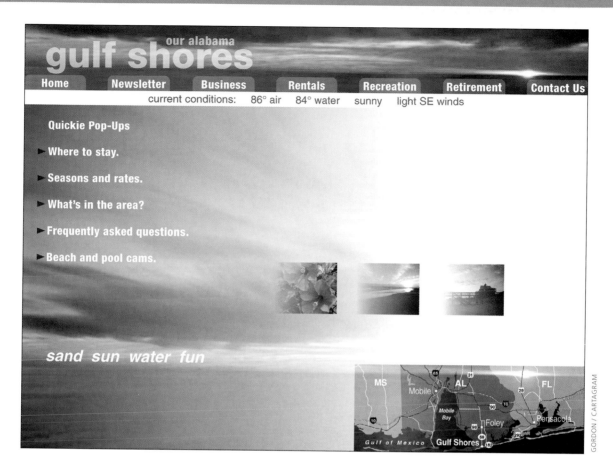

Steven Gordon / Cartagram

To build image-mapped buttons at the top of a travel web page, Steven Gordon first placed a TIFF image in Illustrator to serve as a background image. Next, he drew a button shape with rounded corners and gave it a white Fill and a 25% Opacity using the Transparency palette. He copied the button six times and arranged the buttons in a row above the background image. To space the buttons evenly, Gordon positioned the left and right buttons, selected all buttons, and then clicked the Horizontal Distribute Space icon in the Align palette. To map the buttons to URLs, he selected each button shape and in the

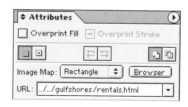

Attributes palette (Window: Attributes) chose Rectangle from the Image Map pop-up menu. He then keyed in the button's URL link in the URL field. In the Save for Web dialog, Gordon selected JPEG as the output file format, clicked Save, and then chose HTML and Images from the Format pop-up menu. He entered a file name in the Name field and clicked Save.

Illustrator & Other Programs

12

Illustrator & Other Programs

Prevent color shifts

If at all possible, you'll want to avoid color space mismatches and conversions, especially if you use any kind of transparency. If you use color management, choose your settings in Illustrator and then use the same settings in Photoshop and InDesign; and when you exchange PSD files between Illustrator, Photoshop, and InDesign, include the color profiles in the files.—*Pierre Louveaux*

Is EPS obsolete?

If your application (e.g., Illustrator, Photoshop 6 or 7, or InDesign 2) can place or open the native AI, native PSD, or PDF 1.4 formats, it's better to use those than EPS, because they may preserve transparency, layers, and other features.

Which formats can you link?

Any BMP, EPS, GIF, JPEG, PICT, PCX, PDF, PNG, Photoshop, Pixar, Targa, or TIFF file can be placed linked (rather than embedded).

So you think it's linked?

If you apply a filter to a linked image, Illustrator will automatically embed the image. In addition to increasing the file size, Illustrator will no longer be able to update the link.

This chapter showcases some of the ways you can use Illustrator in conjunction with other programs. Although the range of work you can create using Illustrator is virtually limitless, using other programs together with Illustrator increases your creative opportunities, and in many instances can save you significant time in creating your final work. One of this chapter's highlights is a step-by-step technique by renowned artist Rob Magiera for bringing Illustrator images into Photoshop.

We'll begin by discussing how you can place artwork in Illustrator, and then we'll provide a general look at how Illustrator works with other programs. We'll then examine how Illustrator works with a number of specific programs, including Photoshop, InDesign, Acrobat, Streamline, Dimensions, and other 3D programs. For information about working with Illustrator and other web or animation programs, see the *Web & Animation* chapter.

PLACING ARTWORK IN ILLUSTRATOR

Illustrator can place more than a dozen different types of file formats. The major choice you'll need to make is whether to link or embed the file. When you link a file, you don't actually include the artwork in the Illustrator file; instead a copy of the artwork acts as a placeholder, while the actual image remains separate from the Illustrator file. This can help reduce file size, but keep in mind that linking is supported only for certain formats (see Tip at left). On the other hand, when you embed artwork, you're actually including it in the file. The Links palette keeps track of linked files, but also lists all the raster images used in your document, regardless of whether they were created within Illustrator or embedded via the Place command (see the *Illustrator Basics* chapter for more). For details on how to place artwork (by linking and/or embedding it), see "Setting Up Artwork in Illustrator," in Chapter 2 of the *Adobe Illustrator User Guide*.

In general you should embed artwork only when:

- The image is small in file size.
- You're creating web graphics.
- The placed file interacts with other parts of the document via transparency. Embedding will ensure proper flattening and printing.
- You want more than just a placeholder with a preview (e.g., you want editable shapes and transparency).
- Linking isn't supported for the format your artwork is in.

In contrast to linked images, embedded image objects can be permanently altered.

And you should link (rather than embed) when:

- Your illustration uses several copies of the same image.
- The image is large in file size.
- Your file will be used in Illustrator 88 through version 6.x.

Another argument for linking files is that you can make changes to a linked file and resend only the linked file to your service bureau or client. As long as it has exactly the same name, it'll auto-update without further editing of the Illustrator document itself.

ILLUSTRATOR & OTHER PROGRAMS

The most important consideration when moving artwork between Illustrator and other programs is whether to move it as vectors or rasters. In general, artwork gets rasterized when you move it to another program, so knowing how to maintain your layer structure and move artwork as vectors is the complicated part. Another consideration is whether you're moving the artwork between two open programs on your desktop using Copy and Paste or Drag and Drop, or moving the artwork via a file format using Save, Save As, Save for Web, or Export.

Depending on the application you're dragging or pasting Illustrator objects into, you'll paste either paths or raster objects. In general, any program that supports PostScript drag and drop behavior will accept Illustrator objects via Drag and Drop (or Copy and Paste). For Mac OS only, you need to be sure that the AICB (Adobe

Resolution of placed images

Greatly reduce your printing time and ensure optimal image reproduction by properly setting the pixel-per-inch (ppi) resolution of raster images before placing them into Illustrator. The ppi of images should be 1.5 to 2 times the size of the line screen at which the final image will print. For example, if your illustration will be printed in a 150-lpi line screen, then the resolution of your raster images would typically be 300 ppi. Get print resolution specifications and recommendations from your printer *before* you begin your project!

Open sesame

If you're working in an application that doesn't allow you to save in a format that Illustrator imports (such as EPS or PDF), but does print to PostScript, you may be able to get the vector data by printing to File and then opening the raw PostScript file from within Illustrator.

Illustrator Files and Clipboard Preferences dialog. To copy and paste vectors to Photoshop set the clipboard preferences as shown above. (See the AI10 User Guide for more about these options)

See Bert Monroy's Photoshop and Illustrator lesson, "Pattern Brushes," in the Brushes chapter

Faster and smaller "saves"

Turning off the PDF option when you save reduces file size and makes saving faster. However, if you're going to be importing your artwork into certain programs (like InDesign and LiveMotion), leave PDF compatibility on.

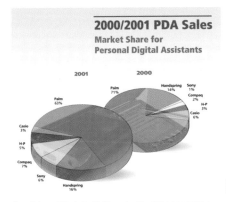

See Adam Z Lein's Gallery in the Transparency chapter to find out how he used Excel Chart Wizard and Acrobat PDF Maker for this Pie Chart

Illustrator ClipBoard) is selected in the Files & Clipboard panel of the Preferences dialog at the time you copy the objects between AI and another application.

When you are dragging and dropping, your Illustrator art will automatically be rasterized at the same physical size, or pixel-per-inch ratio, that you have specified in the *raster-based* program to which you're dragging the art.

You can Save (via Save, Save As, or Save for Web) or Export your Illustrator artwork to many formats, including: Photoshop (PSD), PDF, EPS, SVG, SWF, TIFF, PICT, GIF, JPEG, and PNG. Knowing what file formats your other application supports and the type of information (vector, raster, layers, paths) you want to bring from Illustrator into the other program will help you determine which format to use. See the *Illustrator User Guide* for detailed information about these file formats. Also see the Illustrator & Photoshop.pdf on the *Wow! CD*.

ILLUSTRATOR & ADOBE PHOTOSHOP 7

As the lessons and Galleries in this chapter demonstrate, the creative possibilities for using Illustrator and Photoshop together are endless. With every release, the symbiosis between the programs grows; e.g., most transparency settings can be kept live between Illustrator and Photoshop.

When moving artwork between Illustrator and Photoshop, the main issue is whether to move the artwork as vectors or rasters. By default, artwork that you move from Illustrator to Photoshop using Copy and Paste or Drag and Drop gets rasterized. The trick is to know when and how to move vector artwork without having it rasterized. Moving artwork via a file format is more straightforward because Illustrator can open and export Photoshop PSD files. How to use these methods to move most types of Illustrator objects, such as simple paths, text, compound paths, and compound shapes (singly or in layers) between Illustrator and Photoshop is covered in detail in Illustrator & Photoshop.pdf on the *Wow! CD*.

ILLUSTRATOR & ADOBE INDESIGN 2

When you Copy and Paste artwork from Illustrator into InDesign, the artwork is pasted as either PDF or AICB, depending on which option you specified in the Illustrator Files & Clipboard panel of the Preferences dialog. PDF preserves transparency, while AICB can break your artwork into smaller opaque native InDesign objects that mimic the transparency of your original artwork.

To place Illustrator files in InDesign, you must have saved your Illustrator artwork with the Create PDF Compatible File option enabled. Doing so preserves gradients, patterns, and transparency (which will allow underlying artwork to show through). But your artwork is imported as one object, which is not editable using InDesign, and not listed in InDesign's Links palette. For more about moving artwork between Illustrator and InDesign, search the InDesign online help, using the word "Illustrator."

ILLUSTRATOR, PDF & ADOBE ACROBAT 5

Acrobat's Portable Document Format (PDF) is platform and application independent—this means the format allows easy transfer of files between different operating systems, such as Mac OS, Windows, and even UNIX, as well as between different applications.

Illustrator and Acrobat 5 share many features, including Overprint Preview, the transparency grid, and native PDF 1.4 support. To save your file for use in Acrobat, be sure that you enable the Create PDF Compatible File option in the Illustrator Native Format Options dialog that appears when you first Save your Illustrator file.

PDF files created by other programs can be edited in Illustrator, but you can only open and save one page at a time, and text that appears to be all in one flow or text box in the PDF may be broken up into multiple text boxes when opened in Illustrator.

ILLUSTRATOR & ADOBE STREAMLINE 4

A number of artists use Streamline to creatively translate scanned drawings or photos into Illustrator art.

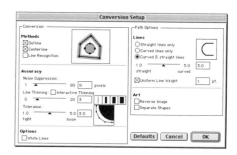

Adobe Streamline Conversion Setup dialog

JACKMORE

Lisa Jackmore's "Wallpaper & Table" image used Adobe Streamline to turn a scanned charcoal mark into an Illustrator custom charcoal Art Brush. See her Gallery in the Brushes, Symbols & Hatches chapter

BATELMAN

In "Liberty & Dollar," Kenneth Batelman used Adobe Dimensions to create a curved rectangle and to wrap his Illustrator artwork of a dollar bill onto it. See his Gallery in the Advanced chapter

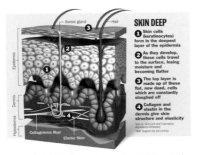

LERTOLA

Joe Lertola's Skin Deep image for TIME used Illustrator and Lightwave 3D. See his Gallery in the Brushes, Symbols & Hatches chapter

Streamline was designed by Adobe to convert scanned black-and-white or color raster images into editable vector paths and fills that can be brought into Illustrator, Photoshop, and other programs that accept Illustrator vector art. For bitmapped art, Streamline gives you much more control for specifying how the auto tracing is done than Illustrator's Auto Trace tool. You can choose whether to trace the outline of shapes, or create vectors that follow the centerlines of the shapes, or a sophisticated combination (see figure on previous page). For raster images, the basic technique is to posterize the image, and then auto trace the resulting shapes and fill them with the corresponding colors, custom colors, or tints of custom colors.

ILLUSTRATOR & ADOBE DIMENSIONS 3

Dimensions allows you to create 3D artwork and save it as vectors that you can edit in Illustrator and/or as rasters.

To create 3D artwork using Dimensions, you can import Illustrator artwork into Dimensions, and bevel, extrude, or revolve it into 3D artwork; or build 3D artwork using primitives such as cubes, spheres, cones, and cylinders. You can color your 3D objects using process and custom colors (which you can import and/or export), or you can wrap vector or raster images onto the 3D objects. You then position light sources and specify the color, shading, highlight, or shininess. Finally, you can set custom camera angles for viewing and output.

You can easily copy and paste or drag and drop artwork between Illustrator and Dimensions, or save your artwork in native Illustrator, EPS, TIFF, PSD, BMP, and PICT 2D formats, or in the 3D format 3DMF.

ILLUSTRATOR & OTHER 3D PROGRAMS

You can import Illustrator paths into 3D programs to use as either outlines or extrusion paths. Once you import the path, you can transform it into a 3D object. Strata's 3D StudioPro, Lightwave 3D, and Carrara Studio are just three of many 3D programs you can use in combination with Illustrator.

MONROY

© Bert Monroy 1999

Bert Monroy
(Photoshop)

Bert Monroy capitalized on layered, resolution-independent artwork that he created in Illustrator and brought into Photoshop to create this image of a neon sign. In the image, Monroy used techniques similar to those detailed in his *Pic n Pac* image (see the lesson "Sketching Tools" on the next page) and in his Rendezvous Cafe image (see the *Brushes* chapter). Monroy's techniques for creating 3D images from 2D software are illustrated in his book, *Bert Monroy: Photorealistic Techniques with Photoshop & Illustrator* (New Riders Publishing).

Software Relay
An Illustrator-Photoshop Workflow

Illustrator with Photoshop Overview: *Create paths in Illustrator; build a registration rectangle; organize layers for Photoshop masking; export as a PSD file; copy Illustrator paths and paste in Photoshop for masking.*

MAGIERA

1

Two stages in the construction of the image in Illustrator: left, the shapes as drawn; right, the shapes with fills

Why crop marks?

Creating crop marks will automatically set the canvas size of a PSD file you export from Illustrator. Also, by making crop marks the same size as the artboard, you can easily register the image after you've modified it in Photoshop. Just choose File: Place, select the image file, click Okay, and then drag a corner until it snaps to a corner of the Artboard.

To illustrate mascots for Salt Lake City's 2002 Olympic Winter Games, Utah artist Rob Magiera drew shapes in Illustrator. He then exported the artwork as a Photoshop (PSD) file so he could airbrush highlights and shadows in Photoshop. While working in Photoshop, Magiera sometimes copied an Illustrator object and pasted it in Photoshop to serve as a selection or to modify a Quick Mask. (See the "Compound Shapes" lesson in this chapter to learn another way to move artwork between Illustrator and Photoshop.)

Although Magiera's illustration would be completed in Photoshop, his client needed the original Illustrator artwork for other uses.

1 Placing a sketch in Illustrator, drawing shapes, and making a registration box. Magiera began by scanning pencil sketches and saving them in TIFF format. He created a new Illustrator file with dimensions that were larger than the drawings he would make and then created crop marks the size of the document by choosing Object: Crop Marks: Make (this will help when you place the Photoshop image back into Illustrator). Next, he placed the scanned image on a template layer in Illustrator (see the *Layers* chapter for more on templates) and drew the mascot shapes with the Pen and Pencil tools. He filled the shapes with color, leaving the outlines unstroked.

In order to more easily modify rasterized shapes once you get them into Photoshop, make sure you organize your major artwork elements onto separate layers (for help see the "Organizing Layers" lesson in the Layers chapter). (On export to PSD, Illustrator preserves as much of your layer structure as possible without sacrificing appearance.) For objects that overlapped other objects (like the bear's arm or the coyote's leg), Magiera created new layers and moved the overlapping objects onto separate layers so he could easily mask them in Photoshop when he began airbrushing them.

The Illustrator Layers palette organized with separate layers for shapes (shown as selected objects) to be masked in Photoshop

Knowing that he would bring some of the paths he had drawn into Photoshop to help with masking, Magiera devised a way to keep paths registered to other pasted paths and to the raster artwork he would export from Illustrator. You can accomplish this by making a "registration" rectangle in Illustrator that will keep your artwork in the same position relative to the rectangle (and the Photoshop canvas) each time you copy and paste. To make this rectangle, first create a new layer in the Layers palette, and then drag it below your artwork layers. Next, draw a rectangle with no stroke or fill that is the same size as the artboard. Center the rectangle on the artboard. With the rectangle matching the size and position of the artboard, copies of the rectangle will be pasted in Photoshop automatically aligned with the canvas.

Now you're ready to export your Illustrator artwork. Select File: Export, and from the Export dialog choose Photoshop (PSD) from the Format pop-up.

2 Working with Illustrator paths in Photoshop. After opening the exported PSD file in Photoshop, Magiera

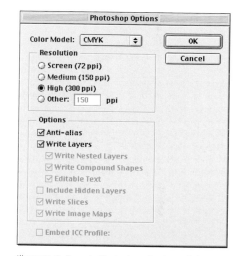

Illustrator's Export: Photoshop Options dialog

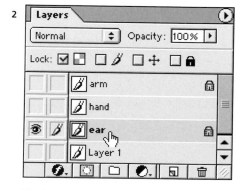

The Photoshop Layers palette showing the layer structure of the Illustrator-exported PSD file

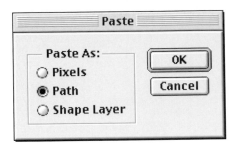

Photoshop's Paste dialog for pasting paths

At top, the bunny figure with the "whole foot" work path selected; bottom, Photoshop's Paths palette showing the selected work path

Masking a shape with a shape

If you mask a raster shape with a pasted Illustrator path in Photoshop, be aware that the mask applies antialiasing to pixels that are already antialiased, resulting in an incorrect appearance. A better way to mask raster shapes in Photoshop is to use the Layers palette's Lock Transparency Pixels option or the Layer: Group with Previous command.

used different masking techniques as he airbrushed highlights and shadows. To mask within a shape, Magiera usually enabled Lock Transparent Pixels for the layer on which the shape was located. If you use the Quick Mask working mode, you can create new masks from objects copied in Illustrator and pasted in Photoshop. To do this, in Illustrator, select both an object *and* the registration rectangle and then choose Edit: Copy. Next, in Photoshop, choose Edit: Paste and in the Paste dialog, choose Paste as Pixels. Notice that the artwork is in the same position on the Photoshop canvas as it was relative to the registration rectangle in Illustrator. With each pasted path, you can generate a selection and either add to or subtract from your working Quick Mask.

As Magiera worked in Photoshop, he occasionally modified a raster shape and then needed to update the Illustrator path that he originally used to generate the shape. To do this, first make a copy of the Illustrator path and the registration rectangle. Then, in Photoshop, choose Edit: Paste and from the Paste dialog, choose Paste as Path. Now you can modify the shape's path with Photoshop's drawing tools. When you finish, Shift-select the modified path and the registration rectangle path (click close to an edge of the canvas to select the rectangle) and choose Edit: Copy. Return to Illustrator, select the original registration rectangle, choose Edit: Paste, and drag a corner of the pasted registration rectangle until it snaps to the corresponding corner of the existing registration rectangle. Now you can delete the original path that you are replacing with the modified path.

When Magiera finished airbrushing in Photoshop, he saved the file (which was still in PSD format).

3 Bringing the Photoshop image into Illustrator. For some of the changes to raster shapes he made in Photoshop, Magiera chose to edit the original path in Illustrator. He selected File: Place and imported the image into the Illustrator file, snapping it to the registration rectangle. He edited the paths using the Pen and Pencil tools.

MAGIERA

Rob Magiera

Rob Magiera created these mascots for the 2002 Olympic Winter Games in Salt Lake City, Utah, using many of the same techniques discussed in the previous lesson. After drawing the mascots in Illustrator, he exported a PSD file and airbrushed the rasterized artwork in Photoshop. Then Magiera edited the Illustrator paths to correspond to the changes he had made to some of the shapes in Photoshop. Finally, he

saved the Illustrator file (used for silk-screened printed versions of the artwork) and sent Illustrator EPS and PSD files to his client.

Shape Shifting

Exporting Paths to Shapes in Photoshop

**Illustrator with Photoshop
Advanced Technique**

Overview: *Draw paths in Illustrator; convert paths to compound shapes; export in PSD format; apply effects in Photoshop.*

HAMANN

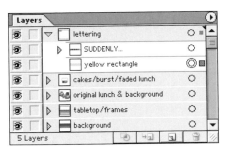

The original Illustrator artwork and the Layers palette shown before the frame, the yellow burst, and the yellow background (behind the type) were turned into compound shapes

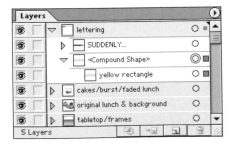

The palette showing objects in a compound shape

Artist Brad Hamann prepared this colorful illustration in Illustrator before exporting it as a PSD file and opening it in Photoshop, where he applied live effects that he could not have created in Illustrator. The key to bringing editable paths into Photoshop is to turn the objects you want to keep as paths into compound shapes. Then, after you export your document as a layered PSD and open it in Photoshop, you will see that your compound shapes have become editable shape layers while the rest of your artwork has been rasterized.

1 Drawing and layering artwork. Hamann used the Pen tool to draw objects and relied on the Blend, Reflect, and Rotate tools to create repeating elements (such as the slanting lines on the side of the milk box). For two of the objects he drew (the yellow burst and the yellow background behind the title), Hamann decided to leave each with a simple fill color in Illustrator and use Photoshop's layer styles and lighting effects to "paint" the objects. Moreover, in order to keep the outer frame looking neat in Photoshop, he had to export it as a single vector object. To do all this, Hamann converted these objects to compound shapes so they would be exported as Photoshop shape layers when he created a PSD file.

Once you've identified the objects you will bring into Photoshop as paths, select each object. From the Pathfinder palette pop-up menu, choose Make Compound Shape. (Choose Release Compound Shape from the Pathfinder palette pop-up menu if you need to turn compound shapes back into regular objects.) Hamann's compound shape frame had two components: a copy of the burst object in Subtract mode, and a rectangular frame. See the *Drawing & Coloring* chapter introduction for details about compound shapes and shape modes.

If a compound shape is to remain an editable path when exported from Illustrator, make sure that it is not inside a group or on a sublayer. If it is, move the shape out of all groups and sublayers (see the *Layers* chapter to learn how to move objects using the Layers palette).

2 Exporting a Photoshop (PSD) file. Export your Illustrator file by choosing File: Export, then choose Photoshop (PSD) format and click OK. In the Photoshop Options dialog, pick a resolution setting that matches the requirements of your printing or display medium and make sure that within Options, all available options are selected. **Important:** *For more information on moving different kinds of artwork between Illustrator and Photoshop, and for help identifying and solving problems that may occur when you try moving certain kinds of artwork, we recommend that you read the AI&PS7.pdf located on the* Wow! CD.

3 Applying effects to shape layers in Photoshop. When Hamann opened the exported PSD file in Photoshop, each Illustrator compound shape appeared as a shape layer in Photoshop's Layers palette. To add a layer effect to a shape layer, Hamann double-clicked the shape layer in the Layers palette. He applied Bevel and Emboss effects to his yellow rectangle and starburst shape layers, and even reshaped the shape paths using Photoshop's Direct-selection tool. Finally, he added effects (such as Strokes) to duplicates of some shape layers, and applied the Add Noise filter (Gaussian) to a duplicate of the background.

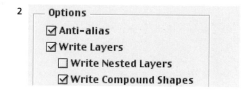

Compound shape to raster

If you turned a stroked object into a compound shape and exported a PSD file, but then found your shape rasterized in Photoshop, don't panic. Either select the object in Illustrator and choose Round Join in the Stroke palette, or remove the object's stroke.

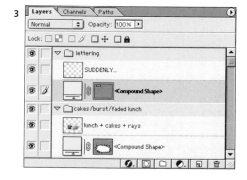

A portion of the Options section of the Illustrator File: Export: Photoshop (PSD) dialog

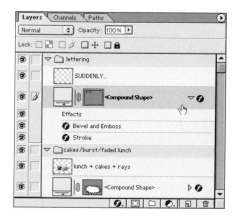

Top shows the Photoshop Layers palette as the PSD is first opened; bottom shows layer effects applied to some of the shape layers

CHAN

Ron Chan
(Photoshop)

Illustrator Ron Chan began this illustration for the Catellus web site by employing many of the same Illustrator techniques described in the "Cubist Construction" lesson (in the *Drawing & Coloring* chapter). After drawing and filling objects with color, Chan brought the artwork into Photoshop, where he selected individual elements and added textures to lend the illustration a more organic look. A similar look can be achieved using Effect menu commands, along with transparency and opacity masks (see the *Transparency & Appearances* and *Live Effects & Styles* chapters for help with effects, the Transparency palette, and opacity masks.)

FISHAUF

Louis Fishauf / Louis Fishauf Design Limited (Photoshop)

For this image about e-commerce, Louis Fishauf brought Illustrator objects into Photoshop, where he created transparency and blurring effects. Fishauf filled the credit card and house front objects with white in Illustrator. Then he pasted them into the Photoshop file and built gradation layer masks to simulate progressive transparency in the objects. Besides using

Illustrator-drawn objects as compositional elements in Photoshop, Fishauf also used the objects to create underlying glows (done with Photoshop's layer effects). To see how similar effects can be achieved using transparency, opacity masks, and live effects in Illustrator, see the *Transparency & Appearances* and *Live Effects & Styles* chapters.

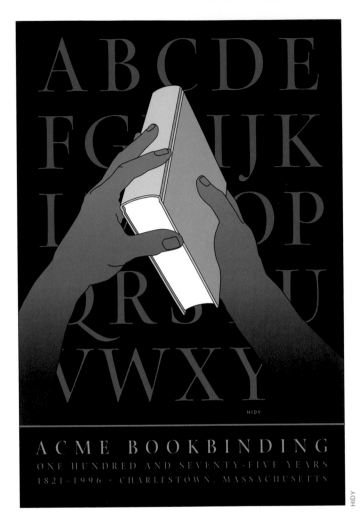

HIDY

Lance Hidy
(Photoshop)

Illustrator Lance Hidy photographed hands holding a book several times until he had a "natural" pose. He scanned the photograph and, in Photoshop, lightened the shadows and other dark tones in the image before printing it. On this print, Hidy drew outlines of the hands directly using a fine-tipped pen. Then he scanned the marked print and placed the resulting TIFF file in Illustrator as a tracing template. He was able to clearly follow the contours and

details of the hands as he traced with Illustrator's Pencil tool.

DONALDSON

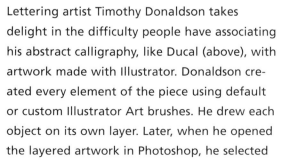

Timothy Donaldson
(Photoshop)

Lettering artist Timothy Donaldson takes delight in the difficulty people have associating his abstract calligraphy, like Ducal (above), with artwork made with Illustrator. Donaldson created every element of the piece using default or custom Illustrator Art brushes. He drew each object on its own layer. Later, when he opened the layered artwork in Photoshop, he selected objects, applied blurs and drop shadows and adjusted transparency. Some of these Photoshop treatments can also be achieved using the Effect menu and the Transparency palette. (See the *Transparency & Appearances* and the *Live Effects & Styles* chapters for more on the Appearance and Transparency palettes and the Effect menu.)

JACKSON / SAN FRANCISCO EXAMINER

Lance Jackson / *San Francisco Examiner* (Adobe Streamline)

To achieve the hard-edged, yet painterly look in this image, Lance Jackson sketched with traditional drawing media, then scanned the drawings into the computer at both high and low resolutions. In Streamline, Jackson translated both resolutions into Illustrator format. Opening both translated files in Illustrator,

Jackson then combined them, mainly using the lower-resolution version while copying and pasting details from the higher-resolution version (the face and hands, for example). Finally, Jackson selected and recolored individual objects until he achieved the final effect in this illustration entitled "Doper."

YIP

Filip Yip
(Adobe Dimensions)

Illustrating computer network hardware that encompasses worldwide service, artist Filip Yip converted flat artwork into 3D objects in Adobe Dimensions and then enhanced them with lighting effects he created with Illustrator gradients. Yip drew the compass tick marks and circular rings in Illustrator, copied and pasted them in Dimensions, and then extruded and angled them as 3D objects. He copied and pasted the objects back into Illustrator where he selected separate surfaces and filled them with gradients, adjusting gradient angles so that highlights fell where he wanted within the composition. Yip drew the transistors and wires of a computer chip in Illustrator and then mapped them to a sphere in Dimensions. He copied the spherized chip and pasted it in Illustrator, and then drew a radial gradient behind the chip to convey the image of a highlighted sphere.

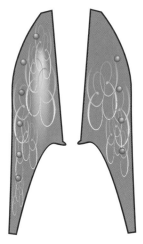

SPOLLEN

Christopher Spollen / MoonLighting Press
(Photoshop and Adobe Dimensions)

Chris Spollen developed Rocket Scientist as a lesson for a class he was teaching and later turned it into a signature piece for his web site. To begin the piece, Spollen opened a scanned public domain image in Photoshop and then adjusted its brightness and contrast. Next, he cleaned up the image using Photoshop's Rubber Stamp tool and applied a tint. He saved the black-and-white image as a TIFF and placed it in Illustrator. Spollen drew most of the other elements in the image as simple objects in Illustrator. For the rocket, he drew flat artwork that he then copied and pasted directly into Adobe Dimensions. He used Dimensions to rotate the flat artwork 360° to create the cylindrical rocket object. Spollen copied the rocket and pasted it in Illustrator, where he decorated the fins and body with symbols from the Zapf Dingbats font that he converted to outlines (Type: Create Outlines).

GROSSMAN

Wendy Grossman
(Photoshop and Adobe Dimensions)

Wendy Grossman brought a Bird of Paradise flower and a bowl from Panama to this composition, titled "Mexico." She began by sketching the layout and then scanning the sketch and placing it in Illustrator as a template. To make the maracas, Grossman constructed the basic shapes and their decorations in Illustrator. Then she brought the artwork into Adobe Dimensions where she turned the flat shapes into 3D objects and mapped the decorations to the surfaces. Grossman copied the maracas and pasted them in Illustrator. Then she rasterized the layered Illustrator file in Photoshop, compositing it with scans of the Bird of Paradise and the bowl, and reworked the entire image using painting and retouching tools. Many of the effects Grossman achieved in Photoshop, like the drop shadows and blurs, can be duplicated using the Effect menu and the Transparency palette. (See the *Transparency & Appearances* and *Live Effects & Styles* chapters for more on using Illustrator's Effects and transparency.)

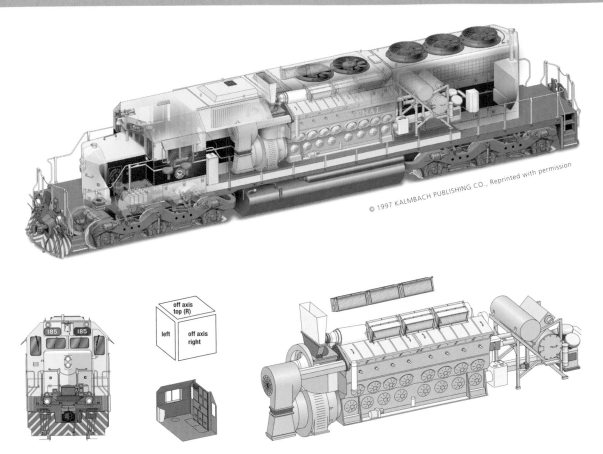

Rick Johnson / Kalmbach Publishing Co. (Photoshop and Adobe Dimensions)

Rick Johnson illustrated this EMD diesel-electric locomotive for *Trains* magazine using engineering drawings, photographs, and field notes. First he drew the front, top, and side view objects in Illustrator as "flat" surfaces. Then he built a cube in Dimensions that conformed to an Off Axis view, and copied and pasted it in Illustrator as a template. Next, he used the Scale, Shear, and Rotate tools to distort the flat surfaces to the angles of the cube template. After distorting the surfaces, Johnson assembled the surfaces into 3D shapes and organized

the illustration by placing interior and exterior shapes of the locomotive on their own layers. When he brought the layers into Photoshop, he selected the layer with the interior surfaces and airbrushed the cut-aways on its layer mask, exposing the locomotive's interior details. To increase or decrease the size of the cut-away, Johnson airbrushed or erased areas of the layer mask, preserving the layer's artwork in case it was needed later. (See the *Transparency* chapter for more on making opacity masks in Illustrator that you can use for cut-aways.)

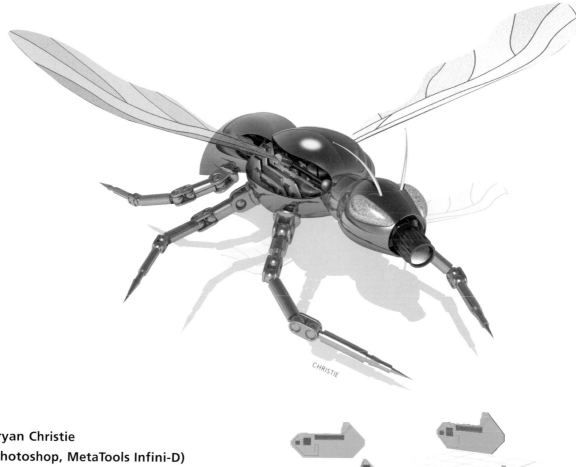

CHRISTIE

Bryan Christie
(Photoshop, MetaTools Infini-D)

Bryan Christie assembled this mechanical bug with Illustrator and later integrated Photoshop and Infini-D, a 3D modeling program. The 3D shapes, such as the leg joints and circuit boards, were first drawn in Illustrator as an outline without detail or color, and then imported into Infini-D and extruded into 3D shapes. To map the color and the details of the circuit boards, Christie drew and colored the circuitry in Illustrator. He then exported the artwork as a PICT and mapped it onto the 3D shapes in Infini-D. Christie created the transparency of the wing by mapping a grayscale image that was origi-

nally drawn in Illustrator onto the wing shape in Infini-D. To complete the mechanical bug, he rendered the artwork in Infini-D, opened it in Photoshop to make minor touchups (such as color correction and compositing separately rendered elements), and finally converted the entire image into CMYK.

Joe Jones: Art Works Studio
(Ray Dream Studio, Bryce, Photoshop)

In this World War II tribute entitled "West Field Yardbird," Joe Jones used Illustrator artwork as components in building the 3D model in Ray Dream Studio, and as texture maps to cover the model in Bryce. To start the artwork that would serve as texture maps for the metal panel seams, window masks, rivets and other elements of the model, Jones drew objects on separate layers with the Pen tool. Then Jones brought the artwork into Photoshop where he applied edge treatments and simulated the effects of weathering by painting onto the art. Then he flattened and saved the files. In Bryce, Jones imported and mapped the images onto the modeled plane parts. In all, he filled the scene with nearly 3000 Illustrator-drawn objects.

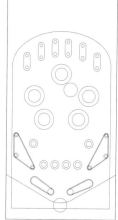

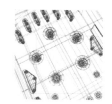

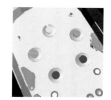

BERGMAN

Eliot Bergman
(Photoshop and Alias Sketch!)

Bergman created this illustration for a trade magazine advertisement with a combination of 2D and 3D programs. He took advantage of the precision possible with Illustrator to draft sections, plans and profiles of objects before importing them into Silicon Graphic's Alias Sketch!, a 3D modeling program. He also made color and bump maps in Illustrator, then retouched them in Photoshop. For this illustration, the first step was to draft the the layout of the pinball machine in Illustrator. The elements in this design served both as a template for 3D objects and as a basis for a color map. Bergman used the gradient tool to create the background, and he used a combination of the Star tool (hidden within the Ellipse tool) and the Filter: Distort: Pucker and Bloat filter to create the starbursts. Bergman imported the artwork into Sketch! where he created 3D objects by extruding and lathing individual items. After rendering a rough preview image, Bergman added the final maps, colors and lights. He brought the finished rendered image into Photoshop for retouching.

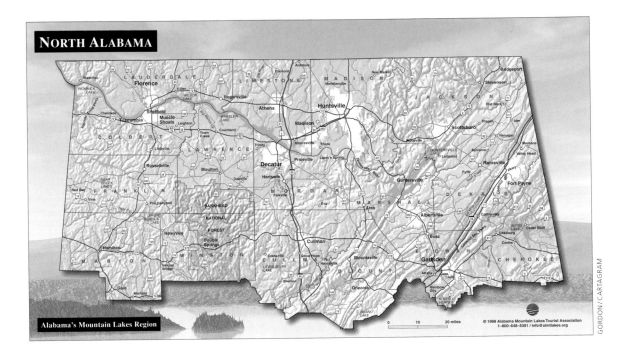

NORTH ALABAMA

Alabama's Mountain Lakes Region

© 1998 Alabama Mountain Lakes Tourist Association
1-800-648-5381 / info@almtlakes.org

GORDON / CARTAGRAM

Steven Gordon
(Painter, Bryce, MAPublisher, Photoshop, and FreeHand)

For this map of northern Alabama, cartographer Steven Gordon downloaded terrain data from the Internet, processed it in a data reader, and imported the resulting PICT image into Painter. He built a color gradation and used the Apply Surface Texture command to create the color relief image. (This process is described in "Building a Terrain Map" in *The Painter 6 Wow! Book*.) Gordon couldn't find a photograph that flowed well around the map, so he developed the background landscape in Bryce by making an "artificial" terrain and adding surface texture, water, and clouds (lower right). Gordon combined the relief and landscape images in Photoshop and then placed this new composite image in Illustrator. Using the MAPublisher suite of filters, he imported map data (roads, rivers, boundaries) into Illustrator, colorized the

linework, resized it to fit the relief, and added symbols and type. To register the Photoshop image with the map's Illustrator artwork, he drew a rectangle that matched the image and turned it into cropmarks with the Make Cropmarks command (see Tip "Creating cropmarks..." in the *Type* chapter). This enabled him to save the national forest shape (lower left on map) as a separate file, import it into Photoshop, and use it as a registered selection for masking and darkening terrain in the forest area. (To reduce the number of points in your file, try using Object: Path: Simplify.)

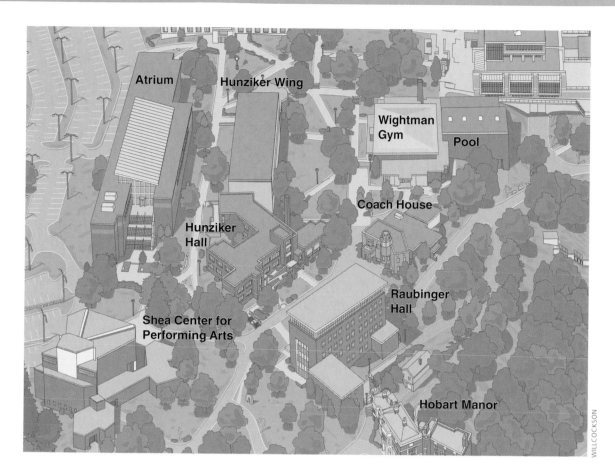

Tom Willcockson / Mapcraft
(Bryce)

Cartographer Tom Willcockson visited the campus of William Paterson University to acquire photographs, building floor plans and other materials. Then in Illustrator, he built a base map of the campus roads, rivers, vegetation areas, building outlines and other features. After scanning a contour map, Willcockson drew closed contour lines, filling them with gray shades based on elevation. He exported two JPEG images to serve as source images in Bryce: the grayscale contour layer and the base map artwork. In Bryce, Willcockson imported the contour JPEG and generated a 3D terrain image. Then he imported the base map JPEG and draped it across the terrain. He rendered the image and exported it as a JPEG, which he placed on a template layer in Illustrator. He traced the streets, building footprints and other features in Bryce-rendered perspective view. Willcockson drew the buildings, and then added trees and shrubs as Scatter brush objects from a brush library he had created for other maps. (See the *Brushes* chapter to learn about using scatter brushes for map symbols.)

Artists

Acme Design Company
see also Michael Kline
215 North Saint Francis #4
Wichita, KS 67201
316-267-2263

Erik Adigard, *see* M.A.D.

Adobe Systems, Inc.
345 Park Avenue
San Jose, CA 95110-2704
408-536-6000
see also Laurie Szujewska, Ted
Alspach, Mordy Golding,
sMin Wang

Agnew Moyer Smith, Inc.
503 Martindale Street
Pittsburgh, PA 15212
412-322-6333
rhenkel@amsite.com

Bjørn Akselson
Ice House Press & Design
266 West Rock Ave.
New Haven, CT 06515
203-389-7334
bjorn@akselson@yale.edu
www.icehousedesign.com

Jen Alspach
jen@bezier.com
www.bezier.com

Ted Alspach
Adobe System, Incorporated
345 Park Ave., Mailstop W11
San Jose, CA 95110
talspach@adobe.com
www.illustrator.com

Sandra Alves
254 Jackson Street
Sunnyvale, CA 94086
408-536-3044

Jack Anderson, *see* Hornall Anderson

Kevan Atteberry
P.O. Box 40188
Bellevue, WA 98015-4188
206-550-6353
kevan@oddisgood.com
www.oddisgood.com

Kevin Barrack
3908 Pasadena Drive
San Mateo, CA 94403
415-341-0115

Rick Barry
DeskTop Design Studio
1631 West 12th Street
Brooklyn, NY 11223
718-232-2484

Jennifer Bartlett
Girvin Strategic Branding &
Design
1601 2nd Ave. The Fifth Floor
Seattle, WA 98101
206-674-7808

Kenneth Batelman
128 Birch Leaf Drive
Milford PA 18337
888-532-0612
Kenneth@batelman.com
batelman.com

Eliot Bergman
362 West 20th Street
New York, NY 10011

Bruce Brashear
124 Escanyo Drive
South Sanfrancisco, CA 94080
650-588-3388
brucebrashear@attbi.com

John Buchmann
261 Tall Pines Drive
West Chester, PA 19380
610-324-5205

Christopher Burke
4408 Chad Court
Ann Arbor, MI 48103-9478
313-996-1316

John Burns
John Burns Lettering & Design
1593 Parkway Drive
Rohnert Park, CA 94928
707 585-7604

Peter Cassell
1185 Design
411 HIgh Street
Palo Alto, CA 94301
650-325-4804
peterc@1185design.com
www.1185design.com

Ron Chan
24 Nelson Ave.
Mill Valley, CA 94941
415-389-6549

K. Daniel Clark
3218 Steiner Street
San Francisco, CA 94123
415-922-7761
www.artdude.com

Sandee Cohen
33 Fifth Avenue, #10B
New York, NY 10003
212-677-7763
sandee@vectorbabe.com
www.vectorbabe.com

Scott Crouse
755 W. Cummings St.
Lake Alfred, FL 33850
863-956-8891

d'JAXN
Portland, OR 97229-7609
503-526-9573

Shayne Davidson
Medical Illustration & Graphics
1301 Granger Ave.
Ann Arbor, MI 48104
734-994-6223
sdmedill@umich.edu
www.medicalart.net

Rob Day & Virginia Evans
10 State Street, Suite 214
Newburyport, MA 01950
508-465-1386

Timothy Donaldson
Domus Crossheads
Colwich Staffordshire ST180UG
England
01889 88 20 43
e@timothydonaldson.com
www.timothydonaldson.com

Linda Eckstein
201 W. 70th St. #6G
New York, NY 10023
212-721-0821

Eve Elberg
60 Plaza Street East, Suite 6E
Brooklyn, NY 11238
718-398-0950

Mindi Englart
145 Cottage Street
New Haven, CT 06511
203-752-1959

Virginia Evans, *see* Day & Evans

Gary Ferster
  756 Marlin Ave., Suite 4
  Foster City, CA 94404
  650-577-9696
  gferster@attbi.com
  www.garyferster.com/

Louis Fishauf
  47 Lorne Ave.
  Kettleby, Ontario
  Canada L0G1J0
  905-726-1597
  fishauf@reactor.ca
  www.fishauf.com

Mark Fox
  415-258-9663
  mfox@blackdogma.com

David Fridberg
  Miles Fridberg Molinaroli
  4401 Connecticut Ave., NW
  Suite 701
  Washington, DC 20008
  202-966-7700

Guilbert Gates
  145 West 12th/Apt 2-5
  New York, NY 10011
  212-243-7853
  see also Jared Schneidman Design

Kerry Gavin
  154 East Canaan Road
  East Canaan, CT 06024
  203-824-4839

Daniel Giordan
  Digi-RAMA Studios
  542 Berkshire Rd
  Southbury, CT 06488

Tim Girvin
  Girvin Strategic Branding &
  Design
  1601 2nd Ave. The Fifth Floor
  Seattle, WA 98101
  206-674-7808
  www.girvin.com

Janet Good
  Industrial Illustrators, Inc.
  P.O. Box 497
  Harrison City, PA 15636-0497
  800-683-9316
  janet@ix3.com
  jlgood524@earthlink.net
  ix3.com

Steven H. Gordon
  Cartagram, LLC
  136 Mill Creek Crossing
  Madison, AL 35758
  256-772-0022
  wow@cartagram.com
  www.cartagram.com

Caryl Gorska
  414 Jackson Street/Suite 401
  San Francisco, CA 94111
  415-249-0139
  see also MAX

Laurie Grace
  860-659-0748
  lgrace@aol.com

Adele Droblas Greenberg
  AD. Design & Consulting
  202 Sixth Ave. Suite #2a
  New York, NY 10013
  212-431-9132

Wendy Grossman
  Grossman Illustration
  355 West 51st Street
  New York, NY 10019
  212-262-4497

Brad Hamann
  Brad Hamann Illustration &
  Design
  41 West Market Street
  Red Hook, NY 12571
  845-758-6186 studio
  bhamann@hvc.rr.com
  www.darkdesign.com

Steve Hart
  TIME/Editorial Art Dept
  1271 Sixth Avenue/Rm 2440 D
  New York, NY 10020
  212-522-3677

Pattie Belle Hastings
  Ice House Press & Design
  266 West Rock Ave.
  New Haven, CT 06515
  203-389-7334

Rick Henkel, see Agnew Moyer Smith

Kurt Hess, see Agnew Moyer Smith

Lance Hidy
  2 Summer St.
  Merrimac, MA 01860
  978-346-0075

Kaoru Hollin
  kaoruhollin@attbi.com

John Hornall, see Hornall Anderson

Hornall Anderson Design Works
  1008 Western Ave., Suite 600
  Seattle, WA 98104
  206-467-5800
  info@hadw.com
  www.hadw.com

Ice House Press & Design
  Pattie Belle Hastings
  Bjørn Akselsen
  266 West Rock Ave.
  New Haven, CT 06515
  203-389-7334

Lisa Jackmore
  13603 Bluestone Court
  Clifton, VA 20124
  703-830-0985
  ljackmore@earthlink.net

Lance Jackson
  LSD
  1790 Fifth Street
  Berkeley, CA 94710
  415-777-8944

Jared Schneidman Design
  16 Parkway
  Katonah, NY 10536
  914-232-1499
  see also Guilbert Gates

Rick Johnson
  Kalmbach Publishing Co.
  21027 Crossroads Circle
  Waukesha, WI 53186
  262-796-8776
  www.kalmbach.com

Dave Joly
  15 King St.
  Putnam, CT 06260
  860-928-1042

Joe Jones
  Art Works Studio
  802 Poplar St
  Denver, CO 80220
  303-377-7745
  joejones@artworksstudio.com
  www.artworksstudio.com

Eric Jungerman
  4640 Edgewood Avenue,
  Oakland, CA 94602

Diane Hinze Kanzler

John Kanzler
  800-210-0711
  john@johnkanzler.com
  www.johnkanzler.com

Andrea Kelley
  Andrea Kelley Design
  530 Menlo Oaks Drive
  Menlo Park, CA 94025
  650-326-1083
  andrea@jevans.com

Michael Kline
  Michael Kline Illustration
  1106 S. Dodge
  Wichita, KS 67213
  316-264-4112
  see also Acme Design Company

Adam Z Lein
  3 Woodlands Ave
  Elmsford, NY 10523
  914-347-1710
  adamz@lein.com
  www.adamlein.com

Joe Lertola
  TIME/Editorial Art Dept
  1271 Sixth Avenue/Rm 2434
  New York, NY 10020
  212-522-3721

Randy Livingston
  Bona Fide Design
  206 Ernest Street
  Washington, IL 61571
  309-745-1126

Patrick Lynch
  Yale University C/AIM
  47 College Street/Suite 224
  New Haven, CT 06510
  203-737-5033

M.A.D.
  Patricia McShane & Erik Adigard
  237 San Carlos Ave.
  Sausalito, CA 94965
  415-331-1023

Jacqueline Mahannah
  Medical and Biological Illustration
  Mahannahj@aol.com

Elizabeth Margolis-Pineo
  margolispineo concept, copy &
  design
  138 Glenwood Avenue
  Portland, ME 04103
  207-773-8447

Rob Magiera
  Noumena Digital
  9636 Ruskin Circle
  Salt Lake City, UT 84092
  801-943-3650

Rob Marquardt
  Toast Design
  300 First Ave North, Suite 150
  Minneapolis, MN 55401
  612-330-9863

MAX
  246 1st Street/Suite 310
  San Francisco, CA 94105
  415-543-1333
  see also Caryl Gorska

Greg Maxson
  116 W. Florida Ave
  Urbana, IL 61801
  217-337-6069
  gmaxti@shout.net
  www.portsort.com

Yukio Miyamoto
  3-8 Matuba-cyo
  Tokorozawa-shi
  Saitama-ken 359-0044 Japan
  +81-42-998-6631
  yukio-m@ppp.bekkoame.ne.jp
  www.bekkoame.ne.jp/~yukio-m/
  index_e.html

Scott McCollom
  808 N. Kaufman St.
  Seagoville, TX 75159

Patricia McShane, see M.A.D.

Bert Monroy
  11 Latham Lane
  Berkeley, CA 94708
  510-524-9412

Christopher Morris
  9828 Smoke Feather Lane
  Dallas, TX 75243
  214-690-1328

Joachim Müller-Lancé
  125 A Stillman St.
  San Francisco, CA 94108
  www.kamedesign.com

Bradley Neal, Thomas Neal
  see Thomas•Bradley Illustration

David Nelson
  Mapping Services
  721 Grape St.
  Denver, CO 80220
  303-333-1060

Gary Newman Design
  2447 Burnside Rd
  Sebastapol, CA 95472
  gary@newmango.com
  www.newmango.com

Ellen Papciak-Rose
  In The Studio
  elleninthestudio@yahoo.com
  http://homepage.mac.com/
  inthe studio

Tom Patterson
  National Park Service
  Division of Publications
  Harpers Ferry, WV 25425-0050
  304-535-6020
  t-patterson@nps.gov
  www.nps.gov/carto

Daniel Pelavin
  90 Varick Street, Suite 3B
  New York, NY 10013-1925
  212-941-7418

Cher Threinen-Pendarvis
  4646 Narragansett Ave.
  San Diego, CA 92107
  619-226-6050

John Pirman
  johnpirman@aol.com
  represented by
  Gerald & Cullen Rapp
  212-889-3337

Dorothy Remington
  Remington Design
  632 Commercial Street
  San Francisco, CA 94111
  415-788-3340

Karen E. Roehr
  93 Thorndike St.
  Arlington, MA 02474
  781-646-9933
  purple@gis.net

Javier Romero
  Javier Romero Design Group
  (JRDG)
  Westport, CT
  203-256-0934
  javierr@jrdg.com

San Francisco Examiner
  see Lance Jackson, Chris Morris,
  Joe Shoulak

Ulrik Schoth
Brunnenhof 30
Bochum, 44866
GERMANY
+49-2327-939811

Max Seabaugh, *see* MAX

Jared Schneidman Design
155 Katonah Ave.
Katonah, NY 10536
914-232-1499
jared@jsdinfographics.com
jsdinfographics.com

Charles Shields
Shields Design
415 East Olive Ave.
Fresno, CA 93728
209-497-8060

Mitch Shostak Studios
57 East 11th Street
New York City, NY 10003
212 979-7981

Joe Shoulak
5621 Ocean View Drive #2
Oakland, CA 94618
415-777-7974

Steve Spindler
Steve Spindler Cartography
1504 South St.
Philadelphia. PA 19146
215-985-2839
steve@bikemap.com
www.bikemap.com

Christopher Spollen
Moonlightpress Studio
362 Cromwell Ave.
Ocean Breeze, NY 10305
718-979-9695
cspollen@inch.com
spollen.com

Nancy Stahl
470 West End Ave, #86
New York, NY 10024
212-362-8779

Steven Stankiewicz
artfromsteve@aol.com
www.porfolios.com/
stevenstankiewicz

Sharon Steuer
c/o Peachpit Press
1249 Eighth St.
Berkeley, CA 94710
800-283-9444

David Stillman
Strider Design Studio
4841 Bay Shore Heights
Sturgeon Bay, WI 54235
906-863-7798

Barbara Sudick
California State University
Dept. of Communication Design
Chico, CA 95929
530-898-5028

Laurie Szujewska
shoe yév skä design
7045 Toma Lane
Penngrove, CA 94951
707 664 9966

Clarke W. Tate
Tate Studio
P.O. Box 339/301 Woodford St.
Gridley, IL 61744-0339
312-453-0694
clarke@tatestudio.com
www.tatestudio.com

Thomas • Bradley Illustration & Design
411 Center Street / P.O. Box 249
Gridley, IL 61744
309-747-3266

Threinen-Pendarvis *see* Pendarvis

Kathleen Tinkel
MacPrePress
12 Burr Road
Westport, CT 06880
203-227-2357

Ivan Torres
12933 Ternberry Ct.
Tustin, CA 92782
714-734-4356
ivanjessica@sbcglobal.net
ivanjessica2002@yahoo.com
www.meshsmith.com

Jean-Claude Tremblay
Illustrator Instructor & Prepress
Technician
7180 Des Erables
Montreal (Quebec)
H2E2R3

Jean Tuttle
Jean Tuttle Illustration
800-816-0460
jeantuttle@aol.com
www.jeantuttle.com

Victor von Salza
Digital PhotoGraphic Arts
4918 SW 37th Ave.
Portland, OR 97221
503-246-2146
www.vonsalza.con

Min Wang, *see* Adobe Systems, Inc.

Pamela Drury Wattenmaker
17 South Plomar Drive
Redwood City, CA 94062
415-368-7878

Timothy Webb
Tim Webb Illustration
305 W. Maywood
Wichita, KS 67217
316-524-3881
tim@timwebb.com
www.timwebb.com

Alan James Weimer
67 Bliss St.
Rehoboth, MA 02769-1932
508-252-9236
aljames@mindspring.com

Ari M. Weinstein
ari@ariw.com
www.ariw.com

Hugh Whyte
Lehner & Whyte
8-10 South Fullerton Ave.
Montclair, NJ 07402
201-746-1335

Tom Willcockson
Mapcraft Cartography
731 Margaret Drive
Woodstock, Illinois 60098
815-337-7137

Filip Yip
P.O. Box 320177
San Francisco, CA 94132
877-463-4547
filip@yippe.com
www.yippe.com

Resources

Adobe Systems, Inc.
345 Park Avenue
San Jose, CA 95110-2704
408-536-6000
www.adobe.com

AGFA
prepress, production
Agfa Corp.
100 Challenger Road
Ridgefield Park, NJ 07660
201-440-2500
www.agfa.com

Ambrosia Software, Inc.
SnapzPro,SnapzProX
PO BOX 23140
Rochester, NY 14692
800-231-1816
www.AmbrosiaSW.com

Apple Computer
ColorSync,QuickTime
800-767-2775
www.apple.com

Aridi Computer Graphics
Digital Art
P.O. Box 797702
Dallas, TX 75379
972-404-9171
www.aridi.com

Avenza
MAPublisher
6505-B Mississauga Road
Mississauga, Ontario L5N 1A6
905-567-2811
www.avenza.com

Bare Bones Software, Inc.
BBEdit
P.O. Box 1048
Bedford, MA 01730
781-778-3100
www.barebones.com

Cartesia Software
Digital Maps
PO Box 757
Lambertville, NJ 08530
800-334-4291 (x3)
www.mapresources.com

CE Software, Inc.
QuicKeys,QuicKeys X
P.O. Box 65580
West Des Moines, IA 50265
515-221-1801
www.cesoft.com

Corel Corporation
procreate Painter, Bryce
1600 Carling Ave.
Ottawa, ON Canada K1Z 8R7
1-800-772-6735
www.procreate.com/

CDS Documentation Services
Printer of this book
2661 South Pacific Highway
Medford, OR 97501
541-773-7575

Dantz
Retrospect
www.dantz.com

Dynamic Graphics Inc.
Clip art, etc.
6000 N. Forest Pk. Drive
Peoria, IL 61614
800-255-8800
www.dgusa.com

Eovia Corp.
Carrara Studio
5330 Carroll Canyon Rd, Ste 201
San Diego, CA 92121
858 457-5359 x111
www.eovia.com

EyeWire, Inc.
Fonts, Images
8 South Idaho Street
Seattle, WA 98134
www.eyewire.com

GifBuilder
piguet@ai.epfl.ch

hot door
CADtools,Perspective,MultiPage
101 W. McKnight Way, Suite B
Grass Valley, CA 95949
1-888-236-9540
www.hotdoor.com

ILemkeSoft
GraphicConverter
Erics-Heckel-Ring 8a
31228 Peine, Germany
+495171 72200
www.lemkesoft.de

Macromedia
FreeHand, Director, Flash MX
600 Townsend Street
San Francisco, CA 94103
800-989-3762
www.macromedia.com

Pantone, Inc.
color matching products
590 Commerce Blvd.
Carlstadt, NJ 07072
866-PANTONE
www.pantone.com

PhotoSphere Images Ltd.
stock imgages
380 West First Avenue, Suite 310
Vancouver, BC V5Y 3T7
800-665-1496
www.photosphere.com

procreate (*see* Corel Corporation)

Sapphire Innovations
Illustrator plugins, brushes
PO Box 26064
Chelsea, London, SW10 OWHL,
United Kingdom
www.sapphire-innovations.com

Strata,
Strata3Dplus
567 S. Valley View Dr./Suite 202
St. George, Utah 84770
800-678-7282
www.strata.com

TruMatch, Inc.
Color Matching Software
50 East 72nd, Suite 15B
New York, NY 10021
800-878-9100
www.trumatch.com

Ultimate Symbol
Design Elements, clipart
31 Wilderness Drive
Stony Point, NY 10980
845-942-0003
www.ultimatesymbol.com

Virtual Mirror Corporation
Vector Studio, Retouch Brush Tools
866-386-7328
www.virtualmirror.com

WACOM
Graphics Tablets
1311 SE Cardinal Court
Vancouver, WA 98683
800-922-9348
www.wacom.com

zenofthepen.org
*QuickTime Enhanced Bézier Pen
Tutorials for Illustrator, Photoshop,
InDesign, FreeHand & Fireworks 4+*

General Index

curves
See also geometric objects
Bézier; 6
blends along; 211
color transition; 236
constructing; 79
duplicate; 130
manipulation of; 6
modifying; 7, 138
placing text on; 186
redrawing; 8
reflecting; 130
smooth; 9
customizing
art brushes; 198
calligraphic brushes; 256
drawing grid; 86
graphs; 16
grids; 24
guides; 25, 195
keyboard shortcuts; 4
palettes; 5
spot colors; 92
Startup file; 3
swatch libraries; 63
symbols; 142
text paths; 186
tool sets; 5
transparent brushes and layers;
256
cut shape, changing; 108
"cut-a-ways"; 89
cut-out look; 230
cutting
See also subtracting
holes; 84
objects; 78
paths; 9, 42, 81

D
d'JAXN; 346
dashed lines
end cap style impact on; 70
Flash export considerations; 334
multicolored; 138
outlining; 71
stroke use; 61
data
importing; 16
numeric; 16
sets; 336
data-driven graphics; 335
See also "Illustrator 10 User

Guide"; "Illustrator 10
XML Grammar Guide"
example; 33
XML variables use; 33
database(s)
linking Illustrator files to; 33
using Illustrator as; 336
Davidson, Shayne; 133
Day, Rob; 194
defining
graph design elements; 17
repeating patterns; 110
scatter brushes; 148
symbols; 142
variables; 336
deforming
See distortion
Delete Anchor Point tool; 9, 41, 43
deleting
See also removing
anchor points; 7, 8, 41
appearances; 252
common mistakes; 8
guides; 25
layers; 156
path sections; 9
symbols; 144
density
vs. intensity; 118
symbol; 143
depth
creating; 74
hatch effect use; 119
sense of; 143
sky; 145
deselecting objects; 52, 53
designs/designing
bookcovers; 194
cropping; 317
gradients; 214
graph; 16
Web pages; 348
destructive Pathfinders; 69
details/detailed
accenting; 309
creating; 130
elimination of; 106
level of; 120
renderings; 88
tracing; 166
views; 88
diagrams, technical; 88
Diccolor; 29
dimensions, graph; 16
Dimensions (Adobe)

creating animation sequence in;
342
Illustrator use with; 358, 371, 372,
373, 374
dimming images; 158
Direct-select Lasso tool; 13, 75
Direct-selection tool
animation editing use; 344
bounding box hidden by; 18
modifying paths in a compound
path with; 65
molding mesh selections with; 322
Pen tool impact; 8
Reshape tool use with; 20
selecting; 11, 12, 13, 39
direction
handles; 22
points; 6
Director (Macromedia); 328
disabling
Auto Add/Delete function of Pen
tool; 8
opacity masks; 247
distance, numeric specification of; 20
distortion
See also transformation
dynamics; 100
of envelopes; 284, 296
filters; 71, 72
with Free Transform tool; 18
of letterforms; 202
of meshes; 296
of parts of letters; 185
of paths; 72, 292
skewing vs.; 101
tools; 71
dithering GIF options; 332
divide/dividing
color and; 84
overlapping paths; 84
paths; 107
divisions of grid; 24
docking palettes; 14
document(s)
creating; 2
linked images in; 33
new; 2
setup; 4, 194, 249
sharing custom brushes between;
140
startup; 3
Donaldson, Timothy; 136, 369
dotted lines in Artboard; 3
drag and drop
moving artwork between
Illustrator & Photoshop;

handles
> grabbing; 100
> length and angle; 6
> (term description); 6

Hard Mix effect vs. filter; 281

hardware
> calibration; 28
> requirements; 2

Hart, Steve; 214

Hastings, Pattie Belle; 202

hatches; 146, 147
> *See also* "Pen & Ink Hatch
>> Effects.pdf" in *Wow! CD*
> applying; 119
> (chapter); 114
> painting with; 148
> teddy bear fuzz use; 346
> working with; 118

Hebrew font; 189

height of curve; 7

help, obtaining; 32

Henkel, Rick; 89, 90, 92, 211

Hess, Eric; 20, 212

Hess, Kurt; 90

hidden/hiding
> edges; 26
> layers; 25, 156, 157, 160, 175
> objects; 161
> page parameters; 3
> palettes; 14

Hidy, Lance; 368

highlights(ing)
> basic techniques; 264
> blending with shadows; 222
> circular; 76
> creating; 74, 75, 288
> objects; 25
> in Photo Crosshatch; 120

hinting technology impact on small
> type; 185

holes
> *See also* mask(ing)
> cutting; 84
> in letters; 185
> *see*-through; 65
> simple; 65

Hollin, Kaoru; 142

hollow snap-to arrow; 8

Horizontal-type
> *See* Type tool, regular

Hornall, John; 191

houses; 38

"How to Use This Book"; 2

HSB (Hue, Saturation, Black) color
> space

CMYK, RGB, and; 328
> coloring meshes with; 296, 324

HTML (Hypertext Markup
> Language)
> creating; 330
> saving Illustrator files as; 348

human
> eye; 135
> face; 241

I

I-beam cursor; 180

ICC(M) printers printing profiles; 28

icons/iconic
> appearance; 251
> images; 44
> layer; 161
> triangle-circle-square; 123

identifying
> elements; 248
> objects; 25

illustrations
> *See also* images; photorealism
> baseball; 306
> Bicycle brand playing card style;
>> 291
> botanical; 218
> butterfly; 221
> children's book; 235
> computer chip board; 74
> fish; 238
> goldfish; 146
> goldfish bowl; 260
> landscape; 236
> Liberty; 315
> magazine; 228, 232, 272
> medical; 135, 141
> overlapping object use in; 78, 84
> pencils; 306
> product; 224, 227, 262, 308
> realistic; 74, 130, 224
> salamander; 268
> stylized; 229
> technical; 74, 88, 222
> transparency use with; 260

Illustrator
> *See* Adobe Illustrator

image(s)
> black and white; 168
> complex; 18
> cropping; 259
> dimming; 158
> fitting to current window; 3

formats; 30
> grayscale; 248
> imported; 31
> linked; 29, 33
> maps; 330, 351
> monotone; 248
> objects; 32
> placed; 110, 166
> placing; 106
> placing letters on top of; 192
> raster; 249
> rasterizing; 28
> saving; 30
> scaling; 3
> size; 4
> tiling; 3
> tracing; 254
> viewing; 23
> visibility; 106

importing
> brush paths into Illustrator; 136
> brushes; 138
> data; 16
> documents; 17
> EPS images; 30
> images; 31
> raster images; 106
> type created in other applications;
>> 180

in-between(s)
> for animation; 71
> blend editing impact on; 210
> Blend tool use; 344, 345
> lines; 177

InDesign (Adobe)
> Illustrator use with; 357
> PDF format use; 21

Infini-D (MetaTools); 375

infographics; 226

ink
> brush; 122
> hatch effects; 118
> transparent overlapping; 198
> washes; 255

insets; 87

instances
> *See also* symbol(s)
> symbol; 117, 143

intensity
> vs. density; 118
> symbol; 143

interlacing GIF options; 332

interlocking chain links; 130

intersections
> of objects; 78

leaves, drawing; 148
legacy documents; 29
Lein, Adam Z.; 121, 263, 356
Lemke, Thorsten; 328
lens (image); 87
Lertola, Joe; 141, 272, 280, 358
letter(s)
    See also characters; fonts; text;
        type
    converting to outlines; 192
    drawing; 127
    hand-drawn; 198, 290
    letterforms; 136, 191, 198, 202
    masking; 192
    placing; 192
    spacing; 184, 185
Liberty illustration; 315
libraries
    color matching; 29
    object component; 90
    swatch; 63
light source, incorporating into a
        sketch; 222
lighting
    ambient effects; 224
    landscape; 236
Lightwave 3D; 358
limiting view; 23
line(s)
    attaching to circles; 80
    attaching to curves; 7
    dashed; 71
    definition of; 5
    graphs; 17
    in-between; 177
    joining; 7
    length; 80, 189
    manipulation of; 6
    multiple; 253
    refining; 165
    straight; 7
    stroked; 44, 70
    weights; 4
    working with; 5
Line tool; 79
linear
    architectural shading; 216
    fills; 214
    gradients; 149, 229, 236
linked images
    color space issues; 29
    vs. embedding images; 31
    filters impact on; 354
    generating a list of; 33
    impact on file size; 32

printing problems with; 32
linking
    vs. embedding images; 354
    opacity masks; 247
    reasons for; 355
    text; 180
Liquify distortion tools; 71
live
    See blends; effects
Live Motion (Adobe); 21, 347
locating
    clipping masks; 303, 304, 305
    objects; 158
    vanishing points; 177
    windows; 23
location map; 266
locking
    guides; 25, 177
    layers; 25, 156, 157, 175
logos, multiple ways of constructing;
        44
Louveaux, Pierre; iv, 69, 71, 213, 246,
        250, 253, 357
    Wow! CD: Ch12:
        AI&PS7.pdf
luminous colors; 142

M

Macintosh
    finger dances; 52
    OS X; 17
    OS9; 5
    requirements; 2
    scaling images relative to Page
        Setup; 3
Macromedia
    Director; 328
    Flash; 333, 338
macros
    See actions
magazine illustrations
    glow effect use; 272
    gradients use in; 228
    palette of gradients use in; 232
Magic Wand tool; 137
Magiera, Rob; 360, 363
Mah, Derek; 210
Mahannah, Jacqueline; 135
manipulating
    See also adjusting; changing;
        modifying
    anchor points of tonal
        boundaries; 222

blend spine; 211
    color; 69
    gradients; 212, 214
    layers; 174
    letterspacing; 184
    meshes; 322
    objects; 10
    paths; 280
    stacking order; 160
    symbols; 142
    text; 186
    type; 180
manual
    creation of geometric objects; 10
    cutting with Scissors tool; 81
    joining open paths; 81
    transformations; 20
    trapping; 98
mapping buttons; 351
Mapping Services; 163
maps
    bike; 134
    creating; 166
    image; 330, 351
    Layers palette use; 163
    location; 266
    point; 210, 223
    road; 138
    symbols; 138
    techniques; 138
    terrain; 274
MAPublisher
    Illustrator use with; 378
Margolis-Pineo, Elizabeth ; 67
markers, graph design elements as;
        17
marks
    See also cropping
    organization of; 256
    painterly; 122
    registration; 194
    tick; 140
    trim; 110
Marquardt, Rob; 66
mask(ing)
    See also blends/blending;
        gradients; layers; stacking
        order;
        transparency/transparent
    across multiple layers; 304
    blends; 213, 227, 306, 308
    clipping; 109, 192, 240, 256, 259,
        263, 300, 302, 303, 304,
        305
    compound path use for; 65

objects *continued*
  cutting; 78
  editable; 210
  filling; 15
  grouping; 11, 260
  identifying; 25
  inserting into; 211, 304
  joining; 42, 78
  like-colored; 87
  moving; 159, 173
  moving between Illustrator &
    Photoshop; *Wow! CD*:
    Ch12: AI&PS7.pdf
  multiple; 14, 212
  organization of; 256
  overlapping; 78, 84, 86
  rasterizing; 298
  reflecting; 43
  repeating; 111
  selected; 252
  selecting; 11, 159, 160
  stroking; 15
  transforming; 88
  ungrouping; 11
  working with; 5
observation, as key to realism; 74
offset/offsetting
  blends; 224
  paths; 87
  shadows; 74
  strokes; 286
  type; 310
Olson, Robin AF; 115, 158
on-screen display
  See also Web
  preparing artwork for; 328
opacity/opaque
  See also transparency
  assigning to default brushes; 254
  of image; 106
  of layers; 260
  masks; 247, 248, 272, 274, 278,
    318
  modifying; 270
  setting; 256
  translucence blending with; 318
  transparency use with; 246, 265
open
  See path(s), open
optimization
  See also performance
  of GIF files; 330
  of repeating patterns; 111
  of Web graphics; 331
order
  of appearance attributes; 251

blend; 211
layers; 158
of operations; 51, 100
stacking; 81, 137, 144, 156, 157,
  159, 160, 253
organization
  of artwork; 174, 361
  of brushes; 256
  of color palette; 94
  of layers; 170
  layers as aid to; 156, 361
  of marks; 256
  naming brushes; 115
  of object categories; 256
  spot color use for; 92
  of swatches; 95
  of Web page layouts; 348
orientation of page; 3
origin (ruler), changing; 24
out-of-gamut
  indicator; 62
  warning; 30
Outline mode
  advantages of working in; 38
  anchor points and paths visible in;
    5
  interrupting preview to; 22
  as most useful working mode; 51
  setting a layer to; 157
  viewing all text paths with; 186
outlines/outlining
  See stoke
  converting type to; 184, 185, 192,
    270
  dashed lines; 71
  extracting from an enveloped
    mesh; 320
  of letterforms; 198
  paths; 87
  small fonts; 185
  transforming; 185
overlapping objects
  applying Soft Mix to; 86
  creating an illustration from; 78
  creating and positioning; 82
  creating illustrations with; 84
  tracing template use of; 78
overprinting
  1-bit TIFF problem; 169
  Christopher Burke's techniques;
    98
  preview; 248
  previewing; 22
  registration handling with; 28

P

Pacific Ocean trench infographic;
  226
package design, gradients use; 231
page
  orientation; 3
  parameters in Artboard; 3
  setting up; 2
  setup; 3, 4
  size; 3
Page tool; 3
PageMaker; 28
Paint bucket tool; 63, 184
Paintbrush tool; 122, 123, 203, 254,
  256
Painter; 378
painterly marks; 122
painting
  with areas of color; 238
  with gradient meshes; 148
  with hatches; 148
  with pattern brushes; 148
  with scatter brushes; 148
palettes
  See under specific palette names
Pantone Process color matching
  system; 29, 95
Papciak-Rose, Ellen; 127, 205, 235,
  286
paper
  colored; 246
  size; 3
Paragraph palette; 180
pasting
  appearance attributes; 159
  into Flash; 340
  key frames into Photoshop; 345
  retaining layer order for; 158
path(s)
  See also curves; geometric objects;
    stroke(s)
  adding; 11, 182, 186
  adjacent; 116
  adjusting type on; 186
  applying brush strokes to; 114
  blends along; 211
  brush; 101, 115, 136
  changing; 22
  circular; 102
  clipping; 268, 281, 304
  closed; 107, 128, 182
  closing; 7, 81
  complex; 213
  compound; 45, 64, 65, 68, 69, 82,
    83, 85, 193, 210, 213, 238,

Toyo; 29
tracing
    compositions; 122
    details; 166
    imported photos; 106
    layer; 168
    preparing an image for; 254
    templates; 78, 122, 164
tracking type to fit; 194
Transform palette; 18, 19
transformation(s); 17
    See also distortion; filters; Free
        Transform tool; morphing;
        moving; reflecting;
        rotating; scaling; shearing;
        Transform palette
    applying as effects; 280
    bounding box use; 18
    of calligraphic fonts; 290
    creating key frames with; 344
    of gradients; 124, 309
    of groups; 21
    manual; 20
    of objects; 88, 89
    outlines; 185
    parts of letters; 185
    repeating; 18
    Smart Guide help with; 25
    tools; 19, 20
    of type; 206
transitions
    See also blends/blending;
        gradients; morphing
    color; 212, 213, 223, 236
    hard; 223
    irregular; 215
translucence
    opacity blending with; 318
Transparency palette; 246
    blending modes; 322
    blending modes application use;
        260
    creating knockouts with; 270
    drop shadow use; 193
    outlining dashed objects use of; 71
    pie chart use of; 263
transparency/transparent
    See also appearances; mask(ing);
        opacity
    adding to fills and strokes; 253
    applying; 136, 247
    basic; 246, 260
    blends; 264
    brushes; 256
    (chapter); 246

color; 161, 256
creating knockouts with; 270
cumulative effect of; 249
curtains; 275
document setup issues; 249
GIF options; 332
grid; 26, 246
Hard Mix effect equivalents; 281
impact on file size; 32
knockout controls and; 248
layers; 256
luminous color use of; 142
opaque-to-transparent blends;
    265
overlapping inks; 198
PDF version impact; 250
printing problems with; 32
settings; 251, 254
simulating shadows and
    highlights with; 289
symbol; 143
tinting scans with; 268
Web colors and; 333
traps/trapping
    Christopher Burke's techniques;
        98
    manual; 98
    previewing; 22
    registration handling with; 28
trees
    creating the trunks for; 149
    drawing; 148
Tremblay, Jean-Claude; 159
triangle-circle-square icon; 123
trickling type; 186
trim marks
    generating; 110
    placing; 194
troubleshooting
    See also precautions
    appearances; 14
    clipping mask problems; 305
    grouping problems; 11, 12
    layers; 162
    printing; 31, 160, 250
    read me first; xvi
    selecting objects; 159
Trumatch; 29
Tuttle, Jean; 94
Twirl tool; 71, 105
Twist tool; 20
type
    See also Area-type; baseline paths;
        Character palette; fonts;
        Paragraph palette; Path-

type; Point-type; text; Type
    tool(s)
accidental selection; 180
adjusting; 186
applying brushes to; 198, 290
calligraphic fonts; 290
(chapter); 180
contouring; 310
converting to outline; 184, 185
crunching; 206
expanding; 207
export; 185
flowing; 181
greeking; 181
hand setting of; 197
letterspacing; 184
manipulation; 180
masking with; 185
moving between Illustrator &
    Photoshop; *Wow! CD*:
    Ch12: AI&PS7.pdf
options; 180
path; 183
selecting; 180
stroking; 207
transforming; 206
trickling; 186
Type tool(s); 180, 181, 182
typeface scanning; 197
typing
    accessing Hand tool while; 32
    numbers; 13
    into palettes; 14
    zooming while; 22
typographic controls; 180

U

undos
    finger position for; 50
    levels of; 22
    number left; 21
    setting number of levels; 22
ungrouping
    See also grouping; selecting
    graphs; 16
    objects; 11
uniform letter and word spacing; 189
unifying
    geometric shapes; 40
    gradients; 228
units of measurement
    palette entry; 13
    rulers; 24
unlinking opacity masks; 247

unlocking
    guides; 25, 177
    layers; 157, 175
updating
    colors; 215
    styles; 15
URLs, assigning; 330

V

vanishing points; 177
variables
    defining; 336
    XML; 33
Variables palette; 335
    data-driven graphics use; 33
variant colors; 96
vase, 3D; 322
vector/vectorizing
    See also rasterization
    images; 106
    raster brush strokes; 137
versioning
    when applying permanent
        Pathfinders; 78
    strategies; 21
Vertical Area-type tool; 181
vertical guides; 43
viewing/views
    changing; 22
    detailed; 88
    different versions of current
        image; 23
    direction handles; 22
    grids; 25
    layer problems with New View
        (View menu); 162
    limiting to Artboard area; 23
    and Navigator palette; 23
    opacity masks; 247
    saving; 23
    the transparency grid; 26
visibility
    of anchor points; 5
    image; 106
    of paths; 5
    of template layers; 123
Visual Basic scripting language
    Illustrator support for; 33
visualization as result of Illustrator
        mastery; 36
von Salza, Victor; iv, 68, 147, 213
    Wow! CD: Ch12: AI&PS7.pdf

W

Wacom tablet
    See also pressure-sensitive devices
    calligraphic brush use with; 126
    drawing leaves with; 149
    ink brushes use with; 135
    letterform creating; 203
    tracing use of; 346
Wang, Min; 185
warnings
    See precautions
Warp tool; 71
warps; 282, 283
    See also effects
    applying; 292
    bowing type; 207
    transforming type with; 206
washes, ink; 255
Watanabe, Andrew T.; 334
water
    creating; 149
    reflections; 145
watercolor simulation; 256
waving flag; 292
Web
    See also HTML; monitors; on-
        screen display; RGB
    colors; 333
    image map creation for; 351
    pages; 348
    preparing artwork for; 328
    RGB guidelines; 328
    safe RGB colors; 29, 62, 329, 348
    save for; 331
    symbols and; 117
Web Swatches palette; 329
Webb, Tim; 232, 233
weights
    line; 4
    stroke thickness controlled with;
        61
Weimer, Alan James; 110, 316, 317
Weinstein, Ari M.; 189
wet reflections; 239
Whyte, Hugh; 66, 230
Willcockson, Tom; 379
windows
    fitting image to; 3
    locating; 23
Windows (MS)
    finger dances; 53
    requirements; 2
wire frames, viewing in Outline
        mode; 22
woodcuts, simulating; 233

woodgrain, text knockout showing;
    270
workflow, Illustrator-Photoshop; 360
wrapping
    text; 182
    textures; 320
Wrinkle tool; 71
wrinkles in fabric; 227
WWW (World Wide Web)
    See Web

X

X axis adjustment; 25
XML standard
    variables; 33
    variables based on; 336

Y

Y axis adjustment; 25
Yip, Filip; 164, 229, 371

Z

Zapf Dingbats font, creating symbols
        from; 372
Zen
    dictionary definition; 36
    of Illustrator; 36
zero of ruler; 25
Zoom tool; 24, 165
zooming; 23
    advantages when smoothing; 167
    numerical specification of; 24
    while typing; 22